Th[illegible] Ins and Outs of [illegible] Solitaire

Jo[illegible] [illegible] is a computer consultant and [illegible] long enthusiast for mathematical ga[illegible]. He is the author of *The Mathematics of Games*, another volume in the Re[illegible] in Mathematics series.

Recreations in Mathematics

Series Editor
David Singmaster

1. Hugh ApSimon
   Mathematical Byways in Ayling, Beeling, and Ceiling
2. Hugh ApSimon
   More Mathematical Byways
3. John D. Beasley
   The Ins and Outs of Peg Solitaire
4. John D. Beasley
   The Mathematics of Games
5. Stewart T. Coffin
   The Puzzling World of Polyhedral Dissections

The Ins and Outs of Peg Solitaire

John D. Beasley

Oxford New York
OXFORD UNIVERSITY PRESS
1992

Oxford University Press, Walton Street, Oxford OX2 6DP
Oxford New York Toronto
Delhi Bombay Calcutta Madras Karachi
Petaling Jaya Singapore Hong Kong Tokyo
Nairobi Dar es Salaam Cape Town
Melbourne Auckland
and associated companies in
Berlin Ibadan

Oxford is a trade mark of Oxford University Press

First Published 1985
First issued as an Oxford University Press paperback 1992

British Library Cataloguing in Publication Data
Data available
ISBN 0–19–286145–X

Library of Congress Cataloging in Publication Data
Beasley, John D.
The ins and outs of peg solitaire / John D. Beasley.
p. cm.—(Recreations in mathematics ; 3)
Originally published: Oxford : Oxford University Press, 1985.
Includes bibliographical references (p.) and index.
1. Solitaire (Board game) I. Title. II. Title: Peg solitaire.
III. Series: Recreations in mathematics ; no. 3.
794—dc20 [GV1469.S6B35 1992] 91–27336
ISBN 0–19–286145–X

Printed in Great Britain by
Biddles Ltd.
Guildford and King's Lynn

PREFACE

The puzzle game of Solitaire has a long history and has given pleasure to many, yet there is surprisingly little published material on it. Most game and puzzle books give no more than a description of the rules and a solution to the standard 'central game'. There are more extensive chapters in *The Unexpected Hanging and Other Problems* by Martin Gardner (1969, British edition entitled *Further Mathematical Diversions*) and in *Winning Ways for Your Mathematical Plays* by Elwyn Berlekamp, John Conway and Richard Guy (1982), but the only substantial book to have been published in England appears to have been Ernest Bergholt's *Complete Handbook to the Game of Solitaire on the English Board of Thirty-three Holes* (1920). This has long been out of print, and in any case much has been discovered since it was written.

David Singmaster's invitation to contribute to the present series is therefore particularly welcome. Solitaire can be enjoyed at two levels. It provides attractive and difficult problems which appeal to the puzzle enthusiast. It also has an underlying theory whose fascination appeals to the mathematician. This theory is not particularly difficult, for there are only a couple of sections in this book which go into 'higher' mathematics and the reader unwilling to follow can easily skip and take the results for granted, but it is both subtle and surprising. He who thinks that knowledge of a solution to the standard 'central game' constitutes complete knowledge of Solitaire is wrong indeed.

PREFACE TO THE PAPERBACK EDITION

A little more work has been done since this book was originally written, some of it prompted by the book itself, and one or two sections would now be written rather differently. However, to update the text in detail would require awkward surgery, so I have contented myself with adding a note on page 252 which summarizes the main developments. The reader who reads the book straight through, and then consults this note, will find himself properly in the picture.

Part of the 'look at the future' in Chapter 15 considers the possible use of a computer, and much of this has already become a look at the past. Nevertheless, I have allowed it to remain. I doubt if future readers will find great difficulty in reinterpreting it in terms of the vastly more powerful computers that will soon be available to recreational users; and perhaps some of them will find as much fascination in looking back at the computers of today as I find in studying the pastimes of the court of Louis XIV.

ACKNOWLEDGEMENTS

One of the pleasures of writing this book has been to discover how many people, both private individuals and library staff, have been willing to go out of their way to help me. The book is very much richer as a result. For permission to publish original material, I thank Mike Boardman, Harry Davis, Martin Gardner, Leonard Gordon, John Harris, Bob Hutchings, Kadon Enterprises Inc., and Wade Philpott; for help in finding historical material, I thank R. C. Bell, John Maltby, Eileen Scott, David Singmaster, Jerry Slocum, the Bodleian Library, the British Library (Department of Printed Books, Newspaper Library, and Science Reference Library), the British Museum, Cambridge University Library, the Library of Congress, the John Crerar Library, Hertfordshire County Libraries (Harpenden, Hemel Hempstead, Stevenage Central, and Stevenage Old Town), the Joseph Regenstein Library, the National Library of Scotland, the Library of University College, London, the Victoria and Albert Museum, and the National Library of Wales; for assistance with translation, I thank Diane Bennett, John Finch, Deborah Singmaster, Shirley Welch, and my father; for putting me in touch with others who are interested in Solitaire, I thank in particular Martin Gardner and Wade Philpott; for help with the proof-reading, and for general support and forbearance, I thank my wife; and for assistance with the actual production of the book, I thank David Singmaster and the staff of Oxford University Press.

Two names must be singled out from these. John Maltby, unknown to me, has been writing his own book on Solitaire and researching its history for the purpose. When we found out about each other's activities, as a result of letters from Martin Gardner, we decided to share our discoveries, while reserving our positions as to any conclusions that we might draw from them. David Singmaster also helped in the tracking down of historical material (I owe my Leibniz material and my initial knowledge of Suremain de Missery to him, just as I owe some of my Wiegleb material to Maltby); furthermore, he tried deliberately to put himself in the position of the inexpert reader and made several cogent suggestions in consequence. The relation between editor and author is not always easy; on this occasion it has been very happy.

I also gladly acknowledge three sources of personal inspiration from many years ago: the late Kathleen Halsey, who gave me my first Solitaire set; J. and L. Randall Ltd., who made it and whose posing of the apparently curious problem 'vacate any hole, the aim being to finish with one peg in one of the nine central holes' first caused me to look into the theory underlying the game; and John Conway, whose talk to the Archimedeans at Cambridge in 1961 resurrected my interest and whose personal imprint on these pages is large. Others have made major contributions to the study of Solitaire, as will become apparent, but his has been as great as any.

I have tried, in the text, to give correct detailed acknowledgement of all previous work by others. If a reader thinks that I have not properly acknowledged any piece of work, let him please tell the publisher or myself, and we will put the record straight in any subsequent printing.

CONTENTS

Non ita pridem increbuit ludi genus singulare, quem *Solitarium* appellant, ubi ego ipse solus ludo, sed collusore velut teste & arbitro, an faciam officio satis. Plena est area calculis in foramina infixis, qui ordine eximendi sunt, sed nullus, (demto primo, qui pro arbitrio eligitur eximi potest, nisi alium calculum transsiliendo devenire possis proxime in vacuum locum, ut in ludo Damico caeditur. Qui ea lege servata omnes ad novissimum usque eximit, vincit; Sed qui uno plures tandem relinquere in area cogitur, palma excidit. Elegantius inverti potest hic ludus, post unum in area vacua pro arbitrio positum, caeteros collocando, sed ea lege observata ponendi, quae fuit paulo ante dicta eximendi. Ita possumus vel aream implere, vel, quod foret ingeniosius, datam figuram calculis formare; velut trigonum, quadratum, octogonum, aut aliud quiddam, si modo licet; neque enim res semper possibilis foret: atque hoc ipsum magnae artis esset praevidere, quid praestari posset; haberetque aliquid imprimis Geometricum hic processus. Sed ego ad profectum inventricis artis ludendi artificia detexisse, non ludum valde exercuisse laudarem.

Gottfried Wilhelm Leibniz,
Miscellanea Berolinensia **1** (1710) 24.

Not so very long ago there became widespread an excellent kind of game, called *Solitaire*, where I play on my own, but as if with a friend as witness and referee to see that I play correctly. A board is filled with stones set in holes, which are to be removed in turn, but none (except the first, which may be chosen for removal at will) can be removed unless you are able to jump another stone across it into an adjacent empty place, when it is captured as in Draughts. He who removes all the stones right to the end according to this rule, wins; but he who is compelled to leave more than one stone still on the board, yields the palm. This game can more elegantly be played backwards, after one stone has been put at will on an empty board, by placing the rest with it, but the same rule being observed for the addition of stones as was stated just above for their removal. Thus we can either fill the board, or, what would be more clever, shape a predetermined figure from the stones; perhaps a triangle, a quadrilateral, an octagon, or some other, if this be possible; but such a task is by no means always possible: and this itself would be a valuable art, to foresee what can be achieved; and to have some way, particularly geometrical, of determining this. But I claim credit only for having laid bare the techniques of playing for the advancement of the art of invention, not for having worked thoroughly at the game myself.

1

SOLITAIRE INTRODUCED

In this chapter we define the rules of Solitaire, look briefly at its history, and pose some introductory problems.

Rules, notation, and equipment

Solitaire ('Peg Solitaire' in America) is a puzzle game for one person. Its salient features are as follows:

(a) it is played with a board and men, the board containing a number of holes each of which can hold one man;

(b) each move consists of a jump by one man over one or more other men, the men jumped over being removed from the board.

Each move therefore reduces the number of men on the board, and the normal object of play is to start from a position with the board nearly full and play to a target position with the board nearly empty. On a board with a central hole, for example, play in the *central game* starts with a man in every hole except the centre, and the object is to end with just a man in the centre, the rest of the board having been emptied.

We shall concentrate on the standard 'English' board shown in Figure 1.1, though we shall consider some other boards in later chapters. (This board should more properly be called the 'German' board, since it seems to have been current in Germany long before its first recorded appearance in England, but the incorrect description has become customary in English-speaking countries.) The holes in the board are denoted by squares in the figure, and we shall use the notation shown to describe them.

Each hole may be occupied by one man, and the permitted move is to jump a man horizontally or vertically (but not diagonally) over an adjacent man into an empty hole immediately beyond, the man jumped over being removed. Thus at the top of Figure 1.2 we can

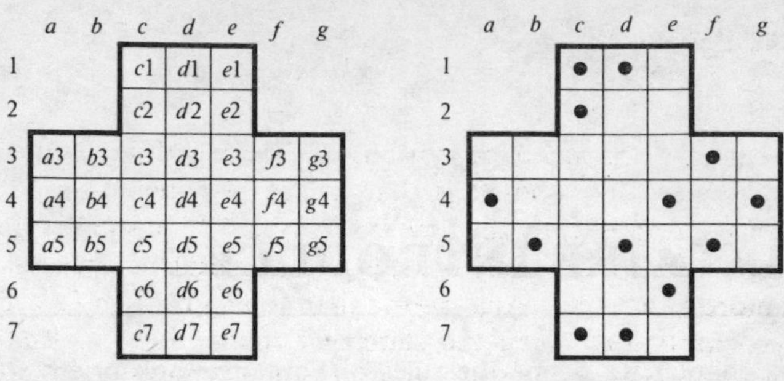

Figure 1.1

Figure 1.2

play *c*1–*e*1 removing *d*1 or *c*1–*c*3 removing *c*2, but we cannot play the diagonal move *d*1–*b*3 removing *c*2. At the bottom of the figure, we can if we wish play *c*7 all the way round to *a*3, removing *d*7, *e*6, *e*4, *f*3, *g*4, *f*5, *d*5, *b*5, and *a*4.

Most modern Solitaire sets contain plastic pegs which fit into holes in a plastic board. Before the invention of plastic, wood was normally used for the board and any convenient material for the men. The traditional English board, for example, is of wood, and has hollows to receive glass marbles or small stones. J. C. Wiegleb (1779) uses the word *Spitzen* (pegs) for the men. C. Bizalion (1871) describes a typical French set 'as it is sold still in our days' as consisting of a small board of thin wood, pierced with holes to receive pegs of bone or ivory, and having a handle so that it can be held in the left hand while the right executes the moves. Those that I have seen have a small sliding drawer underneath to hold the pegs. Several luxury sets also exist in private collections and museums. Wooden peg-boards in the French style appear no longer to be made, modern plastic pocket sets no doubt having proved cheaper and more convenient, but my local High Street currently offers a choice of pocket plastic sets, larger plastic sets, and traditional wooden boards with glass marbles. The construction of the board does not affect the play, of course, and some of the work for this book was done with cheap sets (and even with a pocket chess set when nothing more suitable was to hand); but the use of attractive equipment, whatever its price and material, adds charm to the play of any game.

Whatever equipment is used, it is desirable for some of the men to be distinguished in colour, size, or shape, so that they can be used for 'marked man' problems.

History

The origins of the game are no longer known with certainty. The legend most widely quoted is that it was invented by a French nobleman to while away the time in a prison cell, but I have found no support for this in early sources and fear that its perpetuation owes more to its picturesque nature than to any basis in fact. Similarly unsubstantiated are the statement in the *Encyclopédie méthodique: dictionnaire des jeux mathématiques* (1799) that American Indians played it with their arrows on returning from a hunt, the German tradition that it was a nun's or hermit's game, and the suggestions of various writers that it originated in China, Chaldaea, or ancient Rome. The earliest clear evidence known to me is an engraving by Claude-Auguste Berey, entitled *Madame la Princesse de Soubize joüant au jeu de Solitaire* and dated 1697. This engraving merely shows a lady with a Solitaire board, and the earliest description of the game known to me is in the passage quoted at the front of this book, which comes from a paper written by Leibniz for the Berlin Academy in 1710. Nevertheless, I doubt if this is the whole truth; the rules are so simple that I believe that games which we would recognise as Solitaire were indeed played, even if not recorded, in very early times. John Maltby, who has looked as deeply as anyone into the early history of the game, concurs with this opinion.

(I have not seen an original print of the Berey engraving, and the date on the reproduction that I have seen appears to have been written in. Nevertheless, there are good reasons for believing it: it is consistent with Berey's known period of activity, as recorded in the Inventaire of the Bibliothèque Nationale; the Princess's clothes would have been fashionable for a date around 1695–1700, according to the Victoria and Albert Museum; and the Princess herself died in 1709. So I regard the existence of Solitaire at the court of Louis XIV as adequately proven.)

Neither in the paper cited above nor in a frequently quoted letter written in 1716 does Leibniz describe the size and shape of the board customary at the time, but the Berey engraving shows a 37-hole board obtained by adding holes at *b*2, *f*2, *b*6, and *f*6 to the board of Figure 1.1. This was still sufficiently standard in 1765 to be the only board mentioned by Chevalier Louis de Jaucourt in an article in

Volume 15 of the *Encyclopédie*. It is still made in France, and can occasionally be purchased in this country. The earliest reference that I have found to the 33-hole board of Figure 1.1 is in the first volume of *Unterricht in der natürlichen Magie*, written by J. C. Wiegleb in 1779, which contains one example each of play on the 33-hole board, the 37-hole board, and the 45-hole board obtained by making each of the arms of the 33-hole board three rows deep instead of two.

It is not even certain that the early rules of Solitaire prohibited diagonal moves. Leibniz's word 'proxime' can reasonably be construed as implying that only orthogonal moves were permitted, and only such moves appear in the earliest examples of play known to me (in *Unterricht in der natürlichen Magie* and in the *Encyclopédie méthodique*), but Leibniz and the *Encyclopédie* of 1765 both use the phrase 'as in Draughts' to describe the act of capture, and the move in Draughts is diagonal. It is reasonable to suppose that orthogonal play has normally been required, but the evidence is not quite conclusive.

Leibniz refers to the problem of deciding whether a given target position can be reached from a given starting position. Wiegleb addressed this point, but his statements are so inaccurate that it is impossible even to conjecture what might have lain behind them. (Either his readers were very imperceptive or he ignored their comments, for the statements reappear without change in two subsequent editions.) The first sound investigation of which details have survived was performed by Antoine Suremain de Missery, '*ancien officier au corps royal d'artillérie, membre non residant de l'Académie*', though it is now known only through a report by J.-N. Vallot in 1842. Suremain de Missery investigated many classes of position, distinguished between positions which can be reduced to a single man and those which cannot, and gave the transformations which still remain the simplest way of generating potential starting positions. This theory was republished in 1857 by M. Reiss, to whom it is normally attributed, and extended by H.-A.-H. Hermary (another former officer of French artillery) in 1879.

Nevertheless a question remains. The results discovered by Suremain de Missery, once suspected, are not difficult to prove; I did so myself when I was about twenty, not knowing of previous work, and many others have done the same. In my own case, the trigger which caused me to look was the posing in my set's instructions of the problem: 'Vacate any hole, and play to leave a single survivor in one of the nine central holes.' It occurred to me to wonder why the last man could not always be left in the centre itself, so I looked, and in due course I found out. This particular trigger existed only because somebody else had already analysed the game and set the problem, but the 37-hole board provides more obvious triggers for the inquisitive, for it is impossible on that board to vacate any initial hole and play to leave a single survivor in the hole initially vacated, and it is also impossible to start by vacating the central hole and then play to leave a single survivor in any hole whatever. I cannot believe that only one man sat down between 1697 and 1842 and worked out why. I can believe that the others did not write down their results, or wrote them down only in letters or private jottings that have since been lost, but I would not be surprised if relevant material awaits discovery in a manuscript collection or obscure publication. Perhaps a reader with the time and energy to search likely archives will be able to throw light on the matter.

The theory developed by Suremain de Missery and his successors is very elegant, so elegant that most who have read or rediscovered it have looked no further, but it has a serious limitation: it applies to 'additive' moves (jumping over an empty hole and putting a man in) just as to ordinary 'subtractive' moves. A full theory of the game must take account of the distinction between these moves. Some elementary results (for example, that the men in the board can be divided into four classes and that men of particular classes are needed to clear the corners) must have been discovered in ancient times, but no more general theory appears to have been developed until a group of students studied the game at Cambridge University in 1961–2. (Part of this theory may have been discovered by T. R. Dawson in 1943, for Dawson published with confidence though without proof a result whose difficulty prompted some of its development in 1961, but his method of proof is not known to me and his result could have been proved by the laborious application of elementary arguments.) The principal inspiration of the Cambridge group was J. H. Conway, who has since become a benefactor of many branches of recreational mathematics, but contributions were also made by R. L. Hutchings, J. M. Boardman, M. J. T. Guy, and myself. The fact that this work was first written up by me for an undergraduate journal has caused my part in it to have been thought greater than it really was; in fact the major theoretical discoveries were the work of the others, my role having been in the discovery and analysis of particular problems. The theory of the game is still not complete, in the sense that no discriminant yet exists which is guaranteed to decide the solubility of a problem without an exhaustive analysis of variations, but in practice the solubility of a problem can normally be determined without undue effort unless some special condition (such as the minimisation of the number of moves) is involved.

Sadly little actual play appears in the early sources, and the oldest solution to the central game on the 33-hole board that I have seen was published by A. L. Crelle as late as 1852. (W. Ahrens, writing in 1910, quotes several problems from an anonymous pamphlet *Neueste Anweisung zum Kreuz- Einsiedler- oder Kapuziner-Spiel* which was published in Regensburg in 1807, and it is possible that this pamphlet may have contained such a solution, but I have not seen it myself and Ahrens does not report it as having contained one. The same may be true of an 1815 article by A. W. Schmolck, also cited by Ahrens.) Crelle did not attempt to minimise the number of separate moves required, and the earliest reasonably short solution known to me was one in 19 moves by W. H. Peel in 1890. The frequently quoted solution given by H. E. Dudeney in 1908 is very similar to Peel's. Ernest Bergholt reduced the number of moves to 18 in 1912, and it is characteristic of the fragmented state of Solitaire literature, which has had to find homes where it could, that such a discovery should first have been published in a weekly paper chiefly devoted to ladies' fashions. Bergholt's solution was finally proved to be the shortest possible in 1964.

The central game is only one of the problems possible on the standard board. Reiss gave solutions to all the soluble single-vacancy single-survivor problems in 1857, Peel gave solutions in between 17 and 20 moves to each of the 'complement' problems (in which the final survivor must finish in the hole initially vacant) in 1890, Bergholt gave several 16-move solutions in his *Complete handbook to the game of Solitaire on the English board of thirty-three holes* (1920), and Harry O. Davis gave a 15-move solution to the *c*3-complement problem (see Figure 1.1) in 1963. This is the shortest solution yet found to a single-vacancy single-survivor problem on the standard board and nobody who has seriously studied the game expects to find a shorter one. Davis took up Solitaire in retirement, having been introduced to it by an article in Martin Gardner's 'Mathematical Games' column in *Scientific American* in 1962.

A number of extensions have been made to the basic game.

Bizalion proposed some 'man-on-the-watch' problems, in which a nominated man remains motionless until the final move and then sweeps off all the other remaining men to become the only survivor, and Bergholt and others have since studied such problems extensively. Dawson suggested playing additive Solitaire with numbered counters, the objective being to place specific counters in particular positions. Occasional problems have been published using diagonal moves, and Davis, Wade E. Philpott and John W. Harris have looked in detail at their effect. Maltby introduced Colourtaire, in which men of various colours are used to enhance the central game, a multi-coloured layout being set up and the men being removed one colour at a time. There is little doubt that problems involving marked and distinguished men will receive greater prominence in the future, now that simpler problems have been extensively studied.

Other boards have also received attention: the 37-hole 'French' board; various draughtsboards; the infinite board, on which there exists the beautiful problem of the Solitaire Army, the subject of Chapter 12; the 6 × 6 square board, which is the smallest board on which it is possible to nominate both the initial vacancy and the last man to remain on the board; boards on triangular and other lattices; three-dimensional boards; linear boards; and many others. There are even some two-person versions of the game, one of which we consider briefly in Chapter 14.[1]

A brief survey of this book

Chapters 1 to 3 contain introductory problems and general advice on play.

Chapters 4 to 7 explore the underlying theory of the game on the 33-hole board and develop techniques for deciding whether a given problem is in fact soluble.

Chapter 8 looks at the question: If a problem is soluble, in how few moves can it be solved?

Chapters 9 and 10 contain further problems on the 33-hole board.

Chapters 11 to 14 consider other boards and other rules of play: general symmetrical boards, infinite boards, three-dimensional boards, hexagonal boards, jumps over two or more adjacent men, and various fancies.

[1] It has now become clear that the view taken in the earlier part of this section is altogether too cautious, and that Solitaire was in fact highly fashionable at the court of Louis XIV. See page 252.

Chapter 15 summarises the whole and makes suggestions for further research.

Most chapters contain problems for the reader to solve. This is not a textbook and the exercises are not compulsory. Some interesting results are included in these problems, however, use being made of them in later chapters. If you prefer just to read the answer, which is normally given at the end of the chapter in which the problem appears, fine; but if you prefer to solve, it is normally necessary to do so before reading on since later material may give away the answer.

Introductory problems

For a gentle start, try 'Cross', 'Diamond', 'Crossbow', and 'Longbow' (Figures 1.3 to 1.6). In each of these problems, '●' denotes a hole which is occupied at the start of play and 'x' the hole in which the last man is to finish; so the objective in 'Cross' and 'Diamond' is to leave the last man in the centre, whereas that in 'Crossbow' and 'Longbow' is to shoot a man to *d*1. (Note that the centre is initially occupied in 'Cross' but empty in 'Diamond'.) 'Cross' and 'Diamond' are traditional problems which date back at least to Busschop (1879); I cannot recall having seen 'Crossbow' and 'Longbow' in print before, but problems so simple cannot be new.

Now can you solve the 'central game' (start by vacating the centre and play to finish with the last man in the centre)? If you cannot, read Chapter 2 and then come back. If you can, then try 'Not quite dead'. It was discovered many years ago that if we start the central game with the moves *d*2–*d*4, *d*5–*d*3, *d*7–*d*5, *b*4–*d*4, *e*4–*c*4, and *g*4–*e*4 then we reach 'Dead' (Figure 1.7) and no further move is possible:

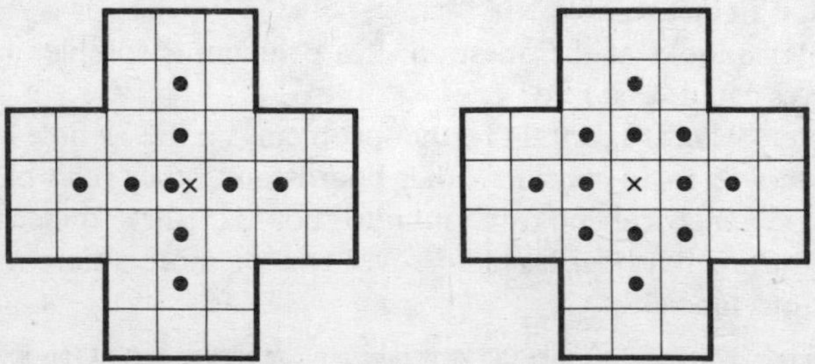

Figure 1.3 'Cross' **Figure 1.4** 'Diamond'

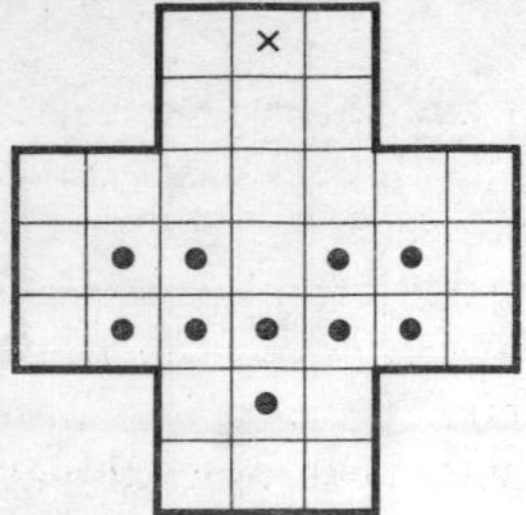

Figure 1.5 'Crossbow'

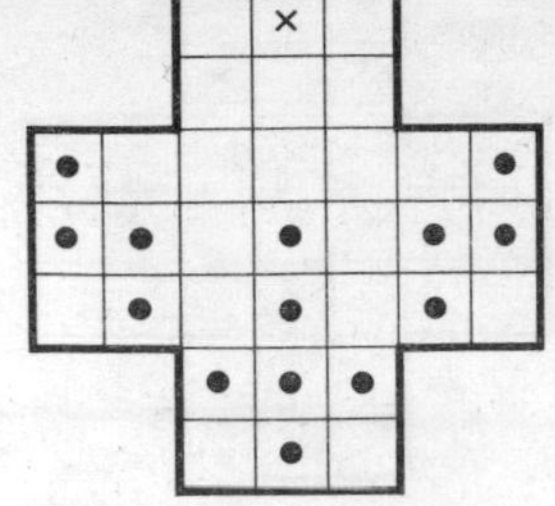

Figure 1.6 'Longbow'

we have failed utterly after only six moves. In 'Not quite dead' (Figure 1.8) we have played the first five of these moves but a solution is still possible; complete one.

After this, start by vacating *c*7 and play to reach 'Snake' (Figure 1.9) or 'Zip' (Figure 1.10), from each of which it is easy to end with a single man in *c*7. Alternatively, start by vacating *e*4 and play to reach letter 'B' (Figure 1.11), or by vacating *d*4 and play to reach letter 'D' (Figure 1.12). In these figures, 'o' denotes the hole which is initially *empty*, all the other holes being initially occupied, and 'x' again denotes the holes to be occupied at the finish. (Our notations '•' for a hole initially occupied and 'o' for one initially empty are alternative, and we shall use whichever is the more convenient for the problem in hand.) 'Snake' is due to Bergholt and 'Zip' to Conway; the letters are surely ancient.

Finally, try some problems with marked men, denoted by '*' in the figures. The general rule is that a marked man must *not* be captured during the course of play. In 'The lecturer and his audience' (Figure 1.13) the marked man at *d*1 represents the lecturer and the

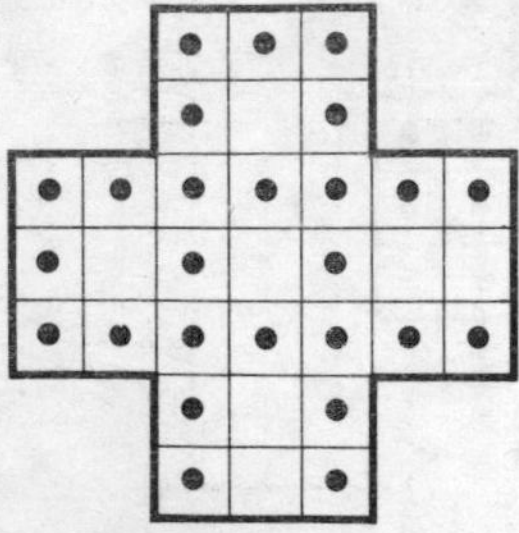

Figure 1.7 'Dead'

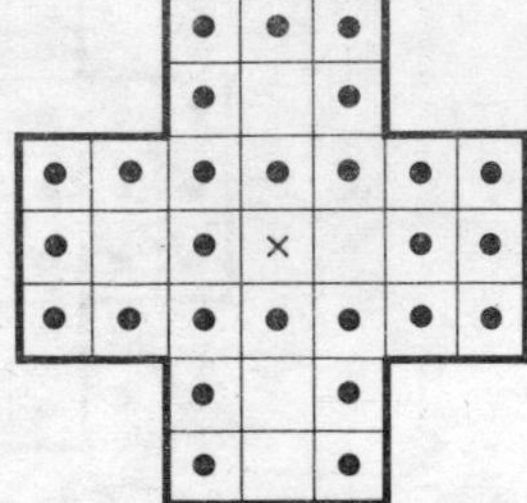

Figure 1.8 'Not quite dead'

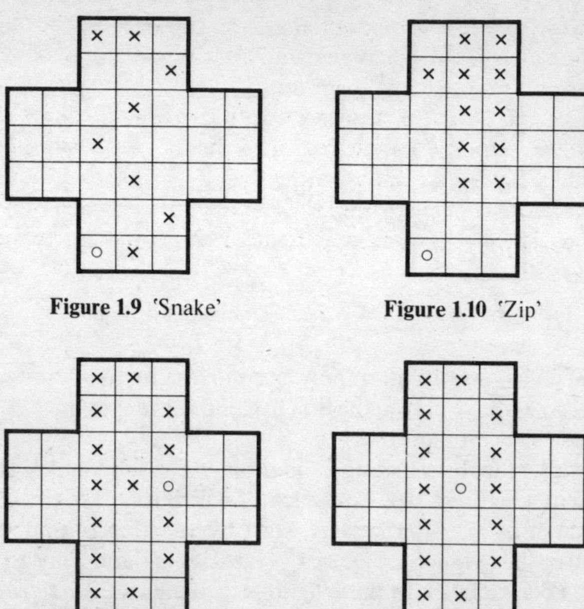

Figure 1.9 'Snake'

Figure 1.10 'Zip'

Figure 1.11 'Letter B'

Figure 1.12 'Letter D'

objectives of play are three-fold: to reduce his audience to three men in *c*7/*d*7/*e*7, or to reduce it to two men in *a*5/*g*5, or to make it vanish altogether. In the first two problems, the lecturer remains a motionless gongoozler at *d*1; in the third, he stays there as long as he can and then, disgusted with the course of events, collects the few remaining students and marches out of the back door (*d*7).

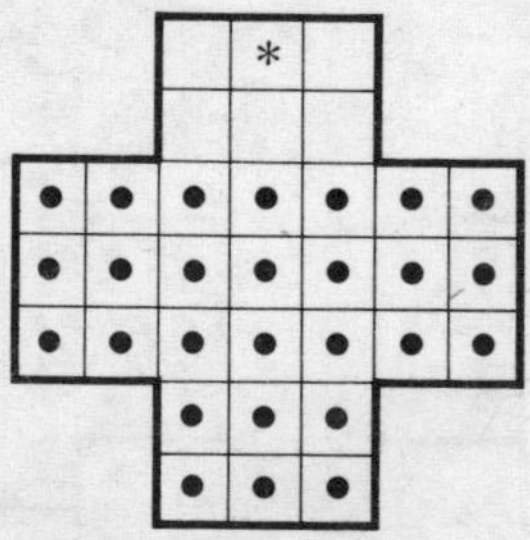

Figure 1.13
'The lecturer and his audience'

In 'Swap' (Figure 1.14) the initial vacancy is at *d*3 and the objective is to interchange the marked men and clear the rest of the board. In 'Triple cross' (Figure 1.15) there are *three* initial vacancies, *b*3, *g*3, and *e*7, and the objective is to end with the marked men *f*5, *a*5, and *c*1 in these holes as shown, the rest of the board again being cleared. Both can be solved as 'man on the watch' problems, the marked men remaining motionless until the last few moves, when they move to their assigned positions and remove the remaining unmarked men.

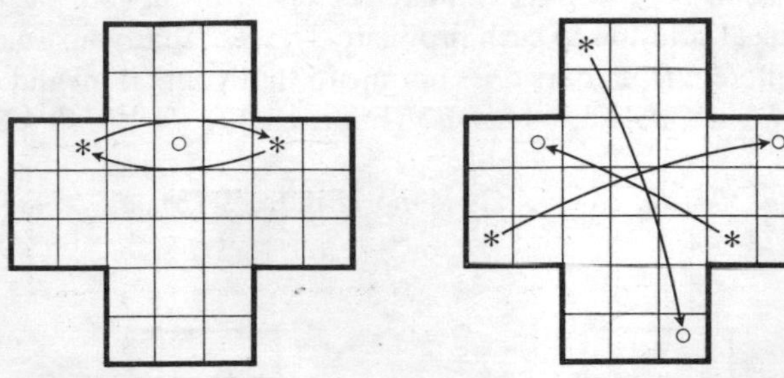

Figure 1.14 'Swap'

Figure 1.15 'Triple cross'

Finally, in 'Whither will he wander?' (Figure 1.16) the initial vacancy is at *d*1 and the objective is once more to remove all except the marked man at *d*3, but the hole in which this man is to finish is not specified. (We shall discover in due course that there is only one hole in which he *can* finish, but we shall let this fact emerge during the next few chapters.)

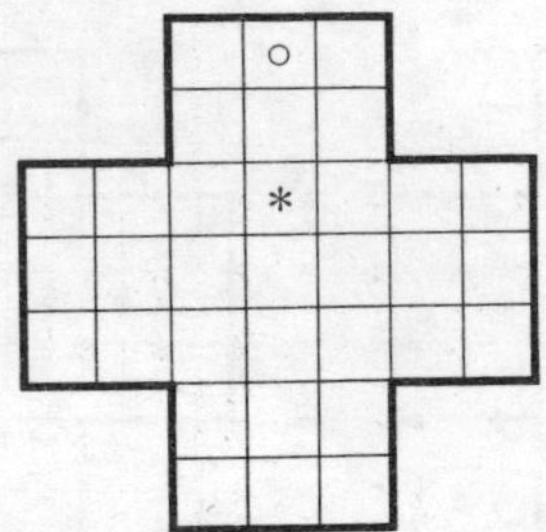

Figure 1.16
'Whither will he wander?'

Each of these problems is soluble but none is easy. If you cannot solve them, read Chapter 2 and then come back. If you *can* solve them, either after reading Chapter 2 or before, then you are well on the way to becoming an expert player.

Solutions to Chapter 1

It is unusual for a Solitaire solution to be unique; even in 'Longbow', where the moves to be played can be shown to be uniquely determined, the player has considerable choice over the order in which he plays them. We therefore content ourselves throughout the book with a typical solution to each problem. The fact that your solution may be different from ours does not mean that yours is invalid.

Cross: *d*3–*d*1, *d*5–*d*3, *b*4–*d*4–*d*2 (Figure 1.17); *f*4–*d*4, *d*1–*d*3–*d*5, *d*6–*d*4.

Diamond: *b*4–*d*4, *e*4–*c*4, *d*2–*d*4–*b*4 (Figure 1.18); *d*5–*b*5–*b*3–*d*3–*f*3–*f*5–*d*5, *d*6–*d*4.

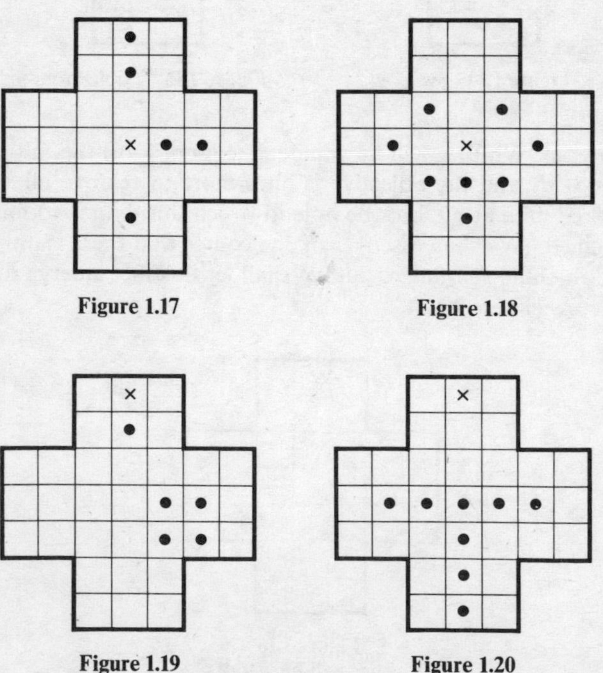

Figure 1.17

Figure 1.18

Figure 1.19

Figure 1.20

Crossbow: *d*6–*d*4, *b*5–*d*5–*d*3, *b*4–*d*4–*d*2 (Figure 1.19); *f*4–*d*4, *f*5–*d*5–*d*3–*d*1.

Longbow: *a*3–*a*5–*c*5, *c*6–*c*4, *g*3–*g*5–*e*5, *e*6–*e*4 (Figure 1.20); *d*5–*d*3, *b*4–*d*4–*d*2, *f*4–*d*4, *d*7–*d*5–*d*3–*d*1.

We postpone the remaining solutions until Chapter 2.

2

SOLITAIRE MADE EASY

In this chapter we make a fundamental classification of the Solitaire men and describe some techniques which simplify the finding of solutions.

The four classes of men

We can make a very simple classification of the rows and columns of a Solitaire board into 'odd' and 'even', counting as 'odd' rows *a*, *c*, *e*, and *g* and columns 1, 3, 5, and 7. This enables us to divide the holes into four classes, as follows:

Row	Column	Class	
even	even	m	(Figure 2.1)
odd	odd	c	(Figure 2.2)
odd	even	s	(Figure 2.3)
even	odd	t	(Figure 2.4)

The reason for our choice of letters will appear in due course.

This simple classification proves to be very important in the theory and play of Solitaire, because every Solitaire move takes the man

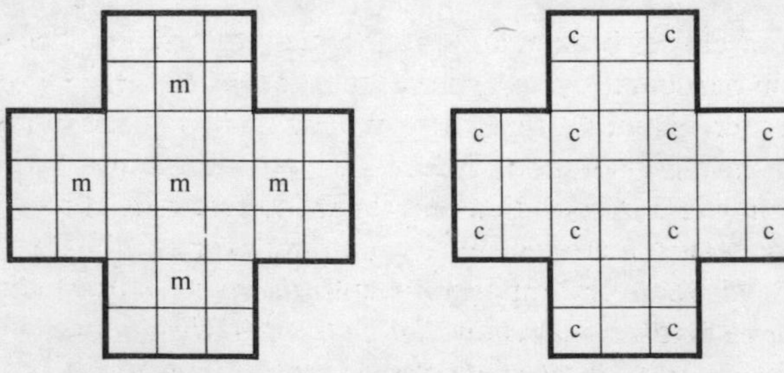

Figure 2.1 **Figure 2.2**

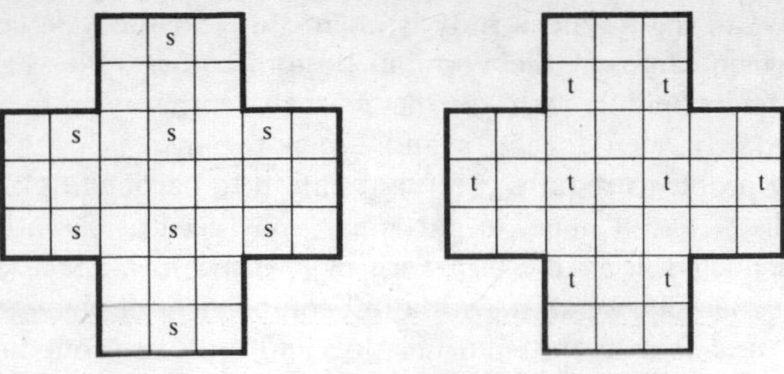

Figure 2.3 Figure 2.4

moved an *even* number of holes in each direction. If the man starts in an even row then it either stays in that row or moves to another even row, and similarly for columns; a man cannot move between an even row or column and an odd one. It follows that *a man stays in the same class of hole throughout its career*. A consequence is that *the number of men in holes of a particular class cannot increase during the course of a solution.*

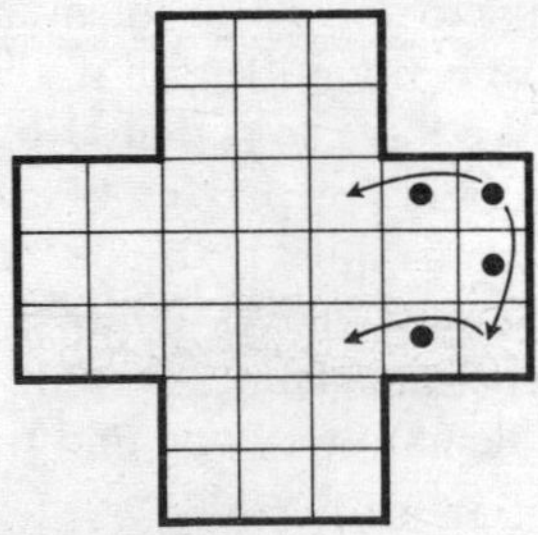

Figure 2.5

The four classes of men are not of equal importance. The 's' and 't' men, in particular, have a special role in the clearance of corners. Suppose, for example, that there is a man at *g*3 which must be removed during a solution (Figure 2.5). Now it cannot be jumped over where it is, but must first be brought to an inside corner, and it can move to such a corner only by jumping over an 's' man at *f*3 or *f*5. This leads to a very important result: *the removal of a man at a*3, *a*5, *g*3, *or g*5 *involves the removal of an 's' man; the removal of a man at c*1, *e*1, *c*7, *or e*7 *involves the removal of a 't' man.* This explains our notation: only 'm' men can move to the Middle; only 'c' men can move to the Corners; only 's' men can clear the Side corners; only 't' men can clear the Top and bottom corners. We shall also use the terms 'middle men' for the 'm' men, 'corner men' for the 'c' men, and 'edge men' for the 's' and 't' men together.

Many problems require careful attention to particular classes of men. The 's' and 't' men, in particular, may need preservation because of their role in the clearance of corners. In 'Snake' (Figure 1.9), for example, we start with a full complement of eight 's' men, but we need four in the final position and must use four more to clear the side corners, allowing *none at all* to be removed by other moves. Did you start by playing *e*7–*c*7? Probably you didn't, but you won't have succeeded if you did. In 'Letter B' (Figure 1.11) it is the 't' men that are most precious, since we start with only seven, must use two to clear *e*1 and *e*7, and need the other five in the final position. Similarly, in 'Letter D' (Figure 1.12) we start with eight 't' men, must use two to clear *e*1 and *e*7, and need the other six in the final position.

Although it is usually the edge men that are the most precious, there are problems in which other men must be carefully preserved. For example, an attempt to solve a problem in which the last man must finish in the centre is bound to fail if all the middle men are removed during play. We have seen that 'Not quite dead' (Figure 1.8) can be killed immediately by playing *g*4–*e*4, but it can be killed just as surely, if not quite as quickly, by playing *e*2–*e*4, *g*3–*e*3, and *f*5–*f*3, since the last of these moves removes the only remaining middle man. Mail order firms claim to supply goods more cheaply by cutting out the middleman; we hope that they don't spend their spare time trying to play Central Solitaire!

Block moves and removals

Some patterns of men occur repeatedly in Solitaire problems, and much time and effort can be saved by using standard sequences of moves to handle them. We now explore some of these. The reader may find it useful to play through the next few examples with board and men. We use a notation similar to that which we used for problems: '●' for a hole which must be occupied at the start of the play, 'o' for a hole which must be empty at the start of the play, and 'x' for a hole in which a man is to finish. Unmarked holes are neither used nor affected by these block moves, so it does not matter whether they are initially occupied or empty.

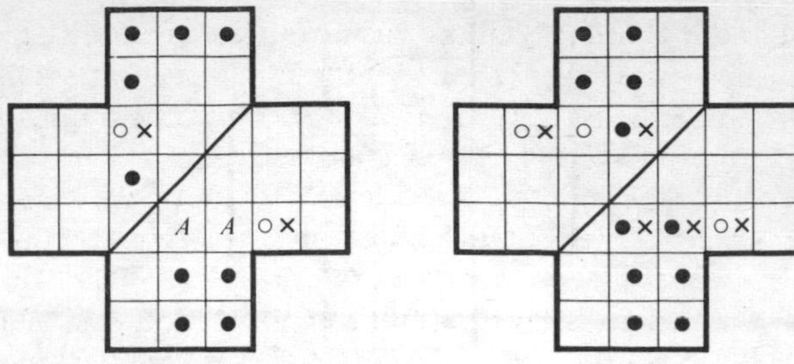

Figure 2.6 Figure 2.7

The upper half of Figure 2.6 shows the well-known *L-move*. The moves *c*1–*c*3, *c*4–*c*2, and *e*1–*c*1–*c*3 replace the L by a single man at *c*3.

Less well known but also useful is the *four-move*, shown in the lower half of Figure 2.6. This requires the two auxiliary holes denoted by *AA*, and its effect is to replace the four men *d*6/*e*6/*d*7/*e*7 by a single man at *f*5. For example, if the holes *AA* are empty then we simply play *e*7–*e*5 and *d*7–*d*5–*f*5. But *the holes AA need not be empty*. In the lower half of Figure 2.7, for example, they are both full, but the moves *d*5–*f*5, *d*7–*d*5, and *e*7–*e*5 still replace the four men *d*6/*e*6/*d*7/*e*7 by a single man at *f*5 *and restore the holes AA to their original state*. Similarly, in the upper half of Figure 2.7 the holes corresponding to *AA* are *c*3 and *d*3, and we notice that one of them is full and the other empty; but we can still play the four-move, for the moves *c*1–*c*3, *d*3–*b*3, and *d*1–*d*3 replace the four men *c*1/*d*1/*c*2/*d*2 by a single man at *b*3 and refill *d*3. Reverting to the lower half of Figure 2.6, the reader may verify that *whatever the initial occupancy of the holes AA, it is possible to play the moves d*7–*d*5, *e*7–*e*5, *and d*5–*f*5 *in some order, thus replacing d*6/*e*6/*d*7/*e*7 *by a single man at f*5 *and restoring the holes AA to their original state.*

We call a set of holes such as *AA*, which are necessary for the performance of a block move but are left unchanged by it, a *catalyst*.

Also useful are *block removals*, in which complete sets of men are removed without affecting the rest of the board. A catalyst is always needed for such a removal. The upper half of Figure 2.8 shows the *three-removal*, for which the necessary catalyst is a pair of holes *UU one of which is full and the other empty*. We call such a pair an *unlike pair*. In Figure 2.8, for example, if *b*3 is full and *d*3 empty then we can play *b*3–*d*3, *c*1–*c*3, and *d*3–*b*3, removing the line of three and

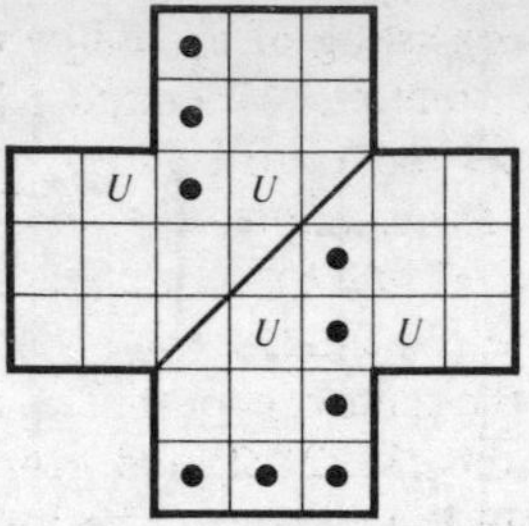

Figure 2.8

restoring the catalyst to its original state. The lower half of the figure shows the similar *L-removal*, which also requires an unlike pair *UU*. If *d*5 is full and *f*5 empty, for example, then we can play *d*5–*f*5, *e*7–*e*5, *e*4–*e*6, *c*7–*e*7–*e*5, and *f*5–*d*5, removing the complete L and restoring the catalyst.

Figures 2.9 to 2.11 show the *six-removal*. The upper half of Figure

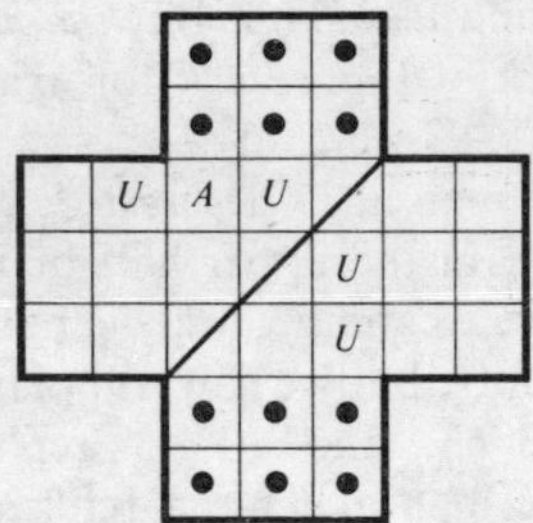

Figure 2.9

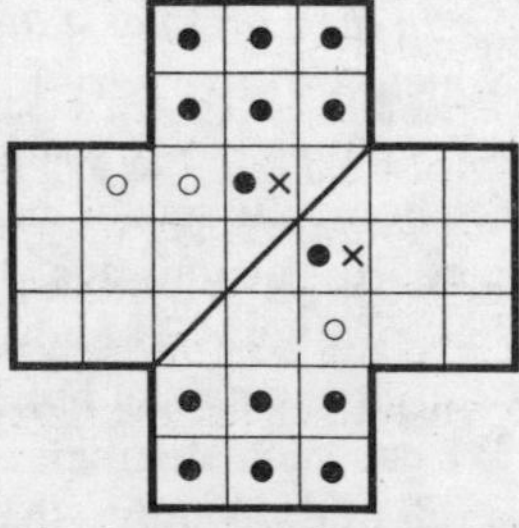

Figure 2.10

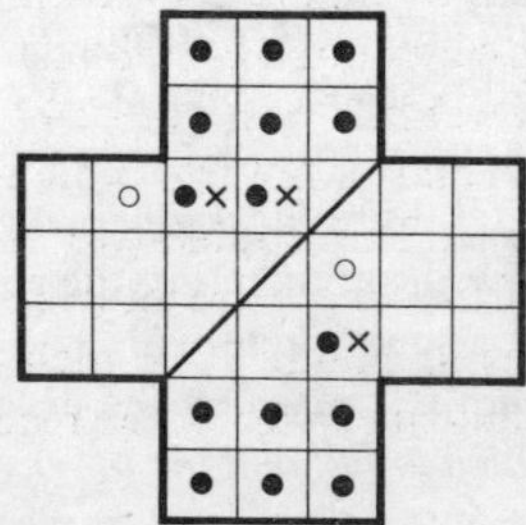

Figure 2.11

2.9 shows a catalyst consisting of an unlike pair *UU* and a hole *A* whose contents do not matter. (Mnemonic: *UU* must be *Unlike*; *A* is *Arbitrary*.) The upper halves of Figures 2.10 and 2.11 show two cases. In Figure 2.10, for example, *b*3 and *c*3 are empty and *d*3 is full, and the moves *c*1–*c*3, *d*3–*b*3, *e*2–*c*2, *e*1–*c*1–*c*3, and *b*3–*d*3 clear the top six and restore the catalyst to its original state. The upper half of Figure 2.11 is the same except that *c*3 is initially full, and the moves *d*3–*b*3, *c*1–*c*3, *b*3–*d*3, *e*2–*c*2, and *e*1–*c*1–*c*3 once more clear the top six and restore the catalyst. The lower half of Figure 2.9 shows an alternative catalyst for the six-removal; the two possible configurations of the catalyst are shown in the lower halves of Figures 2.10 and 2.11, and we leave to the reader the task of showing that the six can indeed be removed and the catalyst restored in each case.

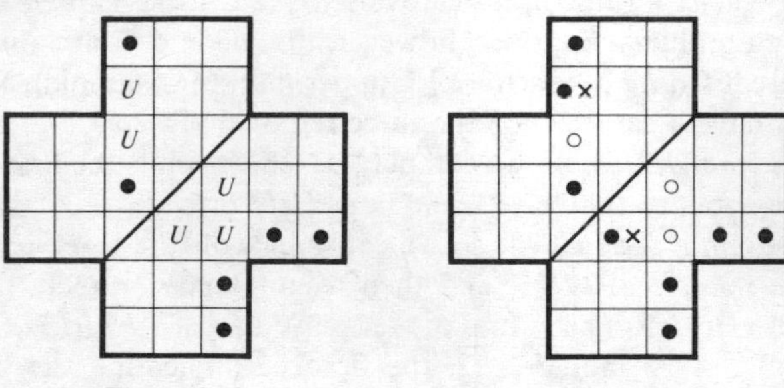

Figure 2.12 **Figure 2.13**

The upper half of Figure 2.12 shows a useful removal called by Bizalion the *call and answer*, for which the required catalyst is again an unlike pair *UU*. For example, if *c*2 is full and *c*3 empty, as in the upper half of Figure 2.13, then the call is *c*1–*c*3 and the answer *c*4–*c*2, removing *c*1 and *c*4 and restoring the catalyst.

The lower half of Figure 2.12 shows the *double-two*, for which the required catalyst is a trio of holes *UUU* not all alike. We call this an *unlike trio*. The double-two is really a combination of a three-removal and one extra move; for example, if *d*5 is full and *e*4/*e*5 empty, as in Figure 2.13, then we can play *g*5–*e*5 followed by the three-removal *e*7/*e*6/*e*5. The reader may wish to check the remaining cases.

Figures 2.14 and 2.15 illustrate an important technique in which two block moves or removals are performed in conjunction, the first

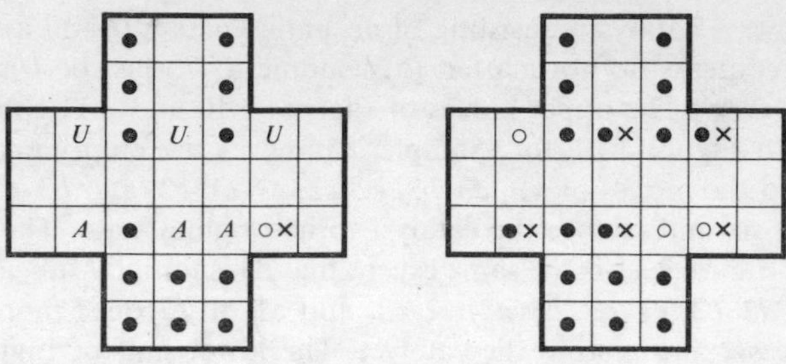

Figure 2.14 Figure 2.15

providing a catalyst for the second. The upper half of Figure 2.14 shows the *double-three*, which is a combination of two three-removals. If *d3* is different from both *b3* and *f3* then we have catalysts for each of the three-removals *c1/c2/c3* and *e1/e2/e3*, and there is no problem. Suppose, however, that *d3* and *f3* are alike but are different from *b3* (Figure 2.15, upper half, for example). We do not now have a catalyst for the three-removal *e1/e2/e3*, but we do have one for *c1/c2/c3*. So we can play *d3–b3*, which is the first move in the three-removal *c1/c2/c3*, and now *d3/f3* provides a catalyst for the three-removal *e1/e2/e3*; so we can break off the three-removal *c1/c2/c3*, remove *e1/e2/e3*, and then resume and complete the removal of *c1/c2/c3*. The actual moves played are *d3–b3*, (*f3–d3*, *e1–e3*, *d3–f3*), *c1–c3*, and *b3–d3*, the brackets indicating the 'inner' three-removal *e1/e2/e3*, and their effect is that both sets of three are removed even though initially we have a catalyst for only one of them. The reader may verify that the double-three can indeed be performed whenever *UUU* (Figure 2.14, upper) is an unlike trio.

The lower half of Figure 2.14 shows the similar *four-three*, which is a combination of a four-move and a three-removal. If we cannot initially remove *c7/c6/c5* then we can start playing the four-move from *d6/e6/d7/e7* into *f5*, break off as soon as a catalyst for the three-removal appears, perform this removal, and then resume and complete the four-move. The lower half of Figure 2.15 shows a case of frequent practical occurrence; the play here is *e7–e5*, *d5–f5*, (*b5–d5*, *c7–c5*, *d5–b5*), and *d7–d5*.

Finally, Figure 2.16 gives an example of a *chain-removal*. It is obvious that a chain such as that shown in Figure 2.16 can be removed if precisely one of the holes *UUUUUU* is occupied, since we can then run the *U* man around the chain. But in fact we can remove the chain provided only that the holes *UUUUUU* are not all alike, for we can run each *U* man in turn as far as it can go and then let the one behind take over. The *U* men do not end in their original holes, but the same *U* holes are left occupied and the chain is removed.

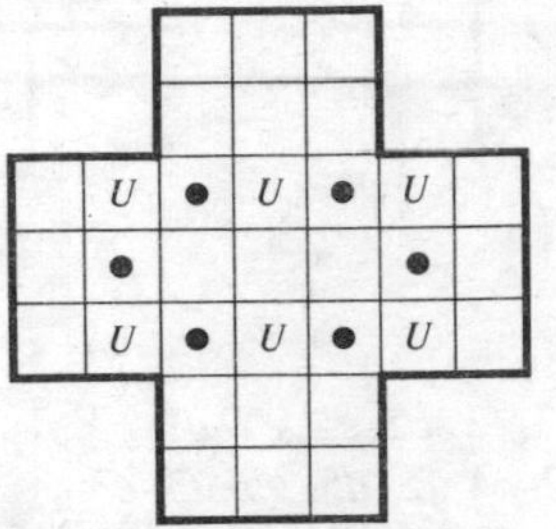

Figure 2.16

These are not the only block moves and removals possible on a Solitaire board and we shall meet some others in later chapters, but they form a very useful set and mastery of them will pay handsome dividends. To see them in action, let us consider the *d*2-complement problem (Figure 2.17). We can solve this as follows:

1. Play the move *d*4–*d*2.
2. Remove the top six, *d*3/*e*3/*f*3 now providing a *UAU* catalyst (Figure 2.9, top).
3. Remove the right-hand six similarly, *e*2/*e*3/*e*4 providing the catalyst.
4. Remove the bottom six similarly.
5. Perform the three-removal *e*3/*e*4/*e*5, *d*5/*f*5 providing the catalyst.
6. Perform the L-removal *a*3/*a*4/*a*5/*b*5/*c*5/*d*5, *c*4/*c*6 providing the catalyst.
7. Make the four-move *b*3/*c*3/*b*4/*c*4–*d*2, completing the solution.

This solution is shown in diagrammatic form in Figure 2.18. Such diagrammatic solutions are frequently more readily comprehensible than lists of moves, and we shall make extensive use of them. On this first occasion, however, it is perhaps desirable to write the moves in full to demonstrate that the solution does indeed exist. We therefore detail the steps above as follows:

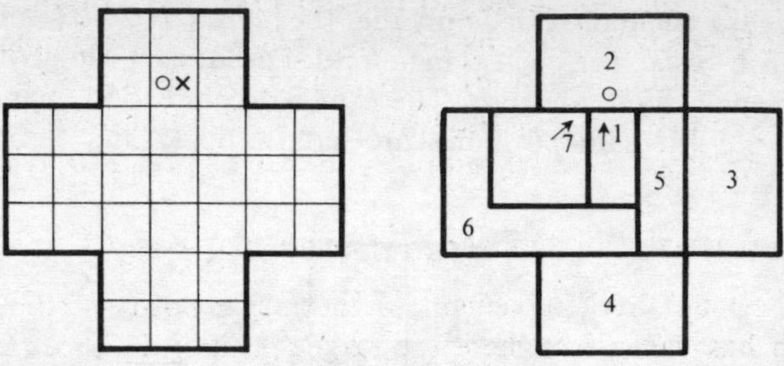

Figure 2.17 **Figure 2.18**

1. *d*4–*d*2.
2. *f*3–*d*3, *e*1–*e*3, *d*3–*f*3, *c*2–*e*2, *c*1–*e*1–*e*3.
3. *e*4–*e*2, *g*3–*e*3, *e*2–*e*4, *f*5–*d*5, *g*5–*g*3–*e*3.
4. *d*5–*f*5, *e*7–*e*5, *f*5–*d*5, *c*6–*e*6, *c*7–*e*7–*e*5.
5. *d*5–*f*5, *e*3–*e*5, *f*5–*d*5.
6. *c*4–*c*6, *a*5–*c*5, *d*5–*b*5, *a*3–*a*5–*c*5, *c*6–*c*4.
7. *b*3–*d*3, *b*4–*d*4–*d*2.

Solitaire made easy indeed!

At this point, we suggest that the reader try the other single-vacancy complement problems. There are only seven such problems which are essentially different (*c*1, *d*1, *c*2, *d*2, *c*3, *d*3, and *d*4), since the rest can be transformed into these by reflection or rotation. The *d*1-complement is probably the hardest to solve and is certainly the easiest in which to make a fatal mistake.

My personal knowledge of block play owes a lot to Conway and something to Bizalion, but this is largely historical accident since the three-removal, double-three, call-and-answer, L-move, and four-move are present even in the play of Wiegleb. Wiegleb does not draw specific attention to the blocking, but the three-removal, in particular, occurs with such frequency that accidental juxtaposition of moves must be ruled out. Block play is also used extensively in the *Dictionnaire des jeux mathématiques*, though again without the drawing of specific attention to it.

Playing backwards

A difficulty encountered in some problems is that of visualising the target position while play is in progress. This difficulty can sometimes be removed by solving the problem backwards, starting from the target position and playing to reach the starting position. This can most obviously be done by making *additive moves* (jumping over a hole and putting a man in). T. R. Dawson suggests doing this with numbered counters, putting them on the board in order 1, 2, 3 and so on, since the required solution can then be obtained by removing them in reverse order.

Alternatively, the following technique may be used:

(a) set up the complement of the target position (the position which has vacancies where the target position has men and men where it has vacancies);

(b) play to reach the complement of the starting position, remembering or writing down the moves as they are made;

(c) rewrite any 'multiple moves' (moves consisting of two or more consecutive jumps by the same man) as sequences of single moves;

(d) set up the starting position normally and play the moves just found in reverse order.

This always gives a solution to the original problem.

For a simple example, suppose that we are asked to vacate the centre and play to 'Wall' (Figure 2.19). By what we have just said, we can solve this problem by setting up the complement of 'Wall', which is 'Cross' (Figure 1.3, repeated for convenience as Figure 2.20), and playing to finish with just a man in the centre, which is the complement of our starting position. Now we solved 'Cross' in Chapter 1 by the following moves:

*d*3–*d*1, *d*5–*d*3, *b*4–*d*4–*d*2, *f*4–*d*4, *d*1–*d*3–*d*5, *d*6–*d*4.

If we write the multiple moves *b*4–*d*4–*d*2 and *d*1–*d*3–*d*5 in full, we get

*d*3–*d*1, *d*5–*d*3, *b*4–*d*4, *d*4–*d*2, *f*4–*d*4, *d*1–*d*3, *d*3–*d*5, *d*6–*d*4.

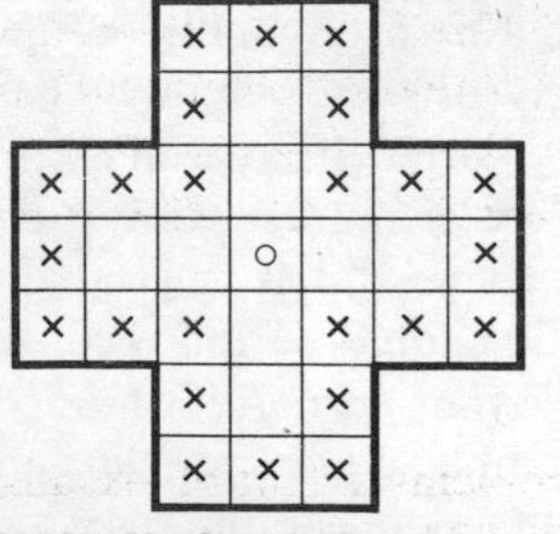

Figure 2.19

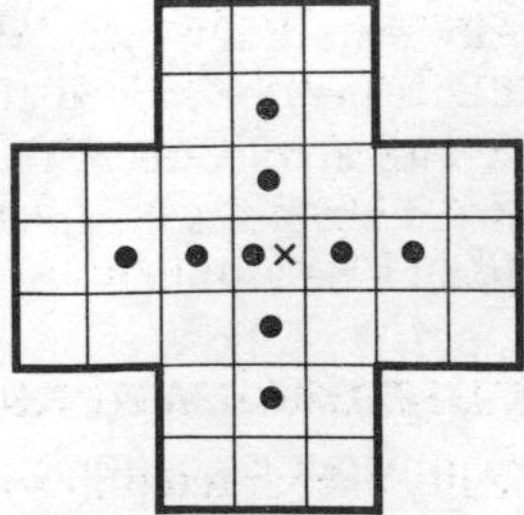

Figure 2.20

Writing these moves in reverse order gives

*d*6–*d*4, *d*3–*d*5, *d*1–*d*3, *f*4–*d*4, *d*4–*d*2, *b*4–*d*4, *d*5–*d*3, *d*3–*d*1;

and it may be verified that this does indeed give a solution to the problem posed.

At first sight it seems impossible that playing backwards should be easier than playing forwards, since the solutions are logically the same. It is easier to visualise a simple target position than a complicated one, however, so backwards play may reduce the risk of oversight, a point of importance in practice if not in theory. The number of alternative lines of play may also be greater in one direction than in the other. Even a problem as simple as 'Wall' gives an example of this. If we try to play forward to 'Wall', we find that moves such as *b*5–*d*5 can be played after the first move and similar moves at most later stages; they may be useless, but they are legally playable and in a more difficult problem we might waste time trying them. No such move can ever be made when playing forward from 'Cross'.

Two warnings

If you were unable to solve any of the problems in Chapter 1, now is the time to try again. You should find them a lot more tractable. We give two warnings, however.

(a) The use of six-removals, L-removals and L-moves to clear corners removes *three* edge men for each pair of outside corners, and so cannot be adopted when there is a critical shortage of edge men. If we have no spare 's' men, for example, then we cannot use such a move or removal to clear the top or bottom.

(b) Although our block moves and removals restore all catalyst *holes* to their original state of fullness or emptiness, they do not necessarily restore the original *men*; a man originally occupying a catalyst hole may be moved elsewhere or removed altogether. In a problem with marked men, this may matter. It is certainly possible to construct problems in which the use of marked men as parts of catalysts may be harmless or even beneficial, but in general this is not so, and the following simple rule should be followed: *no hole containing a marked man should be used as part of a catalyst*. There are a few obvious exceptions; for example, a marked man can form part of a *UU* pair in Figure 2.8 without risk of capture since it merely moves across and then back; but even such uses as these are barred from 'man-on-the-watch' problems where the marked man must not move before the end. It is best to use block play only where it does not affect marked men and to work out play involving marked men in detail.

Solutions to Chapter 2

We first give diagrammatic solutions to the single-vacancy complement problems. We repeat the *d*2-complement in the interests of completeness, although we gave it in Figure 2.18, and we work from the centre outwards so that the hardest case (*d*1) is left until last. We use the following notation in these solutions:

'o' for an initial vacancy;
a straight arrow for an ordinary move;
a diagonal arrow for a four-move;
a bent arrow for an L-move;
a number in a block for a block removal.

In the case of L-moves and other moves involving two separated blocks, we attach '*a*' and '*b*' to the numbers to indicate that the blocks are associated. It should be possible to follow most of these solutions from the diagrams, but a board and men should be used if there is any difficulty.

Figures 2.21 to 2.26 show solutions to the *d*4-, *c*3-, *d*3-, *c*2-, *d*2-, and *c*1-complements respectively. It will be found that the catalysts necessary for the block removals are always present. In Figure 2.21, for example, we make the three-removal *e*4/*e*3/*e*2 (catalyst *d*4/*f*4), the six-removal on the right (catalyst *e*4/*e*6 or *d*3/*e*3), the six-removal at the bottom (catalyst *d*5/*f*5 or *e*4/*e*5), and so on round.

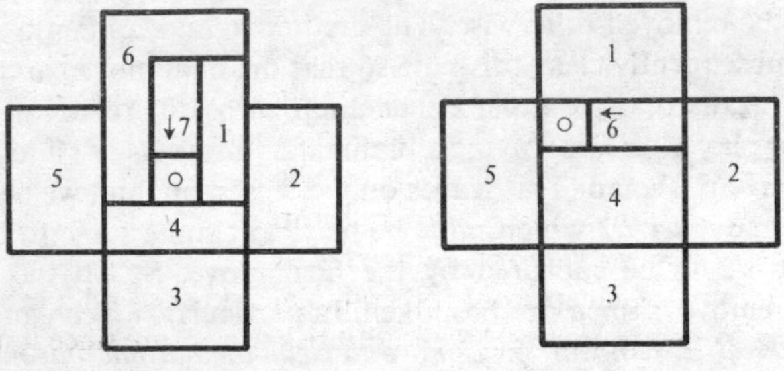

Figure 2.21 **Figure 2.22**

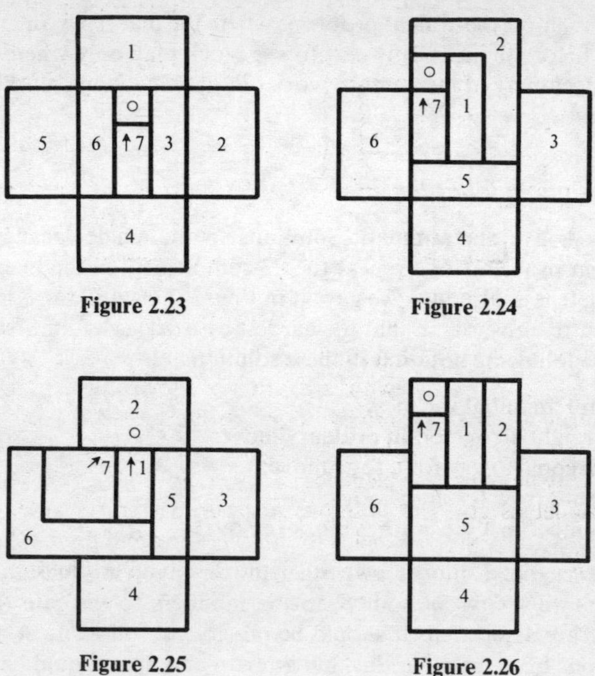

Figure 2.23

Figure 2.24

Figure 2.25

Figure 2.26

Figures 2.27 and 2.28 illustrate a solution to the *d*1-complement. The play shown in Figure 2.27 produces the position shown in Figure 2.28, and the move *d*7–*d*5–*f*5–*f*3–*d*3–*d*1 completes the solution.

Why is the *d*1-complement the easiest in which to make a fatal mistake? Consider the 's' men. We start with seven, of which one must be the final man. This leaves six to be removed during the solution. Four of these must be used to clear the side corners, leaving two to be removed otherwise. The first move puts a man in *d*1. We must subsequently clear this hole so that the final move can refill it, which means that we must either jump across it, removing an 's' man, or play *d*1–*d*3, involving a preliminary move *d*4–*d*2 and so also removing an 's' man. This leaves only one 's' man, and we need this for the move *d*4–*d*2 which must be played at some stage to bring a man to *d*2 to be captured by the final move. So all the moves which remove 's' men are bespoken. In particular, *we cannot play a six-removal, L-removal, or L-move to clear the bottom, but must use the moves c*7–*c*5, *d*7–*d*5, *and e*7–*e*5. We shall prove this more el-

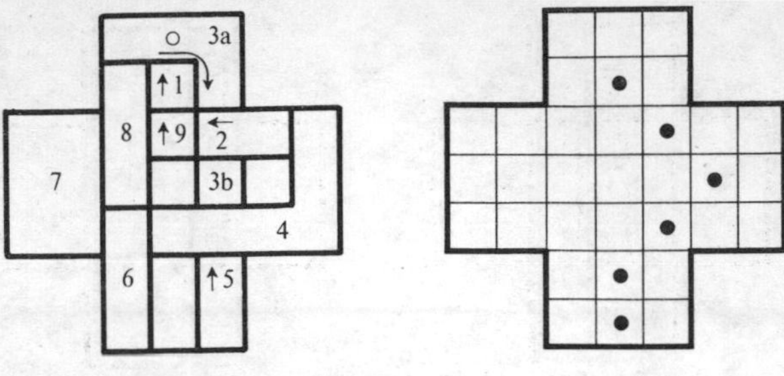

Figure 2.27 Figure 2.28

egantly in Chapter 5, and shall also prove that we must clear at least one of the sides by a downwards L-removal or L-move.

The solutions above are by no means the shortest possible, as we shall see in Chapter 8, but they are logically simple and their very simplicity has a certain elegance.

Now let us give the solutions postponed from Chapter 1. 'Not quite dead' (Figure 1.8) yields to the play shown in Figure 2.29. This produces the position shown in Figure 2.30, and the solution can be completed by the two three-removals *e*3/*d*3/*c*3 and *e*5/*d*5/*c*5 and the move *f*4–*d*4.

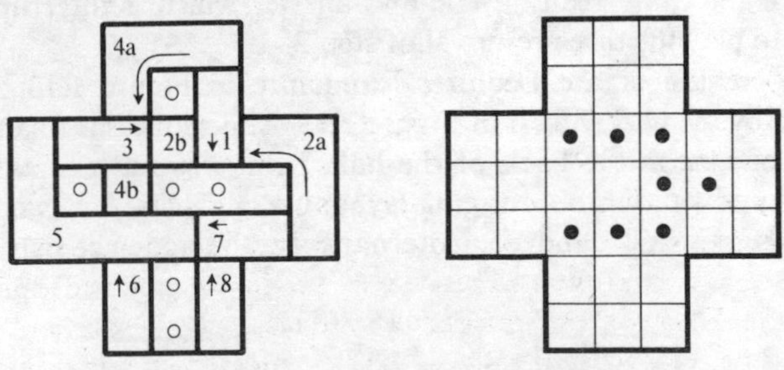

Figure 2.29 Figure 2.30

'Snake' (Figure 1.9) yields to the play shown in Figure 2.31. The holes *c*6/*c*7 provide a catalyst for the opening six-removal.

'Zip' (Figure 1.10) can be reached by the play shown in Figure 2.32. Step 2*a*/2*b* is a double-two removal, and step 3 places a man in *c*5 which is promptly swallowed by step 4. Having reached 'Zip', we can place a man in *c*7 by the zip finish which occasioned the name: *e*1–*c*1–*c*3, *e*2–*c*2–*c*4, *e*3–*c*3–*c*5, *e*4–*c*4–*c*6, and *e*5–*c*5–*c*7.

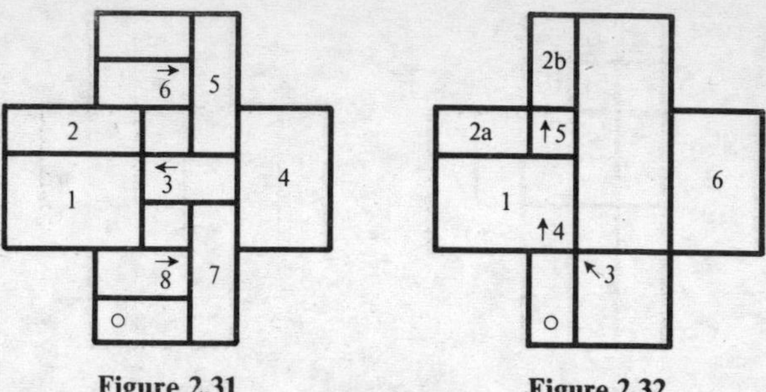

Figure 2.31 Figure 2.32

'Letter B' (Figure 1.11) can be reached by the play shown in Figure 2.33, steps 1*a*/1*b* and 4*a*/4*b* being double-two removals and step 6*a*/6*b* a call-and-answer. There are some subtle restrictions affecting the middle men in *d*2, *d*4 and *d*6: the original man in *d*4 must be jumped over vertically (*not* horizontally), *d*4 must be refilled by a move from *d*2 or *d*6, and the man not moving to *d*4 must be jumped over horizontally. We shall invite the reader to prove these statements after reading Chapter 6.

'Letter D' (Figure 1.12) can be reached by the play shown in Figure 2.34. This is very similar to that of Figure 2.33; in particular, steps 1 and 3 are really a call-and-answer which is interrupted in order to play the three-removal of step 2.

The erosion of the Lecturer's audience in Figure 1.13 can be started by the play shown in Figure 2.35. This reduces it to a square block of nine at the back of the hall, from which it can easily be brought down to three lounging layabouts in *c*7/*d*7/*e*7 or two skulking solitaries in *a*5 and *g*5. Alternatively, the audience can be re-

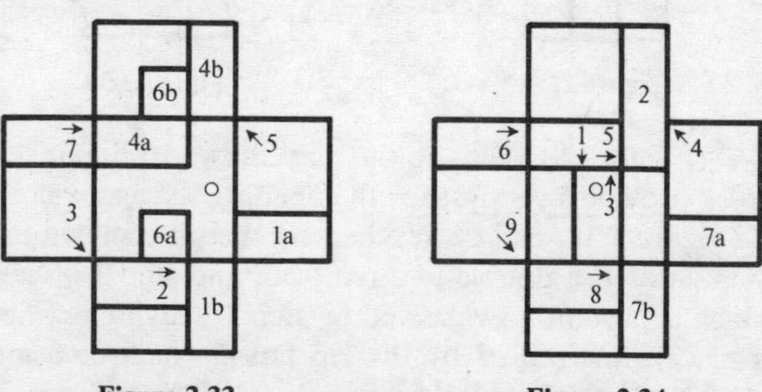

Figure 2.33 Figure 2.34

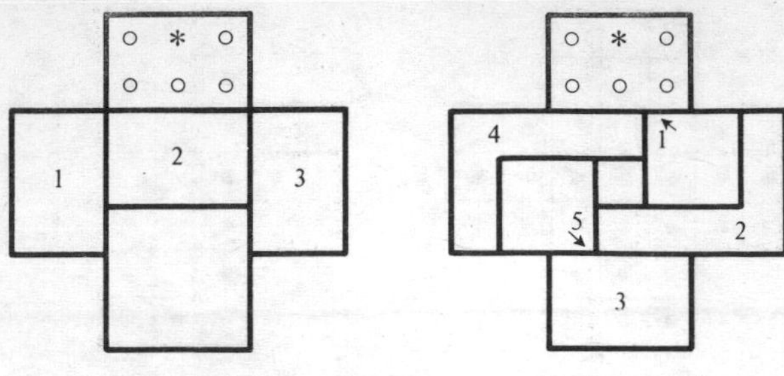

Figure 2.35 Figure 2.36

moved altogether by the play shown in Figure 2.36 and the move *d*1–*d*3–*d*5–*d*7. A final sweep via *b*3 and *b*5 is also possible.

A solution to 'Swap' (Figure 1.14) is shown in Figure 2.37. This play produces the position shown in Figure 2.38, and round we go. The first fatal mistake that we can make in attempting a man-on-the-watch solution is to start by playing *d*5–*d*3. We shall need the man initially in *d*5 to clear one of the side corners, and to move it to *d*3 would put it too far away. So we must start by playing *d*1–*d*3 and *d*4–*d*2, which constitutes step 1*a*/1*b* of the solution. Step 9*a*/9*b* shows a very common manoeuvre which we call an 'extended L-move', the man needed at *d*5 being put there by the move 9*b*.

'Triple cross' (Figure 1.15) is one of the hardest problems in this set and for once it is easier to list moves than block removals. Play *d*3–*b*3, *a*3–*c*3, *f*3–*d*3–*b*3, *e*1–*e*3, *d*1–*d*3–*f*3 (Figure 2.39), *g*5–*g*3–*e*3, *d*5–*d*3–*f*3, *f*4–*d*4, *b*5–*d*5–*d*3, *c*7–*c*5, *e*6–*c*6 (Figure 2.40), and home we go: *a*5–*a*3–*c*3–*e*3–*g*3, *f*5–*d*5–*b*5–*b*3, and *c*1–*c*3–*c*5–*c*7–*e*7.

Finally, whither indeed will he wander (Figure 1.16)? On the face

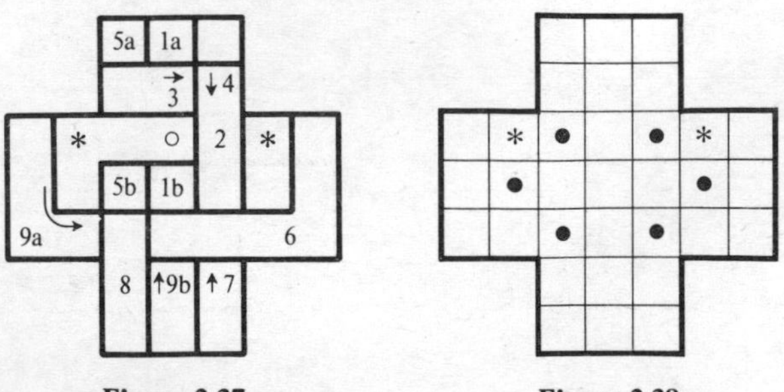

Figure 2.37 Figure 2.38

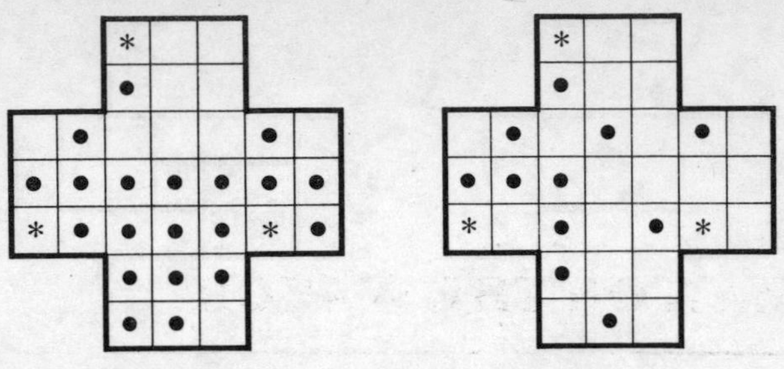

Figure 2.39

Figure 2.40

of it, he can finish in any of the eight 's' holes, but we shall show in Chapter 4 that the choice is more restricted than this and in Chapter 6 that it is very restricted indeed. We accordingly postpone the solution until then.

3

A MAN ON THE WATCH

Having solved a problem, we can do several things: have a rest, or try to find the 'best' solution in some sense, or try to solve it again under more restrictive conditions. In this chapter we shall consider the single-vacancy complement problems under the following conditions:

(a) the man to remain on the board at the end is nominated before play starts;

(b) it must remain motionless (a 'man on the watch') until the very end of the solution, when it must sweep off all the remaining men;

(c) the number of men cleared in this final sweep must be as large as possible.

These conditions produce a very attractive set of problems first proposed by Bizalion and extensively investigated by Bergholt. The implied requirement, that we *prove* the final sweep to be the longest possible, is at first sight forbidding, but we shall see that in most cases the proof is straightforward. Bergholt's own treatment, as recorded in his 1920 book, was not exhaustive, but he covered the most interesting problems.

Odd and even paths

Let us start by looking more closely at the geometry of the Solitaire board.

Figure 3.1 indicates the 's' and 't' holes and shows a single man at *c*1. Now suppose that we require this man to move, and that we allow it to remove as many 't' men as it likes but no 's' men. Then plainly it cannot move off column *c*. If now we require it to remove precisely one 's' man then it must move to column *a* or *e*; it cannot stay in column *c*, nor can it move back there. If we require it to

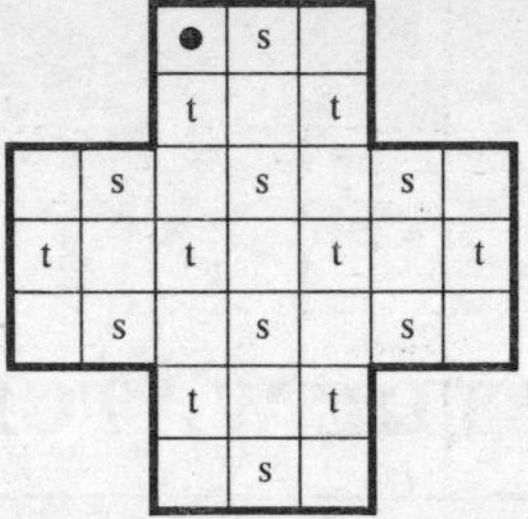

Figure 3.1

capture precisely two 's' men then it can move to column *g* or come back to column *c*, but it cannot stay in the column to which the first move took it. And so on.

We can generalise this result as follows: if we require a 'c' man to remove an *even* number of 's' men then it must finish $4n$ columns away from its starting column, for some n; if we require it to remove an *odd* number then it must finish $(4n+2)$ columns away from its starting column. A similar property holds with respect to the rows and the 't' men.

It follows that if we require a 'c' man to travel between two specified holes, then the *parity* (oddness or evenness) of the number of 's' men captured is determined even though the number itself may not be, and similarly for the 't' men. For example, suppose that we wish the man in Figure 3.1 to move from *c*1 to *e*5. Then whatever path we choose, it must involve an odd number of 's' men and an even number of 't' men.

Similar results apply to the other men. Figure 3.2 shows the 'c' and 'm' holes together with an 's' man at *b*3, and it will be noticed that the rows and the 'm' men are related, and similarly the columns and the 'c' men. If we want to move from *b*3 to *f*5 then we must remove an even number of 'c' men and an odd number of 'm' men. Figure 3.3, rather trivially, shows some 's' and 't' holes, together with an 'm' man at *d*2, and shows that, for moves of an 'm' man, the rows are related to the 's' men and the columns to the 't' men.

These results lead to a simple classification into 'odd' and 'even' of the holes that a man can reach. For example, Figure 3.4 shows the holes that can be reached by a man at *c*1, and it will be noticed that those marked 'o' can be reached only by paths involving an odd

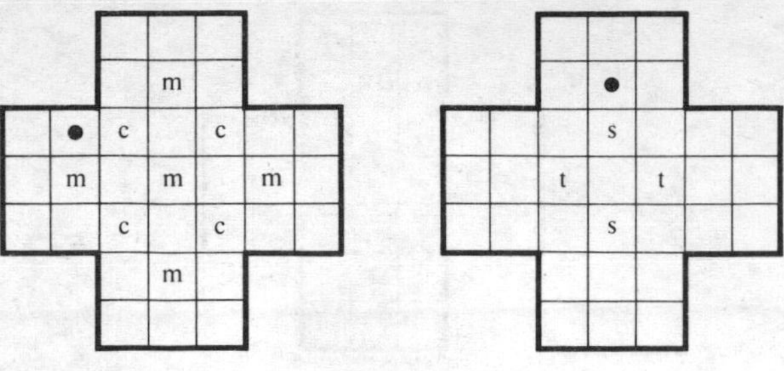

Figure 3.2　　Figure 3.3

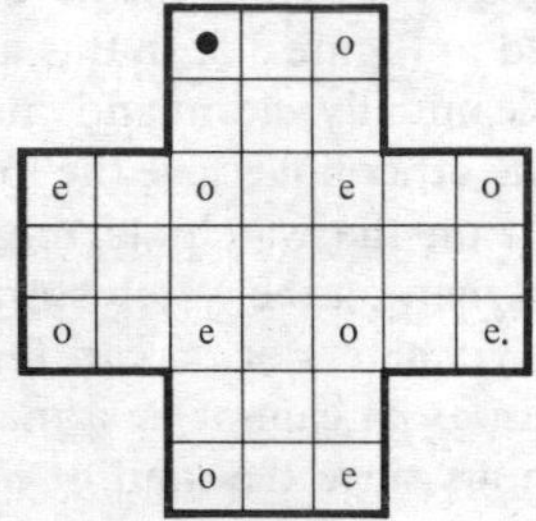

Figure 3.4

number of men and those marked 'e' only by paths requiring an even number.

Having demonstrated this piece of Solitaire geometry, let us consider the men on the watch. There are seven essentially different single-vacancy complement problems, but for present purposes it is convenient to divide them into three classes depending on whether the initial vacancy is a middle, edge, or corner hole. The man on the watch must of course be in a hole of the same class.

Middle man problems

The central problem (*d*4-complement) is of no interest as a man-on-the-watch problem, since any of the remaining middle men may be nominated as the man on the watch and only a one-move final sweep is possible. The solution shown in Figure 2.21 is in fact a man-on-the-watch solution, the man on the watch starting at *d*2.

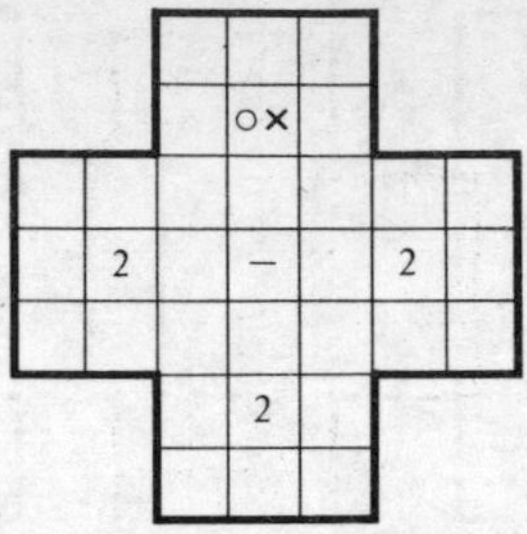

Figure 3.5

The other middle man problem is the *d*2-complement, whose behaviour is summarised in Figure 3.5. In this and subsequent figures, 'ox' represents the hole initially vacant and finally occupied, as usual, and the numbers in the other holes give the longest final sweeps that can be made by men on the watch starting in these holes. Thus Figure 3.5 says that a man on the watch starting at *b*4, *f*4 (which is equivalent to *b*4 by symmetry) or *d*6 can finish at *d*2 with a two-sweep, but that a man at *d*4 cannot be a man on the watch at all. This last fact is obvious since the man at *d*4 must make the first move.

The reader may wish to find solutions finishing with these various sweeps. We give a complete set at the end of the chapter.

Edge man problems

Problems with edge men offer much more variety. The *d*1-, *b*3-, and *d*3-complements come into this category.

(a) *The d1-complement*

There are five essentially different candidates for the man on the watch: *b*3, *d*3, *b*5, *d*5, and *d*7. Figure 3.6 summarises the results, which are explained as follows:

*b*3: No longer path is geometrically possible.

*d*3: This man cannot be a man on the watch since it must make the first move.

*b*5: The only longer path that is geometrically possible is the seven-sweep *b*5–*b*3–*d*3–*f*3–*f*5–*d*5–*d*3–*d*1, but this would remove four middle men, and we need one for the first move and another for the

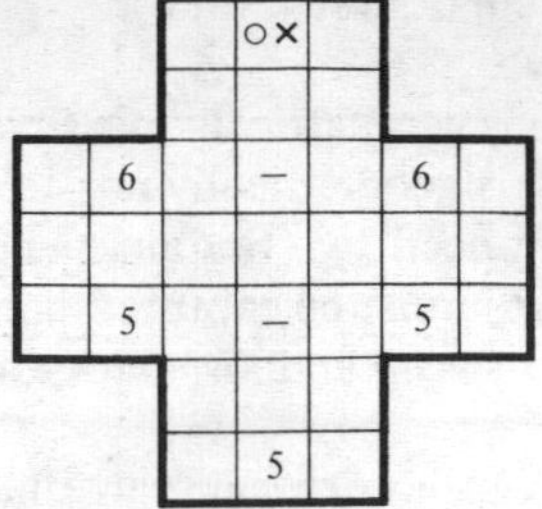

Figure 3.6

move *d*7–*d*5 which we showed in the solutions to the last chapter to be needed in every solution to the *d*1-complement.

*d*5: This man cannot be a man on the watch, for it must move before the end in order to allow the necessary move *d*7–*d*5.

*d*7: The only longer path that is geometrically possible is the nine-sweep *d*7–*d*5–*b*5–*b*3–*d*3–*f*3–*f*5–*d*5–*d*3–*d*1, but this would remove all five middle men and we need one for the first move.

(b) *The b3-complement*

There are seven candidates for the man on the watch. Figure 3.7 summarises the results, which are explained as follows:

*d*1: No longer path is geometrically possible.

*d*3: The middle man at *d*2 must be captured unmoved, since any move by it would remove the man on the watch, and the middle man originally at *b*4 is captured by the first move. Furthermore, the clearances of the right and left sides each involve the removal of a middle man. We shall give a rigorous proof of this in Chapter 6, but a little experiment should bring conviction. All this leaves only one

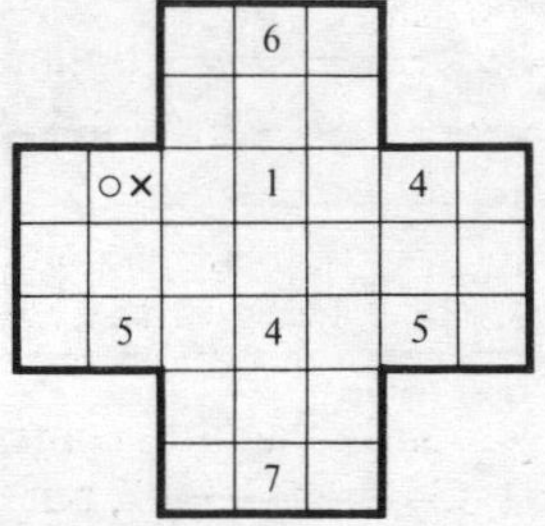

Figure 3.7

middle man for the final sweep, and any path longer than a one-sweep would need two.

*f*3: No longer path is geometrically possible.

*b*5: No longer path is geometrically possible.

*d*5: As with *d*3, we need two middle men to help clear the sides and a third (that at *d*6) must be captured unmoved, so only two are available for the final sweep and any path longer than a four-sweep would need three.

*f*5: No longer path is geometrically possible. The five-sweep gives an attractive miniature version of 'Snake'.

*d*7: No longer path is geometrically possible.

(c) *The d3-complement*

There are five essentially different candidates for the man on the watch: *d*1, *b*3, *b*5, *d*5, and *d*7. Figure 3.8 summarises the results, which are explained as follows:

*d*1: No longer path is geometrically possible.

*b*3: No longer path is geometrically possible.

*b*5: No longer path is geometrically possible.

*d*5: Once more we have a shortage of middle men. Two are needed to clear the sides and one must be captured unmoved, so only two are available for the final sweep. Any path longer than a three-sweep would need three.

*d*7: No longer path is geometrically possible.

Some of this group were considered by Bizalion and his readers in 1871. N. M. Panday (or Pauday) proposed the seven-sweep finish from *d*1, and D. Fawcett found the eight-sweep finish from *d*7; but Bizalion refused to publish the latter on the ground that he had asked only for a seven-sweep from *d*5!

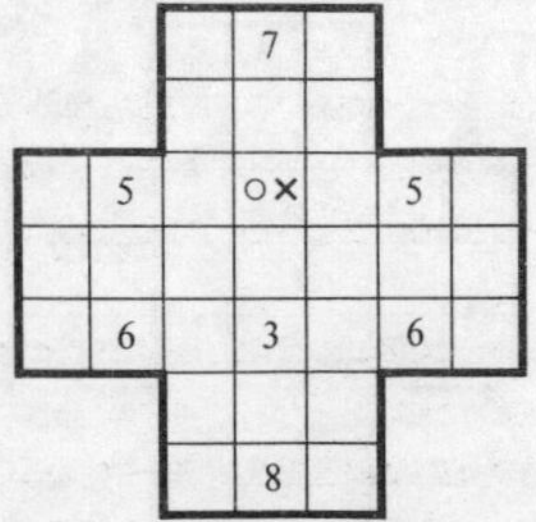

Figure 3.8

Corner man problems

These are the most interesting of all. The final sweeps involve the removal of edge men, so their lengths are limited by the number of these men needed to clear the outside corners. The invariance of the oddness or evenness of path lengths which we proved at the beginning of this chapter is very important here.

There are two cases, the *c*1- and *c*3-complements.

(a) *The c1-complement*

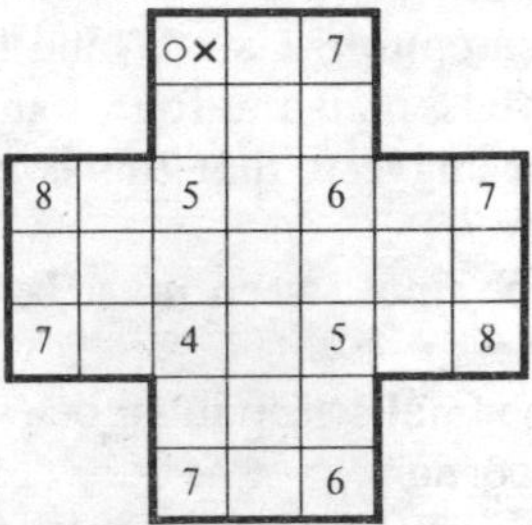

Figure 3.9

There are eleven candidates for the man on the watch. Figure 3.9 summarises the results, which are explained as follows:

*e*1: The first move must be *c*3–*c*1, removing a 't' man, and seven more edge men must be used to clear corners before the final sweep. This leaves at most eight edge men for the final sweep, but the length of every path from *e*1 to *c*1 is odd, as proved in the first section of this chapter, so a seven-sweep is the best possible.

*a*3: The length of the final sweep must be even and we need seven edge men to clear the corners.

*c*3: The length of the final sweep must be odd and we need ten edge men to clear the corners, for the man initially on *e*1 must play *e*1–*c*1 (first move), *c*1–*e*1, and *e*1–*e*3, and that on *a*3 must play *a*3–*a*5 and *a*5–*e*5.

*e*3: The length of the final sweep must be even and we need nine edge men to clear the corners.

*g*3: The length of the final sweep must be odd and it looks at first sight as if a nine-sweep might be possible, for if the first move is *e*1–*c*1 then we need only six more edge men to clear the corners; but in fact there is no such solution. A little experiment will convince of the truth of this, and we shall prove it in Chapter 6.

*a*5: The length of the final sweep must be odd, and we can demonstrate the impossibility of a nine-sweep more easily here. We can clear the corners with seven edge men only by starting *e*1–*c*1 and using four 's' and three 't' men, leaving four 's' and five 't' men for the final sweep, but any sweep from *a*5 to *c*1 involves an odd number of 's' men and an even number of 't' men.

*c*5: The length of the final sweep must be even and we need ten edge men to clear the corners; furthermore, the only way of clearing the corners using only ten edge men is to start by playing *e*1–*c*1, in which case the ten men comprise six 's' and four 't' men. The only six-sweep involving two 's' men and four 't' men is *c*5–*c*7–*e*7–*e*5–*e*3–*e*1–*c*1, and experiment suggests that this is unattainable. We shall give a proof in Chapter 7.

*e*5: The length of the final sweep must be odd and we need ten edge men to clear corners.

*g*5: The length of the final sweep must be even and we need seven edge men to clear the corners.

*c*7: The length of the final sweep must be odd, and a nine-sweep can be proved impossible by a similar argument to that which we used for *a*5.

*e*7: The length of the final sweep must be even. We need four 's' men to clear corners and the only eight-move paths from *e*7 to *c*1 that do not involve at least five 's' men all involve five 't' men and finish with the move *c*3–*c*1. So an eight-sweep solution must start with *e*1–*c*1 and *d*3–*d*1, else we shall have a deficiency of 't' men, and now how can we use the 's' man just delivered to *d*1? Use it we must, for we need four 's' men for side clearance and three for the final sweep, and we have already used one for the first move. Yet it cannot form part of the final sweep where it is, because this sweep must end with *c*3–*c*1; and it cannot be brought out, since this would involve moving another middle man to *d*2 and we cannot afford the removal of another 's' man at *d*3 that this would entail. So we cannot use the man delivered to *d*1 after all, and it follows that an eight-sweep finish is impossible.

(b) *The c3-complement*

There are six essentially different candidates for the man on the

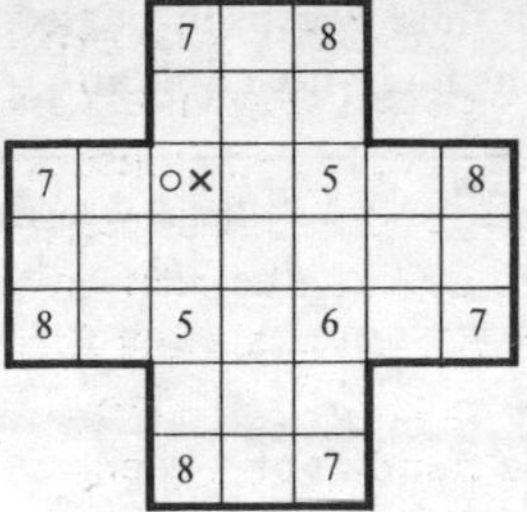

Figure 3.10

watch: *c*1, *e*1, *e*3, *g*3, *e*5, and *g*5. Figure 3.10 summarises the results, which are explained as follows:

*c*1: The length of the final sweep must be odd and a little experiment will convince of the impossibility of a nine-sweep. We shall prove it in Chapter 6.

*e*1: The length of the final sweep must be even and we need seven edge men to clear the corners.

*e*3: The length of the final sweep must be odd and we need ten edge men to clear the corners.

*g*3: The length of the final sweep must be even and we need seven edge men to clear the corners.

*e*5: The length of the final sweep must be even and we need ten edge men to clear the corners.

*g*5: The length of the final sweep must be odd and we need three 's' and four 't' men to clear corners. Any path from *g*5 to *c*3 involves an even number of 's' men and an odd number of 't' men, so no nine-sweep is possible.

Summary

The results of this chapter are summarised in Table 3.1. For each initial vacancy and length of sweep, the table lists the men on the watch which can finish with a sweep of the given length. It also highlights the results which we shall not prove optimal until a later chapter.

We shall consider some other man-on-the-watch problems in Chapter 9. In particular, we shall see that single-survivor problems exist to which a nine-sweep finish is possible, even though no such finish is possible to a single-vacancy complement problem.

Table 3.1: Longest final sweeps in single-vacancy complement problems in 33-hole Solitaire

Final	Initial vacancy						
sweep	*c*1	*c*3	*d*1	*b*3	*d*3	*d*2	*d*4
8	*a*3	*e*1			*d*7		
	*g*5	*g*3					
7	*e*1	*c*1*		*d*7	*d*1		
	*g*3*	*g*5					
	*a*5						
	*c*7						
6	*e*3	*e*5	*b*3	*d*1	*b*5		
	*e*7						
5	*c*3	*e*3	*b*5	*b*5	*b*3		
	*e*5		*d*7	*f*5			
4	*c*5**			*f*3			
				*d*5*			
3					*d*5*		
2						*b*4	
						*d*6	
1				*d*3*			*d*2
—			*d*3			*d*4	
			*d*5				

* Not proved optimal until Chapter 6.
** Not proved optimal until Chapter 7.

Solutions to Chapter 3

Maximal solutions to all the single-vacancy complement problems with a man on the watch are shown in Figures 3.11 to 3.80. A few that have appeared previously are repeated here for completeness. Notes:

Figure 3.17: Step 8*a*/8*b* is an 'extended L-move', in which the move *d*7–*d*5 supplies the man at *d*5 which is swallowed by the L-move.

Figure 3.19: Steps 1 to 4 are single moves which fill *d*1 and clear the T-shaped block *d*3/*b*4/*c*4/*d*4/*d*5; 5*a*/5*b* is a call and answer which clears *c*3 and *c*6; 6*a*/6*b* an extended L-move which refills *c*3; and 7*a*/7*b* an 'extended call and answer' (moves *c*2–*c*4–*c*6, *c*7–*c*5) which clears *c*2, *c*3, and *c*7. The rest is straightforward, 9*a*/9*b* being another extended L-move.

Figure 3.27: Step 7*a*/7*b* is an extended L-move.

Figure 3.29: Step 3*a*/3*b* is an extended L-move.

Figure 3.35: Step 5*a*/5*b* is an extended call and answer.

Figure 3.49: Step 4 is a 'shifted six'. This is really a combination of two three-removals, the second (*e*5/*e*6/*e*7) interacting with the first (*d*4/*d*5/*d*6) and permitting it to be made without the normal catalyst: with *d*3 empty and *f*5 full, play *d*5–*d*3, *f*5–*d*5, *d*6–*d*4, *e*7–*e*5, *d*3–*d*5–*f*5.

Figure 3.55: Step 3 is a shifted six as described in the note to Figure 3.49.

Figure 3.63: Step 6 is a 'Y-removal'. This is a combination of the three-removal *e*3/*f*3/*g*3 with the move *f*5–*f*3 which permits it to be made without the normal catalyst: with *d*3 empty and *f*3 full, play *f*3–*d*3, *f*5–*f*3, *g*3–*e*3, *d*3–*f*3.

Figure 3.67: Step 6 is a Y-removal as described in the note to Figure 3.63.

Figure 3.71: Step 3*a*/3*b* is a double-three, perfectly valid even though the two three-removals are not parallel; the first move (*e*4–*e*2) creates a catalyst for the second three-removal in the usual way.

These are by no means the only solutions to these problems and it is an interesting task to work out alternative final sweeps, but we suggest that serious exploration be left until we have looked at the theory of the game in the next few chapters.

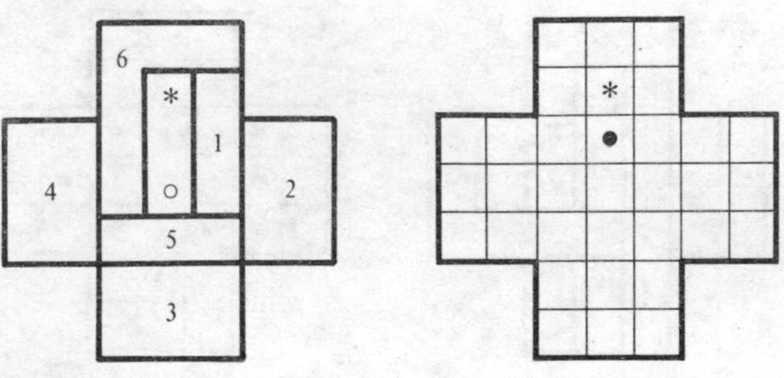

Figure 3.11 Figure 3.12

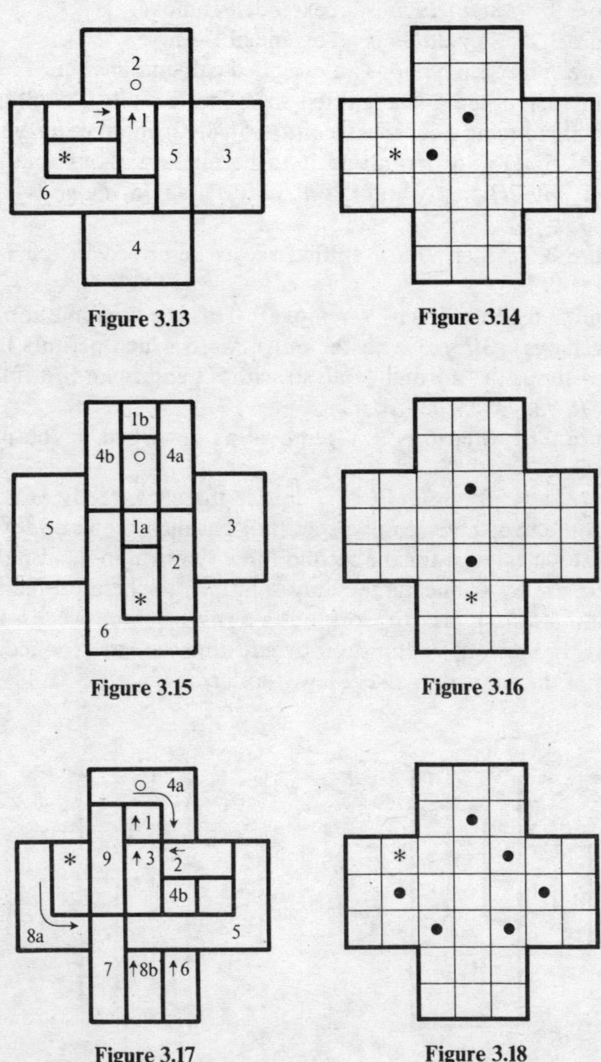

Figure 3.13

Figure 3.14

Figure 3.15

Figure 3.16

Figure 3.17

Figure 3.18

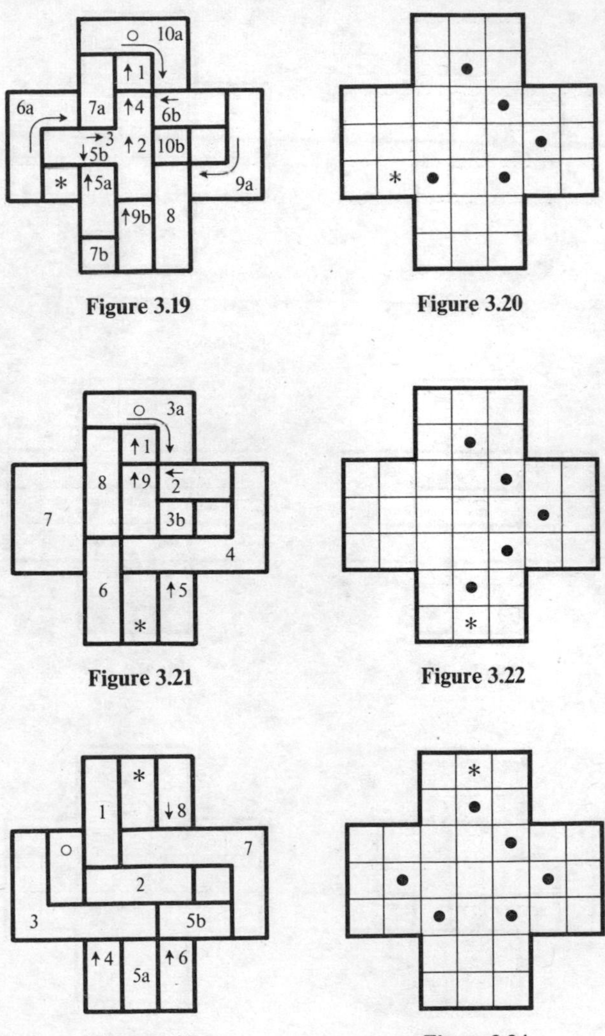

Figure 3.19

Figure 3.20

Figure 3.21

Figure 3.22

Figure 3.23

Figure 3.24

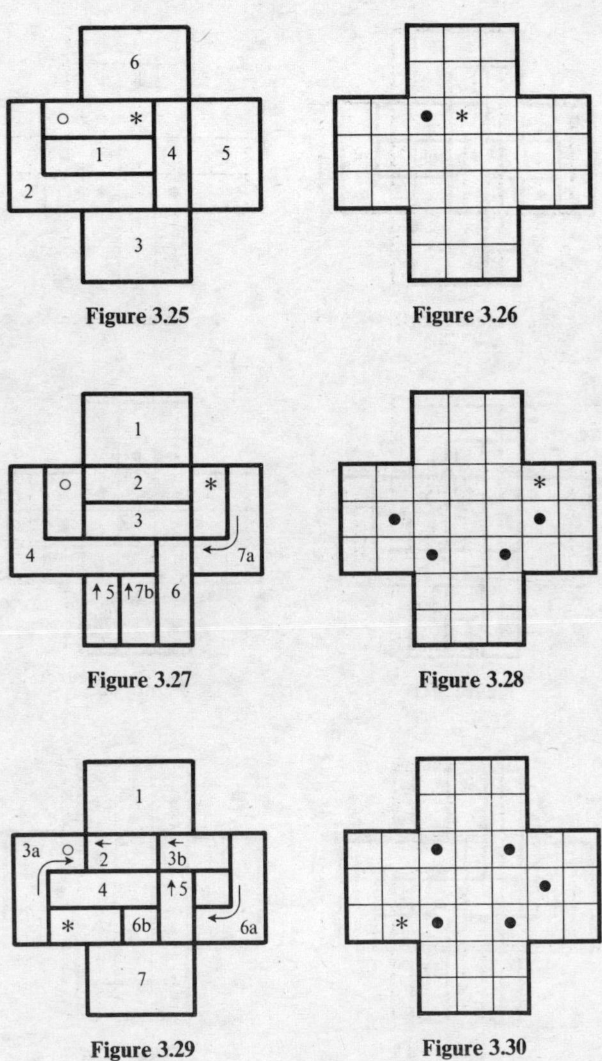

Figure 3.25

Figure 3.26

Figure 3.27

Figure 3.28

Figure 3.29

Figure 3.30

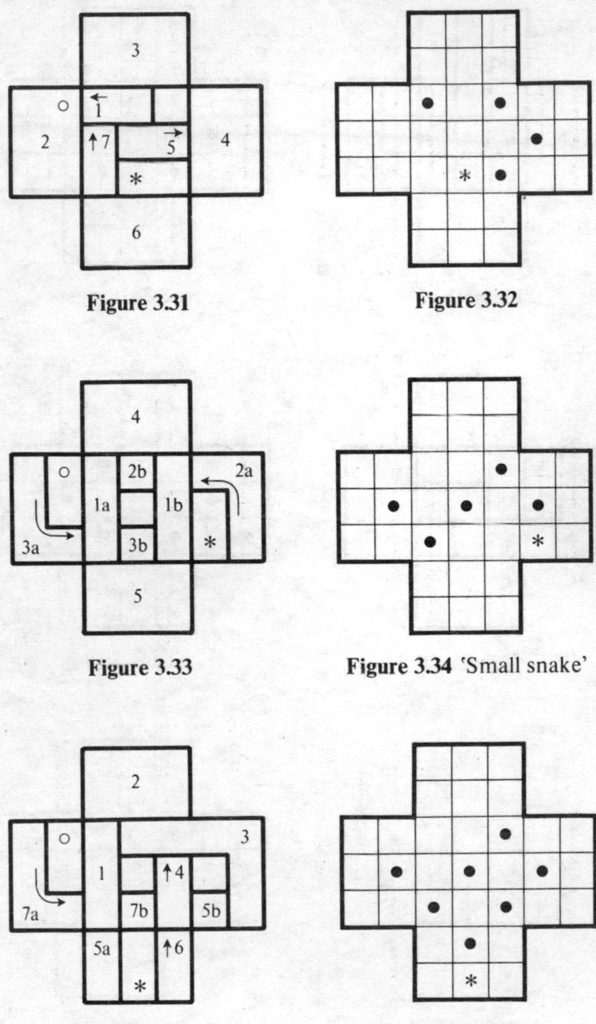

Figure 3.31

Figure 3.32

Figure 3.33

Figure 3.34 'Small snake'

Figure 3.35

Figure 3.36

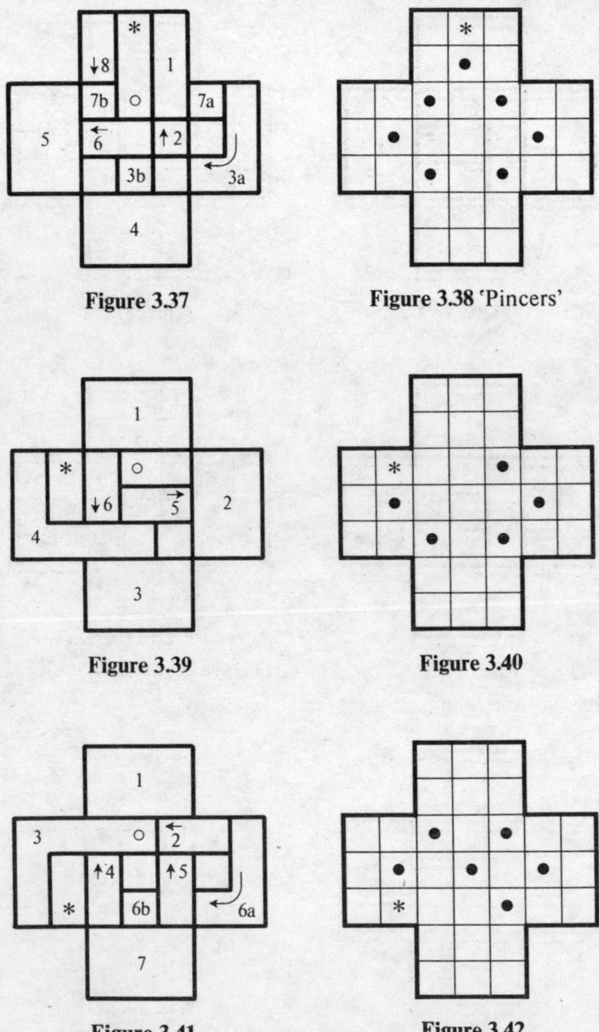

Figure 3.37

Figure 3.38 'Pincers'

Figure 3.39

Figure 3.40

Figure 3.41

Figure 3.42

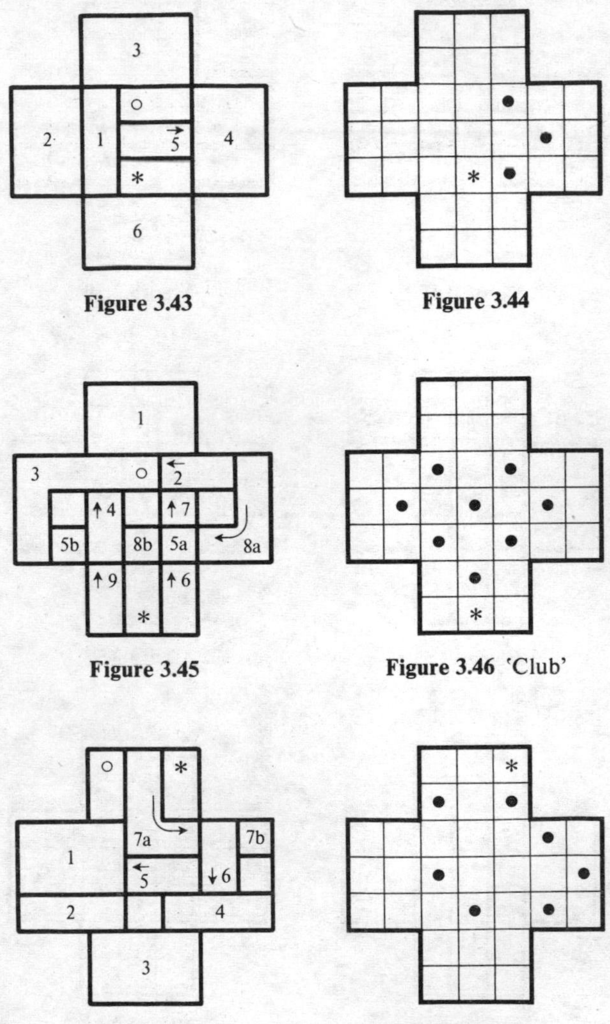

Figure 3.43

Figure 3.44

Figure 3.45

Figure 3.46 'Club'

Figure 3.47

Figure 3.48

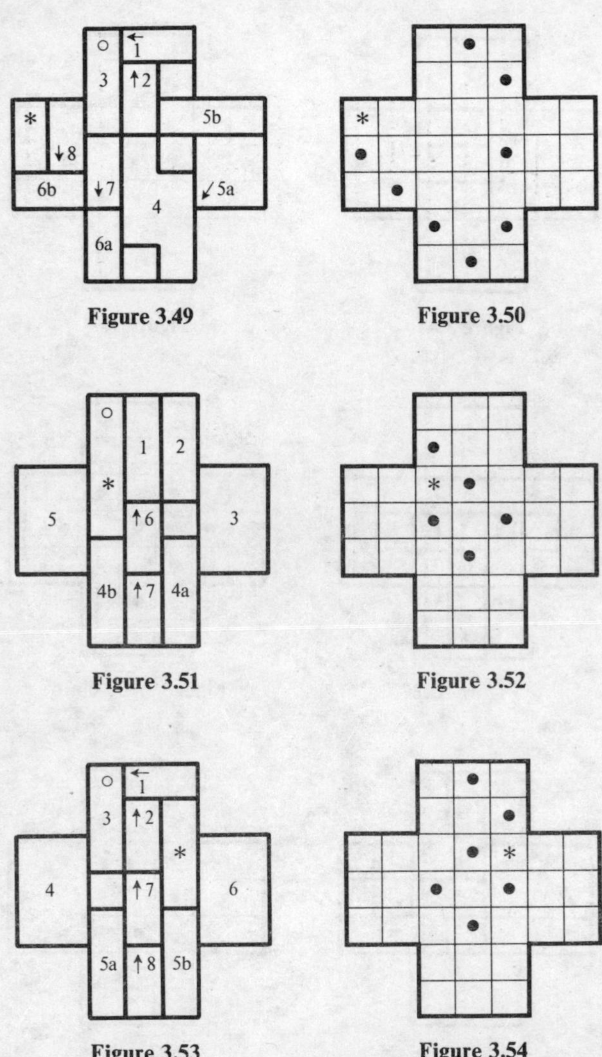

Figure 3.49

Figure 3.50

Figure 3.51

Figure 3.52

Figure 3.53

Figure 3.54

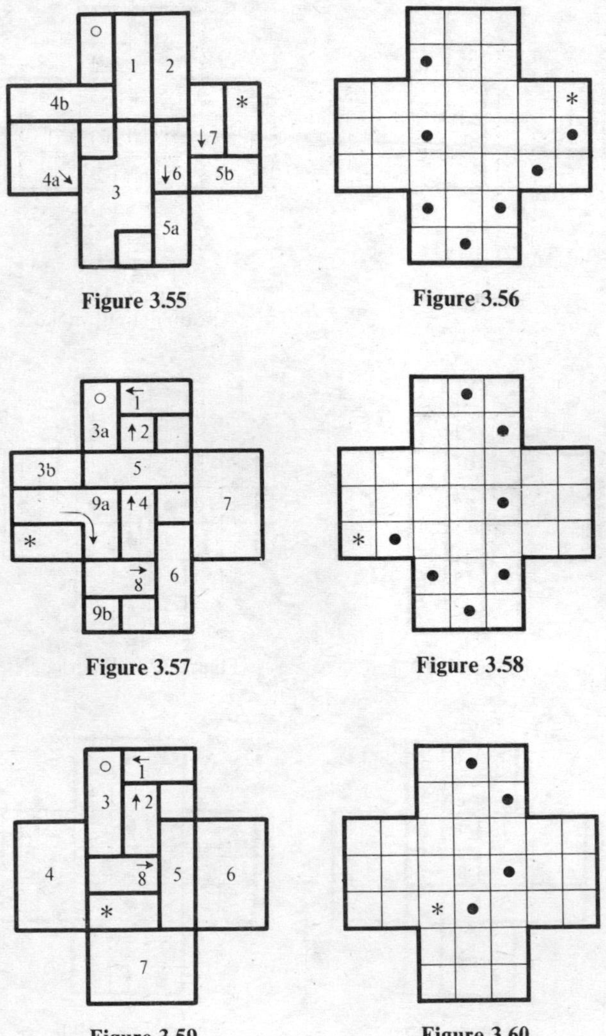

Figure 3.55

Figure 3.56

Figure 3.57

Figure 3.58

Figure 3.59

Figure 3.60

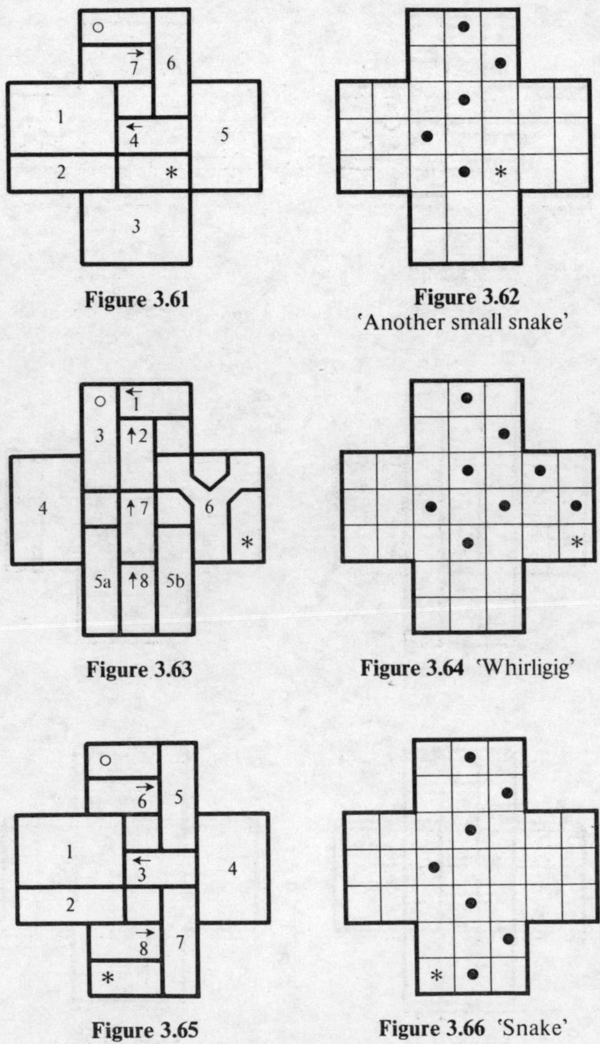

Figure 3.61

Figure 3.62
'Another small snake'

Figure 3.63

Figure 3.64 'Whirligig'

Figure 3.65

Figure 3.66 'Snake'

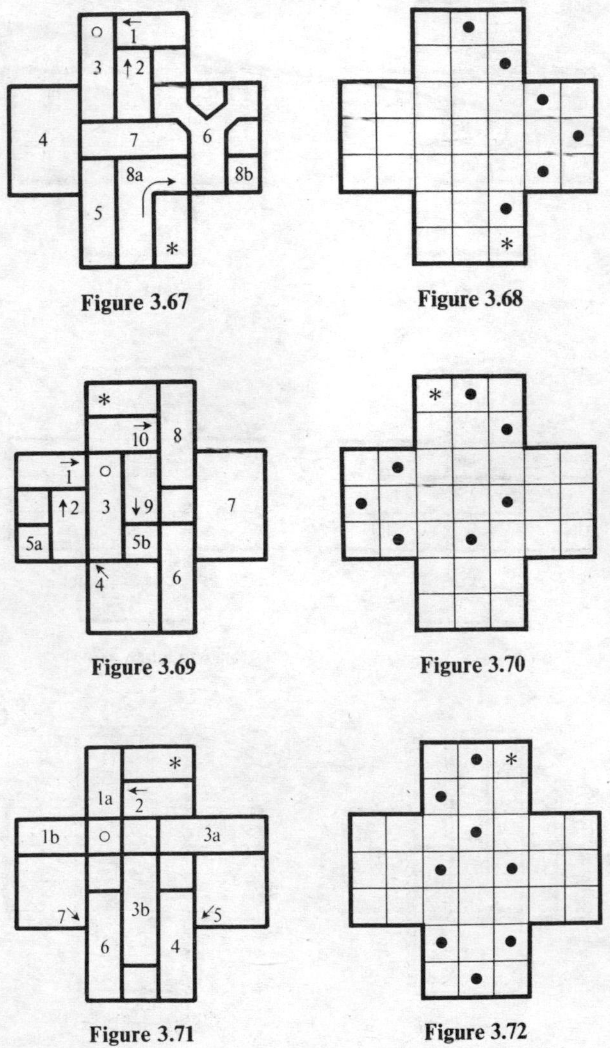

Figure 3.67

Figure 3.68

Figure 3.69

Figure 3.70

Figure 3.71

Figure 3.72
'Faulty arithmetic'

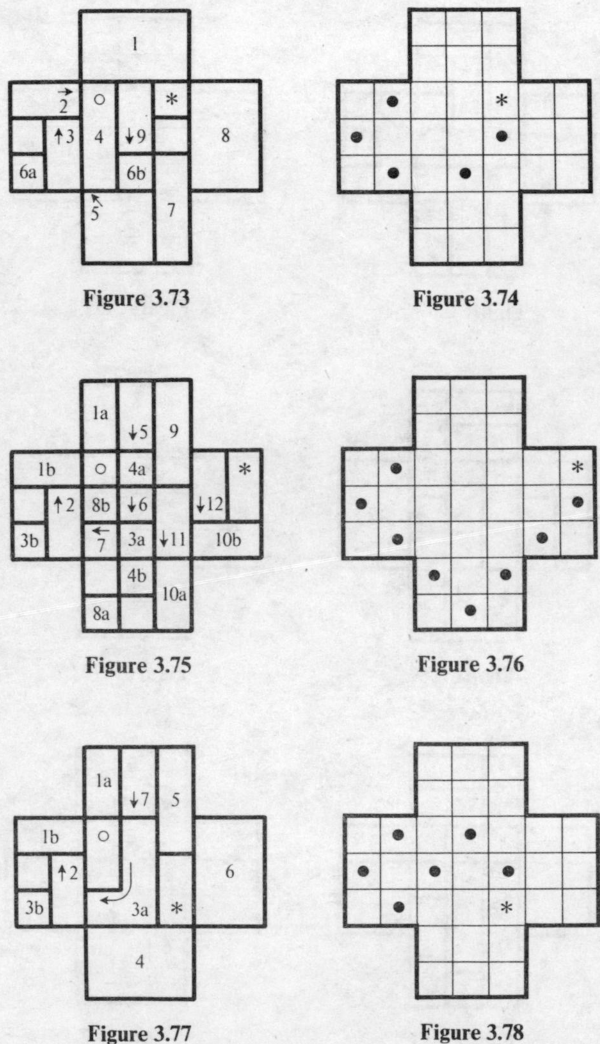

Figure 3.73

Figure 3.74

Figure 3.75

Figure 3.76

Figure 3.77

Figure 3.78

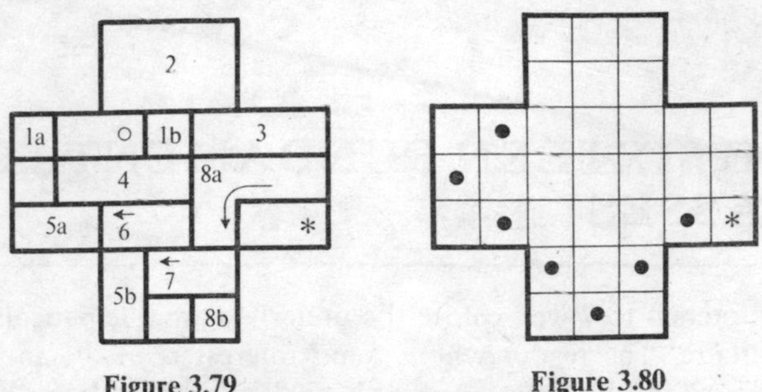

Figure 3.79

Figure 3.80

4

THE SIXTEEN FUNDAMENTAL CLASSES

In Chapters 4 to 7 we explore the underlying mathematical theory of Solitaire. The reader whose main interest is in the solving of puzzles will see this theory primarily as a means of testing whether a given problem is in fact soluble, but the mathematician may see it as a fascinating study in its own right.

In the present chapter we use a parity effect to divide Solitaire positions into sixteen fundamental classes. We have seen parity effects before: in Chapter 2, where we used the fact that each jump moves a man an even number of holes to divide both holes and men into four classes, and in Chapter 3, where we showed that alternative paths between a given pair of holes have lengths of the same parity. The effect that we shall demonstrate here is less immediately obvious, but it is of similar importance since the classes it generates are such that play from a position in one class to a position in another is impossible.

Phase relations

Let us divide the board into the two sets of diagonals shown in Figures 4.1 and 4.2, and then let us set up a position and count the number of men on each diagonal and the total number of men. If we do this for the position of Figure 4.3, we obtain the following:

Diagonal *A*	11 (odd)
Diagonal *B*	10 (even)
Diagonal *C*	11 (odd)
Diagonal *D*	11 (odd)
Diagonal *E*	10 (even)
Diagonal *F*	11 (odd)
Overall total	32 (even)

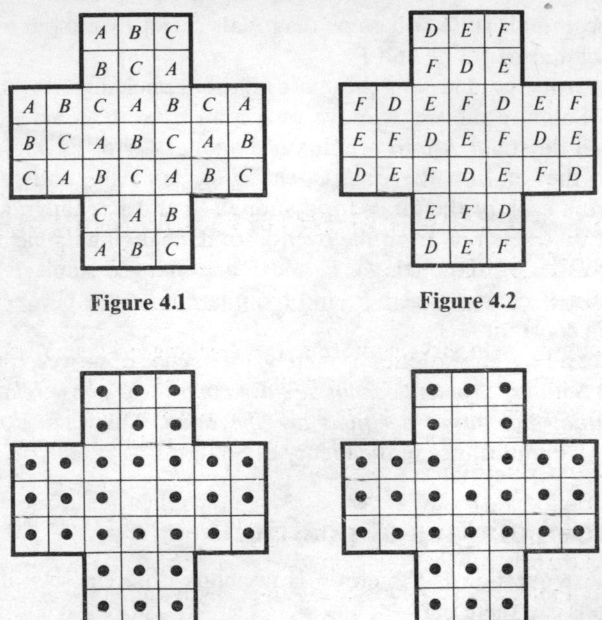

Figure 4.1

Figure 4.2

Figure 4.3

Figure 4.4

We define a position to be *in phase* on a diagonal if the number of men on that diagonal has the same parity as the total number of men, and *out of phase* otherwise. Thus the position of Figure 4.3 is in phase on diagonals *B* and *E*, and out of phase on diagonals *A*, *C*, *D*, and *F*.

If we now play the move *d*2–*d*4, producing the position of Figure 4.4, and repeat this procedure, we obtain:

Diagonal *A* 10 (even)
Diagonal *B* 11 (odd)
Diagonal *C* 10 (even)

Diagonal *D* 10 (even)
Diagonal *E* 11 (odd)
Diagonal *F* 10 (even)

Overall total 31 (odd)

All the parities have changed but *the phase relations have not;* the new position is still in phase on diagonals B and E, and out of phase on diagonals A, C, D, and F.

The property of leaving the phase relations unchanged is possessed by all Solitaire moves. A move by a man from diagonal A over a man on diagonal B into a hole on diagonal C, for example, adds one to the total for diagonal C, changing its parity, and subtracts one from each of the totals for diagonals A and B, changing theirs; and it subtracts one from the overall total, changing its parity also. The parities of diagonals D, E, and F are changed similarly. So all the parities change together, and the phase relations between them remain constant.

Since a Solitaire solution is merely a sequence of moves, it follows that *a Solitaire problem cannot be solved unless the phase relations of the initial and target positions are the same*. This fact is of fundamental importance in the theory of Solitaire.

Sixteen classes of position

The next question is therefore: How many different sets of phase relations can there be?

A first guess might be 64, on the grounds that we have six different diagonals and each can be either in or out of phase. The diagonals cannot be in or out of phase independently, however, for *within each set of three diagonals (ABC or DEF) the number of out-of-phase diagonals must be even*. This can be proved as follows:

(a) if α, β, and γ represent the numbers of men on diagonals A, B, and C respectively, then diagonal A is in phase if α and $\alpha+\beta+\gamma$ have the same parity, i.e. if $\beta+\gamma$ is even, and out of phase if $\beta+\gamma$ is odd;

(b) if an odd number of the terms $\beta+\gamma$, $\gamma+\alpha$, and $\alpha+\beta$ were to be odd then their sum would be odd;

(c) this sum is in fact equal to $(\beta+\gamma+\gamma+\alpha+\alpha+\beta)$, which is equal to $2(\alpha+\beta+\gamma)$ and so is necessarily even.

At most two phase relations within each set of three can be assigned independently, therefore, so the number of different sets of phase relations cannot exceed sixteen. On the other hand, it can be shown that sixteen different sets do exist by the simple expedient of writing down a representative position demonstrating each, as is done in Table 4.1.

The effect of our phase relations is therefore to divide all Solitaire

Table 4.1: Representative members of fundamental classes

Holes occupied	Number of men *A*	*B*	*C*	*D*	*E*	*F*	Total	Phase relations *A*	*B*	*C*	*D*	*E*	*F*
none	0	0	0	0	0	0	0	in	in	in	in	in	in
*d*4, *c*5	0	2	0	0	1	1	2	in	in	in	in	out	out
*c*5, *e*3	0	2	0	1	0	1	2	in	in	in	out	in	out
*e*3, *d*4	0	2	0	1	1	0	2	in	in	in	out	out	in
*d*4, *c*3	0	1	1	0	2	0	2	in	out	out	in	in	in
*c*4	1	0	0	1	0	0	1	in	out	out	in	out	out
*e*5	1	0	0	0	1	0	1	in	out	out	out	in	out
*d*3	1	0	0	0	0	1	1	in	out	out	out	out	in
*c*3, *e*5	1	0	1	0	2	0	2	out	in	out	in	in	in
*e*3	0	1	0	1	0	0	1	out	in	out	in	out	out
*d*4	0	1	0	0	1	0	1	out	in	out	out	in	out
*c*5	0	1	0	0	0	1	1	out	in	out	out	out	in
*e*5, *d*4	1	1	0	0	2	0	2	out	out	in	in	in	in
*d*5	0	0	1	1	0	0	1	out	out	in	in	out	out
*c*3	0	0	1	0	1	0	1	out	out	in	out	in	out
*e*4	0	0	1	0	0	1	1	out	out	in	out	out	in

positions into precisely sixteen classes having the property that play between positions in different classes is impossible. We therefore call these classes the *fundamental classes*.

The earliest surviving reference to the impossibility of play between positions in different fundamental classes is in a report by J.-N. Vallot in 1842 on a now lost work by Antoine Suremain de Missery. Vallot's report neither gives nor refers to a proof, but Suremain de Missery was an able man who made investigations in many fields (mathematics, acoustics, and language) and it is surely reasonable to assume that he did indeed have such a proof.

Null-class boards

The standard 33-hole Solitaire board has a simple but important geometrical property: *if every hole is occupied, the parities of all six diagonals are the same*. It is easily shown that *on such a board, every position is in the same fundamental class as its complement*. We call a board with this property a *null-class* board. It does not matter whether the parities are all odd or all even; null-class boards of both types exist. Null-class boards are of particular interest because only on such a board may play be possible from a position to its complement.

We shall postpone serious consideration of boards other than the standard board until Chapter 11, but as an exercise the reader may care to apply the labelling of Figures 4.1 and 4.2 to the 25-hole diamond board of Figure 4.5 and the 37-hole 'French' board of Figure 4.6, and hence to determine whether these are null-class boards. We also ask a more general question: What is a necessary and sufficient condition on m and n for an $m \times n$ rectangular board to be a null-class board?

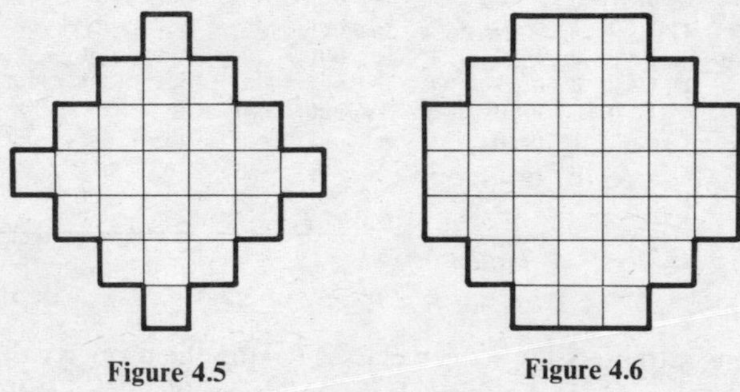

Figure 4.5 Figure 4.6

Single-vacancy and single-man positions

Most of the problems which we have considered so far have started from single-vacancy positions or have required the attainment of single-man positions. Let us therefore look at the fundamental classes to which such positions belong.

It is a simple consequence of our definitions that *a single-man position is in phase on the two diagonals which pass through the occupied hole and out of phase on the other four diagonals*. It follows that a position which is out of phase on fewer than four diagonals *cannot* be reduced to a single-man position; furthermore, if a position can be reduced to a single man then this man must finish in one of the holes at the intersections of the two in-phase diagonals. Such holes recur at intervals of three across the board; diagonals A and D, for example, intersect at $c1$, $c4$, $f4$, and $c7$.

On a null-class board, every position is in the same fundamental class as its complement. This leads to similar relations between single-vacancy positions and between single-vacancy and single-man positions; for example, if we start by vacating a single hole then we cannot finish with a single man other than in the hole originally vacated or in one of the holes at intervals of three from it. *This result is not true on a board which is not a null-class board.* We shall discover a general result which applies to all boards later in the chapter.

These various properties can be summarised as follows:

(a) two single-man positions are in the same fundamental class if and only if the rows and columns of the occupied holes differ by multiples of three;

(b) no single-man position is in the same fundamental class as the empty position or as a double-man position in which the occupied holes are on the same diagonal;

(c) two single-vacancy positions are in the same fundamental class if and only if the rows and columns of the vacancies differ by multiples of three;

(d) no single-vacancy position is in the same fundamental class as the full position or as a double-vacancy position in which the vacancies are on the same diagonal;

(e) on a null-class board, a single-man position is in the same fundamental class as a single-vacancy position if and only if the rows and columns of the man and the vacancy are the same or differ by multiples of three;

(f) on a null-class board, no single-man position is in the same fundamental class as the full position or as a double-vacancy position in which the vacancies are on the same diagonal;

(g) on a null-class board, no single-vacancy position is in the same fundamental class as the empty position or as a double-man position in which the occupied holes are on the same diagonal.

We can now say more about 'Whither will he wander?' (Figure 1.16). The initial vacancy is at *d*1, so the finishing *hole* cannot be other than *d*1, *a*4, *d*4, *g*4, or *d*7 by property (e) above. We have seen in Chapter 2, however, that a *man* initially at *d*3 cannot move outside the 's' holes, namely *d*1, *b*3, *d*3, *f*3, *b*5, *d*5, *f*5, and *d*7. The only holes common to both sets are *d*1 and *d*7, so the finishing hole of the marked man cannot be other than one of these.

A similar result applies to all marked man problems. A man is restricted to holes whose rows and columns differ by multiples of two. The rows and columns of single-man positions reachable from a given position differ by multiples of three. The rows and columns of holes in which a marked man can finish as a solitary survivor therefore differ by multiples of six.

At this point, the reader may care to see which of the complete reduction problems on the 33-hole board (start with a single vacancy and play to finish with a single survivor in a given hole) are in fact soluble. We give solutions at the end of the chapter. Those who find this straightforward may then care to attack the more general 'marked man' problems (start with a single initial vacancy, mark a particular man, and play to leave it as the last survivor), though we give warning that a few of these are difficult to analyse and should perhaps be postponed until after Chapters 5 to 7 have been read. We shall leave our own consideration of them until Chapter 9.

The transformations of Suremain de Missery

The fundamental class of a position can always be found by counting the men on the various diagonals and evaluating the phase relations, but this is tedious and prone to error. In any case, we normally wish to find a fundamental class not as an end in itself but in order to choose a simple position in the same class, for example a potential starting or finishing position for a problem. For this purpose, it is sufficient to have a set of transformations which convert one position into another within the same fundamental class. Suremain de Missery gave several such transformations, the most important of them being shown in Figure 4.7.

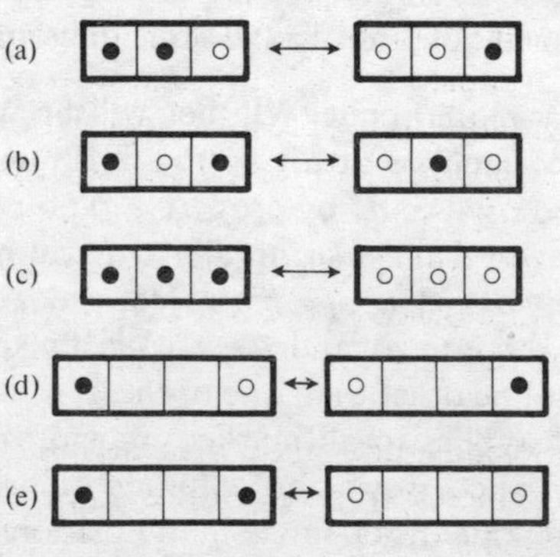

Figure 4.7

The transformations shown in Figure 4.7 are as follows:

(a) play a normal Solitaire move, either forwards or backwards;

(b) replace two men one hole apart by a man in the intervening hole, or vice versa;

(c) empty a line of three adjacent occupied holes, or fill a line of three adjacent vacancies;

(d) move a man three holes in any direction, irrespective of whether the intervening holes are occupied or empty;

(e) remove two men exactly three holes apart, irrespective of whether the intervening holes are occupied or empty, or fill two vacancies similarly.

It will be noticed that each of these transformations is reversible.

Each of the transformations leaves the phase relations of a position unchanged, and hence does not change its fundamental class. Furthermore, it is possible by their use to transform any two positions in the same fundamental class into each other. This is easily seen: by successive use of appropriate transformations, we can transform any position into one in which the occupied holes, if any, are confined to a particular 2×2 square (say *c*3/*d*3/*c*4/*d*4); there are sixteen such positions, one in each fundamental class, so any two positions in the same fundamental class will be transformed by this technique into the same position; and the transformations can be reversed, so if we can get from each of two positions to a third then we can get from either to the other. So we can get from a position to any other in the same fundamental class.

These transformations provide a quick and easy method of finding a position in the same fundamental class as a given position but with only one or two occupied holes. They can also be used directly to obtain positions with only one or two vacancies (the 'direct' method), but *on a null-class board* it is often easier to transform the given position into one with only a few occupied holes and then form the complement of this (the 'complementary' method). The transformations can also be used to see if a board is a null-class board, for if it is then the full position can be transformed into the empty position.

To see the complementary method in action, let us try to find potential single-vacancy starting positions from which to reach the positions of Figures 4.8 to 4.11.

'Fish' (Figure 4.8) can be transformed as follows: (i) replace *c*3/*b*3

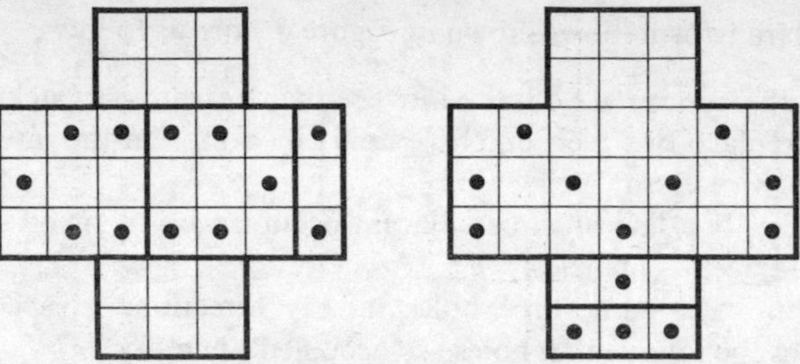

Figure 4.8 'Fish' **Figure 4.9** 'Weeping willow'

by *a*3, replace *a*3/*a*4 by *a*5, and clear *a*5/*b*5/*c*5; (ii) similarly, play *d*3 to *f*5, removing *e*3 and *f*4, and clear *d*5/*e*5/*f*5; (iii) replace *g*3/*g*5 by *g*4 and move *g*4 to *d*4. So 'Fish' is in the same fundamental class as the position with only *d*4 occupied. Since we are using a null-class board, this means that the only single-vacancy positions from which play to it might be possible are those with *d*1, *a*4, *d*4, *g*4, or *d*7 empty. Play to 'Fish' is actually possible from all of these except *g*4.

'Weeping willow' (Figure 4.9) can be transformed as follows: (i) play *a*5 right across to *g*3, removing *a*4, *b*3, *c*4, *d*5, *e*4, and *f*3, and clear *g*3/*g*4/*g*5; (i1) clear *c*7/*d*7/*e*7. This leaves a man on *d*6, and means that the only single-vacancy positions from which play to 'Weeping willow' might be possible are those with *a*3, *d*3, *g*3, or *d*6 empty. In fact it is possible from each of these.

'Arrow' (Figure 4.10) can be transformed as follows: (i) replace *d*5/*d*6 by *d*7 and clear *c*7/*d*7/*e*7; (ii) move *b*3 to *e*3 and clear *d*3/*e*3/*f*3; (iii) clear *c*2/*d*2/*d*2; (iv) clear *d*1/*d*4. This leaves the empty position, and means that there is no single-vacancy position from which play to 'Arrow' is possible.

'Letter J' (Figure 4.11) can be transformed by clearing *e*1/*e*2/*e*3 and *e*4/*e*5/*e*6. This leaves two men in *c*6 and *d*7, and means that there is no single-vacancy position from which play to 'Letter J' is possible.

The reader may care to verify that the direct method does indeed produce the same results. In 'Fish', for example, we can fill *c*1/*d*1/*e*1, fill *c*2/*d*2/*e*2, replace *a*4 by *b*4/*c*4 and fill *a*3/*a*4/*a*5, replace *f*4 by *d*4/*e*4 and fill *f*3/*f*4/*f*5, fill *c*6/*d*6/*e*6, and fill *c*7/*d*7/*e*7, leaving only *g*4 vacant; and the other potential starting vacancies can be obtained from this.

Thus we see the usefulness of these transformations in identifying

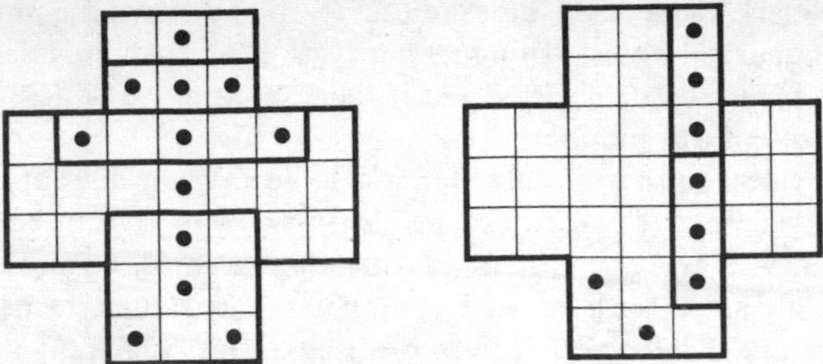

Figure 4.10 'Arrow' **Figure 4.11** 'Letter J'

potential starting positions for problems. It is also a good idea to apply them mentally from time to time during actual play to make sure that the current position is in the same fundamental class as the target position, since the most common errors of play (forgetting to remove a man jumped over and misplacing a man by one hole) change the fundamental class of a position.

Up-and-down Solitaire

We have used parity counts to divide Solitaire positions into sixteen classes. Can we use similar techniques to obtain a finer classification?

The answer is No, and the reason is instructive. It can be shown that if we allow additive moves (jumping over a hole and putting a man in) as well as ordinary subtractive moves, then with sixteen trivial exceptions we can play from a position to any other in the same fundamental class. The exceptions are the sixteen positions in which no move, either additive or subtractive, is possible. The proof is not difficult, for all that is necessary is to show that we can get from any non-exceptional position to a representative position in the same fundamental class, but it is a little tedious to write out in full and we therefore omit it. The reader will find it easy to convince himself of its truth by the study of a few cases.

Hence no further useful subdivision of Solitaire positions is possible using parity effects alone, and any deeper analysis must make use of the fact that a subtractive Solitaire move consumes resources.

Invariant parity counts

The fundamental classes can be derived by an alternative technique which some may prefer.

We mark some of the holes of the board and count the number of men in marked holes, noting its parity. We call such an assembly of marks an *invariant parity count* if there is no move which changes the parity of this number.

The rules for an assembly of marks to be an invariant parity count are very simple: if two adjacent holes in a row or column are unlike (one marked and one unmarked) then the next must be marked, and if they are alike (both marked or both unmarked) then the next must be unmarked. Hence there are precisely sixteen different invariant parity counts, since we can mark the holes of a 2×2 square as we choose but then find that the marking of the rest of the board is determined. One of these is the null count (no hole marked), which tells us nothing. The others can be divided into six 'diagonal' counts typified by Figure 4.12 (three in each direction) and nine 'square' counts by Figure 4.13.

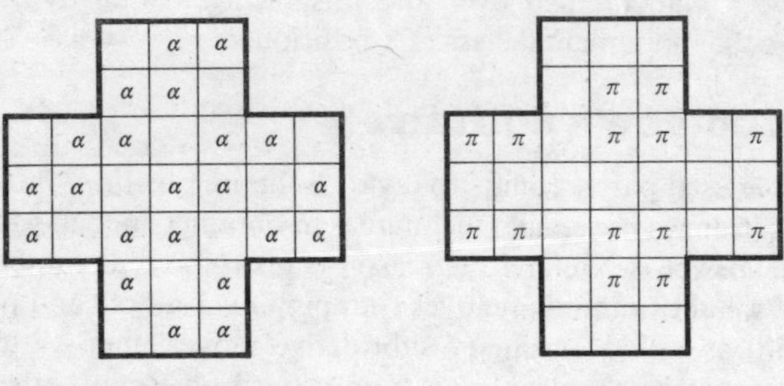

Figure 4.12

Figure 4.13

The count of Figure 4.12 has an obvious connection with the diagonals of Figure 4.1, for the count of men in marked holes in Figure 4.12 is even if and only if the position is in phase on diagonal *A* in Figure 4.1. The connection between the count of Figure 4.13 and the diagonals of Figures 4.1 and 4.2 is less obvious but nevertheless real. In fact the count of men in marked holes is even if the position is in phase on both the diagonals *A* and *D* or on neither of them; if the position is in phase on one diagonal but not the other then the count of men in marked holes is odd.

Invariant parity counts therefore tell us nothing that phase relations have not already told us, but there may be some who find the invariance of a parity count a simpler concept than that of a phase relation. When we consider some alternative rules for removal in Chapter 14, however, we shall find that phase relations provide the more suitable tool, which is why we have given them precedence here.

Algebra of fundamental classes

It is possible to construct an algebra of fundamental classes. This is perhaps of more interest as a piece of mathematics than as a practical contribution to the study of Solitaire and the reader whose primary interests are practical may skip this section, but the theory is quite elegant and we shall use one result from it in Chapter 11. The reader familiar with group theory will recognise the algebra immediately.

We have already seen that there are various ways of selecting a representative member of each fundamental class. In this section we shall represent each class by a position whose occupied holes, if any, are confined to the 2×2 square $c3/c4/d3/d4$. (Any other 2×2 square could have been chosen without affecting the argument.) We shall use the notation $\kappa(P)$ for the fundamental class of position P, and $P(\kappa)$ for the representative position of fundamental class κ.

Now given any two positions P and Q, we can define their *mutual complement* $P \sim Q$ to be that position which has vacancies in those holes which are occupied either in both P and Q or in neither, and men in those holes which are occupied in either P or Q but not in both. It follows, trivially, that if E is the empty position then $P \sim P = E$ for all P, and that if F is the full position then the complement of P is $P \sim F$; also that if P and Q are representative positions of fundamental classes then $P \sim Q$ is also the representative position of a fundamental class.

We can now define an operator + on fundamental classes as follows: if ξ and η are two fundamental classes, then $\xi + \eta$ is the fundamental class of the mutual complement of the representative positions of ξ and η. This can be expressed formally as follows:

$$\xi + \eta = \kappa(P(\xi) \sim P(\eta)).$$

It may be verified that + is associative ($\xi + (\eta + \zeta) = (\xi + \eta) + \zeta$) and commutative ($\xi + \eta = \eta + \xi$), and that $\kappa(E)$ has the behaviour of a zero ($\xi + \kappa(E) = \xi$ for all ξ). We shall therefore denote $\kappa(E)$ by 0. It may also be verified that $\xi + \xi = 0$ for all ξ. This may disconcert readers who have not previously encountered non-zero quantities ξ which have the property $\xi + \xi = 0$, but an analogy is given by the arithmetic of parities; if we denote 'even' by 0 and 'odd' by 1 then the normal rules of arithmetic apply ($0+0=0$, $1+0=0+1=1$) and the relation 'odd + odd = even' is expressed by $1+1=0$.

We shall make extensive use of the operator $+$ in this book, both in relation to ordinary quantities ($x+x=2x$) and in relation to parities ($\xi+\xi=0$). To avoid confusion, we shall use Greek letters whenever parities are involved. We shall also use the operator $-$ ($x-y$ being the value z which satisfies $y+z=x$), but we need only $+$ when dealing with parities since $\xi-\eta$ is always equal to $\xi+\eta$. (Proof: $\xi-\eta$ is the value ζ which satisfies $\eta+\zeta=\xi$, but this is $\xi+\eta$ since $\eta+(\xi+\eta)=\eta+(\eta+\xi)=(\eta+\eta)+\xi=0+\xi=\xi$.)

We have already used 0 to denote the fundamental class of the empty position. There are four fundamental classes whose representative positions have only one occupied hole. Let us denote these by α ($c3$ occupied), β ($d3$ occupied), γ ($c4$ occupied) and δ ($d4$ occupied). All the other fundamental classes can be expressed as selective sums of these (0 being regarded as a special case of a selective sum). For example, the fundamental class whose representative position has $c3$, $c4$ and $d4$ occupied is $\alpha+\gamma+\delta$.

Our definition of the operator $+$ on fundamental classes is equivalent to the relation $\kappa(P\sim Q)=\kappa(P)+\kappa(Q)$ where P and Q are representative positions of fundamental classes. It is very easy to prove that this relation also holds if P and Q are *any* two positions. Now let P be any position and let P' be its complement. We have already seen that $P'=P\sim F$, whence it follows that

$$\kappa(P')=\kappa(P)+\kappa(F).$$

We call this important result the *complementary class theorem*. It is a generalisation of the result that we stated for null-class boards. (The result for null-class boards is $\kappa(P')=\kappa(P)$, which is an immediate consequence of the above result since $\kappa(F)=0$ for a null-class board.)

The reader who is familiar with group theory will long ago have recognised the structure described here as that of the direct product of four cyclic groups of order 2. The sixteen invariant parity counts can be shown to have a similar structure, using the natural definition for the operator $+$. There are also some other ways of looking at this theory which may be of interest to teachers of mathematics wanting unusual illustrative material, and a search through the bibliography at the end of the book is recommended to such readers.

From the viewpoint of Solitaire itself, however, we have now discovered as much as simple parity counts can tell us, and we shall need quite different techniques in the forthcoming chapters.

Solutions to Chapter 4

If we exclude duplication due to symmetry, there are 21 different single-vacancy single-survivor problems on the 33-hole board. They form three groups as follows:

Initial vacancy	Final hole
*c*1	*c*1, *c*4, *f*4, *c*7
*c*4, *f*4	*c*1, *c*4, *f*4
*d*1	*d*1, *a*4, *d*4, *d*7
*d*4	*d*1, *d*4
*c*2	*c*2, *c*5, *f*5
*c*5	*c*2, *c*5

All are soluble, solutions being sketched in Figures 4.14 to 4.19. Each pair of figures refers to one group; for example, to start with *c*1 vacant and finish with a man at *c*7, make the moves *c*3–*c*1, *e*2–*c*2, and *e*3–*c*3, then play as shown in Figure 4.14, producing the position shown in Figure 4.15, and finally make the moves *d*4–*d*6, *e*4–*e*6–*c*6, and *c*3–*c*5–*c*7. Similar 'topping and tailing' can be used to generate all the solutions.

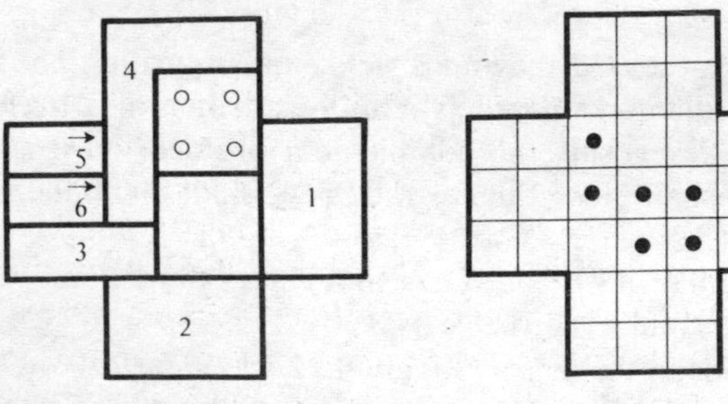

Figure 4.14 **Figure 4.15**

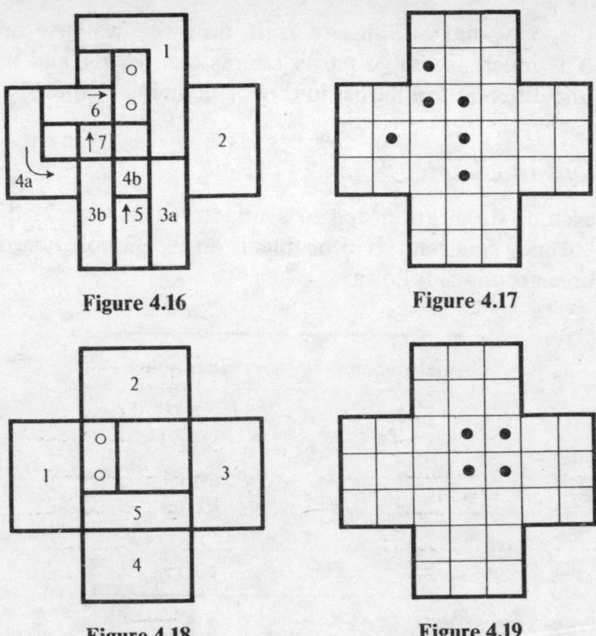

Figure 4.16

Figure 4.17

Figure 4.18

Figure 4.19

The 25-hole diamond board is a null-class board but the 37-hole board is not. If we label them as in Figures 4.20 and 4.21, we obtain the following parity counts:

	A	*B*	*C*
Figure 4.20	odd	odd	odd
Figure 4.21	even	odd	even

By symmetry, the *DEF* diagonals yield similar parities. The fact that the 25-hole diamond board is a null-class board is irrelevant in practice, however, since no complement problem on it is actually soluble. We shall prove this (or rather we shall invite the reader to prove it) in Chapter 5.

A rectangular $m \times n$ board is a null-class board if and only if at least one of m and n is divisible by 3.

'Fish' yields to the play of Figure 4.22 if we start by vacating *d*1, and to that of Figure 4.23 if we start by vacating *a*4. Changing the

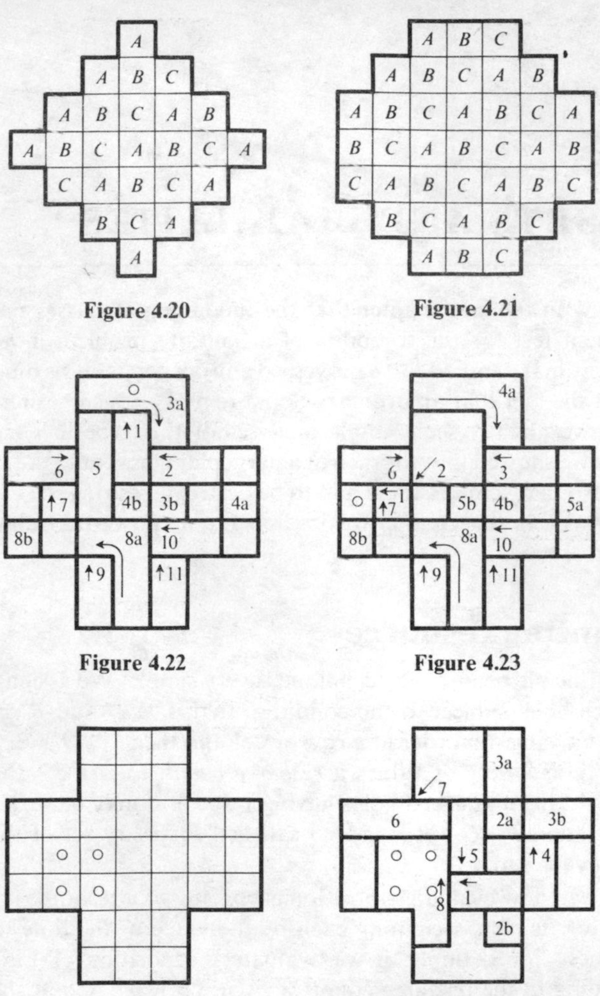

Figure 4.20

Figure 4.21

Figure 4.22

Figure 4.23

Figure 4.24

Figure 4.25

first move of either solution gives one which is valid if we start by vacating *d*4.

It is possible to play from any of the three essentially different initial vacancies for 'Weeping willow' (*a*3, *d*3, and *d*6) to the quadruple-vacancy position shown in Figure 4.24, and the play of Figure 4.25 completes a solution.

5

ASSETS AND LIABILITIES

We saw in the last chapter that the fundamental classes provide a sufficient test for the solubility of a Solitaire problem if we allow both ordinary and additive moves, so any deeper analysis must make use of the fact that an ordinary Solitaire move consumes resources. We have already seen simple analyses of this type in Chapter 2, where we showed that the men in a particular class could not increase and also that some of them had to be destroyed during the clearance of corners. In this chapter we develop a more powerful technique of the same type.

Counting resources

The principle behind our technique is very simple. We assign a value to each hole, subject to the condition that if P, Q and R are three adjacent values in order in a row or column then $P+Q \geqslant R$. We call such an assembly of values a *resource count*. Figure 5.1 shows an example, the unmarked holes having value 0. It may be verified that the relation $P+Q \geqslant R$ is indeed satisfied for every set of three adjacent values in order.

We can now evaluate a position according to a resource count by counting its men, weighting each by the value of the hole which it occupies. For example, if we evaluate the position of Figure 5.2 according to the resource count of Figure 5.1, we obtain the value 6, as shown in Table 5.1.

The importance of resource counts can be explained very simply. The effect on the value of a position of a move from a hole with value P over a hole with value Q into a hole with value R is to replace men with values P and Q by a man with value R. Since $P+Q \geqslant R$ by the definition of a resource count, this change cannot be an increase. So *no play is possible from an initial position to a target position if the target position has a higher value according to a*

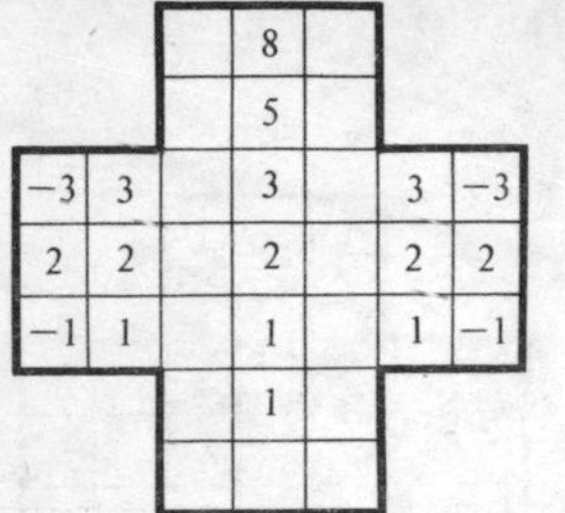

Figure 5.1

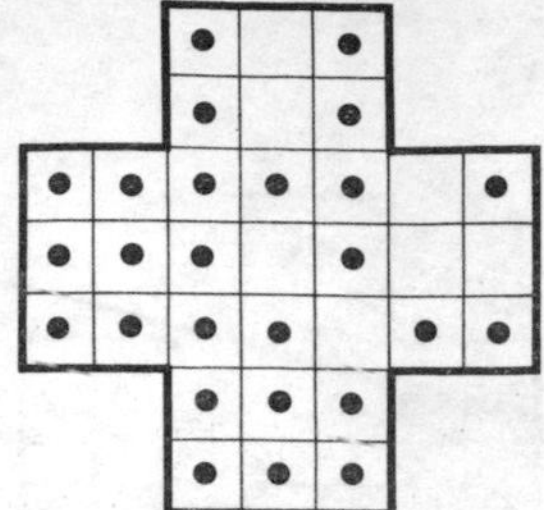

Figure 5.2

Table 5.1: Evaluation of the position of Figure 5.2 according to the resource count of Figure 5.1

*a*3	−3
*b*3	3
*d*3	3
*g*3	−3
*a*4	2
*b*4	2
*a*5	−1
*b*5	1
*d*5	1
*f*5	1
*g*5	−1
*d*6	1
others	0
	6

resource count than the initial position. For example, it is not possible to play from the position of Figure 5.2 to the position containing just a single man in *d*1, for according to the resource count of Figure 5.1 the target position would have value 8 and the position of Figure 5.2 only has value 6.

Resource counts were developed by J. H. Conway and J. M. Boardman in 1961, and were called 'pagoda functions' by Conway after a beautiful example which we shall meet in Chapter 12, but the relatively prosaic name 'resource count' is more descriptive and we shall therefore use it. The count of Figure 5.1 proves to be particularly useful and we shall call it the *spine-count*.

Let us look at some more examples.

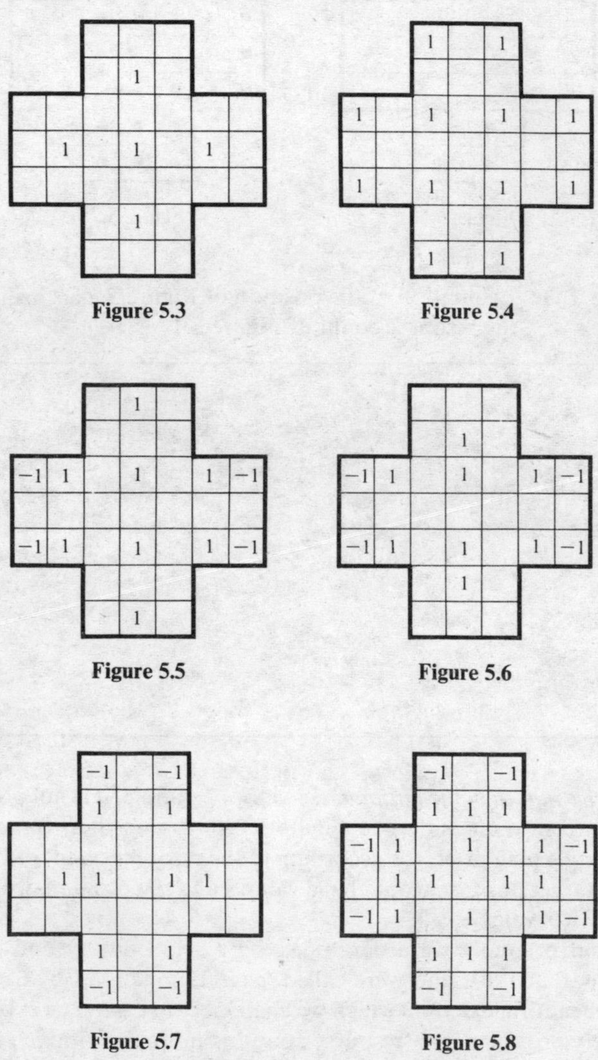

Figure 5.3

Figure 5.4

Figure 5.5

Figure 5.6

Figure 5.7

Figure 5.8

Figures 5.3 and 5.4 show two of the simplest of all resource counts. These simply count the number of middle and corner men present. Figure 5.5 shows a similar count for the 's' men, but here we have added negative values in the side corners so that the count allows for the need to destroy 's' men in clearing these corners. Figure 5.6 shows an important variant of this count, of which we shall make substantial use throughout this book. Figure 5.7 shows the equivalent count of Figure 5.6 for the 't' men, and Figure 5.8 an important combination of Figures 5.6 and 5.7 which we shall call the *cross-count*.

The resource counts shown in Figures 5.3 to 5.8, although important, do not tell us a great deal more than we learned in Chapter 2, but in most cases arguments based on resource counts are simpler and clearer. Figure 5.6, for example, can be thought of as counting the number of 's' men present, allowing both for the need to clear corners and for the fact that in many problems a move into the centre such as *d*2–*d*4 really costs *two* 's' men, not just the one jumped over by the move itself (for if a man is left at *d*1 for later removal then either it must be jumped over where it stands or it must be brought into play via *d*3, and in the latter case a man must be brought to *d*2 for it to jump over, which involves a move over *d*3 and so destroys another 's' man). The contrast between the straightforward arithmetic of Figure 5.6 and this complicated interpretation speaks for itself.

More complicated resource counts allow some results to be proved with spectacular simplicity. Figure 5.9 shows a classic complement problem, using our usual notation: 'o' for an initial vacancy and 'x' for a hole in which a man is to finish. In fact it is insoluble and the resource count of Figure 5.10 proves this immediately, for the value of the target position is 6 and that of the initial position is only 4.

Figure 5.11 shows another insoluble complement problem, and Figure 5.12 a resource count which proves its insolubility; the target position has value 10 and the initial position only value 8.

Construction of resource counts

The construction of valid resource counts is in principle just a matter of assembling values such that $P+Q \geqslant R$ for every set of adjacent values P, Q, R in order. The task is made easier by the following properties:

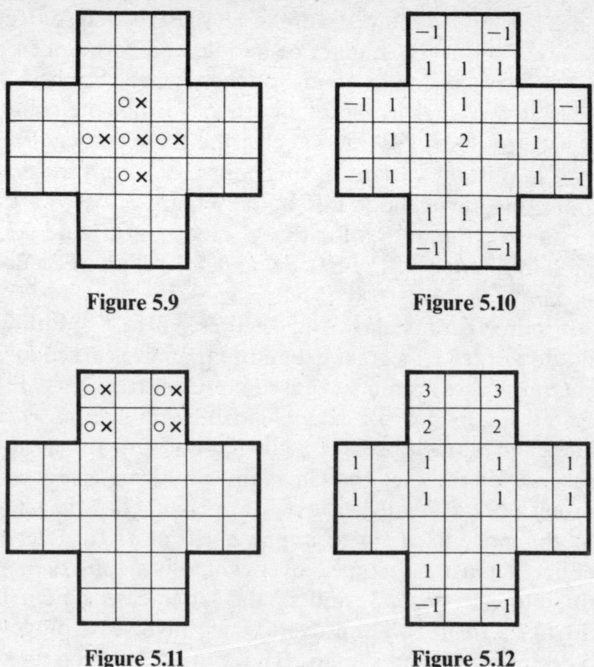

Figure 5.9

Figure 5.10

Figure 5.11

Figure 5.12

(a) a negative value cannot occur in a hole that can be jumped over;

(b) the values on opposite sides of a zero must be equal;

(c) if two adjacent values in a row or column are zero then the whole row or column must be zero.

These results are easily proved. For (a), we notice that if Q is the value between P and R then $P+Q \geqslant R$ and $R+Q \geqslant P$ must both be true, implying $Q \geqslant 0$; for (b), we notice that $P+0 \geqslant R$ and $R+0 \geqslant P$ together imply $P=R$; and (c) is an immediate consequence of (b).

In practice, of course, we normally wish to find resource counts which have high values in some regions of the board and low values in others. The sharpness with which the values of a resource count can rise is limited by the fundamental relation $R \leqslant Q+P$, so the best that we can do if we want a sharply increasing linear sequence $P,Q,R,S,T,\ldots$ is to set $R=Q+P$, $S=R+Q$, $T=S+R$, and so on. This leads immediately to the Fibonacci sequence $-1,1,0,1,$

1,2,3,5,8, ... The Lucas sequence −1,2,1,3,4,7,11, . . . is also occasionally useful.

The construction of valid and useful resource counts is therefore not difficult. Careful and systematic checking of candidates is always necessary, however; wishful thinking is a serious enemy, and it is all too easy to write idiocies such as '0,1,2', '−1,1,1', '1,0,2', and even '−1,0,1'. Only careful checking detects such mistakes before invalid deductions are made from them.

At this point, the reader may care to construct resource counts to prove the problems of Figures 5.13 to 5.18 insoluble. Figures 5.13 to 5.15 are deliberately similar, in order to show how a resource count that decides one problem can be modified to give one that decides another. This is also an appropriate point to prove the assertion in the last chapter that no complement problem is soluble on the 25-hole diamond board of Figure 4.5.

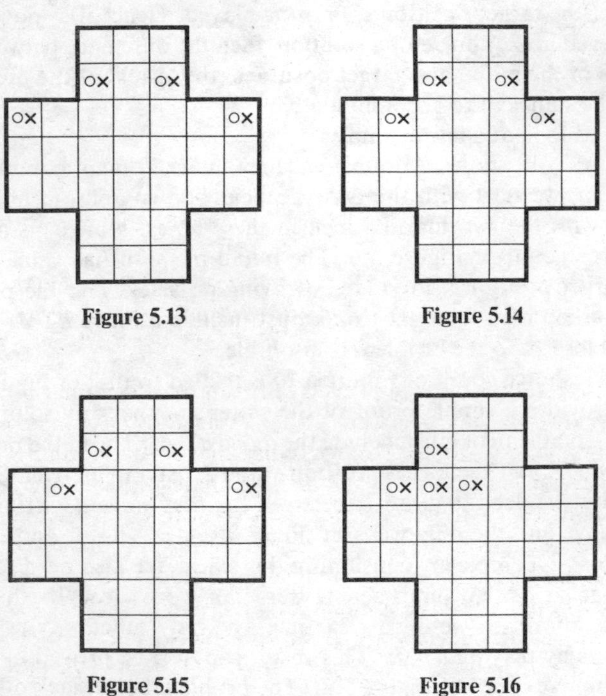

Figure 5.13

Figure 5.14

Figure 5.15

Figure 5.16

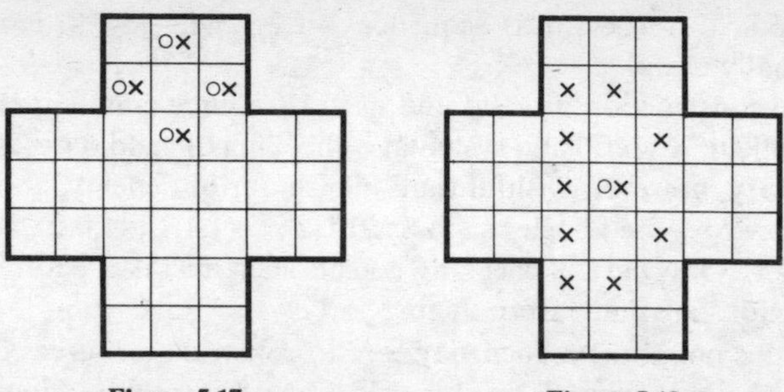

Figure 5.17

Figure 5.18

These moves are forbidden

We have already seen that if the value of the initial position of a problem according to a resource count is lower than that of the target position then the problem is insoluble. Similarly, a move which would reduce the value of the current position to less than that of the target position cannot be played. Hence if a move *must* be played in the course of a solution, then the difference between the values of the initial and target positions (the 'slack' of the problem) must be sufficient to accommodate it.

Let us look at a few examples.

Figure 5.19 shows a double-vacancy 'marked man' complement problem: we start with the two vacancies shown and our aim is to finish with the two marked men in these holes. Now consider the resource count of Figure 5.6. The initial position has value 2 and the target position also value 2, leaving no slack, and the path of the marked man from *d*2 to *d*6 must include a move *d*2–*d*4 which would lose 2. So the problem is insoluble.

The resource count of Figure 5.20 is related to that of Figure 5.5, and provides a simple proof of the statement that any solution to the *d*1-complement must include the move *d*7–*d*5. The initial position has value 4 and the target position value 2, leaving an overall slack of 2, but we need to clear *d*1 between the first move *d*3–*d*1 and the last move and the only ways of doing it (*c*1–*e*1, *e*1–*c*1, and *d*1–*d*3) each lose 2, completely consuming this slack. We also need to clear the man at *d*7. To jump across this man would lose 1, which we cannot afford, so we must clear it in the only other way possible, which is by playing *d*7–*d*5. This result can also be proved by using the resource count of Figure 5.6. (The problem has a slack of 4, but

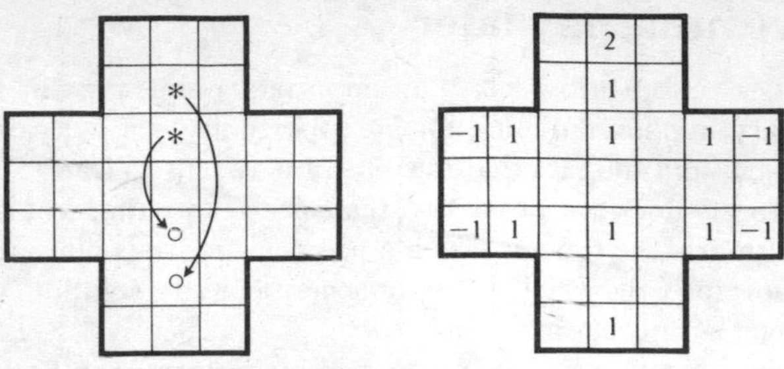

Figure 5.19　　　　Figure 5.20

this is consumed by the first and last moves, each of which loses 2; this leaves nothing for the move needed to clear *d*6.)

The spine-count of Figure 5.1 allows us to prove another result affecting the *d*1-complement. The initial position has value 20 and the final position value 8, leaving a slack of 12, but the necessary clearance of *d*1 during the solution loses at least 8 of this, leaving at most 4 to be lost by the rest of the solution. Now consider the clearance of *a*4 and *g*4. On the face of it, we have a choice between the upward moves *a*5–*a*3 and *g*5–*g*3, the inward moves *a*4–*c*4 and *g*4–*e*4, and the downward moves *a*3–*a*5 and *g*3–*g*5. But the upward moves each lose 4, as do the inward moves, and we can afford at most one such move, so on at least one side we must make the downward move. By an extension of this argument, we can prove a stronger result: we must make either the moves *a*3–*a*5, *a*5–*c*5 (twice), *d*5–*b*5, and *b*3–*d*3, or the corresponding moves on the other side.

A typical use of a resource count therefore has three stages:

(a) we evaluate the slack of the problem (the difference between the values of the initial and target positions), and if it is negative then we declare the problem insoluble forthwith;

(b) we subtract from the slack anything that must be lost by moves that have to be played, and if it is now negative then again we declare the problem insoluble;

(c) we identify any moves that are now banned (because they would lose more than the available slack) and note any that have become compulsory in consequence.

If we are lucky, this procedure leads quickly either to a solution or to a proof of insolubility, and at the very least it may narrow down the possibilities.

Move now, pay later

The last section brings us to an important point: proving a move necessary implies watching for an opportunity when it can legally be played, and the fact that one line of play fails to lead to such an opportunity does not prove that there is no other that would do so. Furthermore, the time at which a necessary move is played may be of importance; playing it at one time may lead to a solution, whereas playing it at another may not.

These difficulties can be postponed by performing a preliminary *analysis of debts and surpluses*, in which we consider a Solitaire problem simply as a collection of debts to be satisfied (holes to be filled) and surpluses to be destroyed (holes to be cleared), and consider the moves that *must* be played in order to liquidate them. The moment that the necessity for a move becomes apparent, we add it to our analysis, and we then see what debts and surpluses it creates in its turn. The outcome of such an analysis is either a proof that no solution exists (because there is ultimately a debt or surplus that cannot be liquidated) or one or more alternative lists of moves that a solution, if one exists, must contain.

For an example, let us analyse 'Longbow' (Figure 1.6). Figure 5.21 represents it in terms of debts (−1) and surpluses (1), the debt at *d*1 arising from the need to fill this hole in the target position. We call such a representation a *task map*. The initial task map of a problem is always obtained by subtracting the target position from the initial position.

Now the first conclusion that we can draw from Figure 5.21 is that a solution must contain the move *d*3–*d*1 to liquidate the debt at *d*1, so we can make this the first item on our list of necessary moves.

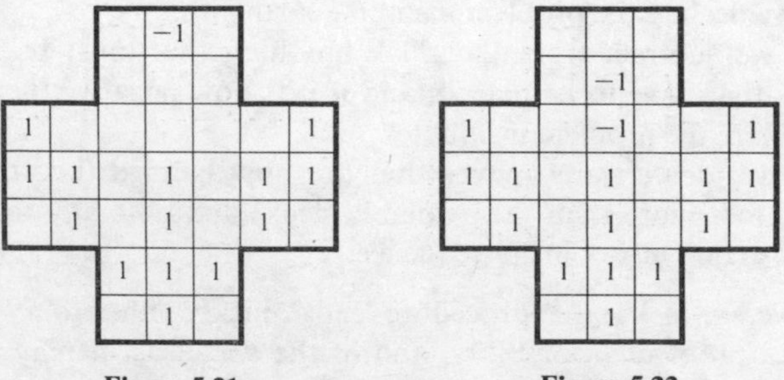

Figure 5.21 Figure 5.22

Never mind that it would be the last move in an actual solution; it *must* be played sooner or later, so we can put it on our list.

The next step is to consider the consequences of the move *d*3–*d*1. Since it puts a man into *d*1 and takes men from *d*3 and *d*2, we can do this on our task map by adding 1 to the number in *d*1 and subtracting 1 from those in *d*3 and *d*2. This duly liquidates the debt at *d*1 but introduces new debts at *d*2 and *d*3, and produces the new task map shown in Figure 5.22.

The new debt at *d*2 can be liquidated only by playing *d*4–*d*2, so this move in turn can be added to our list. It liquidates the debt at *d*2 and also the surplus at *d*4, but introduces a second debt at *d*3 (Figure 5.23).

The debts at *d*3 can apparently be liquidated by several different moves, so let us leave them for a moment and consider some of the surpluses. There is a surplus at *a*4. Now if we evaluate the task map of Figure 5.23 according to the spine-count of Figure 5.1, we find that it has value 0. (Evaluating a task map according to a resource count is straightforward: we multiply each number in the task map by the corresponding value in the resource count, and add the results. In the present case the debts at *d*3 contribute −6 and the surpluses +6, giving an overall value of 0. If a task map yields a negative result when evaluated according to any resource count, then the problem that it describes is insoluble.) This means that the surplus at *a*4 cannot be cleared by *a*5–*a*3 or *a*4–*c*4, since these would lose 4 and we cannot afford any loss, so a solution must contain the move *a*3–*a*5. It must then also contain *a*5–*c*5 to clear the resulting surplus at *a*5, since *a*5–*a*3 is forbidden. The same argument shows that a solution must contain *g*3–*g*5 and *g*5–*e*5. It must also contain *d*7–*d*5, since we must liquidate the surplus at *d*7 and the resource count of

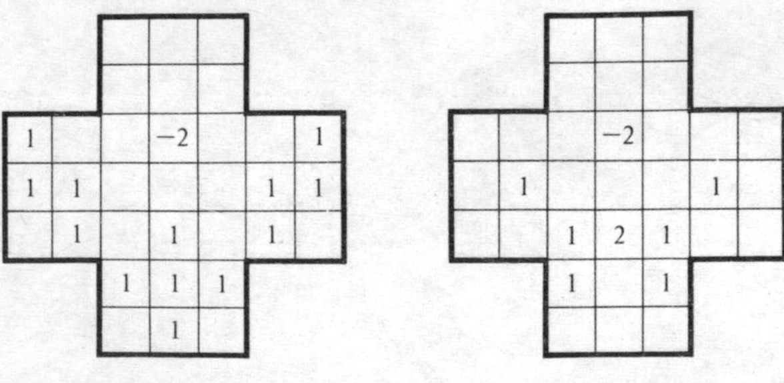

Figure 5.23 Figure 5.24

Figure 5.5 forbids moves across this hole. Adding the effects of all these moves to our task map produces that shown in Figure 5.24.

We now return to the double debt at *d*3. The task map of Figure 5.24 has value 0 according to the resource count of Figure 5.25, and the moves *d*1–*d*3, *b*3–*d*3, and *f*3–*d*3 would each lose at least 1. Hence a solution cannot contain any of them, and so must contain two moves *d*5–*d*3. Their effect is to create a new double debt at *d*4 (Figure 5.26) which can be liquidated only by *b*4–*d*4 and *f*4–*d*4, and the resulting debts at *c*4 and *e*4 (Figure 5.27) can be liquidated only by *c*6–*c*4 and *e*6–*e*4. These moves also liquidate the last remaining surpluses, producing the completely blank task map which has been the object of our endeavours.

Thus we have shown that a solution to 'Longbow' must contain the moves *d*3–*d*1, *d*4–*d*2, *a*3–*a*5, *a*5–*c*5, *g*3–*g*5, *g*5–*e*5, *d*7–*d*5, *d*5–*d*3 (twice), *b*4–*d*4, *f*4–*d*4, *c*6–*c*4, and *e*6–*e*4. These moves are shown in Figure 5.28, which we call a *move map*. The notation is straightforward: 'o' and 'x' denote the holes initially vacant and finally

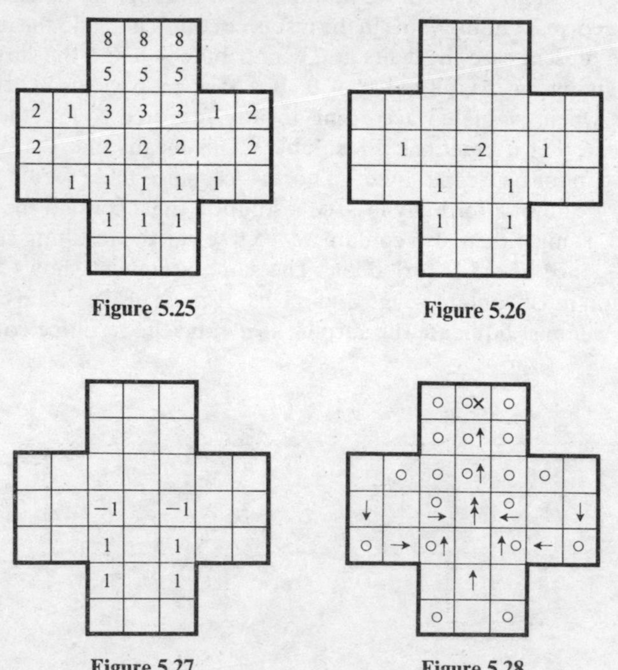

Figure 5.25

Figure 5.26

Figure 5.27

Figure 5.28

occupied, as usual, and the arrows denote the moves. Move maps provide a notation which is very convenient for further analysis, and we shall make extensive use of them.

Single and double surpluses

It must be stressed that an analysis of debts and surpluses is complete only when both debts *and surpluses* have been liquidated. It is not sufficient to liquidate the debts. In this respect there is an important difference between odd and even surpluses. A *double* surplus that is not in an outside corner can always be liquidated by a move across it and a move back. In Figure 5.29, for example, the double surplus at *c*5 can be cleared by *b*5–*d*5 and *d*5–*b*5, or by *c*4–*c*6 and *c*6–*c*4, in each case without creating any new debt or surplus elsewhere. So even surpluses are not a problem. The single surplus at *b*4 cannot be liquidated, however. The task map of Figure 5.29 has value 1 according to the resource count of Figure 5.30, so the move *b*3–*b*5, which would lose 2, is barred, and other resource counts can be used to show that the moves *b*5–*b*3, *a*4–*c*4, *c*4–*a*4, and *b*4–*d*4 are also barred. It can be shown similarly that the surplus at *e*3 cannot be liquidated, while the triple surplus at *e*5, though it can be reduced to a single surplus by an opposing pair of moves across it, cannot be liquidated entirely. We shall return to this point in Chapter 6.

The analysis of Figure 5.21 shows one other point. Look back for a moment at Figure 5.23. This shows a double debt at *d*3 but does not make clear how this debt is to be liquidated. It can be liquidated only by moves of 's' men, however, and all the 's' men are currently in rows 5 and 7. It follows that we must have at least two moves from the set *b*5–*b*3, *d*5–*d*3, and *f*5–*f*3 to get them to row 3. To put it

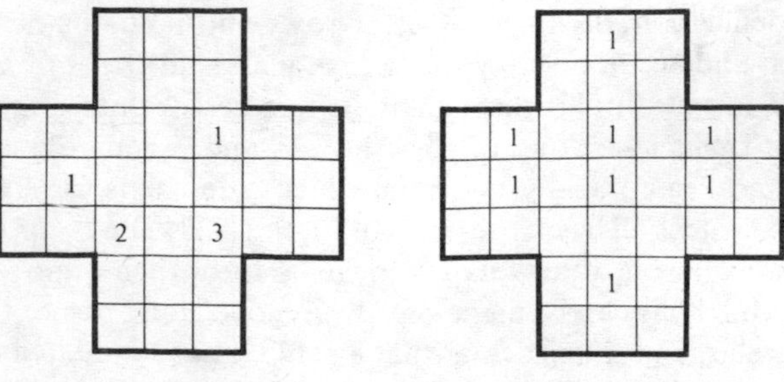

Figure 5.29

Figure 5.30

another way, there is an *overall* double debt over the holes *d*1, *b*3, *d*3, and *f*3 which can be liquidated only by moves to these holes from outside; the only such moves that are available are *b*5–*b*3, *d*5–*d*3, and *f*5–*f*3; therefore a solution must contain at least two of them.

How obvious is obvious?

It is clearly desirable to terminate the detailed analysis of a task map once the remaining moves have become obvious. But what is obvious? Take a look at Figure 5.31. It is obvious, is it not, that the surplus man at *c*2 can be liquidated only by playing *c*2–*c*4? Yet, far from being obvious, it is not even true, as the move map of Figure 5.32 demonstrates; we can play another man to *c*2 and then liquidate both by a pair of vertical moves across *c*2.

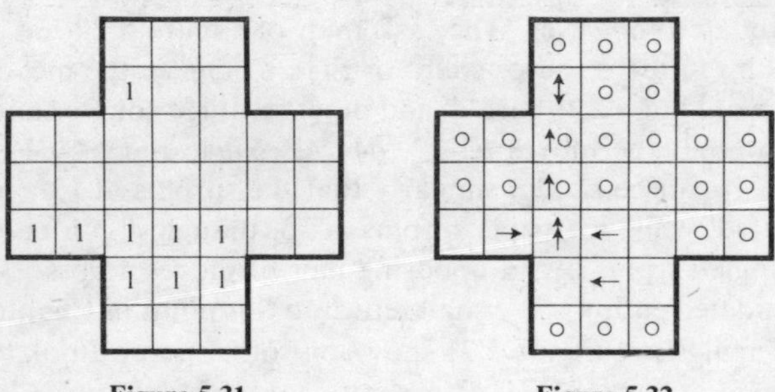

Figure 5.31 Figure 5.32

It may therefore seem that we have to resort to the detailed construction of a resource count every time that we wish to prove a move impossible, but fortunately there is a useful and large class of situations in which this is not so.

We define a *trellis* to be a set of rows and columns no two of which are adjacent, and say that a task map is in *trellis form* if it is possible to put a trellis through all its non-zero values. Figure 5.33 shows a trellis consisting of rows 1, 3, 5, and 7 and columns *a*, *c*, and *f*, and Figure 5.34 a task map which is in trellis form since its non-zero values all lie on the trellis of Figure 5.33. The *trellis theorem* now states that if a task map is in trellis form then a move into a hole of the trellis can be made only by a move along one of the lines of the trellis, and in particular that a debt can be liquidated only by such a move. Thus in Figure 5.34, the debt at *d*3 can be liquidated

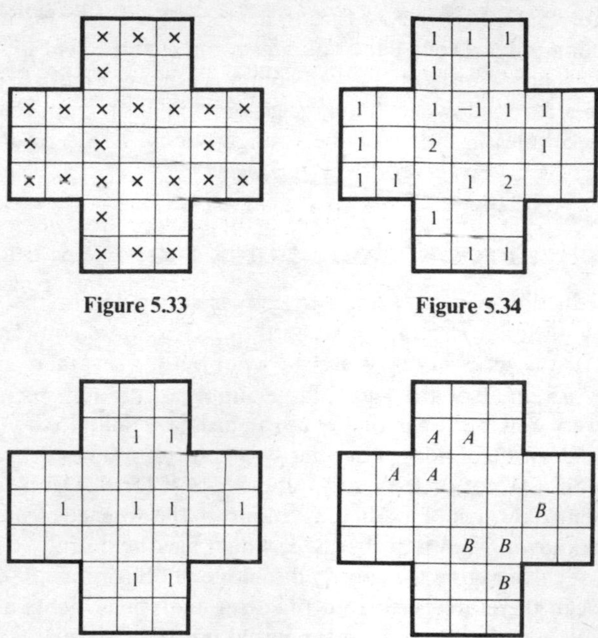

Figure 5.33

Figure 5.34

Figure 5.35

Figure 5.36

only by one of the moves *b*3–*d*3 and *f*3–*d*3; it cannot be liquidated by *d*1–*d*3 or *d*5–*d*3.

The proof of the trellis theorem is very simple: the definition of a trellis ensures that the giving of value 0 to holes on the lines of the trellis and 1 to holes elsewhere produces a valid resource count which has value 0 for the task map under consideration, and a move which places a man in a hole with value 0 must therefore remove men only from holes with value 0. Figure 5.35 shows the resource count derived from the trellis of Figure 5.33, and it may be verified that the moves *d*1–*d*3 and *d*5–*d*3 would each lose 1 according to it.

Note that the trellis theorem applies only to moves which *finish* in a hole on the trellis. It does not apply to other moves. In Figure 5.34, for example, the surplus at *f*4 and one of the surpluses at *c*4 can be liquidated by the move pair *c*4–*e*4 and *f*4–*d*4, neither of which is along a trellis line; but neither of these moves delivers to a trellis hole, so the theorem does not apply.

Most trellises which occur in practice are much simpler than that of Figure 5.33. Figure 5.26 is in trellis form, for example, the trellis consisting only of row 4 and columns *c* and *e*, and so is Figure 5.27, the trellis now consisting only of columns *c* and *e*. Figure 5.24 is *not* in trellis form, however, and in general no task map containing non-zero holes in either of the configurations *AAAA* or *BBBB* in Figure 5.36 is in trellis form.

Practical reduction of task maps

The reduction of a task map to zero is so similar to the normal playing of Solitaire that it is natural to use Solitaire equipment for it. All that is necessary is to find a way of putting several men in one hole. A draughtsboard and a large supply of draughtsmen would work very well, but I personally use an ordinary Solitaire board with pegs laid on their sides, pointing N-S (regarding myself as South) for 2, NE-SW for 3, E-W for 4 and SE-NW for 5. Debts are best represented by men of a different colour. In the absence of such men, I have known peanuts to be used, which has the morally desirable effect of encouraging the speedy discharge of obligations.

We can therefore perform a practical analysis of debts and surpluses very easily. We set up the initial position as usual, and then subtract the target position from it to get the initial task map as we did for Figure 5.21. Subtracting a man from an empty hole leaves a debt, so the initial task map of a complement problem has a particularly simple form: every hole contains either a single surplus or a single debt. Now we proceed as in normal play, but as soon as a move becomes necessary, either because a resource count bars the alternatives or for any other reason, we note it on a move map and make it on the board. We continue this process until we have an empty board. If we have two alternative ways of liquidating a debt or surplus then we note both and see where they lead. If we cannot achieve an empty board then the problem is insoluble; if we can achieve one then we have listed the alternative sets of moves from which a solution, if one exists, must be formed.

A straightforward generalisation of Chapter 4 applies to task maps, the fundamental class of a task map being evaluated by treating *even* surpluses and debts as *empty* holes and *odd* surpluses and debts as *occupied* holes. This leads to the following important result: *if a problem is soluble then the fundamental class of its task map must be that of the empty position.* This is never a difficulty in practice since the initial and target positions of a soluble problem must be in the same fundamental class, and their difference, which forms the initial task map, is then automatically in the fundamental class of the empty position, but it provides a useful check that the initial task map has been set up correctly. It may be verified that each of the task maps shown in the analysis of Figure 5.21 is indeed in the fundamental class of the empty position.

The normal objective of the analysis of a task map is to produce a move map, and it is normally convenient to draw this as the analysis proceeds. A common error in practice is to omit a move from it, however, and it is therefore useful to check that the number of symbols in the completed map (including all symbols 'o' and 'x') is equal to the number of holes in the board. It may be verified that Figures 5.28 and 5.32 satisfy this check.

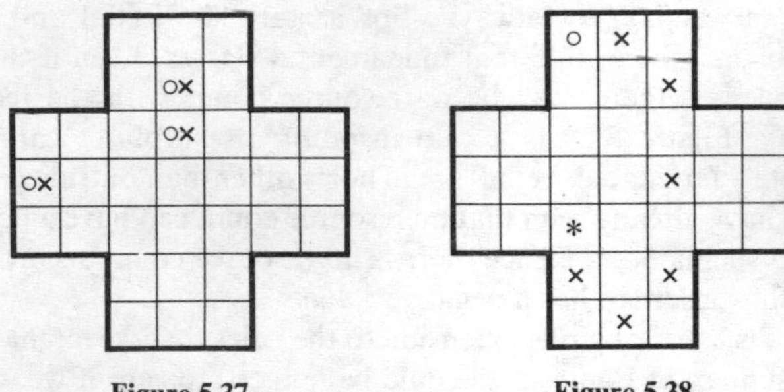

Figure 5.37 **Figure 5.38**

At this point we suggest the analysis of the problems shown in Figures 5.37 and 5.38 by this means. Figure 5.38 shows an attempted solution of the $c1$-complement by a six-sweep by a man on the watch at $c5$. We shall need the results of this analysis when we consider this problem in Chapter 7.

Unconstrained Fractional Solitaire

An analysis of debts and surpluses does not always resolve a problem in ordinary Solitaire; it may provide a list of moves which liquidate all the debts and surpluses but cannot be arranged in order without trying to take a man from an empty hole or put one into an occupied hole. We shall see some examples of this in Chapter 7. It is therefore natural to ask whether we can extend or modify the rules of Solitaire to produce a game for which it would provide a complete resolution. It will be recalled, for example, that the sixteen fundamental classes and the sixteen immovable positions together provide a complete resolution for the game of Up-and-down Solitaire (see Chapter 4).

The most obvious extension is to the game of *Unconstrained Solitaire*, in which we allow a hole to contain any integral number of men, positive, negative, or zero. No constraint on move order applies to this game, since a set of moves forming a solution may be played in any order, so a set of moves liquidating all debts and surpluses automatically provides a solution. Indeed, we have in effect been playing Unconstrained Solitaire in performing the reduction of a task map to zero with board and men.

The next question is therefore: Given that a problem in Unconstrained Solitaire is insoluble, can we prove it by finding a resource count according to which the task map has negative value?

The answer is 'Not always'. For a start, the initial and target positions may be in different fundamental classes. Even if they are not, however, there may be no resource count with the required property. Figure 5.29 is a case in point; its surpluses cannot be completely liquidated, yet all are in holes other than outside corners, and we have already seen that no resource count can have a negative value in such a hole. Hence there is no resource count according to which this task map has a negative value.

There is a less obvious extension to the rules that we might make. The task map of Figure 5.29 could be reduced to zero if we were to allow *fractional* moves, for a single surplus in a hole other than an outside corner could then be liquidated by making half a move across it and half a move back. (Half a move jumps half a man from one hole to another and removes half a man from the hole jumped over.) Such half-move pairs would liquidate all the surpluses in Figure 5.29.

Let us therefore define *Unconstrained Fractional Solitaire* to be Solitaire in which fractional moves are permitted and in which a hole can contain any integral or fractional number of men, positive, negative, or zero. We can now revise our question: Given that a problem in Unconstrained Fractional Solitaire is insoluble, can we prove it by finding a resource count according to which the task map of the problem has negative value?

The answer to this question is 'Yes', but the proof involves a standard result of multi-dimensional geometry. Multi-dimensional geometry is beyond the intended scope of this book, so we confine ourselves to a brief sketch which the reader can skip if he wishes. The task map of a problem can be represented by a point in 33-dimensional Euclidean space, and a resource count by a hyperplane through the origin of this space. Each resource count then divides space into two parts such that task maps with positive or zero values are 'inside' it and those with negative values 'outside'. Now although the number of resource counts is infinite, each can be expressed as a non-negative linear combination of the resource counts in a finite basic set, and the hyperplanes representing this set define a convex cone whose apex is at the origin and whose edges represent the moves. If the point representing a problem lies within this cone then it can be expressed as a linear combination with non-negative coefficients of the unit points along the edges, implying solubility; if it does not lie within the cone then there is at least one hyperplane outside which it lies, implying the existence of a resource count with the required property. The relevance of this result to Solitaire was first noted by Boardman in 1961.

There was a time when it seemed that the 'irreducible' resource counts (those which form the basic set mentioned above) would play as important a role in practice as they do in theory, and some effort was put into computing them. The task is well defined; take a set of 32 independent relations $P+Q=R$ and a normalising condition, solve the 33 resulting equations, and lo and behold: one irreducible resource count. Unfortunately there are 76 different relations $P+Q=R$, so the number of different sets of 32 of them is $\binom{76}{32} \simeq 2.7 \times 10^{21}$. Complete calculation is therefore impracticable, but some progress was made by Conway in the enumeration of particular subsets. In practice the techniques that we shall develop in Chapter 6 have proved much more effective and this has become a backwater, but it is an elegant backwater none the less.

Solutions to Chapter 5

The problems of Figures 5.13 to 5.18 can be proved insoluble by the resource counts of Figures 5.39 to 5.44 respectively. The similarity of Figures 5.39, 5.40, and 5.41 will be noted. It is frequently possible to modify resource counts by interchanging values at the edge with values one hole away from the edge in this way (witness the interchange of *d*1/*d*2 and *d*7/*d*6 between Figures 5.5 and 5.6), though

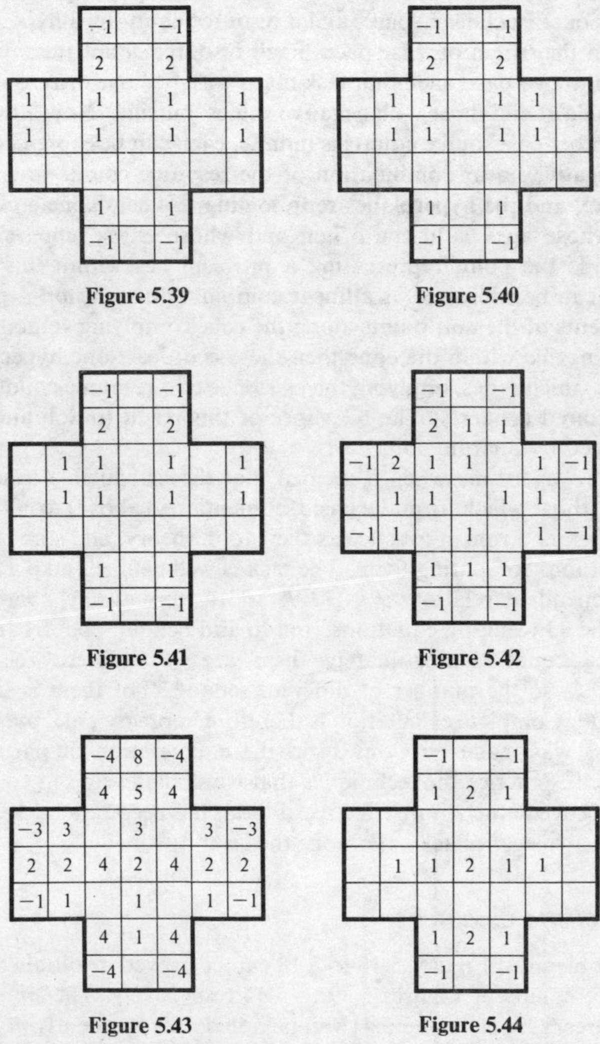

Figure 5.39

Figure 5.40

Figure 5.41

Figure 5.42

Figure 5.43

Figure 5.44

we repeat our warning about the necessity for careful checking of the resulting candidates.

Figure 5.42 shows a modification to the cross-count of Figure 5.8 which is frequently useful in the resolution of problems which feature a debt in an inside corner. We call it the 'North-West modified cross-count' since the modification is confined to the North-West corner (*c*2/*b*3/*c*3). Other modifications of the cross-count are possible: we have already seen the centrally modified cross-count (Figure 5.10), and Figure 5.45 shows the 'North modified cross-count'. Furthermore, any number of similar modifications can be applied independently; the result is still a valid resource count. Figure 5.46 shows the 'NW/NE modified cross-count' and Figure 5.47 the 'fully modified cross-count'. It may be verified that both are valid resource counts.

The insolubility of all complement problems on the 25-hole diamond board can be proved by the set of resource counts shown in Figure 5.48. Each set of three adjacent values *P*,*Q*,*R* in order satisfies

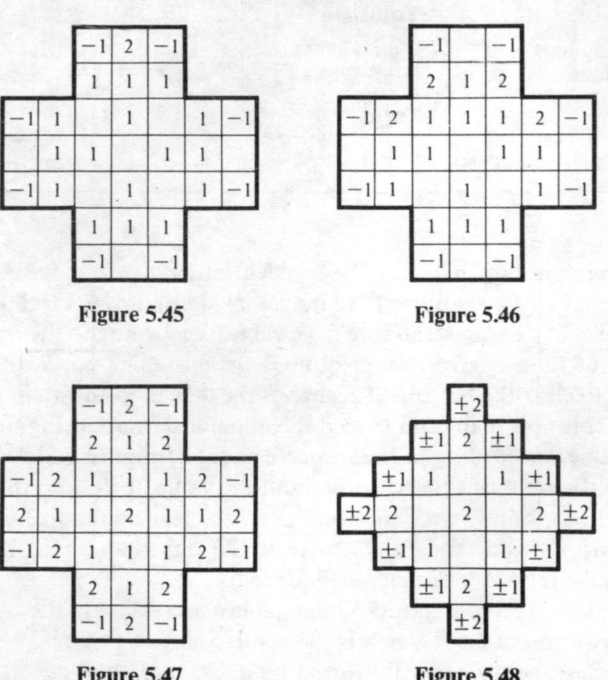

Figure 5.45

Figure 5.46

Figure 5.47

Figure 5.48

$Q \geqslant |P|+|R|$, which is sufficient for $P+Q \geqslant R$ and $R+Q \geqslant P$ both to be true whatever the actual signs of P and R, so each combination of signs in the outside holes produces a valid resource count.

To prove a particular complement problem insoluble, let us assign positive values to the outside holes which are initially vacant and negative values to the remainder. Furthermore, let the sums of the initial vacancies be A (outside holes) and B (inside holes). Then the sums of the initially occupied holes are $-16+A$ (outside holes) and $14-B$ (inside holes). The analysis of Table 5.2 then shows that the slack of the problem is $-2-2B$. This is necessarily negative, since B is either zero or a sum of non-negative quantities, so the problem is insoluble.

Table 5.2: Analysis of a typical complement problem on the 25-hole diamond board

Initial position:	Outside holes:	$-16+A$	
	Inside holes:	$14\quad -B$	
	Total	$-2+A-B$	$-2+A-B$
Target position:	Outside holes:	A	
	Inside holes:	B	
	Total	$A+B$	$A+B$
Slack (initial less target)			$-2\quad -2B$

The initial task map for the problem of Figure 5.37 is shown in Figure 5.49. We shall need the moves *d*4–*d*2 and *c*4–*a*4 to liquidate the debts at *d*2 and *a*4, and we have value 0 according to the resource count of Figure 5.6 so we shall need the moves *c*7–*c*5, *d*7–*d*5, and *e*7–*e*5 to clear the bottom. This leaves the task map shown in Figure 5.50. This task map (and indeed the initial task map of Figure 5.49) has value 0 according to the resource count of Figure 5.51, which is the spine-count of Figure 5.1 without the value at *d*1, and the usual deductions follow: we shall need *a*5–*c*5 to clear *a*5, and *g*3–*g*5, *g*5–*e*5 (twice), *d*5–*f*5, and *f*3–*d*3 to clear the right-hand side. All this leaves the revised task map of Figure 5.52.

The task map of Figure 5.52 has value 4 according to the resource count of Figure 5.53, which is the spine-count of Figure 5.1 turned on its side, so we cannot clear *a*3 by *a*3–*a*5 and shall need to play

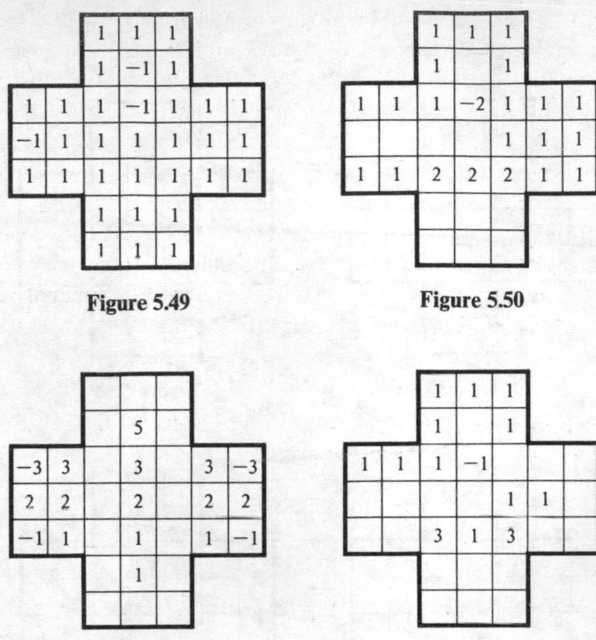

Figure 5.49

Figure 5.50

Figure 5.51

Figure 5.52

*a*3–*c*3. This leaves Figure 5.54. We now have an overall debt over the holes *d*2/*b*3/*d*3/*f*3 which can be liquidated only by playing *b*5–*b*3, *d*5–*d*3, or *f*5–*f*3, but any of these moves will lose at least 1 according to the resource count of Figure 5.53, so the rest of the solution can lose at most 3. We shall therefore need to clear the top by *c*1–*e*1, *e*1–*e*3 (twice), *e*4–*e*2, and *c*2–*c*4, leaving Figure 5.55.

The task map of Figure 5.55 is a trellis map, the trellis lines being rows 3 and 5 and columns *c* and *f*, so all present and future debts must be liquidated by moves along trellis lines. It follows quickly that we shall need the moves *f*3–*d*3, *f*5–*f*3, and *d*5–*f*5, leaving the task map of Figure 5.56, and at last we have a choice: we can play either of the possible opposing pairs of moves (*d*5–*f*5 and *f*5–*d*5 or *e*4–*e*6 and *e*6–*e*4) over *e*5, and either *c*5–*c*3 and an opposing pair over each of *c*3 and *c*5 or *c*3–*c*5 and two opposing pairs over *c*5. The complete move map for the solution is shown in Figure 5.57, the blobs at *c*3/*c*4/*c*5/*e*5 indicating the surpluses which can be liquidated in more than one way.

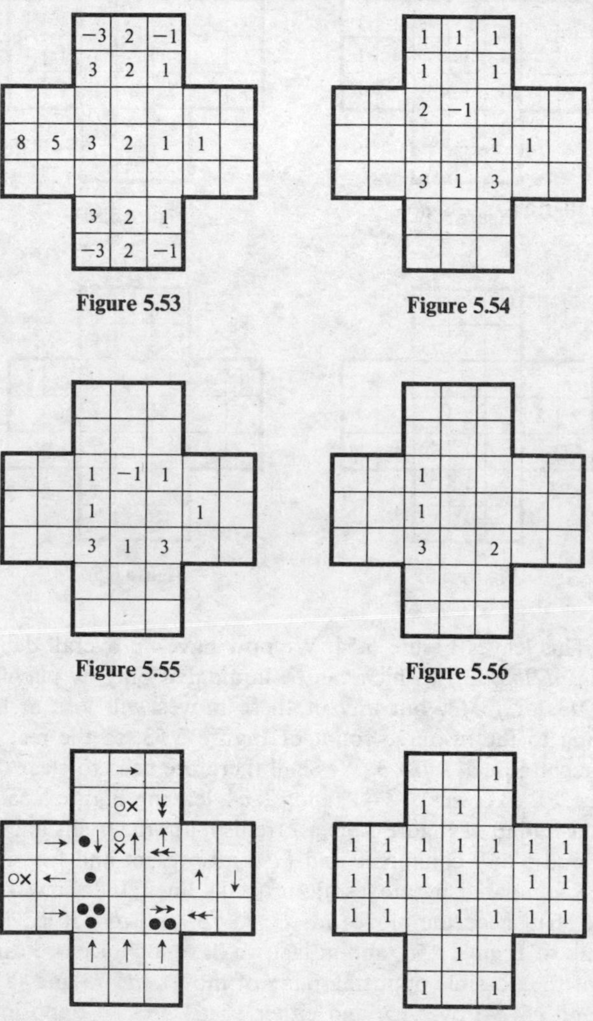

Figure 5.53

Figure 5.54

Figure 5.55

Figure 5.56

Figure 5.57

Figure 5.58

The analysis of Figure 5.38 is perhaps rather easier. The initial task map is shown in Figure 5.58, and the first move must be *e*1–*c*1 since the alternative (*c*3–*c*1) would leave us short of 't' men. This leaves Figure 5.59. We shall now need the following: *c*1–*c*3 to clear *c*1 without loss of an 's' man; *d*3–*d*1 to liquidate the debt at *d*1; *a*5–*a*3, *b*5–*b*3, and *a*3–*c*3 (twice) to clear the left-hand side without disturbing the man on the watch at *c*5; *c*7–*e*7 and *e*7–*e*5 (twice) to clear *c*7/*e*7 similarly; and *g*3–*e*3, *g*4–*e*4, and *g*5–*e*5 to clear the right-hand side without loss of a 't' man. All this leaves Figure 5.60. We shall now need *d*5–*d*7, *e*4–*e*6 (twice), and *c*4–*e*4 to liquidate debts, leaving Figure 5.61, and only now does a choice appear: an opposing pair over *e*5, another over *e*3, and two over *c*3. The complete move map is shown in Figure 5.62.

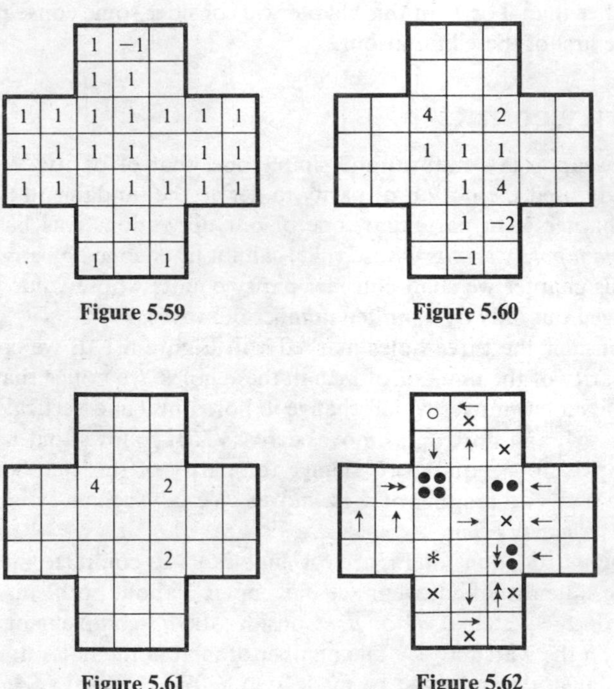

Figure 5.59

Figure 5.60

Figure 5.61

Figure 5.62

6

MATTERS OF BALANCE

The resource counts which we developed in Chapter 5 would provide a complete resolution of Solitaire if we were permitted to make fractional moves and to put any number of men in a hole. Further analysis must therefore take account of the facts that only integral moves are permitted and that the number of men in a hole cannot be other than 0 or 1. In this chapter we consider some consequences of the first of these limitations.

Parity counts

Our weapon is a natural and simple one, that of parity. We have already used the notion of parity to derive the fundamental classes in Chapter 4; in particular, one of our derivations was based on *invariant parity counts* whose value cannot be changed by any move. In this chapter we shall consider parity counts whose value can be changed but only by a limited number of moves.

Consider the three holes marked α in Figure 6.1. If we consider the parity of the number of men in these holes, we notice that there are only a few moves which change it: horizontal and vertical moves across *b*4, and horizontal moves across *c*5. It follows that any solution which is required to change the parity of this number must contain an odd number of these moves. We call such an assembly of values a *parity count*.

The parity count of Figure 6.1 enables us to complete the proof of the statements that we made in Chapter 3 about problems with a man on the watch at *d*3 or *d*5. Consider the *d*3-complement with a man on the watch at *d*5. The number of men in the holes marked α is initially odd and must be made zero before the final sweep. This means that the play before the sweep must contain at least one move which changes its parity, but a horizontal move across *c*5 would disturb the man on the watch on *d*5 so a move across *b*4 must be

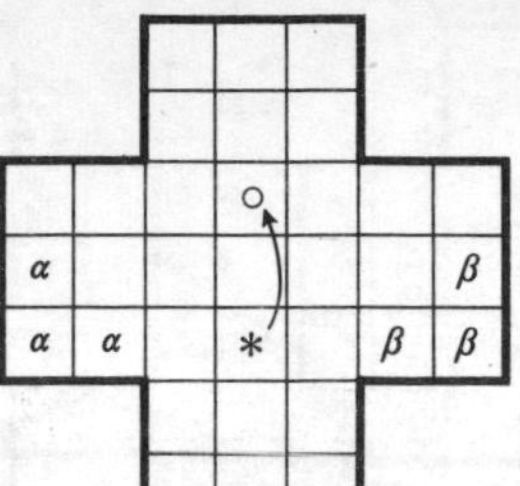

Figure 6.1

played. This move removes a middle man. Similarly, a move across *f*4 is needed to change the parity of β, which removes a second middle man; furthermore, we must play a horizontal move across *d*6 since there is no other way of clearing *d*6 without disturbing the man on the watch on *d*5, and this removes a third. So we can remove no more than two middle men during the final sweep, and anything longer than a three-sweep would need three.

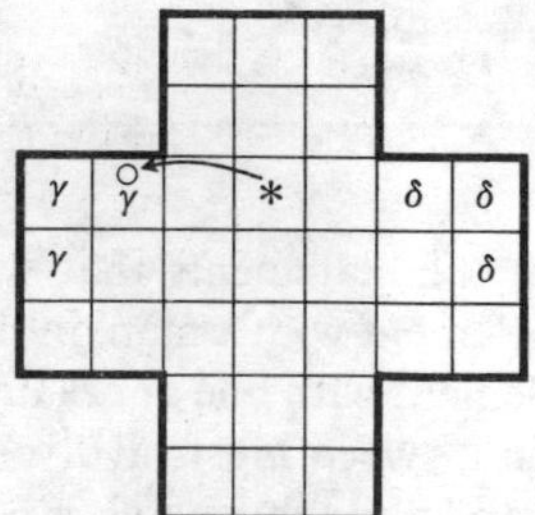

Figure 6.2

The statements about the *b*3-complement with a man on the watch at *d*3 or *d*5 can be proved similarly. Figure 6.2 shows the case with the man on the watch at *d*3. The first move must be *b*5–*b*3, removing a middle man and making γ odd, and we must remove three more middle men before the final sweep: one to change γ again, one to change δ and one to clear *d*2. This leaves at most one for the final sweep, and anything longer than a one-sweep would need two.

Figures 6.3 and 6.4 show another parity count relevant to man-on-the-watch problems. This count can be changed only by moves across *a*4, *c*4, *d*5, or *d*7, each of which removes an edge man. The effects of sweeps by corner men are therefore as shown in Table 6.1.

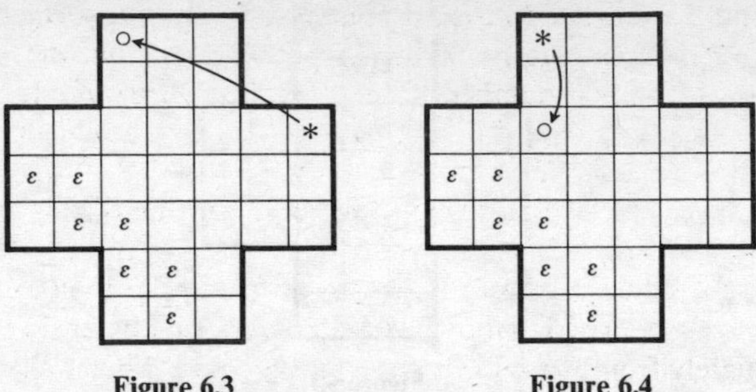

Figure 6.3 Figure 6.4

Table 6.1: The effect of sweeps by corner men on the parity count of Figures 6.3 and 6.4

Starting hole	Finishing hole	Effect of sweep
*a*5, *c*5, or *c*7	*a*5, *c*5, or *c*7	Parity unchanged
*a*5, *c*5, or *c*7	Elsewhere	Parity changed
Elsewhere	*a*5, *c*5, or *c*7	Parity changed
Elsewhere	Elsewhere	Parity unchanged

We can now prove the statements that we made in Chapter 3 regarding the *c*1-complement with a man on the watch at *g*3 (Figure 6.3) and the *c*3-complement with one at *c*1 (Figure 6.4). In each case the play before the final sweep must involve the use of seven edge men to clear corners and an eighth to change the parity of ϵ (since the final sweep does not change it); so no nine-sweep solution is possible.

Into and across the arms

The top half of Figure 6.5 shows another important parity count. This can be changed only by vertical moves across *c*3 or *d*3, and enables us to prove the *arm-balance theorem*, which states that in a solution to a *complement* problem the parities of the vertical moves across *c*3, *d*3, and *e*3 must all be the same: there must be either an odd number of each or an even number of each. The proof is straightforward. The parity count α must be left unchanged by the solution of such a problem, for if it starts even then it must finish even and if it starts odd then it must finish odd, but vertical moves over *c*3 or *d*3 change it, so an odd number of the one must be balanced by an odd number of the other. Similarly, an odd number of vertical moves over *d*3 must be balanced by an odd number of vertical moves over *e*3.

The lower half of Figure 6.5 shows an extension of this theorem: not only must the vertical moves over *c*5, *d*5, and *e*5 have the same parity in a solution to a complement problem, but they must have the opposite parity to that of moves across *d*6. This extension follows immediately from the fact that the parity count β must be changed in any complementation.

The arm-balance theorem plays an important role in the theory of minimal-move solutions to multiple-vacancy complement problems, as we shall see in Chapter 8, and is sometimes of use in proving the necessity of inconvenient moves in problems with marked men. The complement problem of Figure 6.6 shows a simple example of its use. We can remove only three middle men in the course of a solution, so at least one of the holes *d*2, *b*4, *f*4, and *d*6 must be cleared by a move to the centre; but we cannot lose any corner men at all, so we cannot play the required parallel moves across inside corners. Hence the theorem cannot be satisfied, and the problem is insoluble.

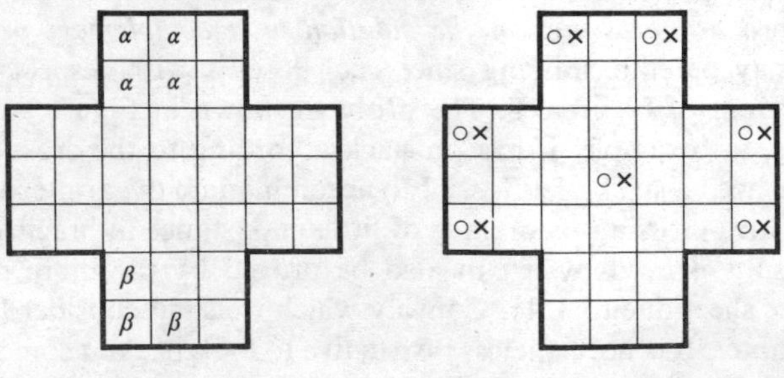

Figure 6.5 **Figure 6.6**

Figure 6.7 displays four parity counts which prove the *arm-crossing theorem*. The only moves that change α are horizontal moves across *d*2 or *d*3 and vertical moves across *b*4 or *c*4. We call these moves *arm-crossings*. (Note that they do *not* include moves across *d*1 or *a*4.) The *arm-crossing theorem* now states that in a solution to a *complement* problem, either the numbers of top arm-crossings

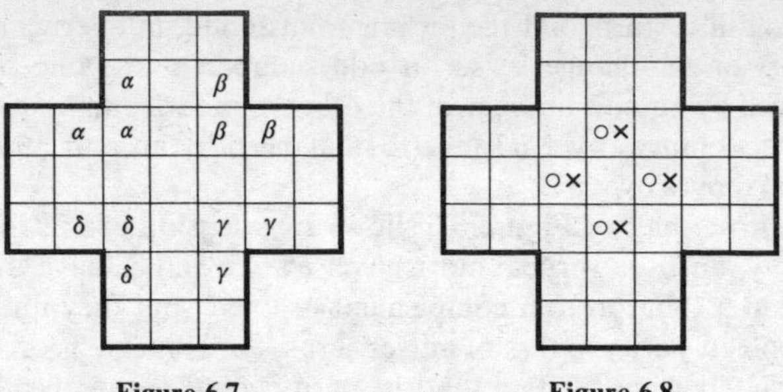

Figure 6.7 **Figure 6.8**

(horizontal moves across *d*2 or *d*3) and bottom arm-crossings (horizontal moves across *d*5 or *d*6) are both even and the numbers of left arm-crossings (vertical moves across *b*4 or *c*4) and right arm-crossings (vertical moves across *e*4 or *f*4) both odd, or vice versa. The proof is very simple. A solution to a complement problem must change the parity of each of α, β, γ, and δ. Suppose we have an even number of top arm-crossings. Then we must have odd numbers of left and right arm-crossings to change α and β, and these also change γ and δ and so must be accompanied by an even number of bottom arm-crossings in order not to change them back again. A similar argument applies if the number of top arm-crossings is odd.

A consequence of the arm-crossing theorem is that *there are at least two arm-crossings in the solution of a complement problem.* This may be embarrassing since each loses 1 with respect to the cross-count of Figure 5.8. The problem shown in Figure 6.8 is insoluble, for example; it has no slack according to the cross-count, and we need a slack of at least 2 to accommodate the arm-crossings.

The arm-crossing theorem is of little importance in practice since the results proved by it can also be proved by the more general balance sheet due to J. H. Conway which we shall consider later in the chapter. It is nevertheless instructive to look back at some of the solutions in Chapters 2 and 3 and verify that they do indeed satisfy the arm-balance and the arm-crossing theorems. For example, consider our simple block-removal solution to the *d*4-complement problem, reproduced for convenience as Figure 6.9. The L-removal *e*1/*d*1/*c*1/*c*2/*c*3/*c*4, the move *d*2–*d*4, and the three-removal *e*2/*e*3/*e*4 involve single vertical moves across *c*3, *d*3, and *e*3 respectively. The six-removals at the left, bottom, and right each involve one arm-crossing, and the three-removal *c*5/*d*5/*e*5 involves a second

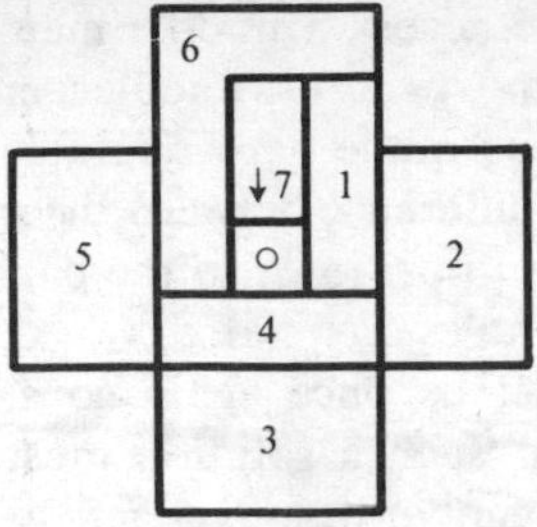

Figure 6.9

bottom arm-crossing. Thus we have an odd number of left and right arm-crossings, an even number of bottom arm-crossings, and no top arm-crossing. The moves of the catalysts involved in the block removals consist of pairs of opposing moves over a single hole and make no net contribution to parities.

Analogous theorems apply to non-complement problems, but it is easier to work them out from first principles as required than to remember the precise conditions under which each is valid.

The removal of middle men

The parity counts shown in Figure 6.7 are not the only useful parities which can be changed only at the expense of a loss with respect to some resource count or specific set of men.

Consider the parity count σ in Figure 6.10. This can be changed only by a move across *d*1, *b*5, *d*5, or *f*5, each of which costs one 's' man, or by a vertical move across a middle man. Similarly, the parity count τ can be changed only by a move across *a*4, *e*2, *e*4, or *e*6, or

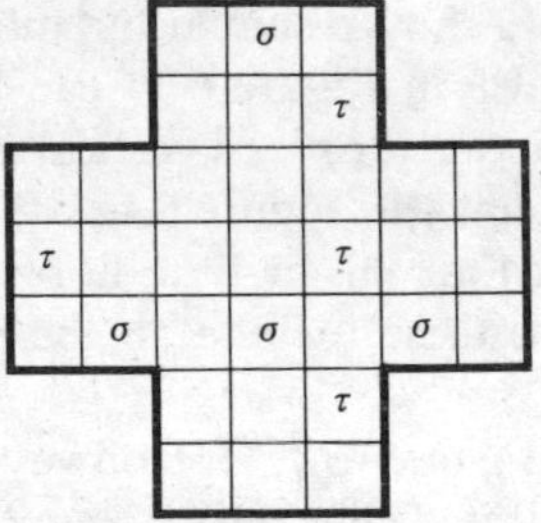

Figure 6.10

by a horizontal move across a middle man. Between them, these cover all the possible moves across middle men. But the total number of moves that must be made across middle men in a solution is known, since it is the difference between the numbers of middle men in the initial and target positions; so the parities of the numbers of moves across σ and τ holes are related.

For an example, let us once again consider the solution of a complement problem. Such a solution must leave the parity of σ unchanged, so if the number of moves across σ holes is odd then the number of vertical moves across middle men must also be odd. But the total number of moves across middle men in a complementation must be odd, so if the number of vertical moves across them is odd then the number of horizontal moves across them must be even; and since the solution must also leave the parity of τ unchanged, it follows that the number of moves across τ holes must be even. In other words, the parities of the numbers of moves across σ and τ holes must be different. *This is a fundamental asymmetry of the 33-hole board with respect to complement problems.*

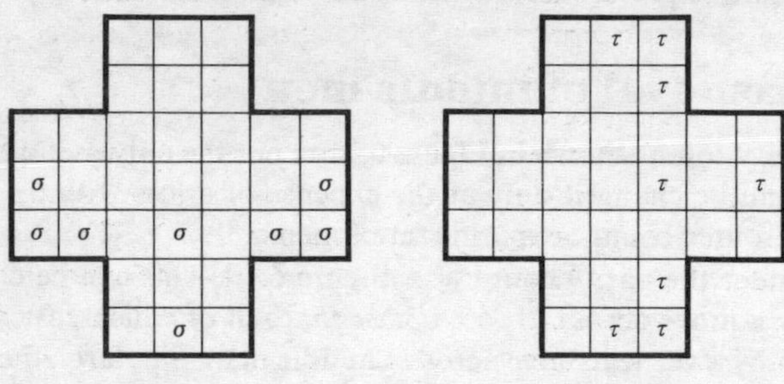

Figure 6.11 **Figure 6.12**

Figures 6.11 and 6.12 show a similar but more sophisticated property. The parity count σ in Figure 6.11 can be changed only by a move across *b*4, *f*4, *d*5, or *d*7, or by a vertical move across the centre. The corresponding count τ in Figure 6.12 can be changed only by a move across *d*2, *e*4, *g*4, or *d*6, or by a horizontal move across the centre. Between them, these include all the possible moves across middle men.

Figures 6.13 and 6.14, due to J. H. Conway and R. L. Hutchings, are even more sophisticated. The parity count α can be changed only by a horizontal move across *d*4, *d*5, or *d*6, or by a vertical move

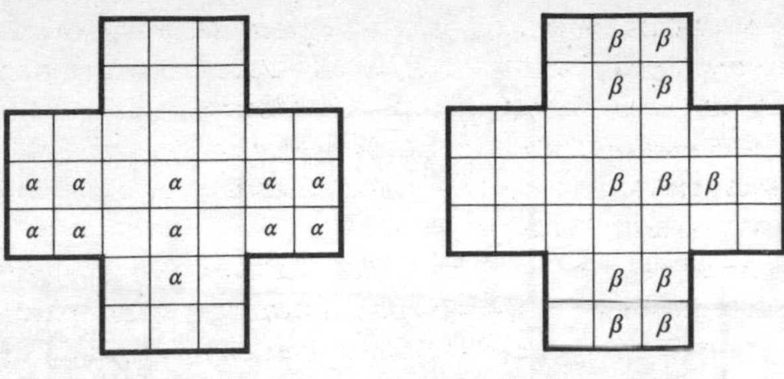

Figure 6.13

Figure 6.14

across *d*3 or *d*5, and the corresponding count β only by a vertical move across *d*4, *e*4, or *f*4, or by a horizontal move across *c*4 or *e*4. Between them, these cover all moves into, over, or out of the centre.

Conway's balance sheet

Some problems require arguments of the form 'We must change parity count *A*, so we must play move *M*, but this reduces our slack according to resource count *R*, so we cannot play move *X* and so must play *Y*, but this in turn changes parity count *B*...'. Such arguments are clumsy and can often be avoided by the use of *multiple-component counts* which combine several elements in one count. The most useful such count on the 33-hole board is the *balance sheet* developed by Conway and illustrated in Figure 6.15. This contains five components: *a* and *b* are the resource counts of Figures 5.6 and 5.7, *c* measures occupancy of the centre, and α and β are the parity counts of Figures 6.13 and 6.14.

The amounts lost according to Conway's balance sheet by the various possible moves are listed in Table 6.2 and illustrated in Figures 6.16 to 6.24. These losses are obtained by algebraic addition and subtraction, a move from a hole with value *P* over one with value *Q* into one with value *R* losing $P+Q-R$; and remember that $\alpha+\alpha=\beta+\beta=0$. The values (a), $(a+\alpha)$, (b), $(b+\beta)$, $(c+\alpha)$, $(c+\beta)$, $(2a-c+\alpha)$, and $(2b-c+\beta)$ cannot be expressed as sums of other values, and so are called the *primitives* of the balance sheet. The values $(2a)$ and $(2b)$ are not primitives, since they can be expressed as sums of other primitives: $(2a)=(a)+(a)=(a+\alpha)+(a+\alpha)$ $=(2a-c+\alpha)+(c+\alpha)$, and similarly for $(2b)$. Every move loss is therefore either a primitive or a sum of primitives, and it follows that

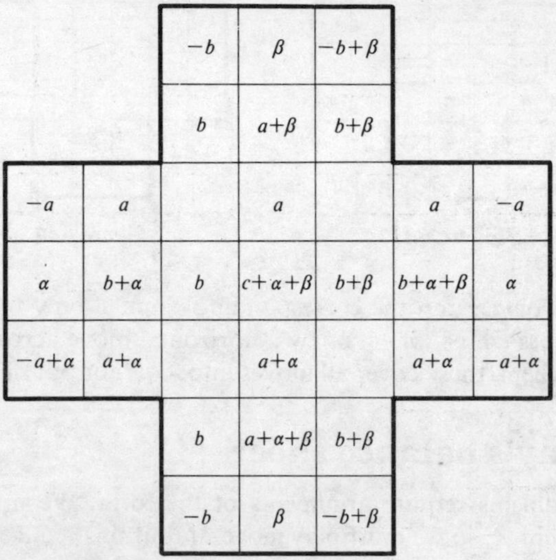

		$-b$	β	$-b+\beta$		
		b	$a+\beta$	$b+\beta$		
$-a$	a		a		a	$-a$
α	$b+\alpha$	b	$c+\alpha+\beta$	$b+\beta$	$b+\alpha+\beta$	α
$-a+\alpha$	$a+\alpha$		$a+\alpha$		$a+\alpha$	$-a+\alpha$
		b	$a+\alpha+\beta$	$b+\beta$		
		$-b$	β	$-b+\beta$		

Figure 6.15

Table 6.2: Move losses according to Conway's balance sheet

Horizontal moves across *d*2 or *d*3	a
Horizontal moves across *d*5 or *d*6	$a+\alpha$
Horizontal moves across the centre	$c+\alpha$
Vertical moves out of the centre	$c+\alpha$
Vertical moves into the centre	$2a-c+\alpha$
Moves into *d*1 or *d*7	$2a$
Horizontal moves into *a*3, *a*5, *g*3, or *g*5	$2a$
Vertical moves across *b*4 or *c*4	b
Vertical moves across *e*4 or *f*4	$b+\beta$
Vertical moves across the centre	$c+\beta$
Horizontal moves out of the centre	$c+\beta$
Horizontal moves into the centre	$2b-c+\beta$
Moves into *a*4 or *g*4	$2b$
Vertical moves into *c*1, *e*1, *c*7, or *e*7	$2b$
Other moves	Nothing

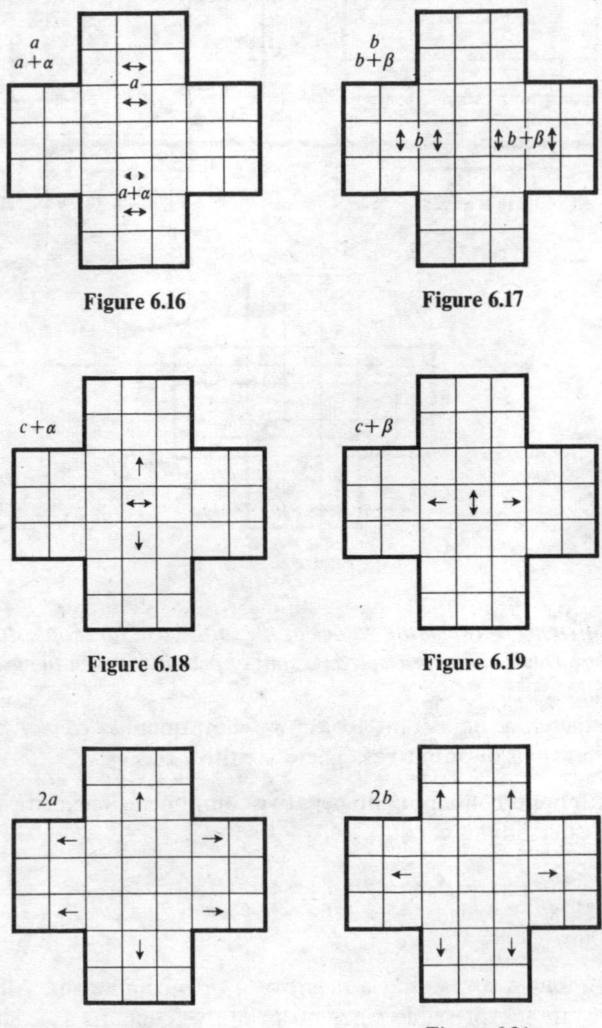

Figure 6.16

Figure 6.17

Figure 6.18

Figure 6.19

Figure 6.20

Figure 6.21

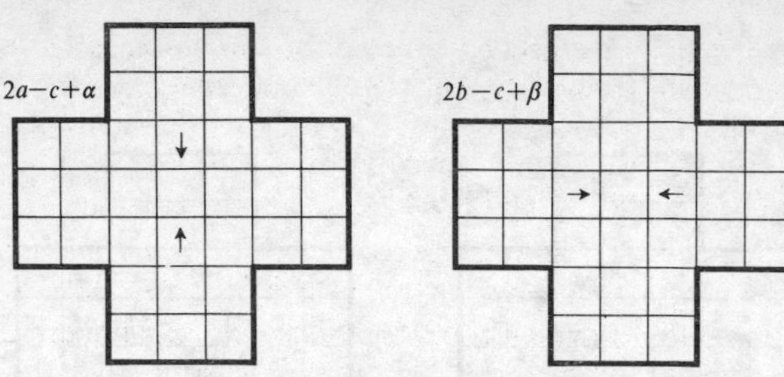

Figure 6.22

Figure 6.23

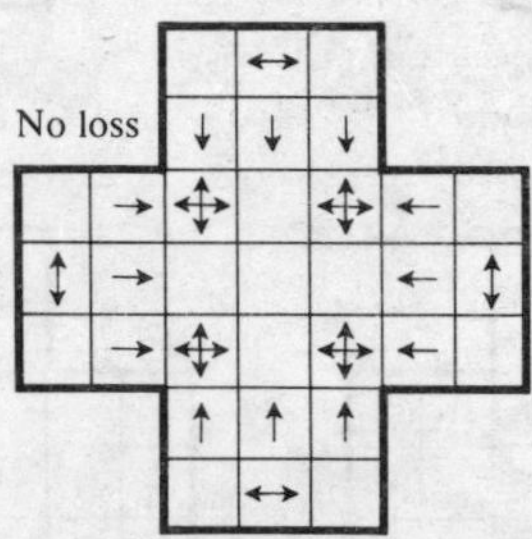

Figure 6.24

if the difference between the values of the initial and target positions of a problem cannot be expressed as a sum of primitives then the problem is insoluble.

It is therefore important to know what amounts *cannot* be expressed as sums of primitives. There are three classes:

(a) Amounts containing no negative component. There are eleven inexpressibles in this class:

(α)	$(a+\beta)$	$(b+\alpha)$	(c)	$(2a+\beta)$	$(2b+\alpha)$
(β)	$(a+\alpha+\beta)$	$(b+\alpha+\beta)$	$(c+\alpha+\beta)$		
$(\alpha+\beta)$					

(b) Amounts containing a negative a or b component. All such amounts are inexpressible since no primitive contains a negative a or b component.

(c) Amounts containing a negative c component. These are most conveniently analysed by removing the multiples of $(2a-c+\alpha)$ or

$(2b-c+\beta)$ which are needed to account for the negative c component and then seeing whether the balance is expressible. For an example, consider $(4a-c+\alpha+\beta)$. The possibilities are $(2a-c+\alpha)$ $+(2a+\beta)$ and $(2b-c+\beta)+(4a-2b+\alpha)$, but the first does not lead to an expression because $(2a+\beta)$ is one of the inexpressibles with no negative component, and the second because $(4a-2b+\alpha)$ has a negative b component. So $(4a-c+\alpha+\beta)$ is inexpressible. We can prove $(4b-c+\alpha+\beta)$ and $(2a+2b-c)$ inexpressible similarly. These three cases prove to be very important in practice.

The use of the balance sheet is similar to that of a resource count. We start by forming the difference between the values of the initial and target positions (most easily done by taking $(4a+4b+c+\alpha+\beta)$, which is the value of the full position, and subtracting the values of the initial vacancies and of the target position), subtract any losses that must be made by forced moves, and analyse the balance. If this is inexpressible then the problem is proved insoluble, and even if it is not inexpressible the possible expressions may be few and so may indicate clearly the pattern which the solution must follow.

Let us look at some examples. First, consider a solution of 'Whither will he wander?' (Figure 1.16) with the marked man finishing at *d*1. Such a solution must include moves *d*3-*d*1-*d*3-*d*1 by the marked man (and also moves *d*3-*b*3-*d*3 or *d*3-*f*3-*d*3 to preserve it while another man moves to *d*2, though these do not affect the argument), and two moves *d*4-*d*2 to remedy the deficiency on *d*2. The balance sheet analysis of Table 6.3 now shows that the rest of the solution must lose $(4b-c+\alpha+\beta)$. We have already noted that

Table 6.3: Analysis of 'Whither will he wander?'

Value of full position		$4a+4b+c+\alpha+\beta$
Less value of initial vacancy		β
Less value of target position		β
Amount to be lost during solution		$4a+4b+c+\alpha+\beta$
Less amounts lost by forced moves:		
Opening move *d*3-*d*1	$2a$	
Final move *d*3-*d*1	$2a$	
Two moves *d*4-*d*2		$2c$
Amount to be lost by rest of solution		$4b-c+\alpha+\beta$

this is inexpressible, so the problem is insoluble. This almost completes our analysis of 'Whither will he wander?', for we have now eliminated every possibility except *d*7; we leave the finding of a solution in this case to the reader.

Figure 6.25 shows a double-vacancy complement problem which was reported as insoluble by T. R. Dawson in 1943. A proof by the balance sheet is quite easy. A solution must contain the move *d*4-*b*4, and the analysis of Table 6.4 then shows that the rest of the solution must lose $(4a+2b-2c+\alpha)$. We can account for the negative c component by using either one term $(2a-c+\alpha)$ and one term $(2b-c+\beta)$ or two terms $(2a-c+\alpha)$, which lead respectively to $(2a-c+\alpha)+(2b-c+\beta)+(2a+\beta)$ and $(2a-c+\alpha)+(2a-c+\alpha)+(2b+\alpha)$, but in each case the residue $(2a+\beta)$ or $(2b+\alpha)$ is inexpressible. Hence $(4a+2b-2c+\alpha)$ is inexpressible, so the problem is insoluble.

Double-vacancy complement problems appear first to have received attention when Dawson set several for solution in *The Fairy Chess Review* in 1943. His accompanying remarks included 'some few fail in practice for lack of elbow room' and 'the case of *b*4, *d*4 is

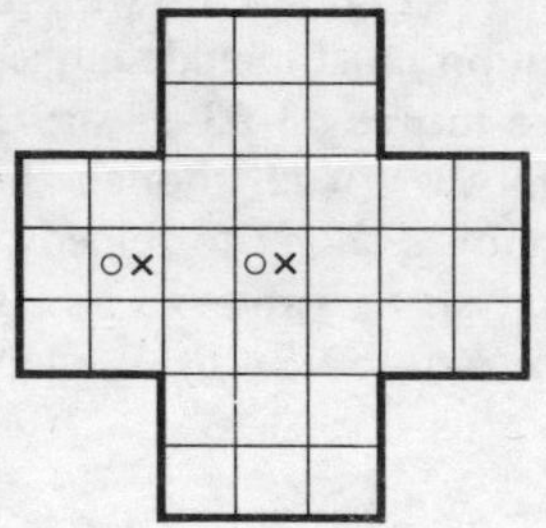

Figure 6.25

Table 6.4: Analysis of the problem of Figure 6.25

Value of full position	$4a+4b+c+\alpha+\beta$
Less value of initial vacancies	$b+c \quad +\beta$
Less value of target position	$b+c \quad +\beta$
Less amount lost by forced move:	
Move *d*4-*b*4 to fill *b*4	$c \quad +\beta$
Amount to be lost by rest of solution	$4a+2b-2c+\alpha$

NOT practicable'. No proof was given, but Dawson, a professional chemist who was also an able mathematician and a chess problemist of genius, was not in the habit of stating a categorical NOT without having proved the matter to his own satisfaction. In fact there are four which are insoluble, the other three being submitted for the reader's attention as Figures 6.28 to 6.30 below. Conway, Hutchings and M. J. T. Guy established this in 1961 with the aid of the parity counts of Figures 6.13 and 6.14 and the resource counts of Figures 5.6 and 5.7, and it was a wish to simplify such analyses that led to the development of Conway's balance sheet. (Dawson's method of proof is not known to me. He may have used elementary arguments: (i) list the alternative moves that can remove the outstanding middle man; (ii) in each case, list the moves now needed to clear *d*1, *a*4, *g*4, *d*7, and the outside corners; (iii) show that we are always short of an 's' or 't' man somewhere. Such arguments are perfectly valid although somewhat laborious. Alternatively, he may have anticipated some of the techniques used here.)

Figure 6.26 shows a triple-vacancy complement problem. What can we say about the solution?

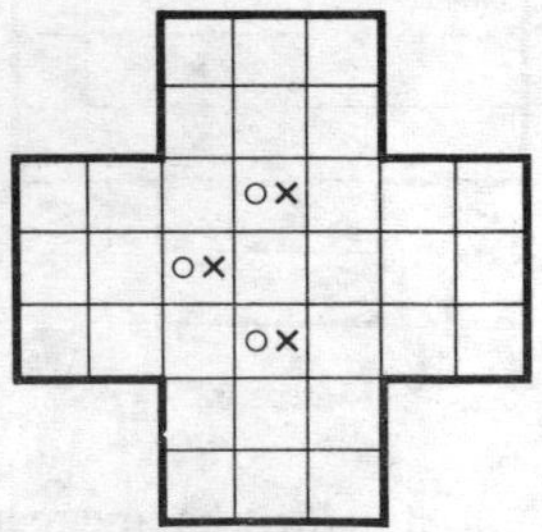

Figure 6.26

A standard balance sheet analysis (Table 6.5) shows that the amount to be lost by the solution is $(2b+c+\alpha+\beta)$. This is expressible only as $(b)+(b+\beta)+(c+\alpha)$, so a solution must contain the following: a vertical move across *b*4 or *c*4, losing (b); a vertical move across *e*4 or *f*4, losing $(b+\beta)$; and either a vertical move out of the centre or a horizontal move across it, losing $(c+\alpha)$. The arm-crossing theorem would have told us about the first two of these but not about the third.

Table 6.5: Analysis of the problem of Figure 6.26

Value of full position	$4a+4b+c+\alpha+\beta$
Less value of initial vacancies	$2a+b+\beta$
Less value of target position	$2a+b+\beta$
Amount to be lost by solution	$2b+c+\alpha+\beta$

Conway and Hutchings analysed all the triple-vacancy complement problems in 1961 and established that there are three classes of insoluble problem: (i) *d*1, *d*2, and any third other than *a*3, *a*5, *g*3, or *g*5; (ii) any two middle men and any third other than an outside corner; (iii) any three from rows 2, 4, and 6. In each case a proof by the balance sheet is straightforward.

Figure 6.27 repeats 'Letter D' from Chapter 1. Again, what can we say about the solution?

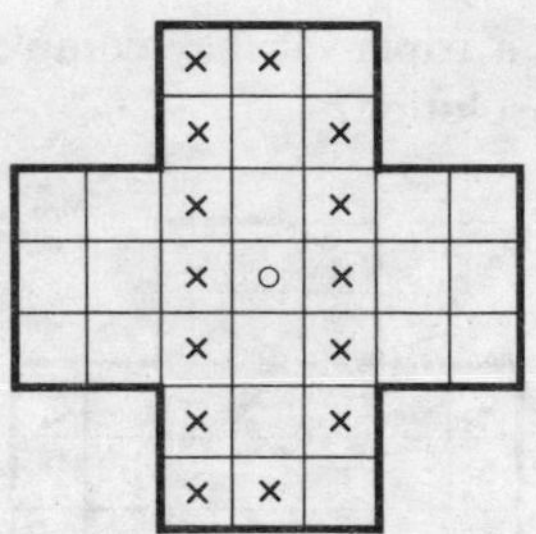

Figure 6.27

Once more we apply a standard balance sheet analysis. We can assume without loss of generality that the first move is *d*2–*d*4, since a horizontal move would remove a 't' man which we cannot afford. The analysis of Table 6.6 then shows that the rest of the solution must lose $(2a+c+\alpha+\beta)$. This is expressible only as $(a)+(a+\alpha)+(c+\beta)$, so a solution must contain the following: a horizontal move across *d*2 or *d*3, losing (a); a horizontal move across *d*5 or *d*6, losing $(a+\alpha)$; and either a horizontal move out of the centre or a vertical move across it, losing $(c+\beta)$. Elementary considerations of debts and surpluses allow us to refine this list; we cannot refill *d*2, since such a move would lose $(c+\alpha)$, which is not one of the amounts that we can lose, so the move losing (a) must be across *d*3; we cannot afford to lose a 't' man other than in the clearance of *e*1 and *e*7, so the move losing $(c+\beta)$ must be a vertical move across *d*4; and we cannot liquidate the surplus at *d*6 other than by the horizontal move losing $(a+\alpha)$, since *d*7–*d*5 would leave an irretrievable debt at *d*7 and other moves lose amounts which we are not permitted to lose.

Figures 6.28 to 6.31 contain some problems which the reader may care to analyse. Figures 6.28 to 6.30 show the other three insoluble double-vacancy complement problems. Figure 6.31 shows a 'marked man' complement problem and our question is: Can the marked man at *c*4 travel to *e*4 via *d*4? The reader may also care to analyse 'Letter B' of Chapter 1 in the same way that we analysed 'Letter D'.

Conway's balance sheet, although easy to use once learned, is harder to master initially than most of the other tools which we have developed. Practice brings fluency, however, and we suggest that the reader should attempt at least some of these problems before reading on. One useful simplification can often be adopted: in a *complement* problem, the value of the initial vacancies equals that of the target

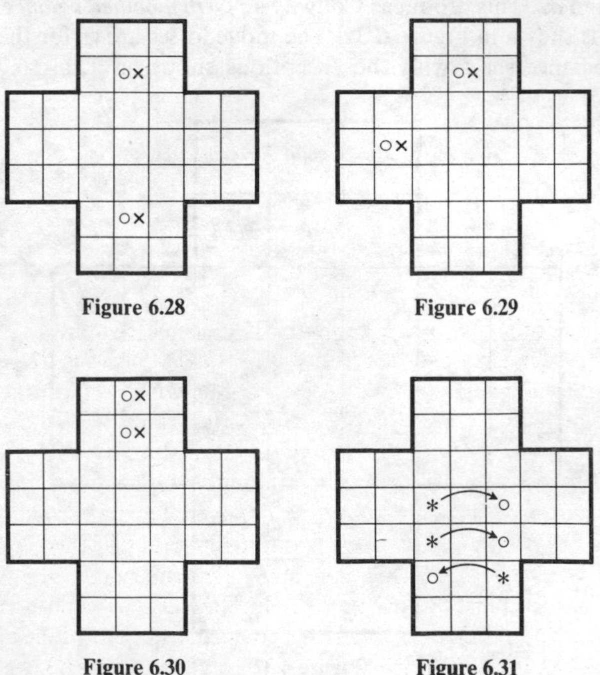

Figure 6.28 **Figure 6.29**

Figure 6.30 **Figure 6.31**

Table 6.6: Analysis of 'Letter D'

Value of full position	$4a+4b+c+\alpha+\beta$
Less value of initial vacancies	$c+\alpha+\beta$
Less value of target position	$4b \qquad +\beta$
Less value to be lost by forced move:	
First move (*d*2–*d*4)	$2a \qquad -c+\alpha$
Amount to be lost by rest of solution	$2a \qquad +c+\alpha+\beta$

position, so the amount to be lost by the solution can be found by subtracting twice the value of the target position from that of the full board.

Modified balance sheets

Conway's balance sheet can be modified by interchanging the values in *d*1 and *d*2. This produces Conway's *North modified balance sheet*, which is shown in Figure 6.32. The move losses are as for the standard balance sheet with the exceptions shown in Table 6.7. The

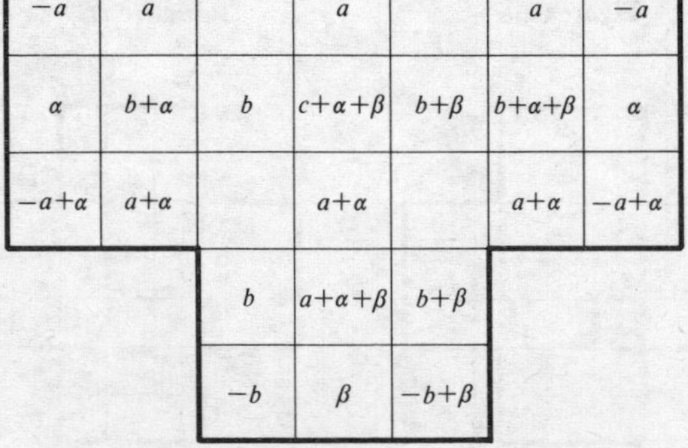

		$-b$	$a+\beta$	$-b+\beta$		
		b	β	$b+\beta$		
$-a$	a		a		a	$-a$
α	$b+\alpha$	b	$c+\alpha+\beta$	$b+\beta$	$b+\alpha+\beta$	α
$-a+\alpha$	$a+\alpha$		$a+\alpha$		$a+\alpha$	$-a+\alpha$
		b	$a+\alpha+\beta$	$b+\beta$		
		$-b$	β	$-b+\beta$		

Figure 6.32

Table 6.7: Move losses according to Conway's North modified balance sheet

Horizontal moves across *d*1:	a	instead of 0
Horizontal moves across *d*2:	0	instead of a
*d*3-*d*1:	0	instead of $2a$
*d*4-*d*2:	$a+c+\alpha$	instead of $c+\alpha$
*d*2-*d*4:	$a-c+\alpha$	instead of $2a-c+\alpha$

introduction of $(a-c+\alpha)$ as a new primitive is a complication, and this modified balance sheet is normally used in practice only when the shortage of 's' men is such that the move losing it cannot be contemplated.

Similar modifications can be performed in any of the arms of the balance sheet, with appropriate modification to the primitives. Figure 6.33 shows thc *fully modified balance sheet*, which can be used to analyse the 'quadruple-cross' problems which we shall meet in Chapter 10.

The description 'standard' for Figure 6.15 and 'modified' for Figures 6.32 and 6.33 is historically correct and reflects the relative

		$-b$	$a+\beta$	$-b+\beta$		
		b	β	$b+\beta$		
$-a$	a		a		a	$-a$
$b+\alpha$	a	b	$c+\alpha+\beta$	$b+\beta$	α	$b+\alpha+\beta$
$-a+\alpha$	$a+\alpha$		$a+\alpha$		$a+\alpha$	$-a+\alpha$
		b	β	$b+\beta$		
		$-b$	$a+\alpha+\beta$	$-b+\beta$		

Figure 6.33

usefulness of the versions on the 33-hole board, but our consideration of general boards in Chapter 11 will suggest that it is really Figure 6.33 which should be regarded as standard and Figure 6.15 as a modification of it, in the same way that the resource count of Figure 5.6 is a modification of the simple 's' man count of Figure 5.5. We nevertheless retain the traditional terminology here.

Conway himself appears to have made little use of these modified balance sheets, and they are not even mentioned in *Winning ways for your mathematical plays*. They are occasionally useful, however, and deserve perpetuation.

Practical analysis using parity counts

Not every problem can be completely decided by the use of Conway's balance sheet and the other parity counts described in this chapter, and in some cases it is still necessary to perform a detailed analysis of debts and surpluses. If an intractable *single* debt or surplus arises during such an analysis, the probability is either that the balance sheet or a parity count has been wrongly evaluated (which is easily done until fluency has been attained) or that a relevant parity count has been overlooked. If all relevant parity counts are correctly evaluated then intractable debts can be expected to arise as *doubles*, and the application of a simple resource count is then normally sufficient to prove insolubility. If the debt arises in an inside corner hole, for example, one of the modified cross-counts typified by Figure 5.46 is likely to be sufficient.

How badly can you play?

We end this chapter with a teasing question. We saw in Chapter 1 that it is possible to kill the *d*4-complement in only six moves by playing to 'Dead' (Figure 1.7). We can still solve the problem after playing the first five of these moves, however. In how few moves from the start of the *d*4-complement can you reach a position from which a solution is no longer possible?

Solutions to Chapter 6

'Whither will he wander?' yields to the solution shown in Figure 6.34. The marked man must finish at *d*7. The reader may have guessed this on the grounds that the man must finish as far away as

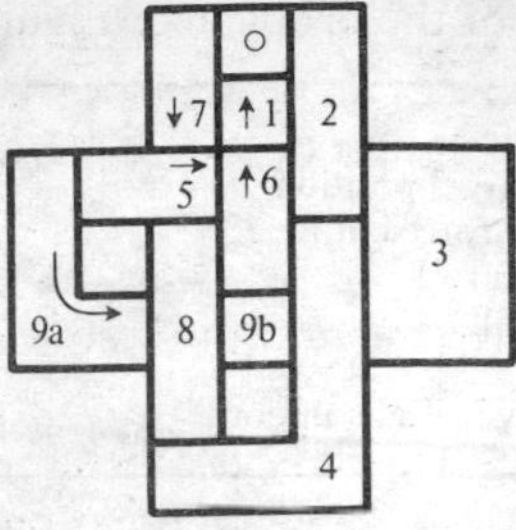

Figure 6.34

possible or the problem would not have been set. Such an argument is not unreasonably cynical; 'wouldn't it be nice if...' is one of the standard techniques for speeding the solution of chess problems, and can reasonably be applied to any form of puzzle in which one line of play seems artistically preferable to another.

The problems shown in Figures 6.28 to 6.30 are analysed in Tables 6.8 to 6.10. Each of these analyses uses the simplification that the amount to be lost by the solution of a complement problem is equal to the value of thc full board less twice the value of the target position. The analyses take account of the moves forced in each solution, and show that the rest of the solutions must lose $(4b-c+\alpha+\beta)$, $(2a+2b-c)$, and $(4b-c+\alpha+\beta)$ respectively. These amounts are irreducible, so the problems are insoluble.

The man at *c*4 in Figure 6.31 can indeed travel to *e*4 via *d*4, but only if the man at *e*6 travels to *c*6 via *d*2. The man at *c*5 is forced to play *c*5-*e*5, since the alternatives would remove a 't' man which we cannot afford. The analysis of Table 6.11 then shows that the rest of the solution must lose $(3a+\alpha+\beta)$. This can be expressed only as (a) $+(2a-c+\alpha)+(c+\beta)$, which forces the move by the man from *e*6

Table 6.8: Analysis of the problem of Figure 6.28

Value of full position	$4a+4b+c+\alpha+\beta$
Less twice value of target position	$4a$
Less amounts lost by forced moves:	
Move *d*4-*d*2 to fill *d*2	$c+\alpha$
Move *d*4-*d*6 to fill *d*6	$c+\alpha$
Amount to be lost by rest of solution	$4b-c+\alpha+\beta$

Table 6.9: Analysis of the problem of Figure 6.29

Value of full position	$4a+4b+c+\alpha+\beta$
Less twice value of target position	$2a+2b$
Less amounts lost by forced moves:	
Move *d*4–*d*2 to fill *d*2	$c+\alpha$
Move *d*4–*b*4 to fill *b*4	$c \quad +\beta$
Amount to be lost by rest of solution	$2a+2b-c$

Table 6.10: Analysis of the problem of Figure 6.30

Value of full position	$4a+4b+c+\alpha+\beta$
Less twice value of target position	$2a$
Less amounts lost by forced moves:	
Move *d*3–*d*1 to fill *d*1	$2a$
Two moves *d*4–*d*2 to fill *d*2	$2c$
Amount to be lost by rest of solution	$4b-c+\alpha+\beta$

Table 6.11: Analysis of the problem of Figure 6.31

Value of full position	$4a+4b+c+\alpha+\beta$
Less twice value of target position	$4b$
Less amounts lost by individual moves:	
Move *c*4–*e*4 (assumed)	$c+\alpha$
Move *c*5–*e*5 (forced)	$a \quad +\alpha$
	α
Amount to be lost by rest of solution	$3a \quad +\alpha+\beta$

across column *d* to be *e*2–*c*2. (The alternatives, *e*6–*c*6 and *e*4–*c*4, would lose $(a+\alpha)$ and $(c+\alpha)$ respectively, neither of which is permitted.) A solution incorporating this path is not difficult to obtain.

The analysis of Table 6.12 shows that a solution to 'Letter B' must lose $(4a+\beta)$. This is expressible only as $(a)+(a+\alpha)+(2a-c+\alpha)+(c+\beta)$, which leads to the results stated. In particular, this proves that we cannot start by playing *c*4–*e*4, since this would lose $(c+\alpha)$, which is not one of the losses that we are allowed. (The problem can also be killed by playing *g*4–*e*4 as the first move, but this is much

Table 6.12: Analysis of 'Letter B'

Value of full position	$4a+4b+c+\alpha+\beta$
Less value of initial vacancy	$b \quad +\beta$
Less value of target position	$3b+c+\alpha+\beta$
Amount to be lost by solution	$4a \quad +\beta$

simpler to prove: it forces the next move to be *d*4–*f*4, which removes a 't' man that we cannot afford.)

The *d*4-complement can be killed in only *four* moves, by playing *d*2–*d*4, *d*5–*d*3, *b*4–*d*4, and *d*3–*d*5 (Figure 6.35). If these moves are made then the analysis of Table 6.13 shows that the rest of the solution must lose $(2a+2b-c)$, which is impossible. Irretrievable wrecks are also possible in five moves: play *d*2–*d*4, *b*3–*d*3, *d*4–*d*2, and now either *b*4–*d*4, *e*4–*c*4 or *f*4–*d*4, *c*4–*e*4.

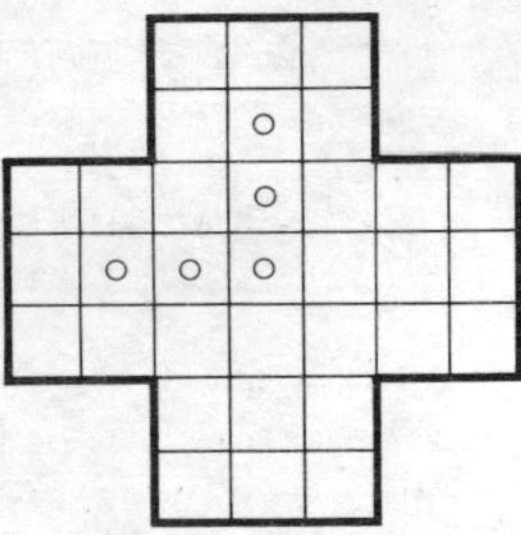

Figure 6.35

Table 6.13: Analysis of the worst possible attempt to solve the central game

Value of full position	$4a+4b+c+\alpha+\beta$
Less twice value of target position	$2c$
Less amounts lost by given moves:	
*d*2–*d*4	$2a \quad -c+\alpha$
*d*5–*d*3	$c \quad +\beta$
*b*4–*d*4	$2b-c \quad +\beta$
*d*3–*d*5	$c \quad +\beta$
Amount to be lost by rest of solution	$2a+2b-c$

The impossibility of solving the *d*4-complement from the position of Figure 6.35 was suspected by Bizalion, who submitted it to his readers in 1871 with a rider that he believed it insoluble, but a proof had to await the attention of Conway and Hutchings in 1961.

7

EXITS, DELIVERIES, AND TRAFFIC JAMS

The tools which we have developed in the last three chapters have taken no account of the fact that a Solitaire move can be played only when the source and capture holes are occupied and the destination hole empty. We now consider the effect of this restriction. The tools which we shall develop will be less systematic than those which we have developed so far, but they are quite powerful and experience suggests that they will prove adequate to resolve most problems occurring in practice.

Exit theorems

If a region starts full, what can we say about the first move affecting it? Answer: it must be a move which removes one or more men from the region and places a man outside it. We call such a move an *exit*. Similarly, if a region finishes empty, what can we say about the last move involving it? Answer: it too must be an exit. These remarks lead immediately to the *exit theorems*:

(a) if a region starts full and ends not full then there must be at least one exit from it;

(b) if a region starts not empty and ends empty then there must be at least one exit from it;

(c) if a region of three or more holes starts full and ends empty then there must be at least two exits from it (for the same move cannot serve as both first and last exit).

These theorems, although obvious as soon as stated, prove to be surprisingly powerful.

For an example, consider the only single-vacancy man-on-the-watch complement problem for which we have not yet determined the longest possible final sweep: the $c1$-complement with a

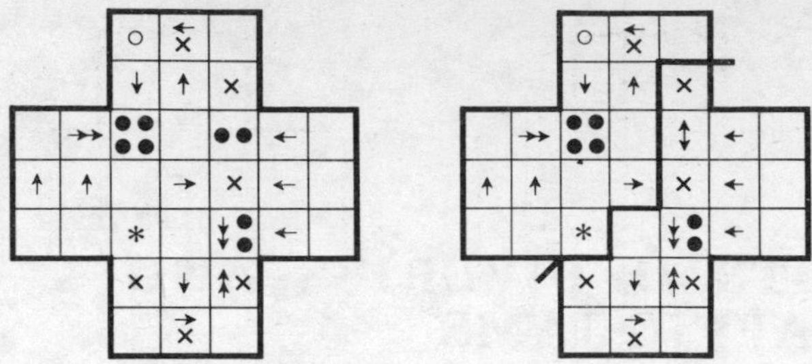

Figure 7.1

Figure 7.2

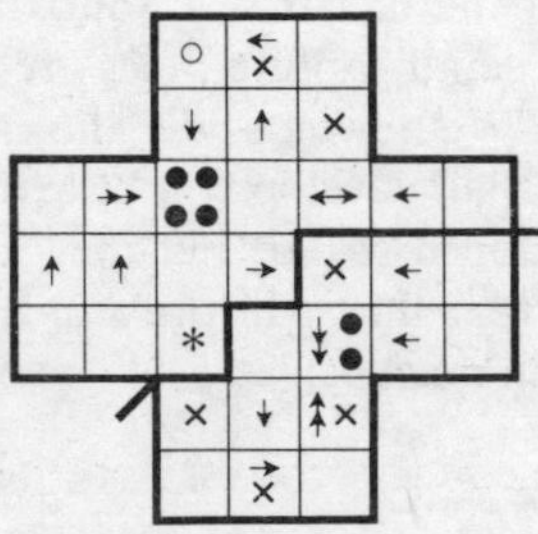

Figure 7.3

man on the watch on *c*5. In Chapter 5, we performed an analysis of debts and surpluses for the only six-sweep finish that might be possible (*c*5-*c*7-*e*7-*e*5-*e*3-*e*1-*c*1), and produced the move map reproduced as Figure 7.1. We still have to liquidate the double surpluses at *e*3 and *e*5 and the quadruple surplus at *c*3.

Now how are we to clear *e*3? We can do so only by an opposing pair of moves across it, but if we use a vertical pair then we obtain the move map shown in Figure 7.2 and if we use a horizontal pair then we obtain the move map of Figure 7.3, and *in neither case is there an exit from the region below the thick line*. The first exit theorem states that we need such an exit, so in neither case do we have a valid solution. The undetermined pairs across *c*3 and *e*5 cannot contribute exits from the relevant regions and so do not affect the issue.

So a six-sweep finish to this problem cannot exist.

The exit theorems apply also to disconnected regions, but the precise wording of the definition should be noted: an exit is a move

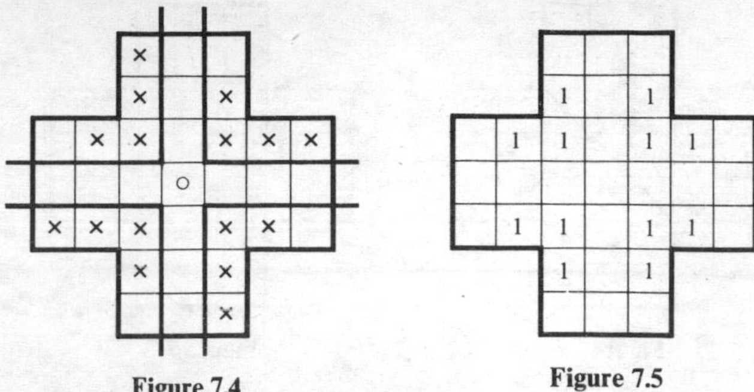

Figure 7.4

Figure 7.5

which delivers a man outside the region, not merely a move across its boundary. Consider the problem shown in Figure 7.4. The four-fold disconnected region outside the thick lines starts full and must finish not full, so a solution must contain an exit from it; but the only such exits are moves such as *b*3–*d*3, each of which loses 2 according to the resource count of Figure 7.5. No such loss is permissible, so the problem is insoluble.

The history of the exit theorems is uncertain. They are attributed to me in *Winning ways for your mathematical plays* and indeed I know of no formal statement of them before my own in 1962, but I cannot believe that so simple a notion genuinely remained undiscovered until then. At the very least, Robin Merson's discovery, mentioned in Chapter 11, was independent and contemporary.

Initial deliveries

Complementary to the idea of a full region which needs an initial exit is that of an empty region which needs an initial entrance. We define a *delivery* to be a move which places a man inside a region and an *initial delivery* to be a delivery to an empty region. The *delivery theorem* now states that an initially empty region which subsequently receives a delivery must receive an initial delivery. This theorem, like the exit theorems, is obvious once stated but nevertheless proves to be useful.

The upper half of Figure 7.6 illustrates the delivery theorem. Suppose that *c*2 and *c*3 are empty, and that *c*1 and *c*4 are to be cleared by the 'call and answer' moves *c*1–*c*3 and *c*4–*c*2. These moves are both deliveries to the initially empty region *c*2/*c*3, but neither is

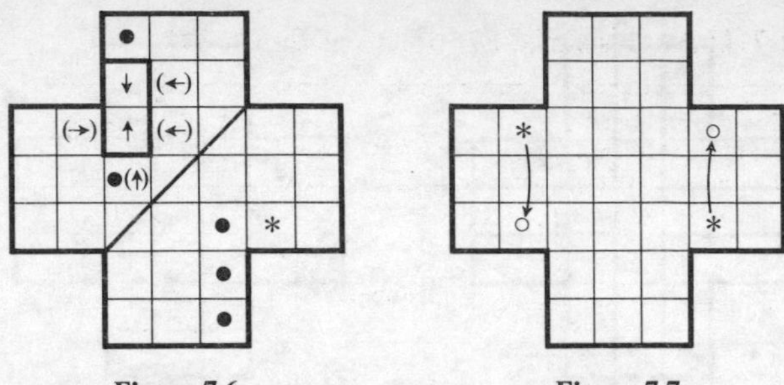

Figure 7.6 Figure 7.7

an initial delivery, so we need an initial delivery as well. The only candidates are *e*2–*c*2, *a*3–*c*3, *e*3–*c*3, and *c*5–*c*3, so at least one of these moves must be made.

The lower half of Figure 7.6 illustrates a useful corollary which we call the *jug-top theorem* (*e*5/*e*6/*e*7 being the jug and *f*5 the handle). Suppose that *e*6 and *e*7 (but not necessarily *e*5) are to be cleared *before the marked man at f*5 *moves*, and that we are short of 's' men and so cannot play a horizontal move across *d*5, *d*6, or *d*7. Then the jug-top theorem states that we must play a vertical move across *e*4. The proof is as follows: (i) we need an initial exit from the region *e*5/*e*6/*e*7, which must be *e*5–*e*3 or *e*6–*e*4 because the alternatives would either make a forbidden horizontal crossing of *d*5/*d*6/*d*7 or disturb or destroy the marked man at *f*5; (ii) if it is *e*5–*e*3 then there is nothing to prove; (iii) if it is *e*6–*e*4 then it leaves *e*5/*e*6 empty, but the move *e*7–*e*5 necessary to clear *e*7 is still to be made and will be a delivery to the region *e*5/*e*6; (iv) an initial delivery to this region must therefore be made, and must be *e*3–*e*5 because the alternatives would again either make a forbidden horizontal crossing of *d*5/*d*6 or destroy the marked man at *f*5.

Figure 7.7 illustrates a double-vacancy man-on-the-watch complement problem which provides a practical application. We have no spare 's' men and so must play *c*1–*c*3, *d*1–*d*3, *e*1–*e*3, *c*7–*c*5, *d*7–*d*5, and *e*7–*e*5. The conditions for the jug-top theorem therefore hold for each of the regions *c*1/*c*2/*c*3 and *e*5/*e*6/*e*7, so we must play vertical moves across *c*4 and *e*4. The balance sheet analysis of Table 7.1 now shows that the rest of the solution must lose $(2b+c+\alpha)$. This is expressible only as $(2b)+(c+\alpha)$, which nevertheless seems hopeful since $(2b)$ can be expressed in several ways. However we need two different primitives from the set (b), $(b+\beta)$ and $(c+\beta)$ for

Table 7.1: Analysis of the problem of Figure 7.7

Value of full board	$4a+4b+c+\alpha+\beta$	
Less twice value of target position	$4a$	
Less amounts lost by forced moves:		
Vertical move across *c*4	b	
Vertical move across *e*4	b	$+\beta$
Amount to be lost by rest of solution		$2b+c+\alpha$

the final paths of the marked men, the term $(c+\alpha)$ does not help, and none of the ways of expressing $(2b)$ contains the two different primitives required. The problem is therefore insoluble.

Out of my way, curse you

Our final technique may seem so simple as to be unworthy of mention, yet it is often of value. It may happen that a necessary move is obstructed by a man which cannot get out of the way. This is particularly likely to happen in problems with marked men. We call such a situation a *traffic jam*.

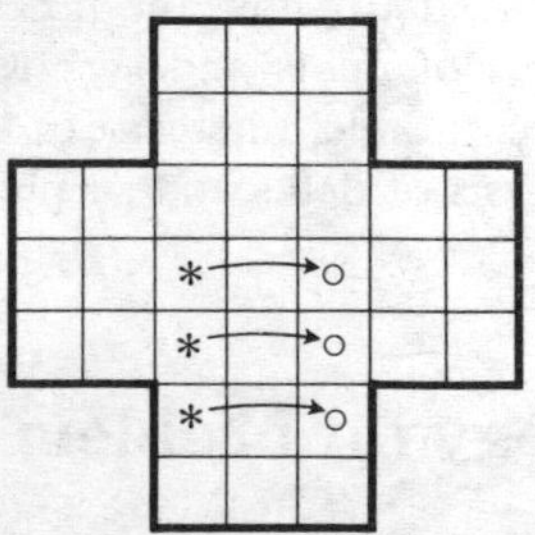

Figure 7.8

Figure 7.8 shows a triple-vacancy complement problem with marked men. The solution must lose $(4a+c+\alpha+\beta)$ according to Conway's balance sheet, so the man at *c*5 must travel to *e*5 by the direct route *c*5–*e*5. This loses $(a+\alpha)$ and leaves $(3a+c+\beta)=(2a)+(a)+(c+\beta)$ to be lost by the rest of the solution. Provision must be made within this for the moves of the marked men from *c*4 and *c*6 across column *d*, which require two primitives from the set (a),

$(a+\alpha)$ and $(c+\alpha)$. The term $(c+\beta)$ does not contribute, so the terms (a) and $(2a)$ must supply both of them. (Remember that $(2a)$ is not a primitive and can be split into $(a)+(a)$, $(a+\alpha)+(a+\alpha)$, or $(2a-c+\alpha)+(c+\alpha)$.) This means that the man at *c*5 must make *only* the move *c*5–*e*5, since *c*5–*a*5 or *e*5–*g*5 would lose a further $(2a)$ which we cannot afford. The restriction of the man at *c*5 to a single move creates a traffic jam which forces the man at *c*6 to travel to *e*6 by the direct route *c*6–*e*6, since a move *c*6–*c*4 cannot be played until the man at *c*5 has played *c*5–*e*5 and the presence of this man at *e*5 then prevents a subsequent move *e*4–*e*6.

The move *c*6–*e*6 loses $(a+\alpha)$, leaving $(2a+c+\alpha+\beta)=(a)+(a+\alpha)+(c+\beta)$ to be lost by the rest of the solution. How can we lose $(a+\alpha)$? Only by another horizontal move across *d*5 or *d*6. But we cannot play such a move across *d*5, for the marked man initially at *c*5 cannot be got out of the way, nor can we play one across *d*6, for the move *d*4–*d*6 necessary to liquidate the resulting deficiency at *d*6 would lose $(c+\alpha)$ which we cannot afford. So the problem is insoluble.

There is a fundamental similarity between exits and traffic jams, and some problems can be attacked by either means; in particular, a full region from which there is no exit can be thought of as an extreme case of a traffic jam. In practice, however, incipient traffic jams are commonly used to show the necessity of moves whose consequences in terms of debts and surpluses are then analysed and shown to be unacceptable, whereas exit theorems are normally applied after an analysis of debts and surpluses has generated one or more move maps.

General strategy for problem resolution

This concludes our investigation into the general theory of Solitaire. We are now in a position to suggest a general strategy for the resolution of a Solitaire problem:

(a) attempt to solve it;

(b) if this attempt is unsuccessful, use Conway's balance sheet and any convenient parity and resource counts to identify moves that must or cannot be played, and try again;

(c) if this does not produce either a solution or a proof of insolubility, perform a detailed analysis of debts and surpluses and write down on blank diagrams the possible sets of moves that a solution must contain;

(d) if it seems impossible to realise these moves in practice, seek regions for which one of the exit theorems does not hold;

(e) alternatively, if the number of possibilities allowed by step (c) is large, try to find reasons to reduce it. In a problem involving marked men, for example, the jug-top theorem or the requirement to avoid traffic jams may identify forced moves which can be incorporated into the analysis and may substantially simplify it.

This strategy is not guaranteed to resolve a problem in the way that the fundamental classes resolve every problem in Up-and-down Solitaire or the irreducible resource counts every problem in Unconstrained Fractional Solitaire, but it will normally be found effective in practice.

The reader may care to try a few problems using the ideas of this chapter.

The holes marked *V* in Figure 7.9 show the initial single vacancies other than *c*1 from which play is possible to a finish with a single man in *c*1. If there is a man on the watch at *c*3, is it possible to end any of the solutions with a move longer than a one-sweep?

Figure 7.10 shows an attractive but unfortunately insoluble problem with rotational symmetry. Prove its insolubility.

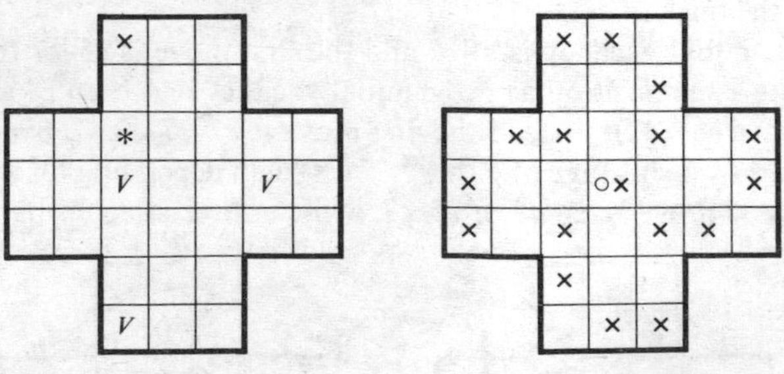

Figure 7.9 **Figure 7.10**

Figure 7.11 shows a triple-vacancy complement problem with marked men. Prove its insolubility. It may be assumed that no move may be made across *d*1; this is not difficult to prove, but its proof makes no use of the ideas of this chapter and its assumption allows concentration on the matters relevant here.

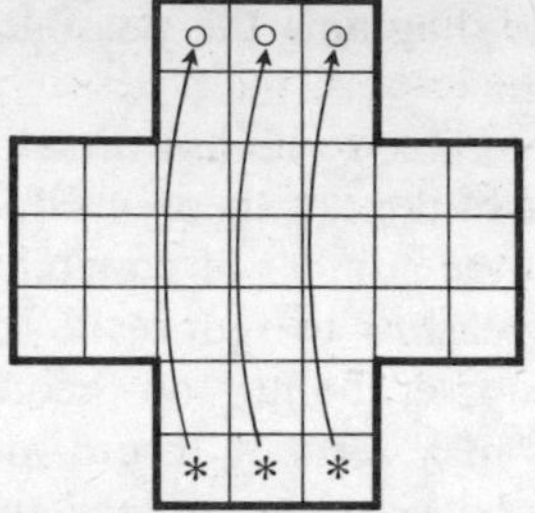

Figure 7.11

Solutions to Chapter 7

Let us take the three initial vacancies in Figure 7.9 in order. The easiest case to resolve is *f*4. A five-sweep is impossible because we do not have enough 't' men, so the best for which we can hope is the three-sweep *c*3–*e*3–*e*1–*c*1. If we try this, however, we find that we cannot liquidate all the debts and surpluses, and the spine-count of Figure 5.1 shows why: we have an initial slack of 26, but the three-sweep will consume 11 and the forced moves *c*1–*e*1, *c*2–*e*2, and *b*3–*b*5 another 17, leaving a deficiency.

If the initial vacancy is at *c*4 then the debts and surpluses that would result from a three-sweep can indeed be liquidated but only as shown in Figure 7.12, and there is no initial exit from the region above the thick line.

If the initial vacancy is at *c*7 and the first move is *c*5–*c*7 then we have the same position as if the initial vacancy had been *c*4 and the first move *c*6–*c*4. If instead the first move is *e*7–*c*7 then a five-sweep is barred by a shortage of either 's' or 't' men depending on whether the second move is *d*5–*d*7 or *e*5–*e*7, while a three-sweep is barred by

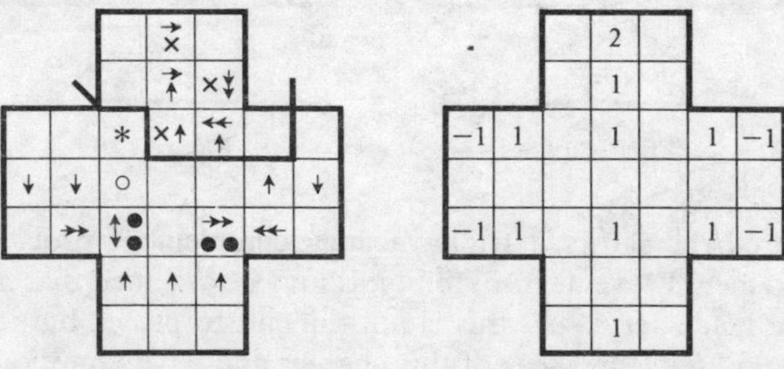

Figure 7.12

Figure 7.13

the resource count of Figure 7.13, for the initial slack is 6, the hypothetical first move loses 1, the necessary moves *c*1–*e*1 and *c*2–*e*2 lose 3, and a three-sweep would lose a further 3.

A one-sweep is possible in each case.

The problem of Figure 7.10 is tough. We note first that there is a debt to be liquidated at *d*4, which means that there must be a move such as *d*2–*d*4 which is not nullified by an opposing move *d*4–*d*2. Without loss of generality, suppose this move actually to be *d*2–*d*4. Then we cannot play *e*1–*c*1 or *c*2–*e*2, for either of these would require *d*4–*d*2 sooner or later to liquidate a debt at *d*2, and so we must play *e*1–*e*3 to clear *e*1 and *e*4–*e*2 to liquidate the resulting debt at *e*2. The task map remaining after these moves is shown in Figure 7.14.

The task map of Figure 7.14 can be resolved in a large number of ways, but we can reduce them by using the fact that a valid solution to the original problem must contain an exit from the region *e*1/*e*2/*e*3. This constraint, together with the prohibition of *d*4–*d*2, reduces the number of move maps that we must consider to three. Two of

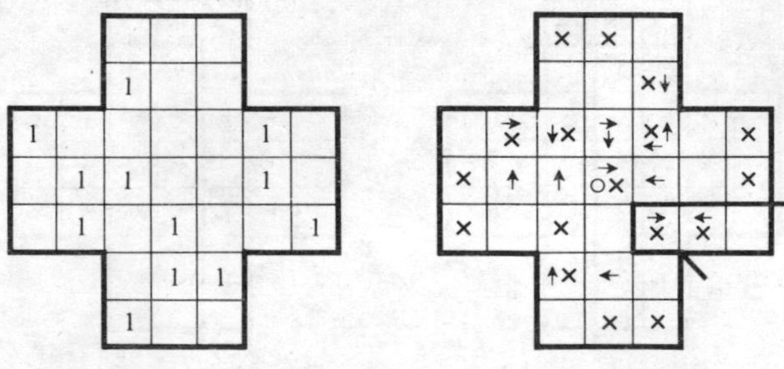

Figure 7.14

Figure 7.15

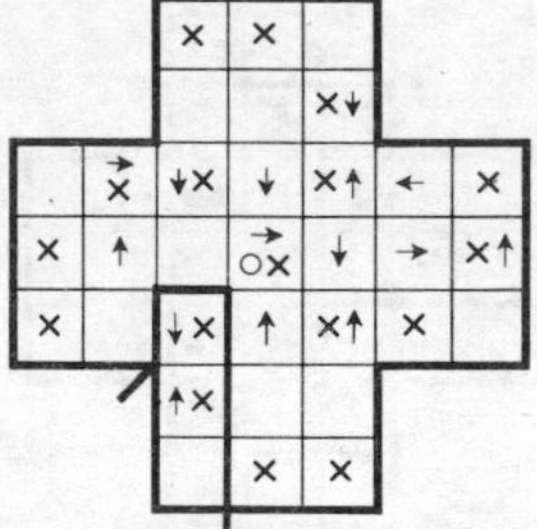

Figure 7.16

these are shown in Figures 7.15 and 7.16, and the third differs from Figure 7.16 only in the replacement of *e*4–*g*4 and *g*5–*g*3–*e*3 by *f*3–*f*5 and *g*5–*e*5–*e*3. None of them represents a valid solution, since Figure 7.15 contains no exit from the region *e*5/*f*5/*g*5 and neither Figure 7.16 nor its cousin contains an exit from the region *c*5/*c*6/*c*7.

The problem of Figure 7.11 is rather easier. Its debts and surpluses can be resolved in the three different ways shown in Figures 7.17 to 7.19, the moves by the marked men being distinguished by triangular arrowheads, and in no case is there a *first* exit from the region to the right of the thick line. (A move by a marked man cannot be the first exit from the region in which it originates unless it is also the first move by the marked man, a condition which does not hold here.)

The fact that all these problems have been resolved by arguments based on exits rather than on deliveries or traffic jams is not accidental, since on the 33-hole board the exit theorems are the most

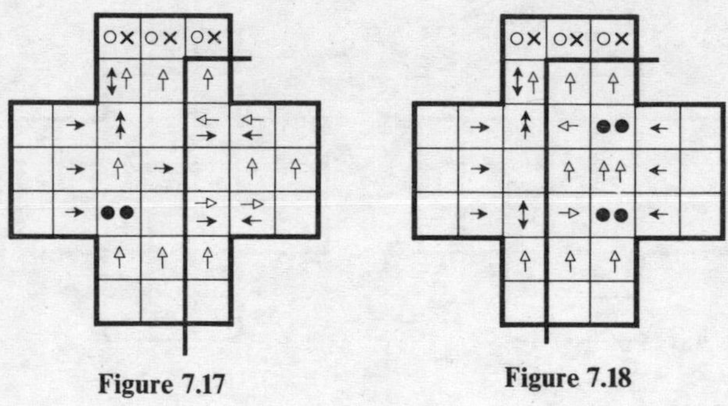

Figure 7.17

Figure 7.18

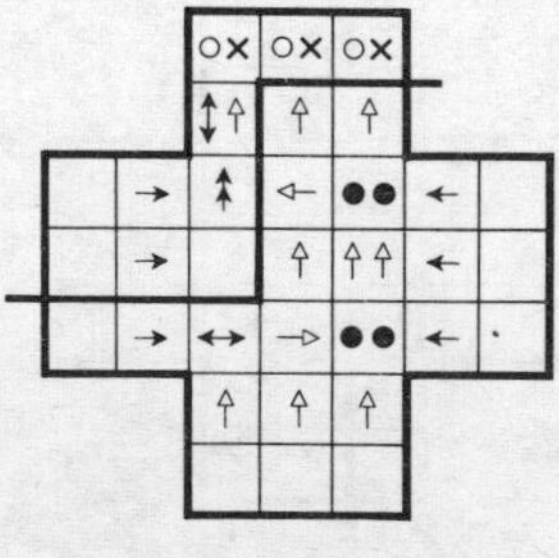

Figure 7.19

useful of the techniques developed in this chapter. The other techniques prove to be more useful on other boards, but they are worth bearing in mind even on the 33-hole board for use in problems where the number of move maps requiring consideration appears to be large.

8

SHORT SOLUTIONS

So far we have considered only the simple question: 'Is this problem soluble?' In this chapter we consider the much more difficult question: 'If a problem is soluble, in how few moves can it be solved?'

Historical survey

Early writers on the game appear to have made little or no attempt to find solutions with few moves, and the earliest reasonably short solutions that I know were published by 'Berkeley' (W. H. Peel) in 1890. Peel's solutions are summarised in Table 8.1. All have since been surpassed, but the best of them, a 17-move solution to the *d*3-complement which ends with a seven-sweep from *d*1, appears to have stood as a record until 1963.

Table 8.1: Solutions by Peel (1890) to single-vacancy complement problems in 33-hole Solitaire

Initial vacancy	Moves required
*c*1	19
*d*1	20
*c*2	17
*d*2	20
*c*3	18
*d*3	17
*d*4	19

Peel's 19-move solution to the central game is as follows:

*d*6–*d*4, *d*5–*d*3, *f*4–*d*4–*d*6 (3 moves made), *f*5–*d*5, *e*7–*e*5, *e*2–*e*4–*e*6, *g*3–*e*3, *b*3–*d*3–*f*3 (8), *c*1–*c*3, *c*4–*c*2, *c*6–*c*4, *a*5–*c*5, *d*5–*b*5 (13), *a*3–

*a*5–*c*5, *c*7–*e*7–*e*5, *e*1–*c*1–*c*3, *g*5–*g*3–*e*3 (17), *c*4–*c*6–*e*6–*e*4–*e*2–*c*2–*c*4, *b*4–*d*4.

The frequently-quoted solution given by H. E. Dudeney in 1908 is very similar, Dudeney's fourth to thirteenth moves being *e*2–*e*4, *g*3–*e*3, *b*3–*d*3–*f*3, *c*1–*c*3, *c*4–*c*2, *c*6–*c*4, *a*5–*c*5, *f*5–*d*5–*b*5, *e*7–*e*5, and *e*4–*e*6. Dudeney's version is slightly more elegant but there is no real difference. Dudeney thought that no shorter solution was possible, but Ernest Bergholt published a remarkable 18-move solution in 1912. The reader may care to try and find it, but he is warned that simple modifications to Peel's solution will not suffice. Bergholt's solution has now been proved to be indeed the shortest possible.

Short solutions have also been found to the other single-vacancy single-survivor problems. Bergholt found several solutions in as few as 16 moves, and his results have been extended by Harry O. Davis. The shortest known solutions to all the single-vacancy single-survivor problems now lie to their credit. A summary is given in Table 8.2. Davis's 15-move solution to the *c*3-complement and Bergholt's 18-move solution to the *d*1-complement are perhaps even more remarkable than Bergholt's 18-move solution to the central game.

Table 8.2: Solutions to single-vacancy single-survivor problems in 33-hole Solitaire (Bergholt and Davis)

Initial vacancy	Final hole	Moves required
*c*1	*c*1, *c*4, *c*7	16
	*f*4	17
*d*1	*a*4	17
	*d*1, *d*4, *d*7	18
*c*2	*c*5	15
	*c*2, *f*5	16
*d*2	*a*5, *d*5	17
	*d*2	19
*c*3	*c*3	15
	*f*3	16
*d*3	*a*3, *d*3	16
	*d*6	17
*d*4	*d*1	17
	*d*4	18

Analytical techniques

In Chapters 4 to 7 we developed some powerful techniques for deciding whether or not a problem is soluble. Are there also effective techniques for deciding how few moves a solution may contain?

Some techniques do indeed exist, though the situation is less satisfactory than that for straightforward decisions on solubility. The simplest is to identify distinct areas within which a move must originate. The criteria for such an area are simple: it must be initially full, and it must be impossible for the first exit from it to be a move originating outside it and jumping over one or more of its men. Figure 8.1 shows the configurations of practical importance: a man in an outside corner hole (*A*), two ajdacent men along an outside edge (*BB*), three adjacent men around an inside corner (*CCC*), and four men in a 2 × 2 square anywhere (*DDDD*). Case *BB* (two adjacent men along an edge) is of no independent importance on the 33-hole board since any such pair must include a man in an outside corner, but it is of importance on other boards.

For example, Figure 8.2 identifies no fewer than twelve such areas for the *d*4-complement, so any solution to this problem must contain at least twelve moves. Additionally, neither the first move nor the last move of the solution can be one of them, and the penultimate move, while it can certainly be an exit from one of the areas of Figure 8.2, cannot be a *first* exit. This determines fifteen distinct moves that a solution must contain, but it is still quite a difficult task to get from fifteen to the known minimum of eighteen.

A second powerful technique is that of the *count with limited gain*. We have already seen resource counts, according to which a move cannot gain at all. A move can indeed gain according to a count

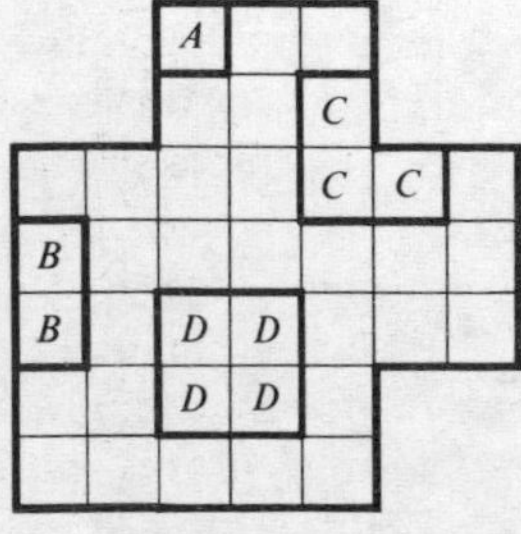

Figure 8.1

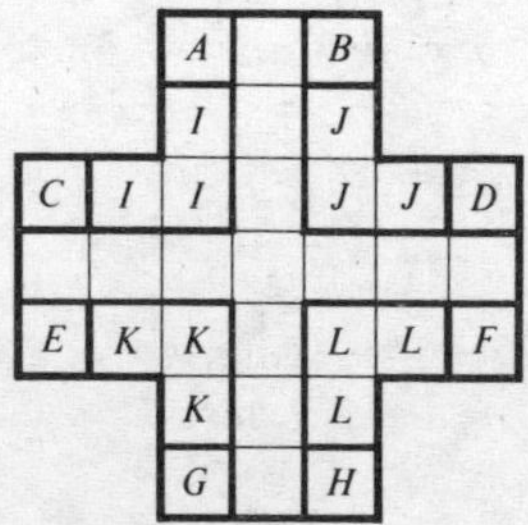

Figure 8.2

with limited gain, but it cannot gain more than a certain amount. Figure 8.3, due to J. H. Conway, shows such a count; there is no move, however complicated, which gains more than 2 according to it. For example, consider the move *b*3–*d*3–*f*3–*f*5–*d*5–*b*5. This removes men from *b*3, *c*3, *e*3, *f*4, *e*5, and *c*5, and puts a man into *b*5. So it loses 0, −1, −1, 2, −1, and −1, and gains 0, giving a net gain of 2. Strictly speaking, of course, any count with finite values has limited gain, but we shall use the term only in respect of counts whose limitations are sufficiently stringent and consistent to be of practical use.

Another technique that is sometimes helpful is to use parity counts to determine starting and finishing holes of moves. We saw in Chapter 5 that the value of a position according to the parity count α in Figure 8.4 could be changed only by a move across *d*2 or a vertical move across *c*3. But we can say more than this: it can be changed only by a move which *starts or finishes* at *d*1 or *c*2. A move which merely alights at *c*2 in passing has no effect.

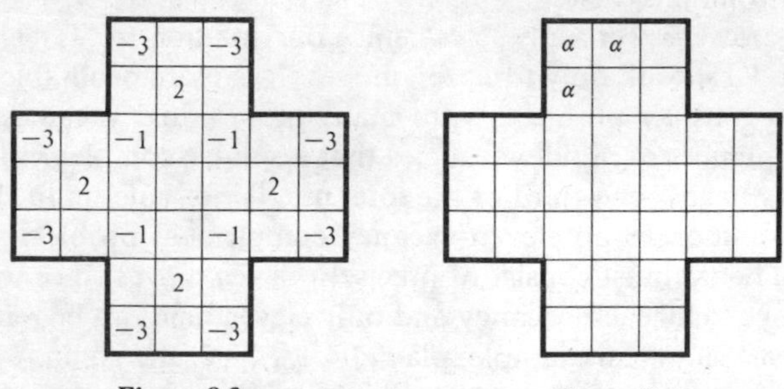

Figure 8.3 **Figure 8.4**

Finally, we can analyse particular classes of moves in detail, perhaps in conjunction with one or more of the above arguments.

This seems to be a reasonable armoury, so why do we say that the situation is less satisfactory than that for simple proofs of insolubility? There are indeed problems where the identification of areas within which moves must originate, perhaps coupled with a little elementary analysis, is sufficient to demonstrate an attainable minimum. In the case of the *d*1-complement, for example, Figure 8.2 identifies twelve areas within which distinct moves must originate, the initial move *d*3–*d*1 makes a thirteenth move, the necessary refilling of *d*2 makes a fourteenth, the necessary moves away from *d*5 and *d*7 make a fifteenth and a sixteenth (for we saw in Chapter 5 that the men originally in these holes cannot be jumped over where they stand), and it is not too difficult, given the constraints on solutions to this problem that were demonstrated in Chapters 5 and 6, to show that there must be at least two more. Thus it can be proved that Bergholt's 18-move solution to this problem is the shortest possible. More usually, however, there is a gap of one or more between the smallest number of moves known and the number that can easily be proved to be necessary, and a long and error-prone analysis of variations is needed to fill this gap. The strength of the techniques of Chapters 4 to 7 is precisely that they normally avoid the performance of such analyses.

Multiple-vacancy complement problems

The shortest known solution to a single-vacancy complement problem takes fifteen moves. Are there complement problems to which shorter solutions exist?

The answer is certainly 'Yes', since our solution to 'Triple cross' (Figure 1.15) took only fourteen moves. It is more profitable, however, to consider problems with many more initial vacancies. The largest number of initial vacancies that a soluble complement problem may have is one-third of the total number of holes in the board, and a solution to an eleven-vacancy complement problem on the 33-hole board must consist of precisely eleven moves since we need one move to fill each vacancy and only eleven men can be removed. Figure 8.5 shows an example; play *e*1–*c*1, *e*2–*c*2, and so on.

So can we beat eleven? Yes, we can. Figure 8.6 can be solved in only *nine* moves; play *a*3–*a*5, *b*3–*b*5, *c*3–*c*1, *e*3–*e*1, *f*3–*f*5, *g*3–*g*5, *c*7–*c*5–*c*3–*e*3–*e*5–*c*5, *d*7–*d*5–*d*3–*d*1, *e*7–*e*5. Many other complement problems exist which are soluble in only nine moves; the reader may care to try Figures 8.7 and 8.8.

No complement problem can be solved in eight moves, however. We shall prove this in stages, showing firstly that a hypothetical eight-move complementation must include at least three moves by edge men and so cannot contain more than five moves by corner men; then that it must contain precisely four moves by corner men, three by edge men, and one by a middle man; and finally that there is always a region from which none of these eight moves provides a first exit.

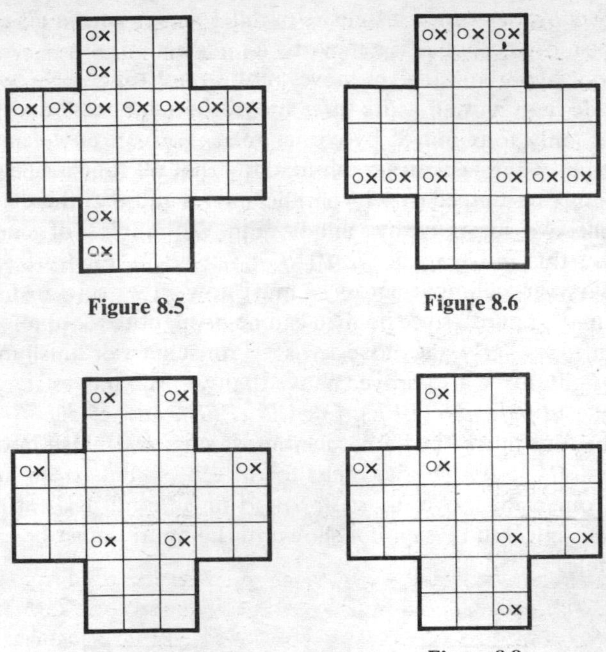

Figure 8.5

Figure 8.6

Figure 8.7

Figure 8.8

Look back at Figure 8.4 and consider the parity count denoted by α. Complementing a position changes the value of this parity count, and therefore requires a move which starts or finishes in *d*1 or *c*2. These are *edge* man moves. The board contains eight such parity counts, and it is easily seen that we need at least three moves to change the values of all of them. (No move changes the values of five of the parity counts, and the only moves which change four are moves such as *d*1-. . .-*d*7 and *a*4-. . .-*g*4. Each such move removes three middle men, so we cannot make more than one of them.)

This leaves at most five moves to be made by corner men, which means that at least two of the twelve corner holes cannot be the source or destination of a move. These holes must therefore be complemented by being jumped over, which means that they must be inside corners and must start full. Suppose, without loss of generality, that *c*3 is one of them and that it is complemented by a vertical move across it. Since *c*3 is not the destination of a move, no other move across it may be made, so by the arm-balance theorem

(Chapter 6) there must also exist parallel moves across *d*3 and *e*3, and the move across *d*3 is a move by a *middle* man.

So our hypothetical eight-move solution must include a move by a middle man as well as its three moves by edge men, and so can contain only four moves by corner men. We can now repeat the argument of the last paragraph to show that all four inside corner holes must be jumped over by parallel moves and that there must be a parallel two-step move by a middle man. Without loss of generality, suppose this move to be *d*2–*d*4–*d*6 (*A* . . . *B* in Figure 8.9). The necessary vertical move across *c*3 must now either start or finish in *c*2 (*C* in the figure), since no man can be brought to *d*2 to allow it to continue. Similarly, the move across *e*3 must start or finish in *e*2 (*D* in the figure). We also proved above that we need moves starting or finishing in *b*3/*a*4/*b*5 (*EEE*), *f*3/*g*4/*f*5 (*FFF*), and *c*6/*e*6/*d*7 (*GGG*); and the four moves by corner men must start and finish in outside corners (*H* . . . *O*). This accounts for fifteen of the sixteen holes in which our eight moves must start and finish, and it is easily seen that the sixteenth (*P* say, not shown in the figure) must be an edge man hole.

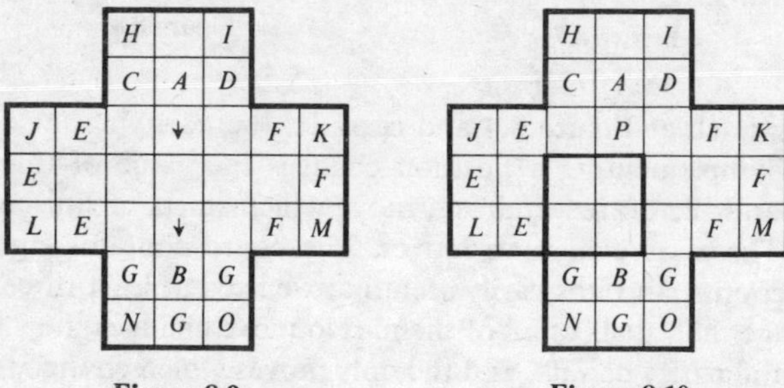

Figure 8.9

Figure 8.10

We now appeal to an exit theorem. Wherever hole *P* may be, there is a 2 × 2 region in which none of the eight moves already identified starts or finishes. In Figure 8.10, for example, *P* is assumed to be at *d*3, and *c*4/*d*4/*c*5/*d*5 is such a region. This region must start full, since none of our eight moves finishes in it, and the first exit from it must be a move other than those already identified. So an eight-move complementation is impossible.

The central game

We now prove that Bergholt's 18-move solution to the central game is indeed the shortest possible. We proceed in three stages: we use various arguments involving Figure 8.3 to prove that no 17-move solution can contain a move into or out of *d*1, *a*4, *g*4, or *d*7; then we use this fact to show that all but one of the moves of such a solution can be accounted for very simply; and finally we enumerate variations, and show that sooner or later we must always violate one of the constraints thus established.

We classify the moves of our hypothetical solution as follows: the first move, the last move, the penultimate move, eight moves to clear outside corners, and six others which we shall call 'free' moves. Now the solution must increase the count of Figure 8.3 from its initial −20 to 0, but it is easily seen that the first move loses 2, the last move loses 2, the penultimate move gains at most 1, and the corner clearances gain at most 2 each, which leaves at least 7 to be gained by the six free moves. We also note that any move into or out of *d*1, *a*4, *g*4, or *d*7 would *lose* at least 1.

Now let us fix our ideas by choosing *d*2–*d*4 as our first move. The second move can now be *b*3–*d*3 or *d*5–*d*3; let us consider *d*5–*d*3 first. This move is one of our six free moves and gains 0, so the remaining five free moves must still gain at least 7. But one of them must be the first exit from the region of Figure 8.11, and there are two possibilities: moves such as *d*1–*d*3 and *d*1–*d*3–*d*5, which each lose 2, and moves such as *b*3–*d*3 and *b*3–*d*3–*d*5, which gain only 1. If we play a move which loses 2 then the four remaining free moves must gain at least 9, which is impossible, and if we play a move which gains only 1 then the four remaining free moves must gain at least 6, which is impossible if any of them loses. Conclusion: a 17-move solution starting *d*2–*d*4, *d*5–*d*3 cannot contain a free move which loses, and hence cannot contain a move into or out of *d*1, *a*4, *g*4, or *d*7.

The argument for solutions with second move *b*3–*d*3 is similar but a little more laborious. The move *b*3–*d*3 is a free move and gains only 1, leaving the five remaining free moves to gain at least 6. Now consider the first exit from the region of Figure 8.12. If it is *c*4–*c*2 then it gains only 1, leaving the four remaining free moves to gain at least 5 and also leaving the first exit from the region of Figure 8.13 still to be made. This exit cannot be *e*4–*g*4 or *d*5–*d*7, since each of these would lose 2 and leave the three remaining free moves to

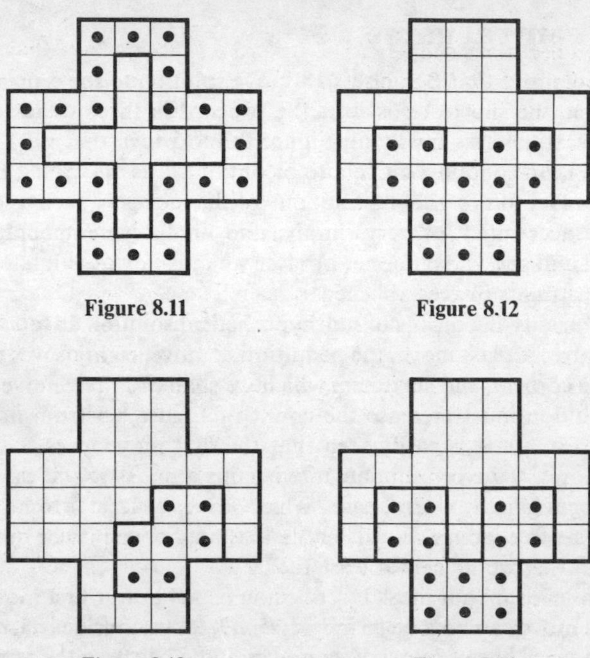

Figure 8.11 Figure 8.12

Figure 8.13 Figure 8.14

gain at least 7; so it must be one of the other possibilities, each of which is a free move gaining at most 1, leaving the three remaining free moves to gain at least 4 and so prohibiting any of them from losing. Similarly, if the first exit from the region of Figure 8.12 is *d*5-*d*3-*b*3 or *d*5-*d*3-*f*3, then it gains only 1; the subsequent first exit from the region of Figure 8.14 also gains at most 1, leaving the three remaining free moves to gain at least 5 and again prohibiting any of them from losing. The other first exits from the region of Figure 8.12 can be analysed similarly and all lead to the same conclusion: a 17-move solution starting *d*2-*d*4, *b*3-*d*3 cannot contain a move into or out of *d*1, *a*4, *g*4, or *d*7. This concludes the first stage of our proof.

We can now say quite a lot about the moves necessary to clear the sides. In the absence of moves into or out of *d*1, *a*4, *g*4, and *d*7, there are only two possibilities: L clearances, typified by *c*1-*c*3, a move to *c*2 (which we shall call a 'necessary delivery'), and *e*1-*c*1-*c*3, and U clearances, typified by *c*1-*c*3, a necessary delivery to *c*2, *e*1–*e*3, a necessary delivery to *e*2, and *c*3–*c*1–*e*1–*e*3. Note that a move to a hole such as *c*2 is classed as a necessary delivery only if the adjacent outside corner is empty. If we start by playing *d*2–*d*4, *b*3–*d*3, *c*1–*c*3 then *c*4–*c*2 would be a necessary delivery to *c*2 but *d*3–*b*3 would *not* be a necessary delivery to *b*3; *a*3 is still occupied, and we shall need another delivery to *b*3 or *b*5 in due course.

The restriction to L and U clearances enables us to refine our classification of the moves of a hypothetical solution. Suppose for a moment that we have four L clearances. These involve four necessary deliveries, each of which must be a free move since it cannot be anything else, and the first exit from the region of Figure 8.11 must also be a free move and cannot be a necessary delivery. This accounts for five of the six free moves, leaving one which we shall call the 'spare'. Similarly, if we have three L clearances and one U clearance then we must have five necessary deliveries and a separate first exit from the region of Figure 8.11, leaving no spare move, and we cannot have two or more U clearances since these would involve at least six necessary deliveries and a separate first exit and we have only six free moves in all. In summary, a solution must contain a first move, a last move, a penultimate move, eight clearances of outside corners, a first exit from the region of Figure 8.11, and either four or five necessary deliveries. In the first case there is one spare move; in the second there is none.

The rest is a matter of enumeration. We proceed systematically through the possible lines of play, following each until further progress is impossible. The enumeration assuming one U and three L clearances is trivial, since in the absence of a 'spare' move no divergence is possible from the single line *d*2–*d*4, *b*3–*d*3, *c*1–*c*3, *c*4–*c*2, *e*1–*c*3 and no further progress is possible. The enumeration assuming four L clearances is shown in Table 8.3, the 'spare' move being in bold face in each line. Each line of play stops when no further move is possible without either violating the constraints described in the previous paragraph, losing too much ground as measured by the count of Figure 8.3, or transposing into a position already reached earlier in the table.

For example, consider line 28. This starts after the four moves *d*2–*d*4, *b*3–*d*3, *e*3–*c*3, *g*3–*e*3, the move *e*3–*c*3 being the 'spare'. All moves other than the three necessary deliveries *b*5–*f*3, *d*5–*f*3, and *f*5–*f*3 are now ruled out because the spare has already been played, and *f*5–*f*3 is ruled out because it would leave too much ground to be

Table 8.3: Analysis of the *d*4-complement problem in 33-hole Solitaire

<table>
<tr><th></th><th>1</th><th>2</th><th>3</th><th>4</th><th>5</th><th>6</th><th>7</th><th>8</th><th>9</th></tr>
<tr><td>1</td><td>d2-d4</td><td>b3-d3</td><td>d4-d2</td><td>c1-c3</td><td>e2-c2</td><td></td><td></td><td></td><td></td></tr>
<tr><td>2</td><td></td><td>|</td><td>|</td><td></td><td>c4-c2</td><td>e1-c3</td><td></td><td></td><td></td></tr>
<tr><td>3</td><td></td><td>|</td><td>b5-b3</td><td>c1-c3</td><td></td><td></td><td></td><td></td><td></td></tr>
<tr><td>4</td><td></td><td>|</td><td>|</td><td>a3-c3</td><td></td><td></td><td></td><td></td><td></td></tr>
<tr><td>5</td><td></td><td>|</td><td>c1-c3</td><td>e1-c1</td><td>c4-c2</td><td>c1-c3</td><td></td><td></td><td></td></tr>
<tr><td>6</td><td></td><td>|</td><td>|</td><td>c4-c2</td><td>e1-c3</td><td>e4-c2</td><td></td><td></td><td></td></tr>
<tr><td>7</td><td></td><td>|</td><td>|</td><td>|</td><td>|</td><td>c6-c2</td><td>a5-c5</td><td>d5-b5</td><td>a3-c5</td></tr>
<tr><td>8</td><td></td><td>|</td><td>|</td><td>|</td><td>|</td><td>d3-b3</td><td>a3-c3</td><td>f3-b3</td><td>a5-c3</td></tr>
<tr><td>9</td><td></td><td>|</td><td>|</td><td>|</td><td>|</td><td>|</td><td></td><td>d5-b3</td><td>a5-c3</td></tr>
<tr><td>10</td><td></td><td>|</td><td>|</td><td>|</td><td>|</td><td>e4-c4</td><td></td><td></td><td></td></tr>
<tr><td>11</td><td></td><td>|</td><td>|</td><td>|</td><td>|</td><td>c6-c4</td><td>a5-c5</td><td>d5-b5</td><td>a3-c5</td></tr>
<tr><td>12</td><td></td><td>|</td><td>|</td><td>|</td><td>e3-c3</td><td>g3-e3</td><td>d5-f5</td><td>g5-e3</td><td></td></tr>
<tr><td>13</td><td></td><td>|</td><td>|</td><td>|</td><td>e4-c4</td><td></td><td></td><td></td><td></td></tr>
<tr><td>14</td><td></td><td>|</td><td>|</td><td>|</td><td>c6-c4</td><td>a5-c3</td><td></td><td></td><td></td></tr>
<tr><td>15</td><td></td><td>|</td><td>|</td><td>|</td><td></td><td>e1-c5</td><td></td><td></td><td></td></tr>
<tr><td>16</td><td></td><td>|</td><td>|</td><td>|</td><td></td><td>a5-c5</td><td>d5-b5</td><td>a3-c3</td><td></td></tr>
<tr><td>17</td><td></td><td>|</td><td>|</td><td>|</td><td></td><td></td><td></td><td>e1-c5</td><td></td></tr>
<tr><td>18</td><td></td><td>|</td><td>|</td><td>|</td><td></td><td></td><td></td><td>a3-c5</td><td></td></tr>
<tr><td>19</td><td></td><td>|</td><td>|</td><td>d3-b3</td><td>a3-c3</td><td>c4-c2</td><td></td><td></td><td></td></tr>
<tr><td>20</td><td></td><td>|</td><td>|</td><td></td><td></td><td>f3-b3</td><td>a5-c3</td><td>c4-c2</td><td>e1-c3</td></tr>
<tr><td>21</td><td></td><td>|</td><td>|</td><td></td><td></td><td>d5-b3</td><td>a5-c3</td><td>c4-c2</td><td>e1-c3</td></tr>
<tr><td>22</td><td></td><td>|</td><td>e3-c3</td><td>e1-e3</td><td>e4-e2</td><td>c1-e3</td><td></td><td></td><td></td></tr>
<tr><td>23</td><td></td><td>|</td><td>|</td><td>|</td><td></td><td>g3-e3</td><td>d5-f3</td><td>c1-e3</td><td></td></tr>
<tr><td>24</td><td></td><td>|</td><td>|</td><td>|</td><td></td><td></td><td></td><td>g5-e3</td><td></td></tr>
<tr><td>25</td><td></td><td>|</td><td>|</td><td>g3-e3</td><td>b5-f3</td><td>c1-c3</td><td>g5-e3</td><td></td><td></td></tr>
<tr><td>26</td><td></td><td>|</td><td>|</td><td></td><td>|</td><td>e1-e3</td><td></td><td></td><td></td></tr>
<tr><td>27</td><td></td><td>|</td><td>|</td><td></td><td>|</td><td>g5-e3</td><td></td><td></td><td></td></tr>
<tr><td>28</td><td></td><td>|</td><td>|</td><td></td><td>d5-f3</td><td>e1-e3</td><td></td><td></td><td></td></tr>
<tr><td>29</td><td></td><td>|</td><td>|</td><td></td><td></td><td>g5-e3</td><td></td><td></td><td></td></tr>
<tr><td>30</td><td></td><td>|</td><td>c5-c3</td><td>a5-c5</td><td>d5-b5</td><td>a3-c5</td><td></td><td></td><td></td></tr>
<tr><td>31</td><td></td><td>|</td><td></td><td>|</td><td></td><td>c7-c5</td><td>c2-c6</td><td>a3-c5</td><td></td></tr>
<tr><td>32</td><td></td><td>|</td><td></td><td>|</td><td></td><td></td><td>|</td><td>e7-c5</td><td></td></tr>
<tr><td>33</td><td></td><td>|</td><td></td><td>|</td><td></td><td></td><td>e4-c6</td><td>a3-c5</td><td></td></tr>
<tr><td>34</td><td></td><td>|</td><td></td><td>|</td><td></td><td></td><td></td><td>e7-c5</td><td></td></tr>
<tr><td>35</td><td></td><td>|</td><td></td><td>c7-c5</td><td>c2-c6</td><td>a5-c5</td><td></td><td></td><td></td></tr>
<tr><td>36</td><td></td><td>|</td><td></td><td></td><td>|</td><td>e7-c5</td><td></td><td></td><td></td></tr>
<tr><td>37</td><td></td><td>|</td><td></td><td></td><td>e4-c6</td><td>a5-c5</td><td></td><td></td><td></td></tr>
<tr><td>38</td><td></td><td>|</td><td></td><td></td><td></td><td>e7-c5</td><td></td><td></td><td></td></tr>
<tr><td>39</td><td></td><td>d5-b3</td><td>b5-d5</td><td>c7-c5</td><td>c4-c6</td><td>e7-c5</td><td></td><td></td><td></td></tr>
</table>

gained according to Figure 8.3. This leaves only *b*5–*f*3 and *d*5–*f*3 to be considered, and both appear in the table (lines 25 and 28). Follow *d*5–*f*3. The only two possibilities for the next move are the corner clearances *e*1–*e*3 and *g*5–*e*3; both appear (lines 28 and 29). Follow *e*1–*e*3, still in line 28. The only possibility for further progress is the necessary delivery *e*4–*e*2, but this produces a position which has already been reached (after seven moves of line 23) and need not be analysed again. So line 28 does not lead to a 17-move solution. Alternatively, follow *g*5–*e*3 into line 29. Now we can make no move that is either a corner clearance or a necessary delivery, so line 29 also fails to lead to a 17-move solution.

Solutions to Chapter 8

Solutions as short as those following were first published by Bergholt, Davis, or T. H. Willcocks, but I have allowed personal fancy rather than historical priority to determine my selection. The sources of the original solutions are given in the Bibliography.

We consider the complements first.

*c*1: *e*1–*c*1, *d*3–*d*1, *f*3–*d*3, *e*5–*e*3, *d*3–*f*3, *g*3–*e*3, *b*3–*d*3–*f*3 (7), *c*5–*e*5, *a*5–*c*5, *f*5–*d*5–*b*5 (10), *c*1–*c*3, *a*3–*a*5–*c*5, *e*7–*e*5, *g*5–*g*3–*e*3 (14), *d*7–*d*5–*d*3–*b*3–*b*5–*d*5–*f*5–*f*3–*d*3, *c*7–*c*5–*c*3–*e*3–*e*1–*c*1. The task of solving this problem in sixteen moves, removing thirteen men in the last two, was set as one of Bergholt's 'special problems' described in the next chapter. A solution was first published by Willcocks in 1952. Willcocks finishes with a seven-sweep *d*7– . . . –*d*5 and a six-loop *c*1– . . . –*c*1; the reader may enjoy filling in the details.

Alternatively, *c*3–*c*1, *e*3–*c*3, *c*4–*c*2, *c*1–*c*3, *c*6–*c*4–*c*2 (5), *e*5–*e*3, *e*7–*e*5, *e*2–*e*4–*e*6 (8), *e*1–*c*1–*c*3, *g*3–*e*3, *g*5–*e*5–*c*5, *c*7–*e*7–*e*5, *g*4–*e*4–*c*4–*c*2–*e*2–*e*4–*e*6–*c*6–*c*4 (13), *a*5–*c*5–*c*3, *a*4–*c*4–*c*2, *a*3–*c*3–*c*1.

*d*1: *d*3–*d*1, *b*3–*d*3, *d*4–*d*2, *c*1–*c*3, *c*4–*c*2, *e*1–*c*1–*c*3 (6), *f*3–*d*3–*b*3, *a*3–*c*3, *e*5–*e*3, *e*2–*e*4 (10), *g*5–*e*5, *d*5–*f*5, *g*3–*g*5–*e*5–*e*3, *e*7–*e*5 (14), *b*5–*d*5–*f*5–*f*3–*d*3–*b*3, *a*5–*a*3–*c*3, *c*7–*c*5, *d*7–*d*5–*b*5–*b*3–*d*3–*d*1. (Bergholt)

*c*2: *c*4–*c*2, *c*1–*c*3, *c*6–*c*4–*c*2 (3), *e*5–*c*5, *e*7–*e*5, *e*4–*e*6, *c*7–*e*7–*e*5 (7), *e*2–*e*4–*e*6, *g*5–*e*5, *e*6–*e*4, *g*3–*e*3–*e*5, *a*3–*c*3–*e*3, *e*1–*c*1–*c*3 (13), *g*4–*e*4–*c*4–*c*2–*e*2–*e*4–*e*6–*c*6–*c*4, *a*5–*c*5–*c*3, *a*4–*c*4–*c*2.

*d*2: *d*4–*d*2, *b*3–*d*3, *c*1–*c*3, *c*4–*c*2, *c*6–*c*4 (5), *a*5–*c*5, *d*5–*b*5, *f*5–*d*5, *e*7–*e*5, *e*4–*e*6, *e*2–*e*4 (11), *g*3–*e*3–*e*5, *d*5–*f*5–*f*3, *g*5–*g*3–*e*3, *e*1–*c*1–*c*3, *a*3–*a*5–*c*5, *c*7–*e*7–*e*5 (17), *c*4–*c*6–*e*6–*e*4–*e*2–*c*2–*c*4, *b*4–*d*4–*d*2.

*c*3: *c*1–*c*3, *c*4–*c*2, *c*6–*c*4 (3), *a*5–*c*5, *d*5–*b*5, *e*3–*c*3–*c*5, *g*3–*e*3, *f*5–*d*5–*d*3–*f*3 (8), *e*1–*c*1–*c*3, *g*5–*g*3–*e*3, *e*7–*e*5, *e*2–*c*2–*c*4–*c*6–*e*6, *a*3–*a*5–*c*5 (13), *b*3–*b*5–*d*5–*f*5–*f*3–*d*3, *c*7–*e*7–*e*5–*e*3–*c*3. (Davis)

Alternatively, *c*5–*c*3, *c*7–*c*5, *c*2–*c*4–*c*6 (3), *e*3–*c*3, *g*3–*e*3, *d*5–*d*3–*f*3, *a*5–*c*5, *f*5–*d*5–*b*5 (8), *e*1–*e*3–*e*5, *g*5–*g*3–*e*3, *e*7–*c*7–*c*5, *e*6–*c*6–*c*4–*c*2–*e*2, *a*3–*a*5–*c*5 (13), *b*3–*b*5–*d*5–*f*5–*f*3–*d*3, *c*1–*e*1–*e*3–*c*3. (Davis)

*d*3: *b*3–*d*3, *c*5–*c*3, *c*7–*c*5, *c*2–*c*4–*c*6 (4), *e*3–*c*3, *g*3–*e*3, *d*5–*d*3–*f*3 (7), *a*5–*c*5, *f*5–*d*5–*b*5, *e*7–*c*7–*c*5, *e*6–*c*6–*c*4–*c*2 (11), *c*1–*c*3, *e*1–*e*3–*e*5, *g*5–*g*3–*e*3, *a*3–*a*5–*c*5, *d*1–*d*3–*b*3–*b*5–*d*5–*f*5–*f*3–*d*3. (Davis)

*d*4: *d*2–*d*4, *f*3–*d*3, *e*1–*e*3, *e*4–*e*2, *e*6–*e*4 (5), *g*5–*e*5, *d*5–*f*5, *g*3–*g*5–*e*5, *c*3–*e*3, *a*3–*c*3, *b*5–*d*5–*f*5–*f*3–*d*3–*c*3 (11), *c*1–*e*1–*e*3–*e*5, *c*7–*c*5, *c*4–*c*6 (14), *e*7–*c*7–*c*5, *a*5–*a*3–*c*3, *c*2–*c*4–*c*6–*e*6–*e*4–*c*4, *b*4–*d*4. (Bergholt)

Most of the non-complement solutions can be obtained from these by suitable re-orientation of the play and modification of the first or last few moves, and we content ourselves with abbreviated descriptions in these cases.

Start at *c*1, finish at *c*4: play *c*3–*c*1 and then follow the *d*3-complement solution reflected about the diagonal *c*3–*e*5. (Davis)

Start at *c*1, finish at *c*7: play the first thirteen moves of the second *c*1-complement solution, giving a position symmetrical about row 4, and finish *a*3–*c*3–*c*5, *a*4–*c*4–*c*6, *a*5–*c*5–*c*7.

Start at *c*1, finish at *f*4: *c*3–*c*1, *e*3–*c*3, *g*3–*e*3, *b*3–*d*3–*f*3 (4), *g*5–*g*3–*e*3, *c*5–*c*3, *f*5–*f*3–*d*3–*b*3 (7), *a*3–*c*3, *e*1–*e*3, *e*4–*e*2, *c*1–*e*1–*e*3, *c*7–*c*5 (12), *e*6–*e*4–*e*2–*c*2–*c*4–*c*6, *a*5–*c*5–*e*3, *e*7–*c*7–*c*5, *a*4–*c*4–*c*6–*e*6–*e*4, *d*4–*f*4. (Davis)

Start at *d*1, finish at *a*4: play *d*3–*d*1 and then follow the *d*4-complement solution, combining the last two moves. (Bergholt)

Start at *d*1, finish at *d*4: play *d*3–*d*1 and then follow the *d*4-complement solution. (Bergholt)

Start at *d*1, finish at *d*7: *d*3–*d*1, *b*3–*d*3, *c*1–*c*3, *c*4–*c*2 (4), *e*1–*c*1–*c*3, *d*3–*b*3, *a*3–*c*3, *f*3–*d*3–*b*3 (8), *e*5–*e*3, *a*5–*a*3–*c*3, *e*2–*e*4, *e*7–*e*5–*e*3 (12), *g*5–*e*5, *d*5–*f*5, *g*3–*g*5–*e*5, *c*6–*c*4–*e*4–*e*6, *c*7–*e*7–*e*5, *b*5–*b*3–*d*3–*f*3–*f*5–*d*5–*d*7. (Bergholt)

Start at *c*2, finish at *c*5: play *c*4–*c*2 and then follow the second *c*3-complement solution reflected about row 4. (Davis)

Start at *c*2, finish at *f*5: play *c*4–*c*2 and then follow the second *c*3-complement solution, reflected about row 4, up to but not including the final move; finish *c*7–*e*7–*e*5, *d*5–*f*5. (Davis)

Start at *d*2, finish at *a*5: *d*4–*d*2, *f*3–*d*3, *e*5–*e*3, *e*7–*e*5, *e*2–*e*4–*e*6 (5), *c*7–*e*7–*e*5, *c*3–*e*3, *c*6–*e*6–*e*4–*e*2 (8), *e*1–*e*3, *g*5–*e*5, *d*5–*f*5, *g*3–*g*5–*e*5, *a*3–

*c*3, *b*5-*d*5-*f*5-*f*3-*d*3-*b*3 (14), *a*5-*a*3-*c*3, *d*1-*d*3-*b*3-*b*5, *c*1-*c*3-*c*5-*a*5. (Davis; Bergholt also has a 17-move solution.)

Start at *d*2, finish at *d*5: play the first fourteen moves of the preceding solution and then finish *c*1-*c*3-*c*5, *a*5-*a*3-*c*3, *d*1-*d*3-*b*3-*b*3-*d*5. (Davis.)

Start at *c*3, finish at *f*3: play the first fourteen moves of the first solution to the *c*3-complement and then finish *c*7-*e*7-*e*5-*e*3, *d*3-*f*3. (Davis; Bergholt gives a 16-move solution ending in a seven-sweep.)

Start at *d*3, finish at *a*3: play *b*3-*d*3 and then follow the second solution to the *c*1-complement reflected about the diagonal *c*3-*e*5.

Start at *d*3, finish at *d*6: play the solution to the problem 'start at *d*2, finish at *d*5' omitting the first move *d*4-*d*2, and then add a final move *d*4-*d*6. The replacement of this final move by *d*5-*d*3 and its incorporation into the previous move gives another 16-move solution to the *d*3-complement. (Davis)

Start at *d*4, finish at *d*1: play the solution to the *d*4-complement, reflected in the diagonal *c*3-*e*5, up to but not including the last two moves, and then finish *b*3-*d*3-*f*3-*f*5-*d*5-*d*3-*d*1. (Bergholt)

The problems of Figures 8.7 and 8.8 yield as follows:

Figure 8.7: *c*3-*c*1-*e*1, *e*2-*c*2, *e*3-*c*3-*c*1, *a*5-*a*3-*c*3-*c*5-*e*5-*e*3-*g*3, *g*4-*e*4-*c*4-*a*4, *d*7-*d*5, *g*5-*e*5-*c*5-*a*5-*a*3, *c*7-*c*5, *e*7-*e*5.

Figure 8.8: *c*5-*c*3-*c*1, *e*3-*c*3-*a*3, *d*1-*d*3, *c*7-*c*5-*e*5-*e*3-*c*3, *g*3-*g*5-*e*5-*e*7, *a*4-*c*4-*e*4-*g*4, *e*1-*e*3-*g*3-*g*5, *d*7-*d*5, *a*5-*c*5-*e*5.

9

LONG SOLUTIONS

In Chapter 3 we considered the single-vacancy complement problems with a man on the watch and found the longest possible final sweeps. In this chapter we consider some other problems whose solutions can contain long sweeps.

The elusive nine-sweep finish

We proved in Chapters 3 and 6 that no solution to a single-vacancy complement problem can finish with a nine-sweep. Can we finish a solution to a single-vacancy *non-complement* problem with such a sweep?

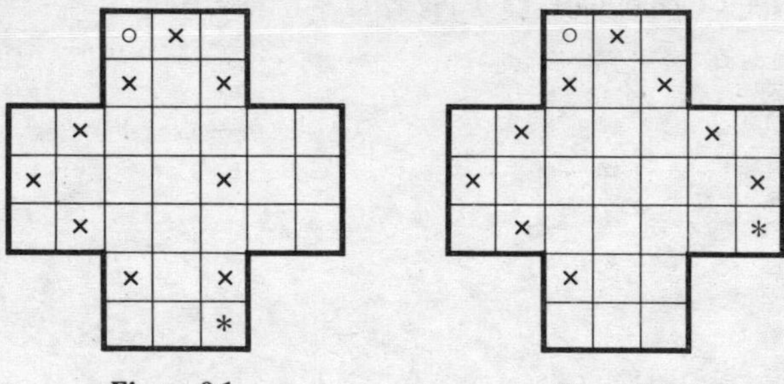

Figure 9.1 Figure 9.2

Yes, we can. We can start by vacating *c*1, mark either *g*5 or *e*7, and play to finish in *c*7. Figures 9.1 and 9.2 show two of the possible final sweeps.

The history of these solutions is not known with certainty. The earliest reference to a nine-sweep finish is in Bergholt's *Complete Handbook* (1920), where five 'special problems' appear under the following rubric: 'The following five problems are of such exceptional interest and difficulty that their solutions have not been included in the book: they have all been worked out by the author, or by Mr. G. L. Moore, and are left to the ingenuity of the reader.' It is difficult to understand why the exceptional interest of a problem should be a reason for omitting its solution, but the book as published is tight to 96 pages and they may have been late additions; had the original text stopped after problem 128, there would have been a gap where the 'special problems' now appear but no corresponding gap at the end of the solutions. Be that as it may, the wording of problem 132, translated into our notation, is as follows:

> Vacate *c*1. Finish the game with a sweep of *nine* at the last move. (This problem also may be solved in two distinct ways).

Now what does 'in two distinct ways' mean? Does it mean 'from two distinct starting points' or merely 'by two distinct paths'? The word 'also' appears to refer to problem 129, which we shall consider later in the chapter, and throws no light.

The known facts are these. Bergholt claimed that he or Moore had found two distinct solutions, a claim I see no reason to dispute. These solutions may or may not have had the same starting point. T. H. Willcocks rediscovered our Figure 9.2, set it as a problem in the August 1950 issue of *The Fairy Chess Review*, and published the solution in a subsequent issue. Harry O. Davis, not knowing this, rediscovered Figure 9.2 in 1964 and published a solution leading to it in the May 1967 issue of *The Mathematical Gazette*. A note published with this paper refers to subsequent work by Davis and Wade E. Philpott in which they proved that only eight distinct nine-sweep finishes to single-vacancy single-survivor problems are possible. No proof appears in the paper but Philpott sent me diagrams of the possible sweeps in 1969. All are to the problem 'vacate *c*1, finish at *c*7'; two of the sweeps start from *e*7 and six from *g*5.

The impossibility of other nine-sweep finishes can in fact be proved fairly easily by the methods of Chapters 3 to 7. The four parity counts typified by ϵ in Figures 6.3 and 6.4 are particularly useful. They do not prohibit the solutions of Figures 9.1 and 9.2, or the other solutions discovered by Davis and Philpott, because the first move of each solution (*e*1–*c*1) changes the values of the parity counts across the NW and NE corners and the final sweep (*e*7– . . . –*c*7 or *g*5– . . . –*c*7) changes the values of the other two.

Other long sweeps

Perhaps the most attractive nine-sweep is that shown in Figure 9.3, and it is a pity that it cannot be made the finish of a single-vacancy to single-survivor problem. To reach it, we must start with at least two vacancies. The two double-vacancy positions which are symmetrical about column *d* and from which play to it is possible are shown as *AA* and *BB* in Figure 9.4. *BB* is given by Bergholt.

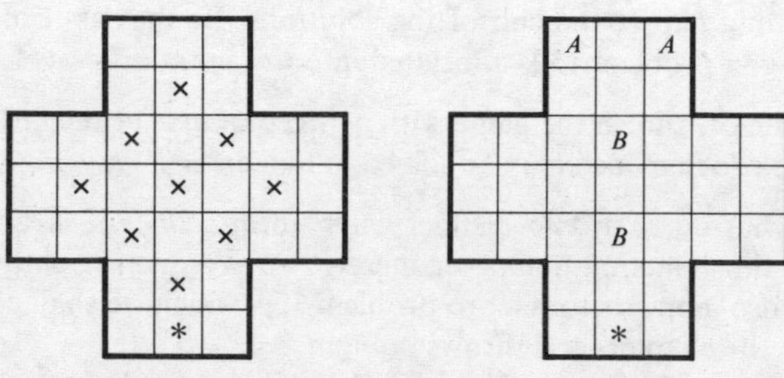

Figure 9.3

Figure 9.4

Although no single-vacancy complement solution can finish with a nine-sweep, a solution to the *c*1- or *c*3-complement problem can contain an *intermediate* nine-sweep. Figures 9.5 and 9.6 show two possibilities. Figure 9.5 solves part of another of Bergholt's 'special problems', the first published solution again having been given by Willcocks. The position of Figure 9.6 can be incorporated in a 16-move solution to the *c*3-complement.

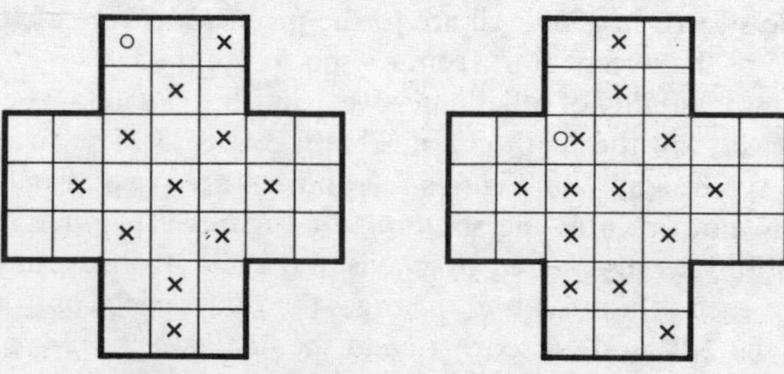

Figure 9.5

Figure 9.6

No single-vacancy to single-survivor problem can contain a move longer than a nine-sweep, but longer sweeps can be obtained in the solutions to other problems. The longest sweep geometrically possible is a sixteen-sweep, Figure 9.7 showing an example. There is no way in which such a position can be reached from a single-vacancy start, but it is possible to reach an eleven-sweep from such a start. Figure 9.8 shows one possibility.

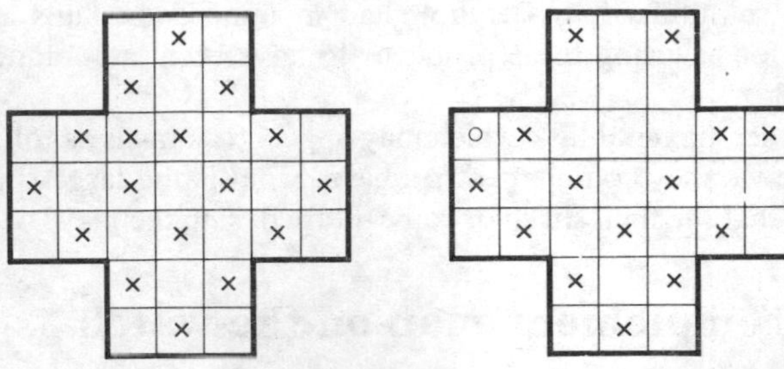

Figure 9.7 **Figure 9.8**

The idea behind Figure 9.7 can be generalised to the construction of positions, not necessarily reachable from single-vacancy starts, from which various multiple sweeps are possible. The subject was opened in a splendid investigation, now largely forgotten, by T. R. Dawson in 1943. Some of Dawson's results are as follows:

(a) thirteen consecutive two-sweeps, leaving the last man in any hole other than *d*4;

(b) seven consecutive three-sweeps, leaving the last man in *a*3, *b*3, *c*3, *d*3, or *a*4;

(c) five consecutive four-sweeps, leaving the last man in *a*3, *b*3, or *c*3;

(d) four consecutive five-sweeps;

(e) three consecutive six-sweeps;

(f) two consecutive eight-sweeps.

Dawson regarded the last two as too trivial to be set as problems for formal solution. I do not agree, certainly as regards (e); and while (f) is indeed trivial since Dawson regards a sixteen-sweep as two consecutive eight-sweeps, it becomes less trivial if we add the condition that the second sweep consume the man that has made the first.

This is an appropriate point to mention the only one of Bergholt's 'special problems' to which no solution was subsequently published by Willcocks. This is problem 129: 'Vacate *c*2. Finish the game in 18 moves, capturing twelve balls in the last two moves. (This problem may be solved in at least two ways).' The precise meaning of 'two ways' is unclear in the absence of Bergholt's own solutions, and in fact the problem can be solved in 16 moves with final sweeps of 7 + 5, and in 17 moves with final sweeps of 8 + 4 or 9 + 3. The existence of shorter solutions than Bergholt had in mind is perhaps another reason for believing these problems to have been late additions to his book.

Another maximal task which may appeal to some is as follows: in a single-vacancy complement problem, what is the largest number of men that the final survivor can capture during the play?

Non-complement man-on-the-watch finishes

A complete table of the longest final sweeps possible in single-vacancy man-on-the-watch problems, both complements and non-complements, is given as Table 9.2 at the end of the chapter. This table, like all others in the book, omits duplicates which are equivalent to listed positions under reflection or rotation. In many cases the man on the watch and the final destination have a greater influence on sweep length than the initial vacancy, a fact reflected in the organisation of the table.

The table includes some 'loop' problems in which the marked man is to finish in its original hole. There are no 'complement' versions of such problems. These apart, there are only three cases in which the a choice of an initial vacancy other than the target hole permits a longer final sweep: the problems '*c*1 to *e*1' and '*c*1 to *a*5', which can be finished with nine-sweeps if the initial vacancy is at *e*7 or *g*5 respectively but only with seven-sweeps if it is at *e*1 or *a*5, and the problem '*d*3 to *b*3', which can be finished with a five-sweep if the initial vacancy is at *e*3 or *e*6 but only with a one-sweep if it is at *b*3. All the solutions in the table can be proved to be the longest possible by the techniques of Chapters 4 to 7.

There are a few problems involving marked men which are soluble only if we allow the marked man to move before the final sweep, and a few in which the marked man can make a longer final sweep if we allow it to move first than if we do not. Such problems are not of great interest, however, and we omit the details. The reader with a desire for completeness will have no difficulty in identifying and solving them for himself, though he may find the process a little tedious.

Loop finishes

Many problems have solutions which finish with loops. We divide such loops into three classes: man-on-the-watch loops, 'go there and stay' loops, and other loops.

Man-on-the-watch loops were considered in the section immediately above.

A 'go there and stay' loop solution involves *two* moves by the marked man: a move to the initial vacancy as the first move of the solution, and a final sweep. The longest final sweeps possible under these conditions are shown in Table 9.1. It will be noticed that no solution to the *c*3-complement longer than a four-sweep is possible under these conditions, and no solution at all to the *d*3-complement unless the marked man is at *b*3. The undoubted star of the class is the eight-sweep finish to the *c*1-complement by a man starting at *e*1, given by Bergholt and shown in Figure 9.9.

Table 9.1: Maximal 'go there and stay' loops in 33-hole Solitaire

Initial vacancy	Marked man	Longest sweep
*c*1	*e*1	8
	*c*3	6
*c*2	*e*2 or *c*4	6
*c*3	*c*1 or *e*3	4
*d*3	*b*3	6

Our third class is of general loops. In fact this does not greatly widen the field; for example, the only complement problem in which the condition 'go there and stay' restricts the length of the final sweep is the *c*3-complement, to which a six-sweep loop finish is possible without this condition. We saw such a finish in 'Faulty arithmetic' in Chapter 3, and another eight-sweep finish incorporating such a loop is shown in Figure 9.10.

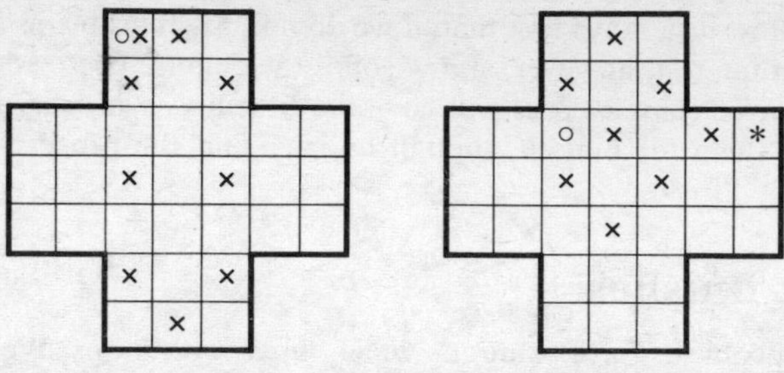

Figure 9.9 Figure 9.10

We end this chapter with an elegant loop problem due to R. L. Hutchings: vacate *c*2, mark *e*2, and let *e*2 make a five-sweep move to *c*2 during the solution and then a six-sweep loop to finish. Hutchings does this in only 17 moves.

Table 9.2: Longest-sweep man-on-the-watch solutions in 33-hole Solitaire

Marked man	Final hole	Initial vacancy	Longest sweep
*c*1	*c*1	*c*7	8
		*c*4, *f*4	6
	*e*1	*e*7	9
		*e*1, *b*4, *e*4	7
	*a*3	*a*3, *g*3	8
		*d*3, *d*6	6
	*c*3	*c*3, *f*3, *c*6	7
	*e*3	*e*3	8
		*b*3, *e*6	6
	*g*3	*a*3, *d*3, *g*3, *d*6	7
	*a*5	*g*5	9
		*d*2, *a*5, *d*5	7
	*c*5	*c*5	8
		*c*2, *f*5	6
	*e*5	*e*2, *b*5, *e*5	7
	*g*5	*a*5, *g*5	8
		*d*2, *d*5	6
	*c*7	*c*4, *f*4, *c*7	7
	*e*7	*e*1, *b*4, *e*4, *e*7	6

Table 9.2: *Continued*

Marked man	Final hole	Initial vacancy	Longest sweep
*d*1	*b*3	*b*3, *e*3, *e*6	6
	*d*3	*a*3, *d*3, *d*6	7
	*b*5	*e*2, *b*5, *e*5	7
	*d*5	*d*2, *a*5, *d*5	8
	*d*7	*a*4, *d*4, *d*7	5
*c*2	*c*2	*c*5, *f*5	6
	*e*2	*e*2, *b*5, *e*5	5
	*a*4	*d*1, *a*4, *d*4, *g*4, *d*7	6
	*c*4	*c*1, *c*4, *f*4, *c*7	5
	*e*4	*e*1, *b*4, *e*4, *e*7	6
	*g*4	*d*1, *a*4, *d*4, *g*4	5
		*d*7	3
	*c*6	*c*3, *f*3, *c*6	4
	*e*6	*b*3, *e*3, *e*6	5
*d*2	*b*4	*e*1, *b*4, *e*4, *e*7	2
	*d*4	*a*4, *d*4, *d*7	1
	*d*6	*a*3, *d*3, *d*6	2
*c*3	*c*1	*c*1	5
		*c*4, *f*4, *c*7	1
	*e*1	*e*1	6
		*e*7	4
		*b*4, *e*4	2
	*c*3	*f*3	4
	*e*3	*e*3, *e*6	5
		*b*3	3
	*g*3	*d*3, *g*3, *d*6	4
		*a*3	2
	*e*5	*e*5	6
		*e*2	4
	*g*5	*d*2, *a*5, *d*5, *g*5	5
*d*3	*b*3	*e*3, *e*6	5
		*b*3	1
	*d*3	*a*3	6
	*b*5	*e*2, *b*5, *e*5	4
	*d*5	*a*5, *d*5	3
*d*4	*d*2	*a*5, *d*5	1

Solutions to Chapter 9

Figures 9.1 and 9.2 yield to the play *e*1–*c*1, *d*3–*d*1, *b*3–*d*3, *c*1–*c*3, *d*3–*b*3, *a*3–*c*3, *c*4–*c*2, *b*5–*b*3, *d*5–*b*5, *a*5–*c*5 (10), *d*7–*d*5–*b*5, *c*7–*c*5, *e*4–*c*4–*c*6, *e*2–*e*4, *g*3–*e*3, *e*4–*e*2, and now either *e*6–*e*4, *g*5–*e*5, *e*4–*e*6, *g*4–*e*4 (Figure 9.1) or *f*5–*f*3, *e*7–*e*5, *d*5–*f*5–*f*3 (Figure 9.2). Davis plays *f*5–*d*5–*b*5 at the eleventh move and reaches Figure 9.2 in 18 moves.

Figure 9.4, *AA*: *c*3–*c*1–*e*1, *a*3–*c*3, *d*3–*b*3, *a*5–*a*3–*c*3, *f*3–*d*3–*b*3, *c*5–*c*3, *b*3–*d*3, *e*1–*e*3–*c*3, *e*5–*c*5, *g*5–*e*5, *b*5–*d*5–*f*5, *e*7–*e*5–*e*3, *g*3–*g*5–*e*5, *c*7–*c*5.

BB: *b*3–*d*3, *c*1–*c*3, *c*4–*c*2, *e*1–*c*1–*c*3, *d*3–*b*3, *a*3–*c*3, *f*3–*d*3–*b*3, *a*5–*a*3–*c*3, *e*5–*e*3, *e*2–*e*4, *e*7–*e*5–*e*3, *g*5–*e*5, *b*5–*d*5–*f*5, *g*3–*g*5–*e*5, *c*7–*c*5.

Figure 9.5: *c*3–*c*1, *e*3–*c*3, *g*3–*e*3, *b*3–*d*3–*f*3, *c*5–*c*3, *a*5–*c*5, *d*5–*b*5, *a*3–*a*5–*c*5, *f*5–*d*5–*b*5, *c*7–*c*5, *b*5–*d*5, *e*7–*e*5–*c*5, *e*1–*e*3–*e*5, *g*5–*g*3–*e*3, *c*1–*e*1. (Davis; Willcocks plays to leave fifteen men symmetrically placed in *b*4/*c*123567/*d*12467/*e*35/*f*4, from which we can finish at either *c*1 or *c*7 as required by Bergholt.)

Figure 9.6: *a*3–*c*3, *d*3–*b*3, *a*5–*a*3–*c*3, *f*3–*d*3–*b*3, *c*1–*c*3, *b*3–*d*3, *e*1–*e*3–*c*3, *e*5–*e*3, *g*5–*e*5, *d*5–*f*5, *b*5–*d*5, *g*3–*g*5–*e*5–*c*5, *e*7–*e*5, *c*7–*e*7.

Figure 9.8: *a*5–*a*3, *c*4–*a*4, *c*6–*c*4, *e*6–*c*6, *c*7–*c*5, *c*4–*c*6, *e*4–*e*6, *e*7–*e*5, *g*4–*e*4–*e*6, *g*5–*e*5, *d*5–*f*5, *e*2–*e*4, *d*3–*d*5, *c*2–*c*4, *a*3–*c*3, *d*1–*d*3–*b*3.

Dawson's 2-sweeps: to end at *a*3, remove *a*3/*c*47/*e*345; at *b*3, remove *a*5/*c*5/*d*3/*e*35/*g*3; at *c*3, remove *c*135/*d*3/*f*3/*g*3; at *d*3, remove *a*3/*b*3/*c*467/*g*3; at *a*4, remove *a*5/*b*3/*c*3/*e*357; at *b*4, remove *c*137/*e*13/*g*3. Dawson gives the play. I quote: 'To this group, I found 6, 1, 8, 2, 1, and 2 solutions respectively and there will be others.' A remarkable achievement.

3-sweeps: to end at *a*3, remove *a*3/*c*247/*d*5/*e*1357/*f*3/*g*3; at *b*3, remove *a*35/*c*135/*d*4/*e*13/*f*4/*g*35; at *c*3, remove *a*3/*c*135/*d*2/*e*135/*f*3/*g*35; at *d*3, remove *a*5/*c*46/*d*2/*e*13567/*g*35; at *a*4, remove *a*3/*c*137/*d*45/*e*13/*f*35/*g*3.

4-sweeps: to end at *a*3, remove *a*5/*b*4/*c*157/*d*6/*e*157/*f*4/*g*35; at *b*3, remove *a*35/*c*247/*d*3/*e*357/*f*4/*g*35; at *c*3, remove *a*35/*c*357/*d*46/*e*37/*f*4/*g*35.

5-sweeps: remove *a*35/*c*137/*d*6/*e*157/*f*4/*g*35.

6-sweeps: remove *a*3/*b*5/*c*1346/*d*26/*e*1357/*g*35. This may have been trivial to Dawson but it wasn't to me.

8-sweeps: remove *a*345/*b*35/*c*1/*d*257/*e*17/*f*35/*g*345.

Bergholt's problem 129 can be solved in 16 moves by *c*4–*c*2, *c*1–*c*3, *c*6–*c*4–*c*2, *e*4–*c*4, *e*1–*c*1–*c*3–*c*5, *a*3–*c*3, *b*5–*b*3, *e*6–*e*4, *g*5–*e*5, *e*4–

*e*6, *e*7–*e*5, *e*2–*e*4–*e*6, *g*3–*e*3, *c*7–*e*7–*e*5, *g*4–*e*4–*e*2–*c*2–*c*4–*c*6–*e*6–*e*4, *a*5–*a*3–*c*3–*e*3–*e*5–*c*5. We leave the 17-move solutions to the reader.

The survivor of a single-vacancy single-survivor problem can capture at most thirteen men during the play. If we vacate *d*3 and mark the man at *b*3 then we can play *b*3–*d*3, *c*1–*c*3, *d*3–*b*3, *d*1–*d*3, *e*3–*c*3, *g*3–*e*3, *b*3–*d*3–*f*3, *e*1–*e*3, *c*5–*c*3, *a*5–*c*5, *d*5–*b*5, *a*3–*a*5–*c*5, *f*3–*d*3–*b*3–*b*5–*d*5, *c*7–*c*5, *d*5–*b*5, *d*7–*d*5, *e*5–*c*5, *g*5–*e*5, *b*5–*d*5–*f*5–*f*3, *d*4–*f*4, *g*4–*e*4, *e*7–*e*5–*e*3, *f*3–*d*3. The marked man can actually consume fourteen men and finish at *d*5, but this leaves a man at *g*4 and he was brought up not to leave food at the side of his plate.

The problems listed in Table 9.2 should give no trouble to a reader who has worked this far and we refrain from giving solutions.

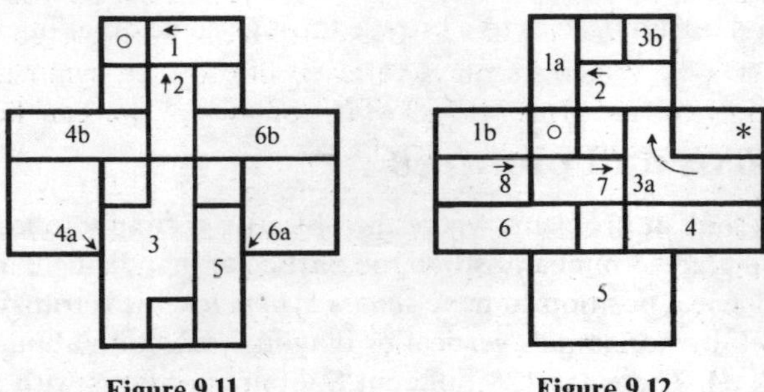

Figure 9.11 **Figure 9.12**

Figures 9.9 and 9.10 can be reached by the play shown in Figures 9.11 and 9.12 respectively. Step 3 in Figure 9.11 is a shifted six. The other loop finishes should give no trouble.

Hutchings plays *c*4–*c*2, *c*1–*c*3, *a*4–*c*4–*c*2, *c*6–*c*4, *e*1–*c*1–*c*3–*c*5, *e*3–*c*3, *e*5–*e*3, *e*7–*e*5, *g*4–*e*4–*e*6, *c*7–*e*7–*e*5 (10), *e*2–*e*4–*e*6–*c*6–*c*4–*c*2, *a*3–*c*3, *a*5–*c*3, *d*4–*d*6, *g*5–*e*5, *g*3–*e*3, *c*2–*c*4–*c*6–*e*6–*e*4–*e*2–*c*2. He comments that the play from move 11 onwards includes a ‘quintuple-three’ block removal!

10

WHIMS AND FANCIES

In this final chapter on the 33-hole board, we forget extrema for a while and treat ourselves to a browse through some other interesting problems.

Patterns and pictures

We first look at problems where the objective is simply to leave the men in a predetermined position, no particular man being marked.

We define a position to have *square symmetry* if it is transformed into itself by horizontal, vertical or diagonal reflection about a line through *d*4. There are 128 different Solitaire positions with square symmetry, but only twelve of them can be reached from the position with only the centre vacant. We have already seen two of these: the position with only the centre occupied, and 'Wall' (Figure 2.19). Figures 10.1 to 10.10 show the other ten.

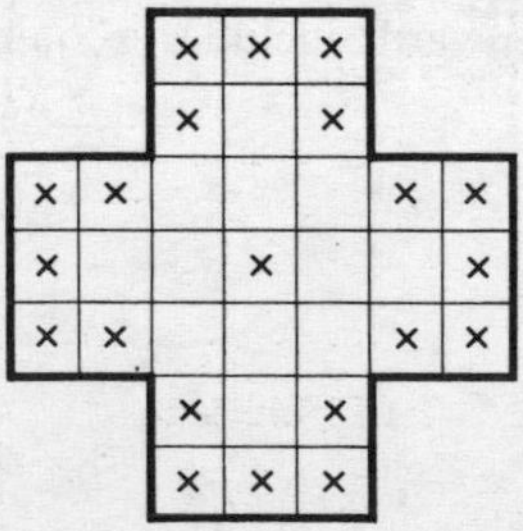

Figure 10.1

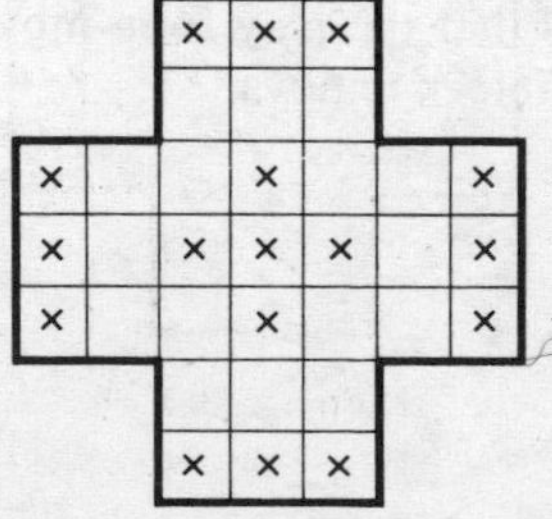

Figure 10.2

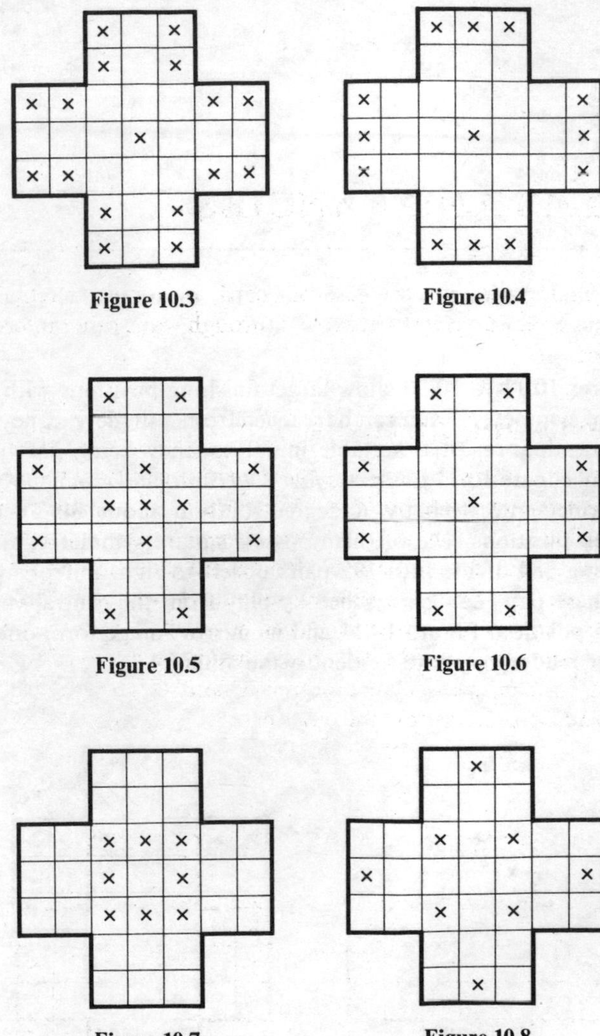

Figure 10.3

Figure 10.4

Figure 10.5

Figure 10.6

Figure 10.7

Figure 10.8

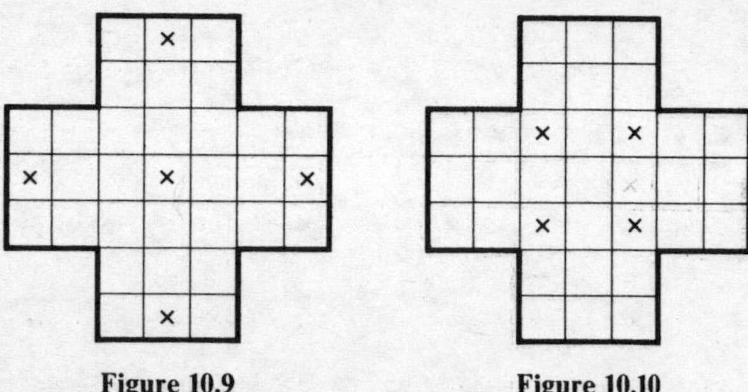

Figure 10.9

Figure 10.10

Figures 10.11 to 10.20 show target finishing positions with other forms of symmetry. Each can be reached from a single-vacancy start, the determination of a suitable initial vacancy being part of the problem. Figure 10.11 possesses *four-fold rotational symmetry*, being transformed into itself by 90-degree rotation about *d*4. There are 512 such positions. 128 of them possess square symmetry, and the remaining 384 divide into 192 pairs of left-to-right mirror images. 25 of these pairs can be reached by play from the central-vacancy starting position. Figure 10.11 and its mirror image form one such pair; the reader may care to identify the other 24.

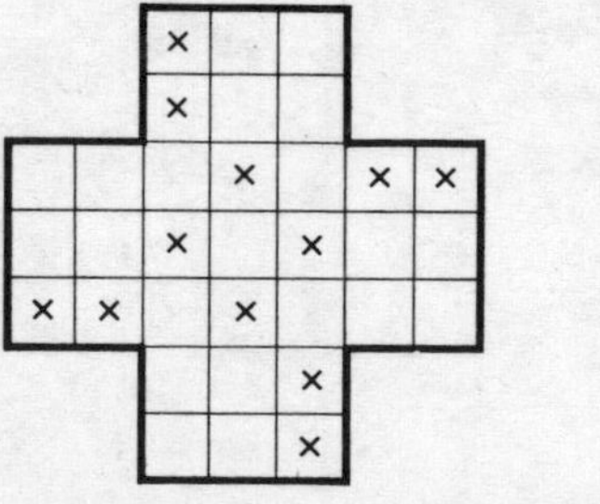

Figure 10.11

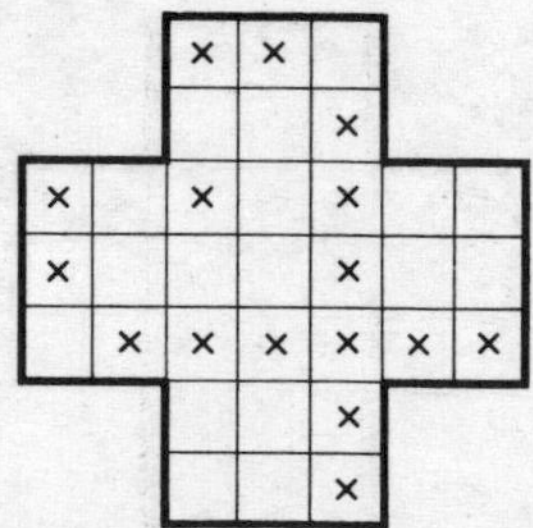

Figure 10.12

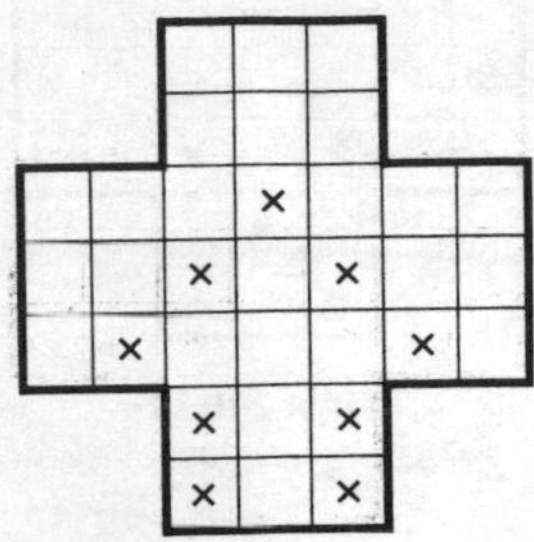

Figure 10.13 'Lych gate'

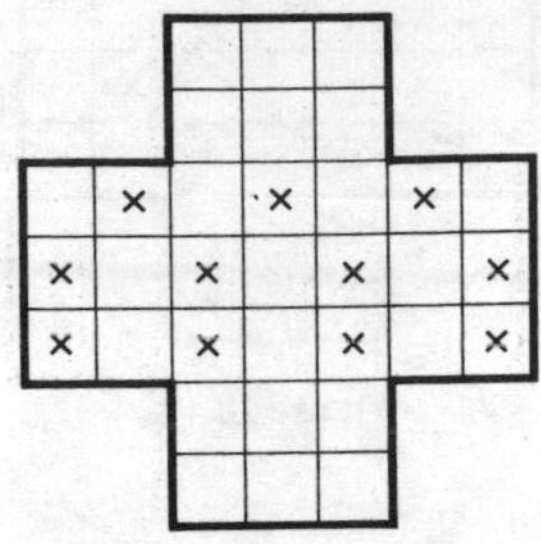

Figure 10.14 'Arcade'

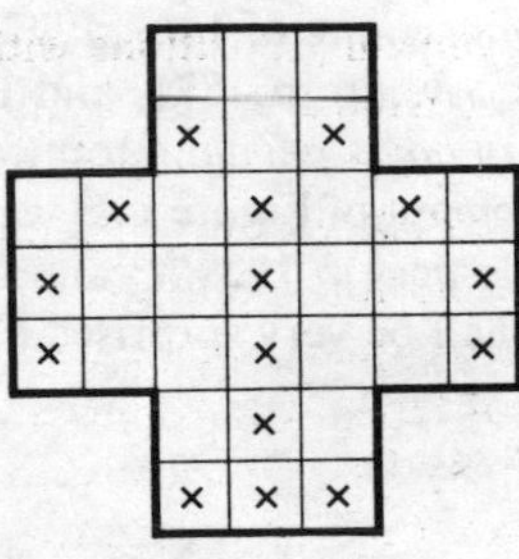

Figure 10.15 'Tree'

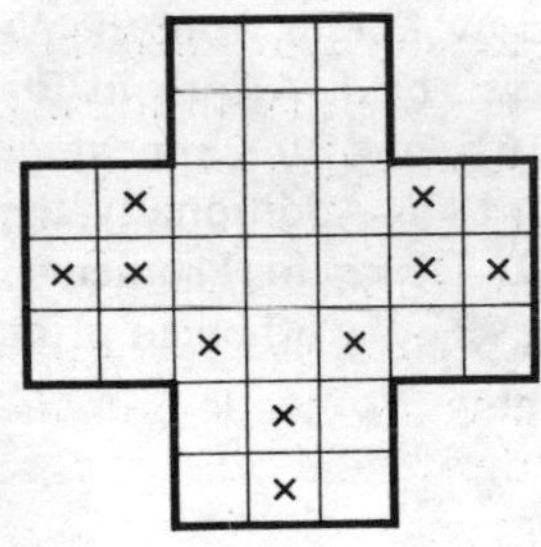

Figure 10.16 'Bush'

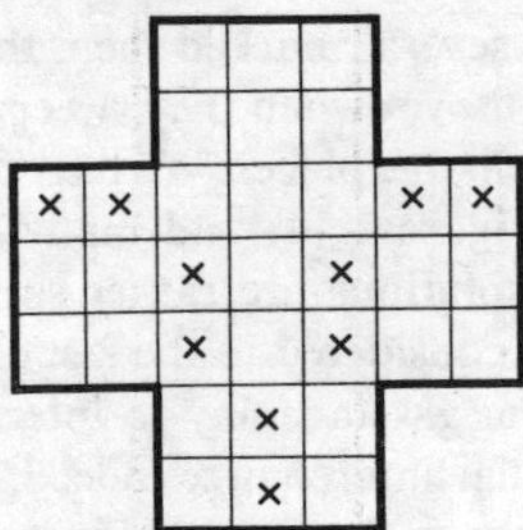

Figure 10.17 'Lily'

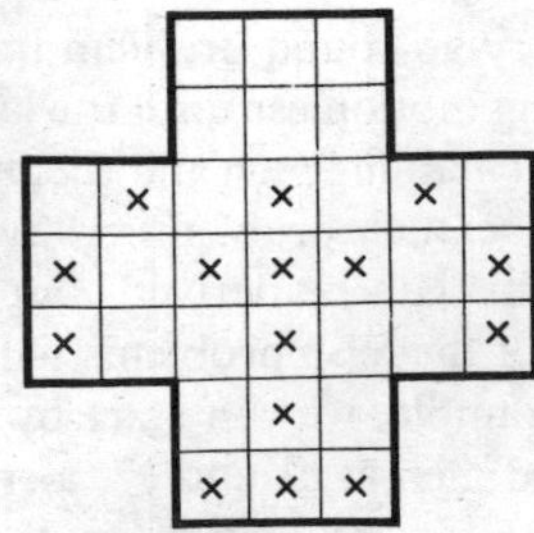

Figure 10.18 'Fountain'

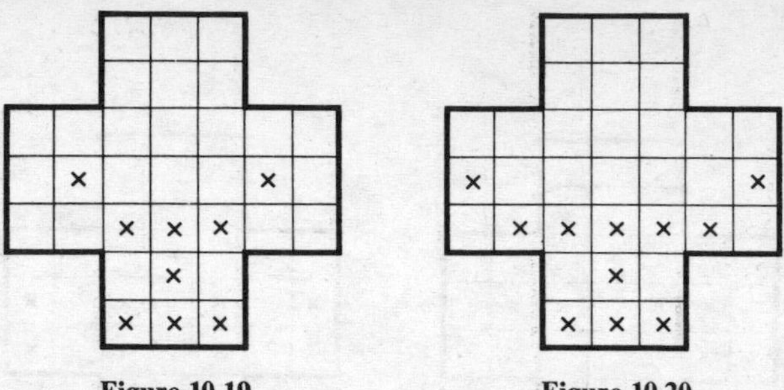

Figure 10.19 **Figure 10.20**

Many positions of this type have appeared in the literature; Figures 10.2, 10.4, 10.7, and 10.9, together with 'Wall', are indeed quoted by Ahrens from the *Neueste Anweisung* of 1807, Figure 10.6 was given by J. Alcorn in Bizalion's column in 1871, and Figures 10.1, 10.5, and 10.8 appeared in *Every boy's annual* (Routledge) in 1875 or 1876. Additionally, the complement of Figure 10.3 was given by A. L. Dewey in 'Problems in Puzzle-peg' in 1929. I cannot recall having seen the others in print but I shall be very surprised if all are original.

Merry-go-rounds

A merry-go-round problem involves several marked men, these remaining motionless until the last few moves when they sweep off the other remaining men and themselves change places. We have already seen one such problem in 'Swap' (Figure 1.14) and many similar problems can be derived, but their solutions are rather similar to those of the loop problems which we considered in the last chapter. For example, we can start by vacating *d*4 and play to interchange marked men at *c*1 and *e*7, a spectacular interchange indeed, but its solution is very similar to that of the eight-sweep loop with the marked man at *c*1 and the initial vacancy at *c*7.

Some slightly different problems are shown in Figures 10.21 to 10.24. Note that all except Figure 10.23 have more than one initial vacancy.

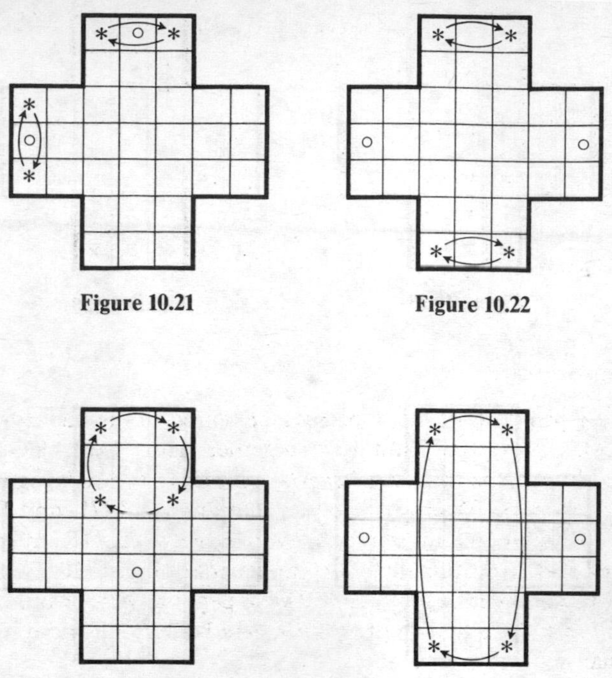

Figure 10.21

Figure 10.22

Figure 10.23

Figure 10.24

Return journeys

In many of our problems with marked men, we have tried to move the marked men as far as possible. The objective in the next few problems is to *return* the marked men to their starting holes. We have already seen single-move return journeys in the loops of Chapter 9, but in the problems given here it is required that the marked man make at least two separate moves. In Figure 10.25, for example, it must make the two moves *d*1- . . . -*d*5 and *d*5- . . . -*d*1, and in Figures 10.27 and 10.28 it must make three moves (*d*2-*d*4-*f*4, *f*4-*d*4-*b*4, and *b*4-*d*4-*d*2 in Figure 10.27).

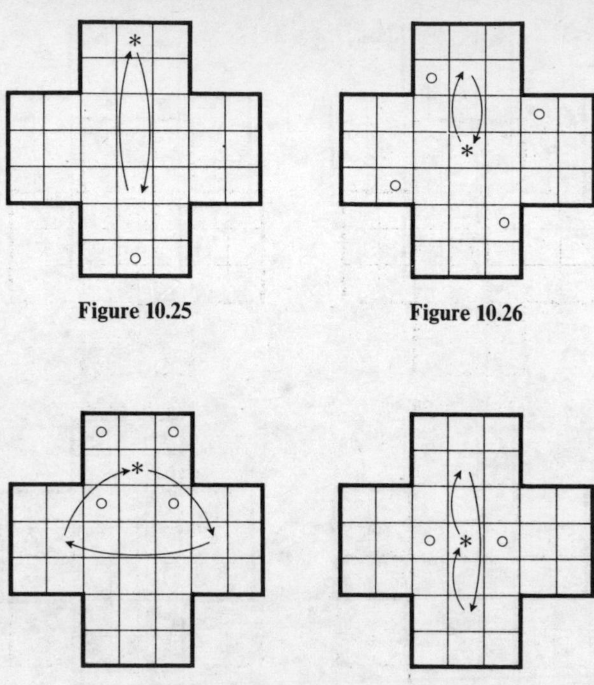

Figure 10.25

Figure 10.26

Figure 10.27

Figure 10.28

Multiple-cross complement problems

As we have seen, any problem can be spiced by nominating in advance the men that are to finish in the specified holes. In the *multiple-cross complement problems*, the nominated men are the men that start in the diametrically opposite holes. We have already seen one such problem in 'Triple cross' (Figure 1.15). 'Triple cross' was soluble as a man-on-the-watch problem, the marked men remaining motionless until the last few moves. Not many multiple-cross complement problems are soluble under this condition, but many are soluble under the less onerous but still attractive condition that each marked man make one move only. Each of the problems in Figures 10.29 to 10.40 has such a solution.

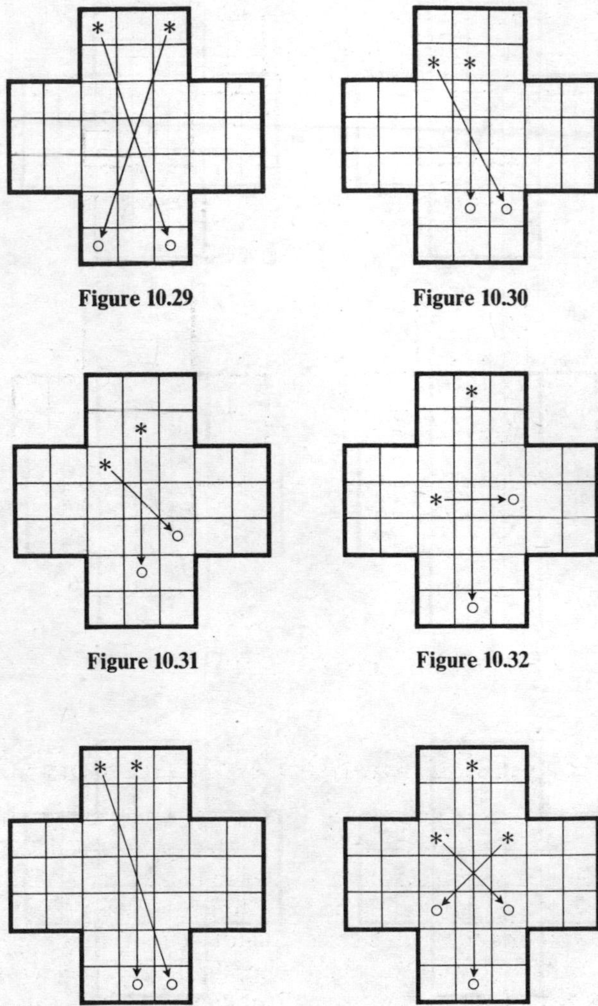

Figure 10.29

Figure 10.30

Figure 10.31

Figure 10.32

Figure 10.33

Figure 10.34

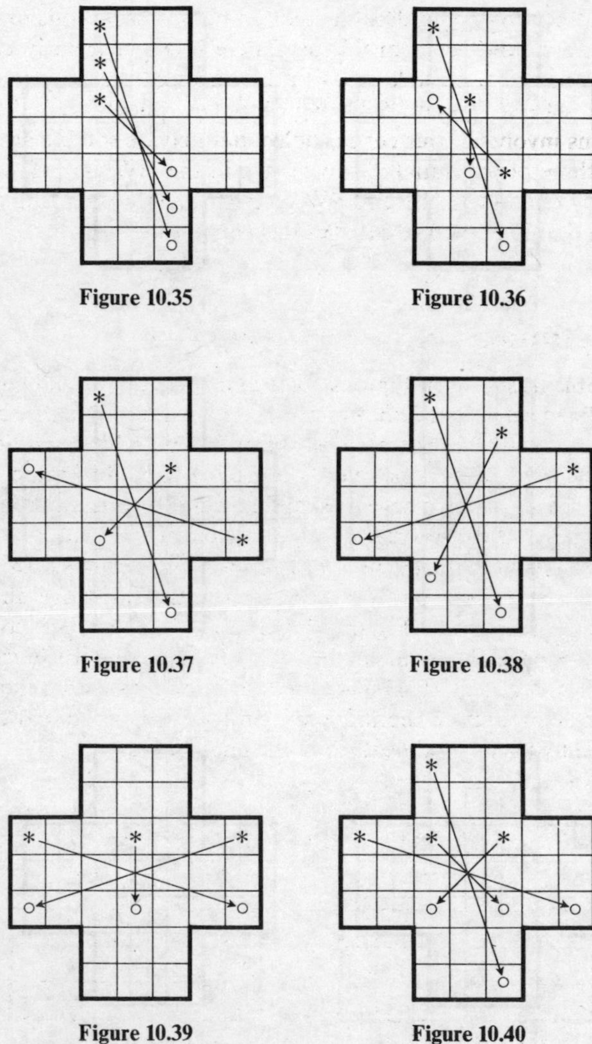

Figure 10.35

Figure 10.36

Figure 10.37

Figure 10.38

Figure 10.39

Figure 10.40

No quintuple-cross or higher-cross complement problem is soluble, and only a few of the quadruple-cross complement problems are. The simplest method of proof is by Conway's balance sheet, which also throws considerable light on possible solutions to triple-cross and double-cross problems. There is a particularly elegant analysis of the quadruple-cross problems using the fully modified balance sheet of Figure 6.33, which shows quickly that the only problems involving four corner holes that may be soluble are those where three of the initial vacancies are in the NW and SE corners and only one in the NE and SW corners (or vice versa). It will be noticed that Figure 10.40 satisfies this condition.

Miscellanea

The problems shown in Figures 10.41 and 10.42 do not fall into any well-defined category but both have taken my fancy. Neither can be solved as a 'man-on-the-watch' problem, but both have solutions in which the marked men make only one move each. In Figure 10.42, the last move can be a seven-sweep, which is surprising in view of the normally obstructive nature of marked men in *d*3 and *c*4.

Figures 10.43 to 10.46 show 'traffic crossing' problems, in which we include the condition that the marked men must travel through the intersection point. Figures 10.43 and 10.44 can be solved as 'man-on-the-watch' problems but Figures 10.45 and 10.46 cannot. The fact that Figure 10.43 has such a solution means that the alternative destinations of the marked men (*c*1 to *a*3, *c*5 to *e*3) can be achieved by trivial modification of the final moves.

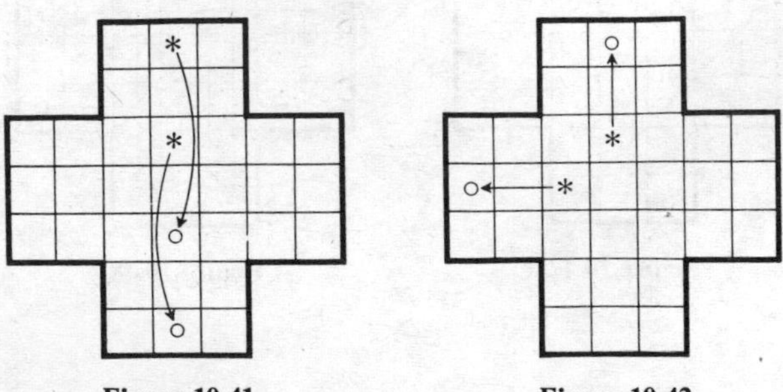

Figure 10.41 Figure 10.42

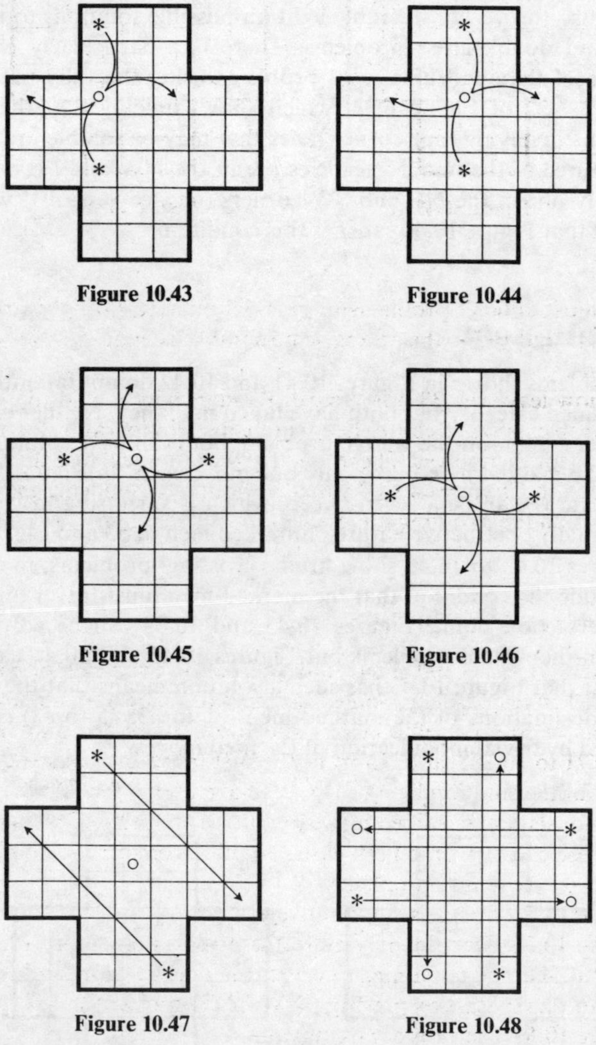

Figure 10.43

Figure 10.44

Figure 10.45

Figure 10.46

Figure 10.47

Figure 10.48

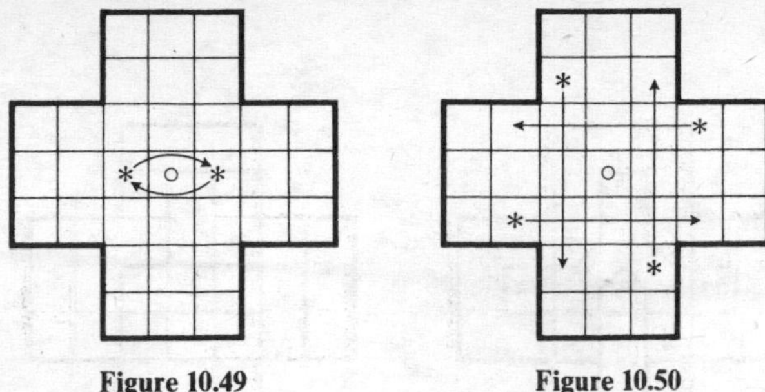

Figure 10.49 **Figure 10.50**

The most difficult problems in the final quartet, fittingly, are Figures 10.49 and 10.50, the others being soluble as 'man-on-the-watch' problems.

We now leave the 33-hole board. Readers who would like to try more problems on it can either search the Bibliography or invent problems for themselves. Those who try the latter will find the theory developed in Chapters 4 to 7 valuable both in diagnosing insoluble problems and in avoiding blind alleys in soluble ones.

Solutions to Chapter 10

Figures 10.51 to 10.100 show solutions to the problems of Figures 10.1 to 10.50 respectively. Some are rather intricate and a board and men may be found useful. Unless stated otherwise, the play in Figures 10.71 to 10.100 stops short of the first move by a marked man, the rest of the solution being easy. We have used a few block moves and removals not described hitherto, but all are in the Glossary and in any case can be worked out easily enough from first principles.

Notes on particular problems:

Figure 10.51: Step 1 is a Y-removal.

Figure 10.56: Start by playing to the position of Figure 10.1 (see Figure 10.51). The remaining moves form a merry-go-round.

Figure 10.58: Start by playing to 'Wall' (Figure 2.19).

Figure 10.59: Step 1 is a Y-removal.

Figure 10.60: The six-removals feature a 'knight's move' catalyst which is occasionally useful. The catalyst for step 1 is the unlike pair *d*4/*f*3, the play being *d*2–*d*4, *f*3–*d*3, *d*4–*d*2, *e*1–*e*3, *d*1–*d*3–*f*3.

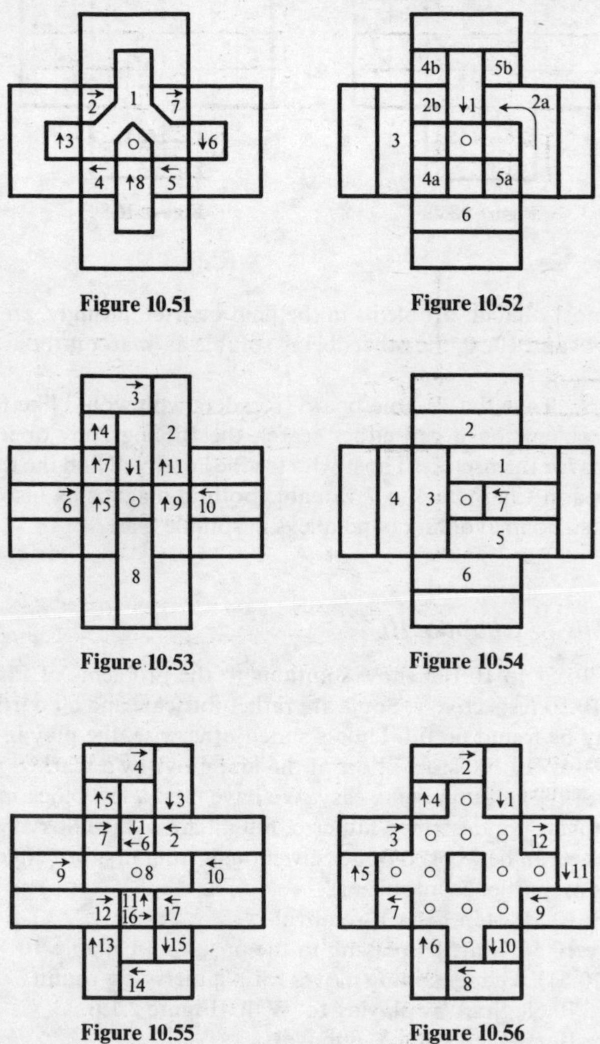

Figure 10.51

Figure 10.52

Figure 10.53

Figure 10.54

Figure 10.55

Figure 10.56

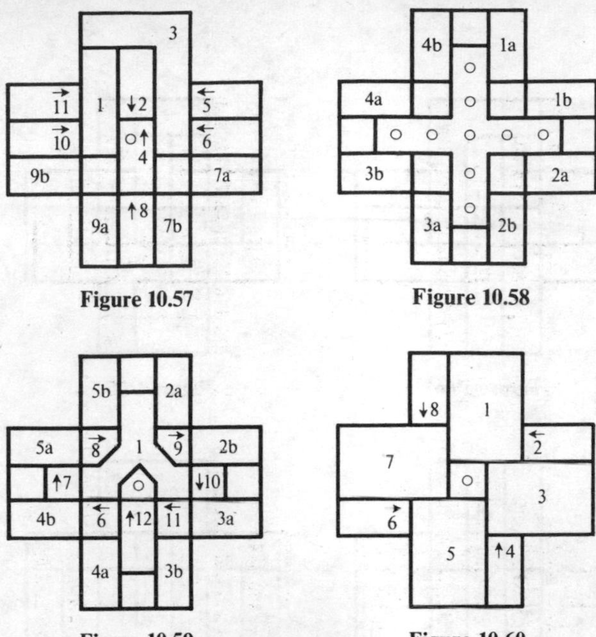

Figure 10.57 **Figure 10.58**

Figure 10.59 **Figure 10.60**

Figure 10.61: The other 24 positions with four-fold rotational symmetry which, with their mirror images, can be reached by play from a central-vacancy start, are shown in Figures 10.101 to 10.124. Many are ancient; Figure 10.114, for example, was given by J. Black in 1871.

Figures 10.62 to 10.70: Solutions also exist with the following initial vacancies:

Figure 10.62	*d*1, *a*4
Figure 10.63	*d*2, *a*5, *g*5
Figure 10.64	*a*3, *g*3
Figure 10.65	*a*5, *g*5
Figure 10.66	*a*5, *g*5
Figure 10.67	*d*2, *a*5, *g*5
Figure 10.68	*a*4, *g*4
Figure 10.69	*d*2, *a*5, *g*5
Figure 10.70	*a*4, *g*4

Step 7*a*/7*b* of Figure 10.69 is an extended L-move, and step 6*a*/6*b* of Figure 10.70 an extended call and answer.

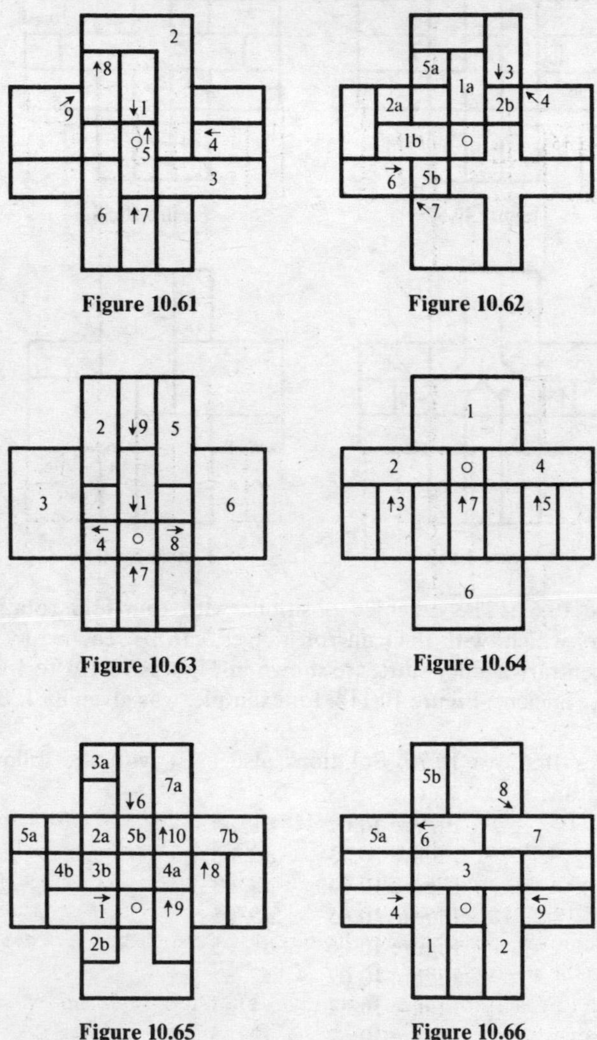

Figure 10.61

Figure 10.62

Figure 10.63

Figure 10.64

Figure 10.65

Figure 10.66

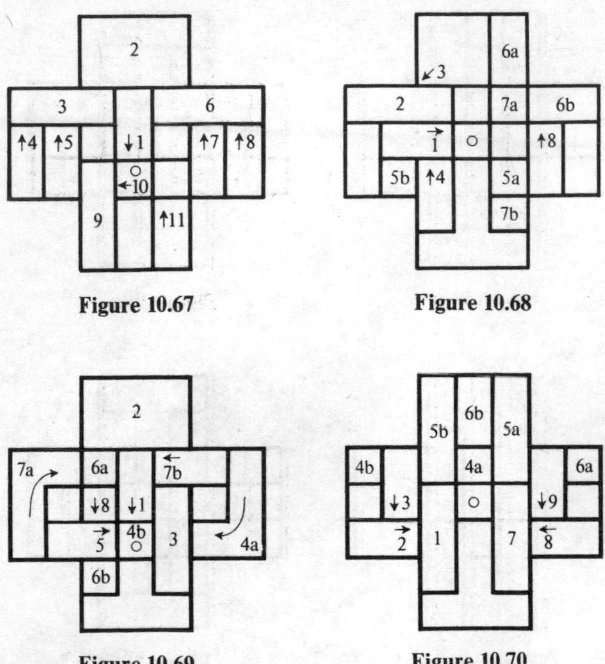

Figure 10.67

Figure 10.68

Figure 10.69

Figure 10.70

Figure 10.73: Step 3*a*/3*b* consists of a six-removal and a three-removal combined in the same way as the two three-removals of a double-three: the opening move of the six-removal (*e*4–*e*6) provides a catalyst for the three-removal (*c*4/*e*4 unlike), so we can break off the six-removal, perform the three-removal, and then resume and complete the six-removal.

Figure 10.75: Step 6 is a Y-removal and step 7*a*/7*b* an extended call and answer.

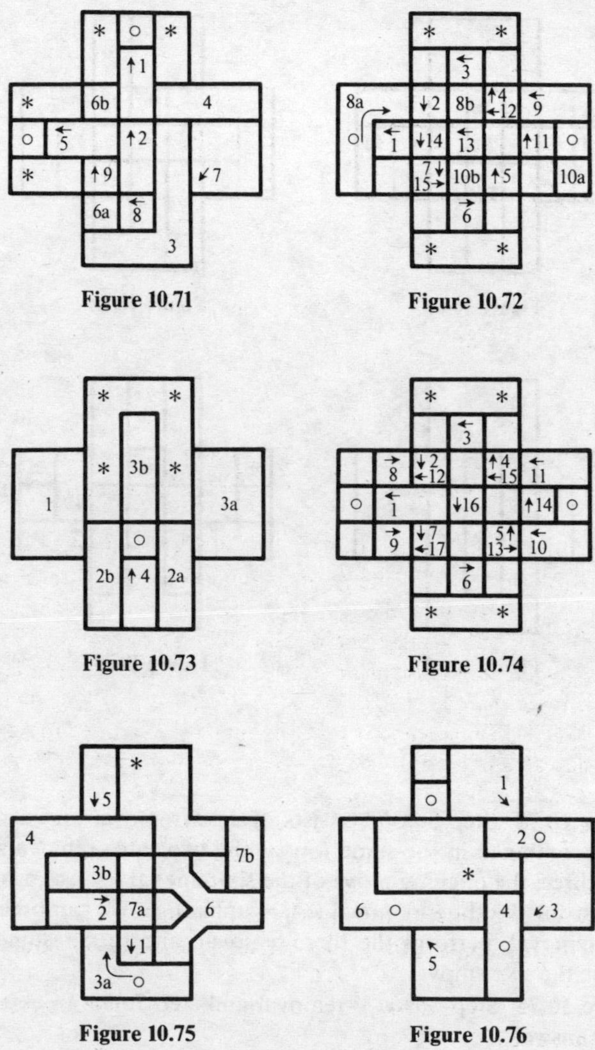

Figure 10.71

Figure 10.72

Figure 10.73

Figure 10.74

Figure 10.75

Figure 10.76

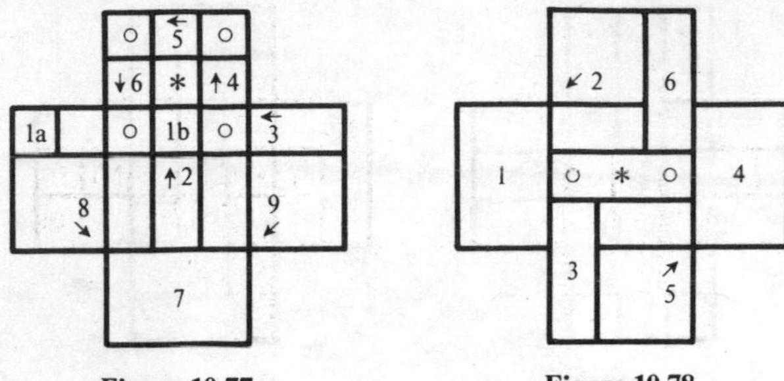

Figure 10.77 **Figure 10.78**

Figure 10.80: Step *2a*/*2b* is a combined L-removal and six-removal, the first move of the former creating a catalyst for the latter.

Figure 10.81: The point of this problem is that the man initially at *c*3 must travel via *d*7. The given play leaves a position in which he can go home by *c*3–*c*5–*c*7–*e*7–*e*5, and the rest is easy.

Figure 10.82: Step 4 takes the man at *c*4 home.

Figure 10.83: Step 6*a*/6*b* is an 'i-move', which is a straight version of the L-move.

Figure 10.84: Steps 3 and 4 take the man at *c*3 home, and steps 7 and 8 that at *e*3. Step 10 is a six-removal with a knight's-move catalyst (*e*2/*d*4 unlike).

Figure 10.86: Step 4 takes the man at *d*3 home.

Figure 10.87: Steps 5 and 6 take the man at *e*3 home.

Figure 10.88: Steps 5 to 8 take the man at *c*1 home. Step 10*a*/10*b* is a 'doubly extended call and answer' (*a*4–*c*4–*c*2, *e*1–*c*1–*c*3).

Figure 10.89: Steps 4 to 7 take the man at *a*3 home, and step 9 that at *d*3.

Figure 10.90: Steps 4 to 7 take the man at *a*3 home, and steps 9 and 10 that at *e*3.

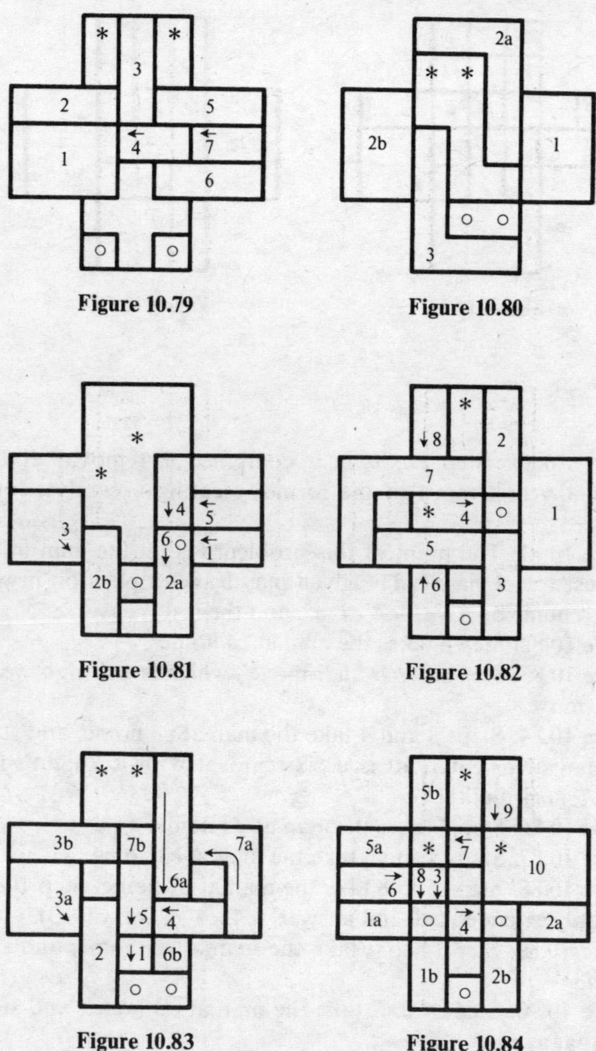

Figure 10.79

Figure 10.80

Figure 10.81

Figure 10.82

Figure 10.83

Figure 10.84

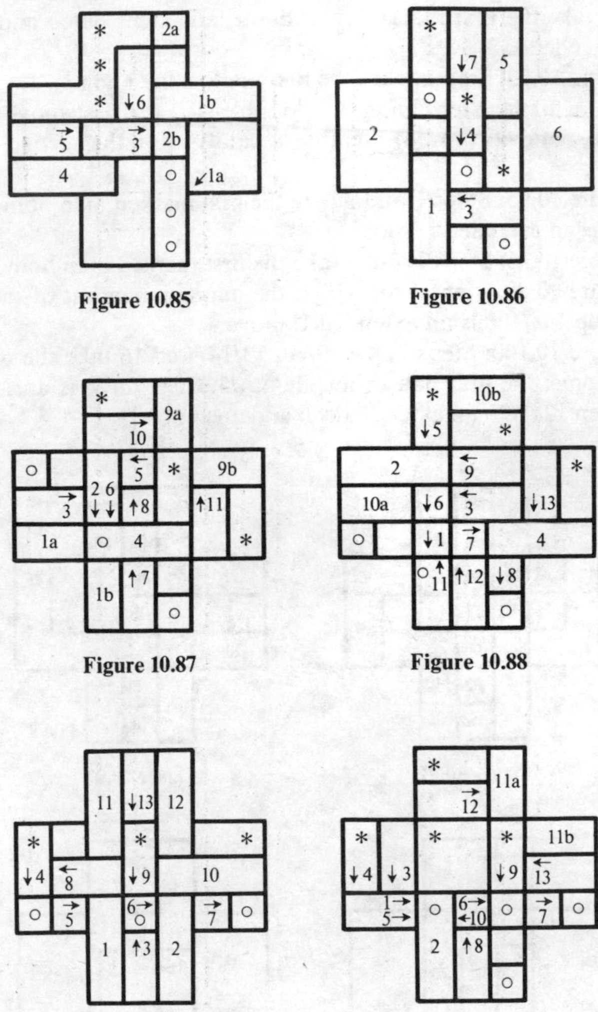

Figure 10.85

Figure 10.86

Figure 10.87

Figure 10.88

Figure 10.89

Figure 10.90

Figure 10.91: The point about this problem is that only one vertical move may be made across the centre (proof by Conway's balance sheet); the other marked man must go round the side. Steps 1 and 2 take the first marked man home, and steps 6*a*/6*b* and 9*a*/9*b* are extended L-moves.

Figure 10.92: Step 1 takes the first marked man home.

Figure 10.94: Step 5*a*/5*b* is a 'double-six', the first move of the first six-removal (*a*4–*c*4) creating a catalyst for the second (*c*4/*c*5 unlike).

Figure 10.95: Steps 1 and 3 take the first marked man home. Step 8*a*/8*b* is an extended L-move.

Figure 10.96: Steps 1 and 5 take the first marked man home.

Figure 10.99: Steps 5 and 7 get the marked men out of the way, and step 10*a*/10*b* is an extended L-move.

Figure 10.100: Steps 2, 4/5, 9/10, 13/14, and 16 take the marked men home; the first pauses awhile at *d*3. Step 7*a*/7*b* is an i-move, and step 12*a*/12*b* an extended call and answer.

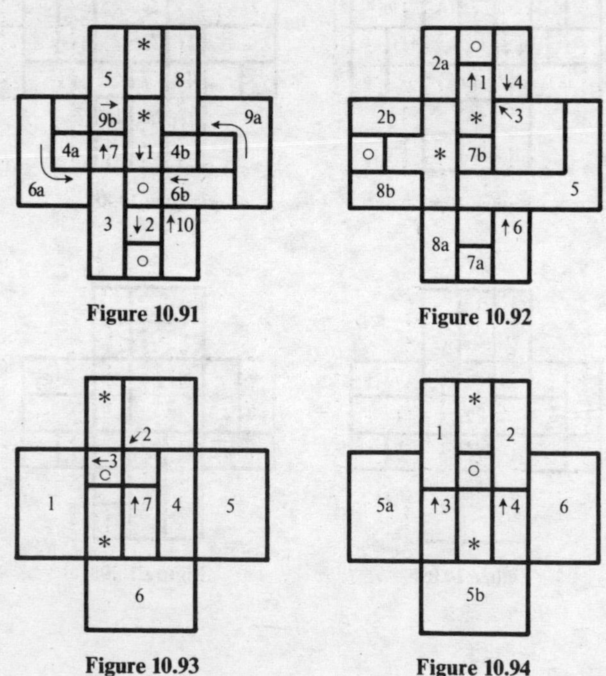

Figure 10.91

Figure 10.92

Figure 10.93

Figure 10.94

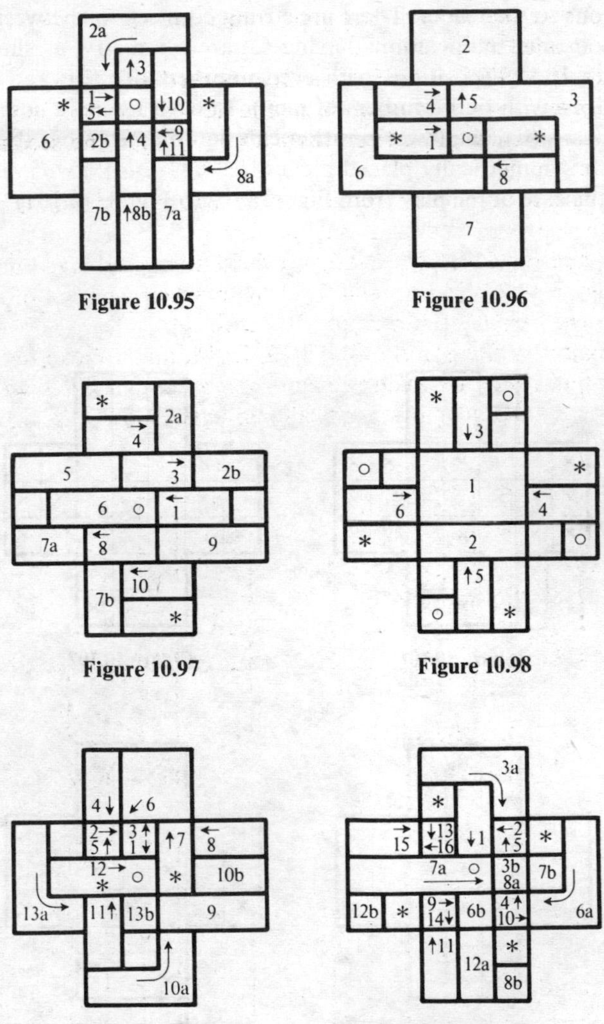

Figure 10.95

Figure 10.96

Figure 10.97

Figure 10.98

Figure 10.99

Figure 10.100

As stated in the note to Figure 10.61, the other positions with four-fold rotational symmetry which can be reached from a central-vacancy start are shown in Figures 10.101 to 10.124. We leave the solutions to the reader. There are strong connections between these positions and the positions having square symmetry, as shown by Figures 10.125 (positions with even numbers of men) and 10.126 (positions with odd numbers of men). In each figure, a connecting line means that the lower position can be obtained from the upper by four symmetrically placed moves (*b*3–*d*3, *e*2–*e*4, *f*5–*d*5, and *c*6–*c*4 in the case of the play from Figure 2.19 to Figure 10.101).

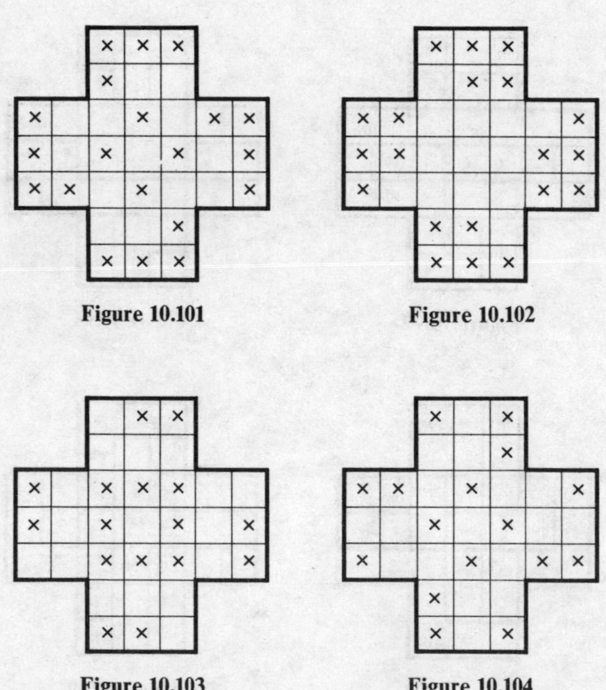

Figure 10.101

Figure 10.102

Figure 10.103

Figure 10.104

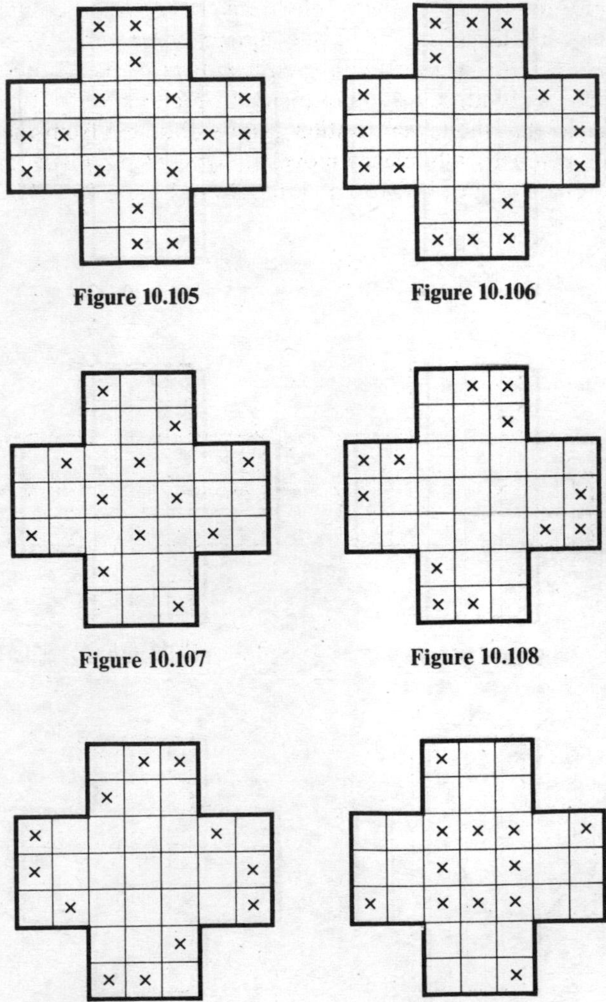

Figure 10.105

Figure 10.106

Figure 10.107

Figure 10.108

Figure 10.109

Figure 10.110

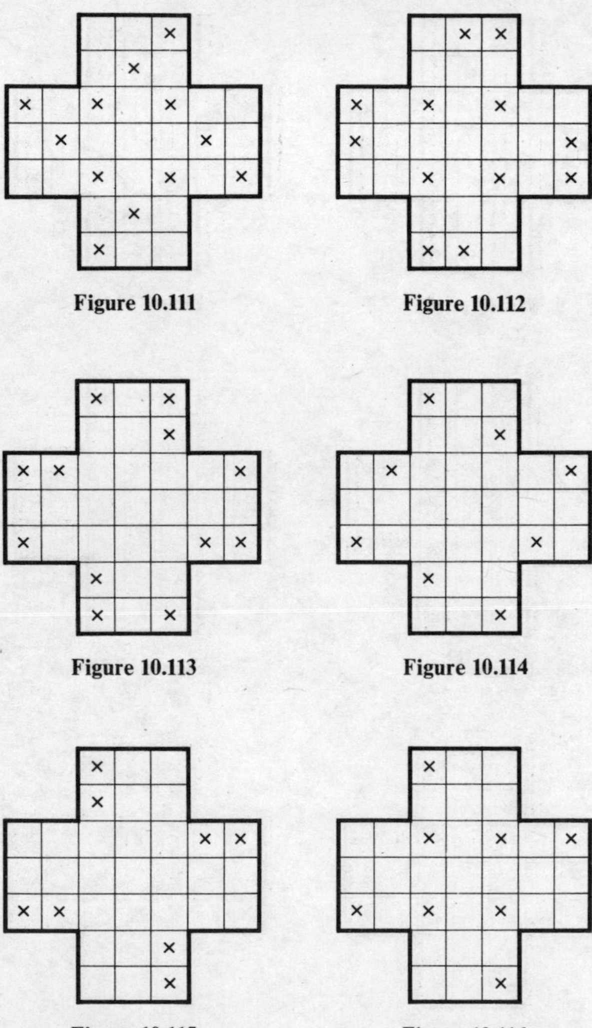

Figure 10.111

Figure 10.112

Figure 10.113

Figure 10.114

Figure 10.115

Figure 10.116

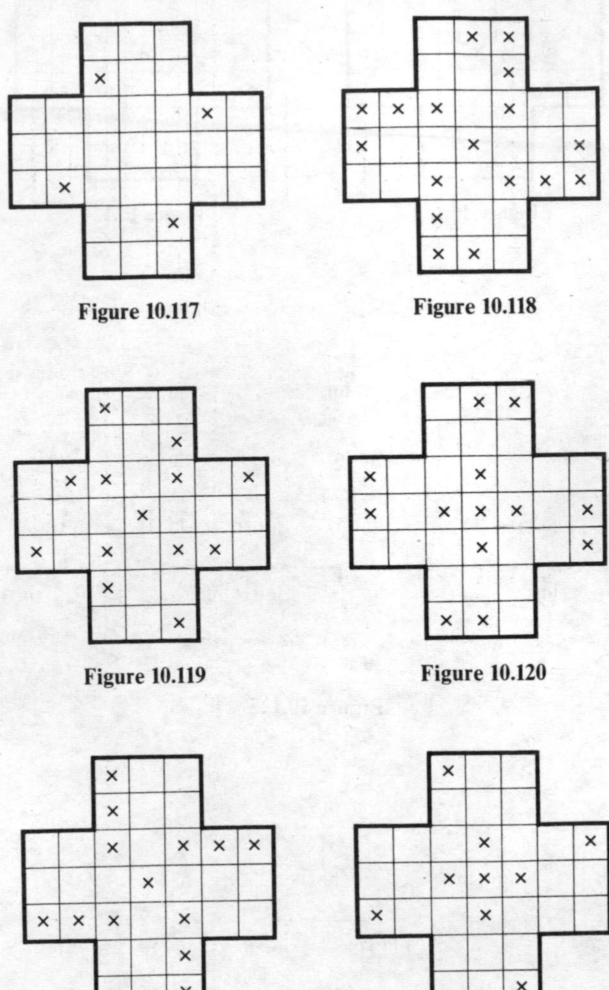

Figure 10.117

Figure 10.118

Figure 10.119

Figure 10.120

Figure 10.121

Figure 10.122

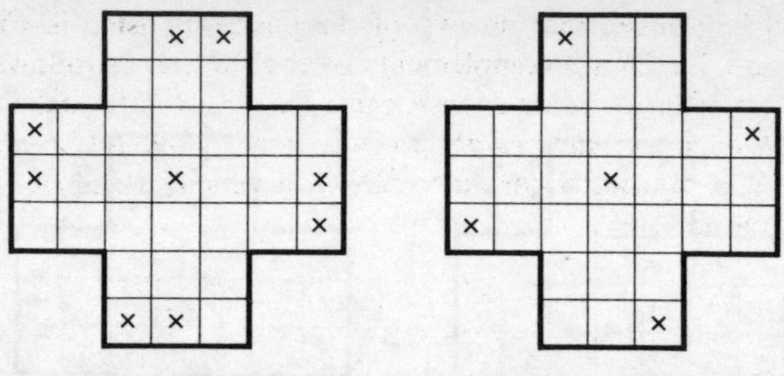

Figure 10.123 **Figure 10.124**

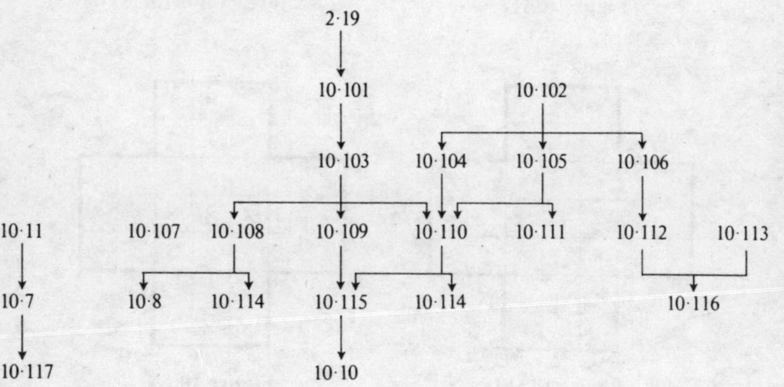

Figure 10.125

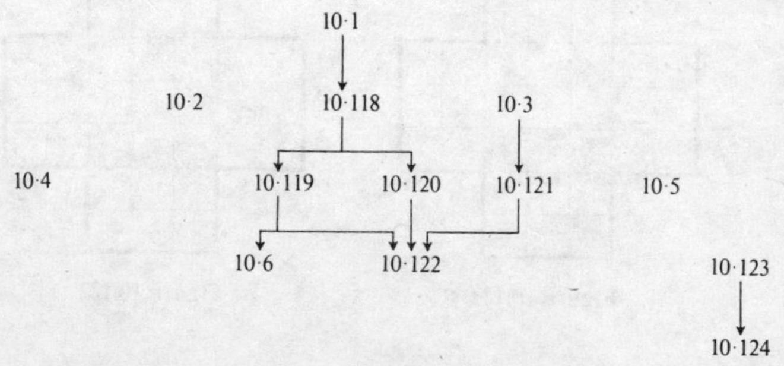

Figure 10.126

It will be noticed that no two of the positions listed in Figures 10.125 and 10.126 are complements of each other. It follows that *there is no solution to the central game on the 33-hole board which passes through an intermediate position having four-fold rotational symmetry*, a pleasantly curious result with which to end our study of this board.

11

GENERAL SQUARE LATTICE BOARDS

We now leave the standard 33-hole board. In this chapter we establish some general results concerning boards whose holes are arranged in square lattices, and look at some boards of particular historical importance.

Rectangular and square symmetry

We start with a few definitions. We define a board to be a *square lattice board* if its holes are arranged in a square lattice, each hole having four neighbours unless the board edge intervenes. *Note that the term refers to the arrangement of the holes* and not to the overall shape of the board. The standard 33-hole board is a square lattice board, as are most of the boards that we shall consider in this book, so we shall continue to use the simple term 'board' to mean a square lattice board unless it is qualified otherwise.

We define a board to be *gapless* if it has the property that if it has holes at any two points in the same row or column of the lattice then it has holes at all the intervening points. The standard 33-hole board is a gapless board, but the boards of Figures 11.1 and 11.2 are not. The concept of 'gaplessness' is not of great importance, but it excludes some pathological boards and enables us to state some general results more simply.

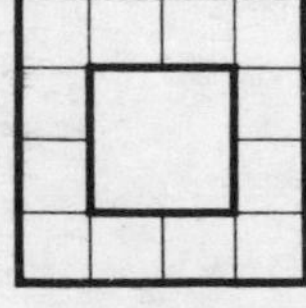

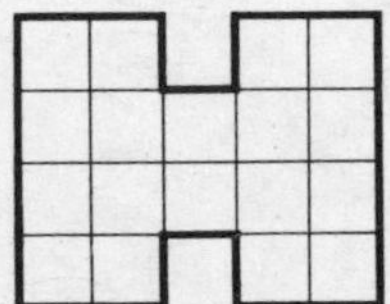

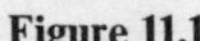

Figure 11.1

Figure 11.2

We define a board to have *rectangular symmetry* if it is transformed into itself by reflection about a horizontal or vertical axis, and to have *square symmetry* if it has rectangular symmetry and is also transformed into itself by reflection about a diagonal axis. The standard 33-hole board and the board of Figure 11.1 have square symmetry; that of Figure 11.2 has rectangular symmetry only.

We call a board with rectangular symmetry *odd–odd* if it has an odd number of holes in each direction, *even–even* if it has an even number of holes in each direction, and *odd–even* if it has an odd number of holes in one direction and an even number in the other. The standard 33-hole board is odd–odd, that of Figure 11.1 even–even, and that of Figure 11.2 odd–even.

We define a draughtsboard to be a board obtained by marking the alternate holes of a square board (Figure 11.3), turning them through 45 degrees, and using them to form a new board (Figure 11.4). Draughtsboards may be odd–odd (Figure 11.4), even–even (Figure 11.5), or odd–even (Figure 11.6). An odd–odd draughtsboard with axis of length n contains $(n^2+1)/2$ holes; an even–even draughtsboard with axis of length n contains $(n^2+2n)/2$ holes; an odd–even draughtsboard with even axis of length n contains $n^2/2$ holes.

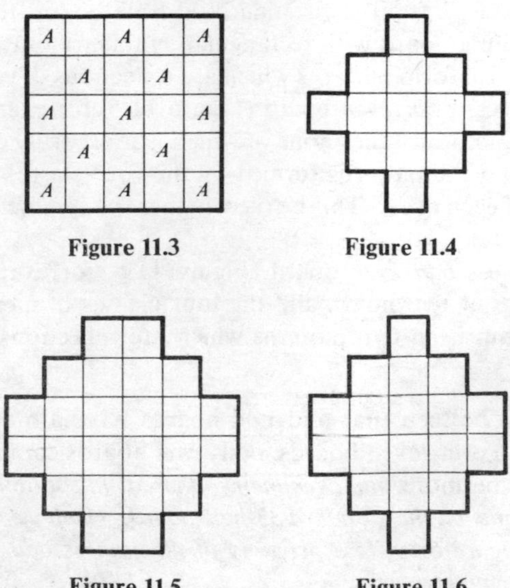

Figure 11.3

Figure 11.4

Figure 11.5

Figure 11.6

Classification of men

The general theory which we developed in previous chapters applies to all boards, though there are differences of detail which we now explore.

We saw in Chapter 2 that the men on a standard board can be divided into four classes according to the holes which they can occupy. This property is shared by all *gapless* boards with rectangular or square symmetry provided that they have at least two holes in each direction. (Clearly a 1×1 board has only one class and a $1 \times n$ board only two classes.) The classes may be characterised as follows:

(a) A gapless *odd–odd* board (Figure 11.4, for example) has a central hole, and its classes comprise men which can reach the central hole, men which can jump vertically over it, men which can jump horizontally over it, and men which can neither reach it nor jump over it. In Figure 11.4, and in other boards with square symmetry, these classes form three distinct patterns. In boards with rectangular but not square symmetry, they form four distinct patterns, unless the two classes of men which can jump over the centre form patterns which are reflections of each other. (If we remove the corner holes *c*1, *e*1, *c*7, and *e*7 from the standard 33-hole board, for example, then we obtain a board with rectangular symmetry only, but the 's' and 't' holes still form patterns which are reflections of each other.)

(b) A gapless *even–even* board (Figure 11.5, for example) has a central group of four holes none of which is more truly central than any other, and the patterns formed by the four classes of men are reflections of each other. This is true whether the symmetry is square or merely rectangular.

(c) A gapless *odd–even* board (Figure 11.6, for example) has a central group of two holes, and the four classes of men form two sets each comprising two patterns which are reflections one of the other.

It can thus be seen that odd–odd boards have a more complex structure than even–even boards, odd–even boards coming between the two. Furthermore, *the asymmetry inherent in solutions of complement problems on the standard 33-hole board, which we described in relation to Figure 6.10, is a property of all gapless odd–odd boards with square symmetry.*

Null-class boards

An important result, easily overlooked by a player leaving the 33-hole board for the first time, is that *not every board is a null-class board as defined in Chapter 4*. The easiest way of determining whether a particular board is indeed a null-class board is to try to obtain the empty position from the full position by the transformations of Suremain de Missery, since this is possible on and only on such a board. Suremain de Missery gives general results for boards of many shapes; we content ourselves with the simplest.

(a) A *square* board is a null-class board if and only if the length of its sides is a multiple of 3. The smallest null-class square board is therefore the 3×3 board, but this board is not of great interest and no single-vacancy complement problem on it is soluble. The next null-class square board is the 6×6 board, which we shall consider later in this chapter.

(b) A *rectangular* board is a null-class board if and only if the length of at least one of its sides is a multiple of 3. The smallest such board of any interest is the 4×3 board, since the 1×3 board is trivial and no single-vacancy complement problem on the 2×3 and 3×3 boards is soluble. The soluble single-vacancy complement problems on the 4×3, 5×3 and 6×3 boards are shown in Figures 11.7 to 11.9 respectively, V indicating the possible places for the initial vacancy.

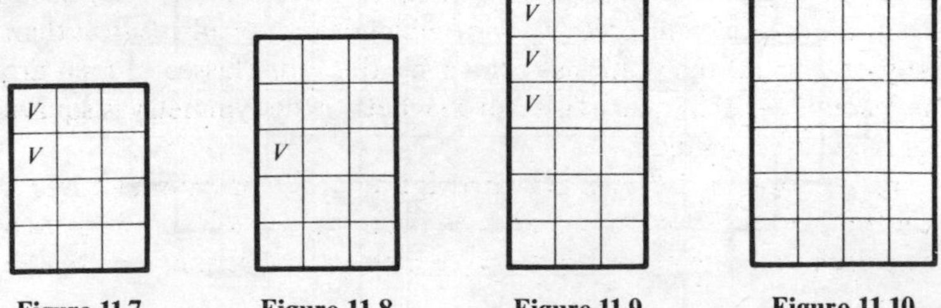

Figure 11.7 Figure 11.8 Figure 11.9 Figure 11.10

(In these and similar figures, we show only positions which are essentially different. It follows from Figure 11.9, for example, that the initial vacancy on a 6×3 board can be any hole along a long side, since each such hole is equivalent to one of the marked holes.) The $n \times 3$ boards with $n > 6$ satisfy the same rule as the 6×3 board, a single-vacancy complement problem being soluble if and only if the initial vacancy is a hole along one of the long sides. The smallest rectangular board on which *all* single-vacancy complement problems are soluble is the 6×4 board shown in Figure 11.10.

(c) An *odd–odd draughtsboard* is a null-class board if and only if the length of its axis is of the form $12n+5$ or $12n+7$. The smallest null-class odd–odd draughtsboard is therefore the 13-hole board that was shown in Figure 11.4, but it is easily seen that no complement problem on this board is soluble. The next null-class odd–odd draughtsboard is the 25-hole board that was shown in Figure 4.5, but we showed in Chapter 5 that no complement problem is soluble on this board either. The smallest odd–odd draughtsboard on which a complement problem is actually soluble is the 145-hole board shown in Figure 11.11, and it may be verified that all the single-vacancy complement problems on this board are indeed soluble.

Figure 11.11

(d) An *even–even draughtsboard* is a null-class board if and only if the length of its axis is of the form $12n$ or $12n+10$. The smallest null-class even–even draughtsboard is therefore the 60-hole board shown in Figure 11.12, and it may be verified that all the single-vacancy complement problems on this board are indeed soluble.

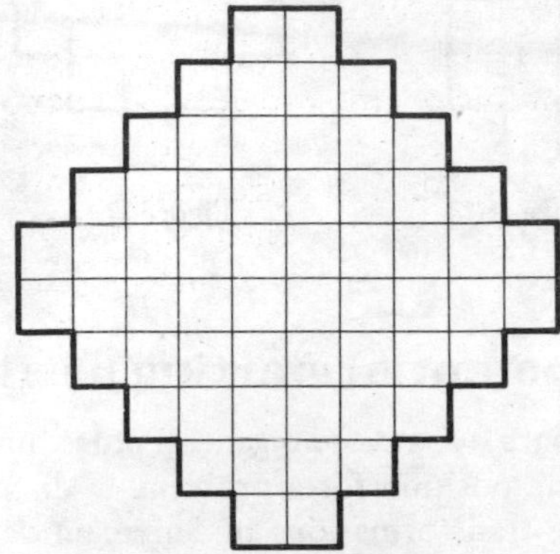

Figure 11.12

(e) An *odd–even draughtsboard* is a null-class board if and only if the length of its even axis is of the form $12n$, $12n+4$, $12n+6$, or $12n+8$. The smallest null-class odd–even draughtsboard is therefore the 8-hole board shown in Figure 11.13, but no single-vacancy complement problem is soluble on this board. The next smallest null-class odd–even draughtsboard is the 18-hole board that was shown in Figure 11.6, on which some but not all single-vacancy complement problems are soluble; the reader may enjoy determining which. The smallest odd–even draughtsboard on which all the single-vacancy complement problems are soluble is the 32-hole board shown in Figure 11.14.

A board with rectangular symmetry which is not a null-class board can be converted into a null-class board by removing its centre (one hole in the case of an odd–odd board, two in the case of an odd–even, and four in the case of an even–even). We call a board with such a piece removed an *annular* board. Such a board is not a gapless board, however; in particular, the asymmetry which we discussed in relation to Figure 6.10, and which adds to the complexity of play on gapless odd–odd boards, does not apply to annular boards.

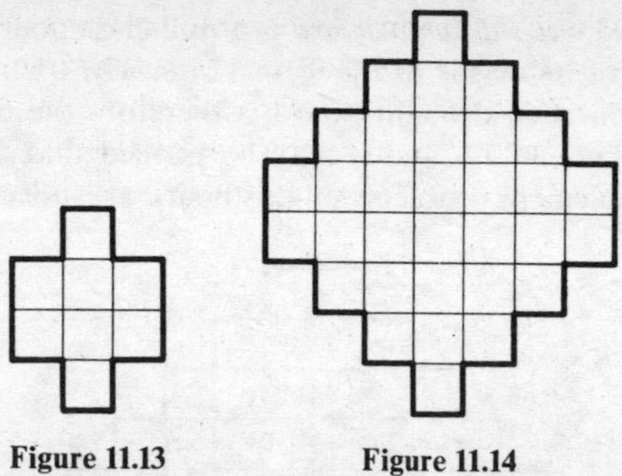

Figure 11.13 Figure 11.14

Obtaining potential starting positions

On the 33-hole board, we gave two general procedures for obtaining a potential starting position for a problem: a 'direct' procedure in which we use the transformations of Suremain de Missery to go directly from the target position to a position with only one or two vacancies, and a 'complementary' procedure in which we use them to go to a position with only one or two occupied holes and then complement this position. The direct procedure is valid on any board, but *the complementary procedure is valid only on a null-class board.*

The complementary procedure is so useful on null-class boards that it is desirable to find a generalisation of it which applies to all boards. Such a generalisation is as follows:

(a) take the target position and add or subtract a position in the same fundamental class as the full position;

(b) use the transformations of Suremain de Missery to obtain a position in the same fundamental class with only one or two occupied holes;

(c) complement the resulting position.

The validity of this generalised complementary procedure can be proved most simply by using the algebra of fundamental classes which we developed in Chapter 4. (It can also be proved without great difficulty from first principles, so readers who skipped the algebra have not missed anything vital, but the algebraic proof is more elegant.) If T is the given target position, F the full position, and F' the position in the same fundamental class as the full position, then step (a) produces a position A whose fundamental class $\kappa(A)$ equals $\kappa(T)+\kappa(F')$, step (b) a position B whose fundamental class $\kappa(B)$ equals $\kappa(A)$, and step (c) a position C whose fundamental class $\kappa(C)$ equals $\kappa(B)+\kappa(F)$ by the complementary class theorem. Hence

$$\begin{aligned}\kappa(C) &= \kappa(B)+\kappa(F)\\ &= \kappa(A)+\kappa(F)\\ &= \kappa(T)+\kappa(F')+\kappa(F)\\ &= \kappa(T)\end{aligned}$$

since F' was chosen so that $\kappa(F')=\kappa(F)$ and $\kappa(F)+\kappa(F)=0$.

The simplified complementary procedure for a null-class board is a special case of this generalised procedure, since on such a board the empty position is in the same fundamental class as the full position and the use of this position in step (a) reduces it to a nullity.

The classical 37-hole board provides a convenient example of this procedure. Suppose that we wish to finish with a man in hole *d*5 (T in Figure 11.15). The full position of this board is in the same fundamental class as the position with only the centre occupied (F' in Figure 11.15), so step (a) gives a position with *d*4 and *d*5 occupied. Step (b) now gives a single-man position whose occupied hole is either *d*3 or one of the holes a multiple of three rows and columns away from it (V in Figure 11.15), and step (c) gives a position in which one of these holes is the only vacancy. Hence the only single-vacancy positions from which play to a single man in *d*5 may be possible are *a*3, *d*3, *g*3 and *d*6. This gives three essentially different starting positions, since *g*3 is symmetrically equivalent to *a*3, and it may be verified that each of the resulting problems is indeed soluble.

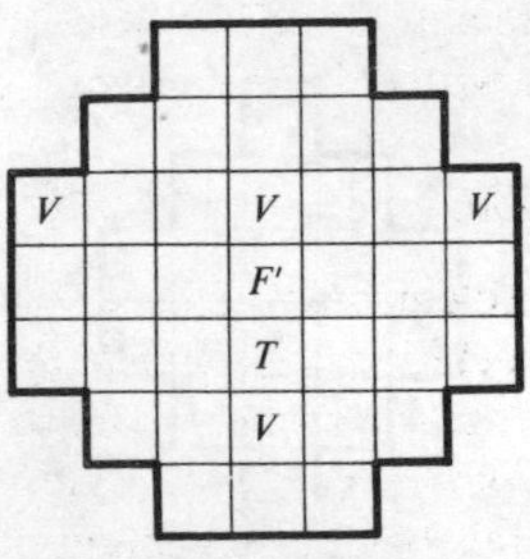

Figure 11.15

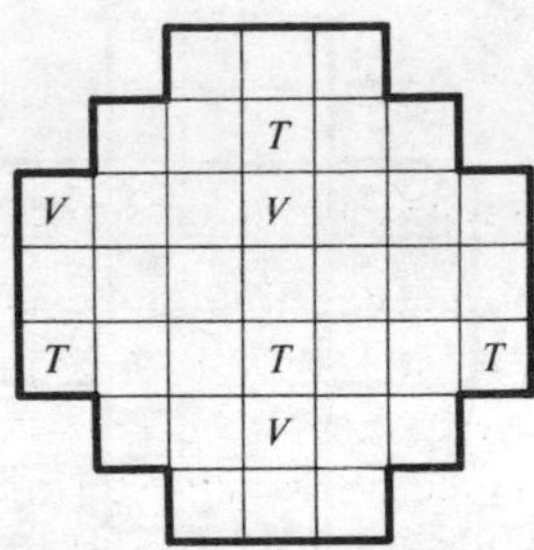

Figure 11.16

By repeating this procedure for each target hole in turn, it can be shown that there are only ten different single-vacancy to single-survivor problems on this board that may be soluble. These are shown in Figure 11.16, *V* indicating the possible initial vacancies and *T* the possible target holes. (Figure 11.16 shows three initial vacancies and four target holes, apparently yielding twelve different combinations, but if the initial vacancy is at *d*3 or *d*6 then the target holes *a*5 and *g*5 are equivalent.) Each of these ten problems is indeed soluble.

Resource and parity counts

The general theory which we derived in Chapters 4 to 7 applies to all boards, though the resource and parity counts which are useful in practice vary from board to board. The resource count of Figure 5.1, for example, can be thought of as a development of the alternate-column Fibonacci count of Figure 11.17. The count of Figure 11.17 can be applied to any board, but it is the addition of values in columns *a* and *g* to allow for the effect of the adjacent edges that makes Figure 5.1 so powerful on the 33-hole board.

The most usual way of allowing for the effect of the board edge is to assign a negative value to an outside corner which is initially occupied. We cannot always do this, however. Figure 11.18 shows a resource count which is useful in identifying insoluble problems on the 18-hole board of Figure 11.6, and it will be noticed that the negative value at *b*5 is not balanced by a negative value at *b*2; indeed the value at *b*2 is as positive as that at *b*5 is negative. This property always holds when outside corners are separated by two other holes, as is easily proved. (Let *P*, *Q*, *R*, *S* be the values of four adjacent

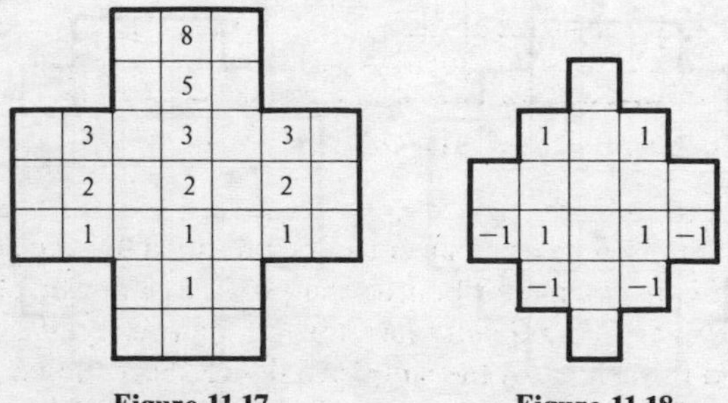

Figure 11.17 **Figure 11.18**

holes in line; then $P+Q\geqslant R$ and $S+R\geqslant Q$ together imply $P+Q+R+S\geqslant Q+R$, whence $P+S\geqslant 0$.)

Conway's balance sheet (Figure 6.15) is particularly dependent on the geometry of the 33-hole board and cannot be applied without change to boards of substantially different pattern. The simplest effective generalisation of it is based on the fully modified balance sheet of Figure 6.33 and is shown in Figure 11.19. The primitives of this generalised balance sheet are (a), $(a+\alpha)$, (b), $(b+\beta)$, $(c+\alpha)$, and $(c+\beta)$, and it will be noticed that moves across successive *rows* of a holes lose (a) and $(a+\alpha)$ alternately and moves across successive *columns* of b holes lose (b) and $(b+\beta)$ alternately. No term containing a negative a, b or c component can be expressed as a sum of primitives, nor can any of the following:

(α)	$(a+\beta)$	$(b+\alpha)$	(c)
(β)	$(a+\alpha+\beta)$	$(b+\alpha+\beta)$	$(c+\alpha+\beta)$
$(\alpha+\beta)$			

c	$b+\beta$	c	b	c	$b+\beta$	c	b	c
$a+\alpha$		$a+\alpha$		$a+\alpha$		$a+\alpha$		$a+\alpha$
c	$b+\beta$	c	b	c	$b+\beta$	c	b	c
a		a		a		a		a
c	$b+\beta$	c	b	c	$b+\beta$	c	b	c
$a+\alpha$		$a+\alpha$		$a+\alpha$		$a+\alpha$		$a+\alpha$
c	$b+\beta$	c	b	c	$b+\beta$	c	b	c
a		a		a		a		a
c	$b+\beta$	c	b	c	$b+\beta$	c	b	c

Figure 11.19

This generalised balance sheet can be modified to take account of the edges of any particular board, and provides a powerful weapon. Often, however, the difficulty lies not in a deficiency of c but in its parity, and in such cases the simpler balance sheet shown in Figure 11.20 is effective. This balance sheet is obtained from that of Figure

ω	$b+\omega$	ω	b	ω	$b+\omega$	ω	b	ω
$a+\omega$		$a+\omega$		$a+\omega$		$a+\omega$		$a+\omega$
ω	$b+\omega$	ω	b	ω	$b+\omega$	ω	b	ω
a		a		a		a		a
ω	$b+\omega$	ω	b	ω	$b+\omega$	ω	b	ω
$a+\omega$		$a+\omega$		$a+\omega$		$a+\omega$		$a+\omega$
ω	$b+\omega$	ω	b	ω	$b+\omega$	ω	b	ω
a		a		a		a		a
ω	$b+\omega$	ω	b	ω	$b+\omega$	ω	b	ω

Figure 11.20

11.19 by replacing c, α and β by a single component ω. Its primitives are (a), $(a+\omega)$, (b) and $(b+\omega)$, and neither an isolated ω nor a term containing a negative a or b component can be expressed as a sum of these primitives.

Block Play

The three-removal and the call and answer are useful on almost all boards, but there are other block moves which play no significant role on the 33-hole board but are useful elsewhere.

The clearance of sharp corners such as those of odd–odd draughtsboards can often be simplified by the *nine-removal*, the *pointed ten*, and the *eleven-removal*, which are shown in Figures 11.21 to 11.23.

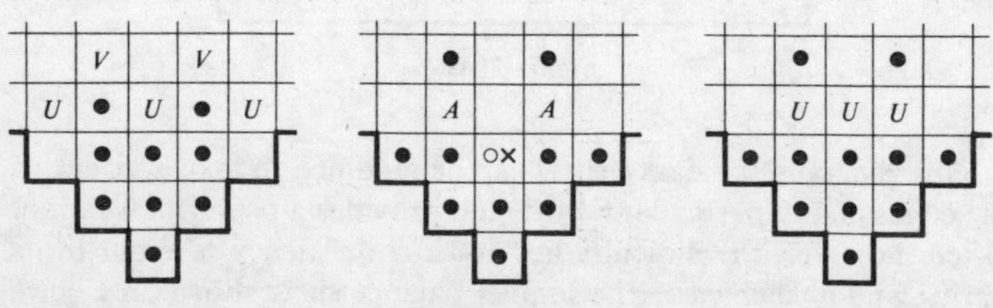

Figure 11.21 **Figure 11.22** **Figure 11.23**

The nine-removal requires either an unlike triple *UUU* or an unlike pair *VV*. The pointed ten and the eleven-removal are closely related; the pointed ten uses the holes *AA*, but can be played irrespective of their initial contents and restores them to their initial state during the play, while the eleven-removal requires an unlike triple *UUU*. The shifted six (Figure 3.55, for example) is also useful for stepping down the sides of draughtsboards and clearing sharp corners. It is sometimes possible to clear the edges of a large odd–odd draughtsboard by using nine-removals for two opposite corners and eleven-removals for the other two, running down the intervening diagonals by three-removals and shifted sixes.

The clearance of blunter corners such as those of even–even draughtsboards can often be simplified by the *tally* and the *anvil*, shown in Figures 11.24 and 11.25. The anvil uses the holes *AA*, but can be played irrespective of their initial contents and restores them to their initial state during the play. The basic principle behind these moves, that of interrupting a sequence of moves in order to perform a call and answer, can frequently be put to good effect.

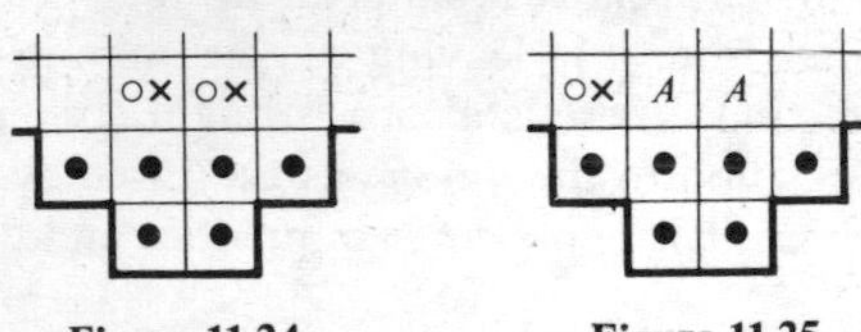

Figure 11.24 Figure 11.25

Even blunter corners such as those of the 37-hole board can sometimes be cleared by the *flat ten* shown in Figure 11.26 and the *seven-plus-one* shown in Figure 11.27. These use the holes *AA* and *A*, but can be played irrespective of their initial contents and restore them to their initial state during the play. The flat ten is very similar to the pointed ten of Figure 11.22 and an eleven-removal can be

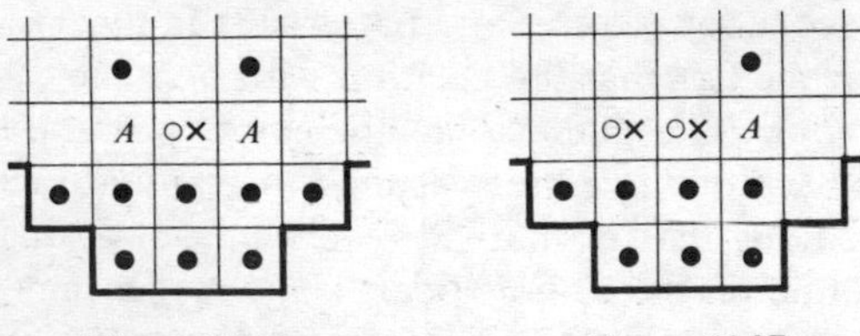

Figure 11.26 Figure 11.27

derived from it in the same way that of Figure 11.23 was derived from the pointed ten, but this eleven-removal is of little practical importance and we do not illustrate it. Further block moves can also be obtained from the seven-plus-one by adding either or both holes marked 'ox' to the region to be cleared.

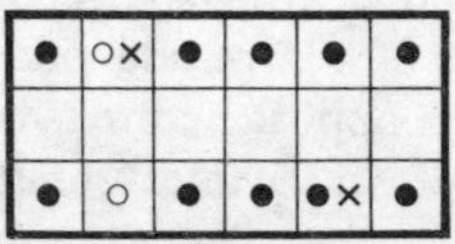

Figure 11.28

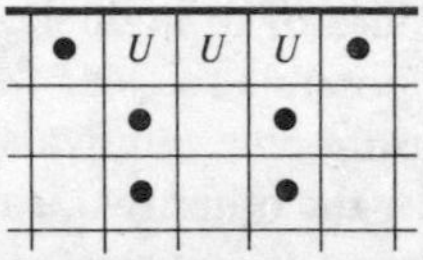

Figure 11.29

The edges of square and rectangular boards can sometimes be cleared by L-moves and six-removals, but these are not sufficient for all problems. Block moves that may help when they are inadequate are the *i-move* (Figure 11.28, top), the *two-five* (Figure 11.28, bottom), and the *double-Y* (Figure 11.29). The double-Y requires an unlike triple *UUU*. The i-move is simply a straightened L-move, and the two-five differs from it in leaving the last man in the fifth hole instead of the second. There is also a 'straight six removal' which bears the same relation to the i-move as the L-removal does to the L-move, but it is of little importance in practice and does not merit illustration.

The 37-hole and 41-hole boards

We now look at some boards of particular historical importance.

The first Solitaire board to be mentioned in print was the 37-hole board. This is not a null-class board, and we have already seen in Figure 11.16 that only ten different single-vacancy to single-survivor problems on it are soluble.

As a partial compensation for this disadvantage, the 37-hole board offers more scope for pictures and patterns than the 33-hole board. In particular, the fact that the position with only the centre vacant is in the same fundamental class as the empty position means that play is possible from a central vacancy to many attractively symmetrical positions that cannot be reached from a single-vacancy starting position on the 33-hole board. The reader may care to try 'Le tricolet' (Figure 11.30) and 'Le lecteur au milieu de ses amis'

(Figure 11.31), both of which come from the *Dictionnaire des jeux mathématiques* of 1799, and also to play to finish with a square of nine men, three different finishing positions being possible though only one is centred on *d*4. Paul Busschop's book *Recherches sur le jeu de solitaire* (1879) includes twenty-three target positions with eight-fold symmetry among its 300 problems, and there are undoubtedly others.

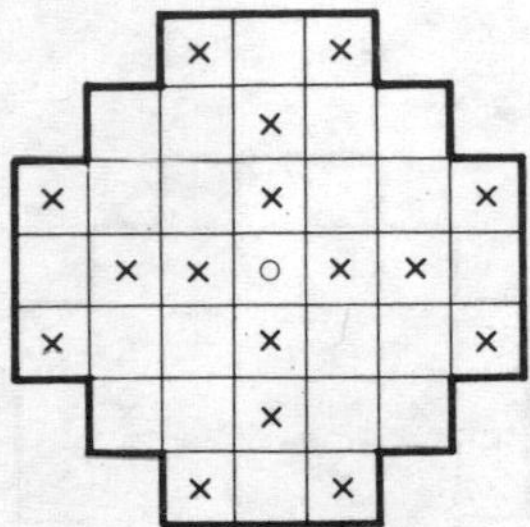

Figure 11.30

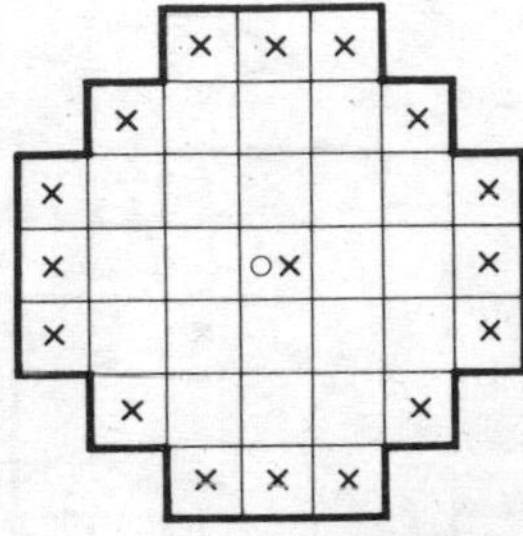

Figure 11.31

None of the writers on the 37-hole board appears to have concerned himself with the number of separate moves needed to solve a problem, and the first attempt to find reasonably short solutions to the single-vacancy single-survivor problems appears to have been made by Leonard Gordon in 1972. Harry Davis subsequently shortened one of Gordon's solutions, and their joint results are summarised in Table 11.1. We know of none shorter.

Table 11.1: Solutions by Gordon and Davis to single-vacancy single-survivor problems in 37-hole Solitaire

Initial vacancy	Final hole	Moves required
*a*3	*d*2, *g*5	21
	*a*5, *d*5	22
*d*3	*a*5, *d*2	21
	*d*5	22
*d*6	*d*2, *a*5	20
	*d*5	21

Little attention has been given to the finding of solutions containing long sweeps. The longest *intermediate* sweep possible in a single-vacancy single-survivor problem is the nine-sweep shown in the well-known problem 'La corsaire' (Figure 11.32), which also comes from the *Dictionnaire des jeux mathématiques*. The longest *final* sweep possible in such a solution is the eight-sweep shown in Figure 11.33, which was surely also discovered in ancient times, though I cannot recall having seen it in print.

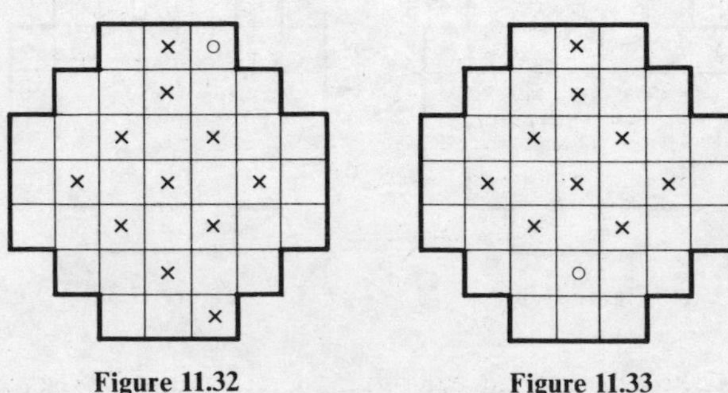

Figure 11.32 **Figure 11.33**

The resolution of difficult problems on the 37-hole board may be simplified by the balance sheet shown in Figure 11.34, which is Conway's balance sheet with the addition of values at *b*2, *f*2, *b*6, and *f*6. It has the extra primitives $(a-b-d+\alpha)$, $(-a+b-d+\beta)$, $(a+b+d+\alpha)$, and $(a+b+d+\beta)$, but these do not reduce the number of inexpressible values; *if a term is inexpressible according to Conway's balance sheet then it is also inexpressible according to the balance sheet of Figure 11.34*. In particular, the terms $(2a+\beta)$, $(2b+\alpha)$, $(2a+2b-c)$, $(4a-c+\alpha+\beta)$ and $(4b-c+\alpha+\beta)$ are all inexpressible according to Figure 11.34. A value expressible in at least one way according to Conway's balance sheet may be expressible in more ways according to Figure 11.34, however; for example, $(2a+\alpha+\beta)$, expressible according to Conway's balance sheet only as $(2a-c+\alpha)+(c+\beta)$, is here expressible also as $(a-b-d+\alpha)$ $+(a+b+d+\beta)$. The reader may find this balance sheet useful in resolving one of the nine-man square problems proposed above.

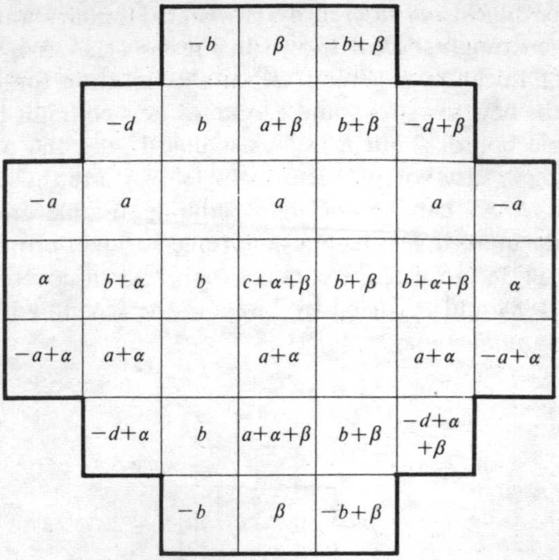

		$-b$	β	$-b+\beta$		
	$-d$	b	$a+\beta$	$b+\beta$	$-d+\beta$	
$-a$	a		a		a	$-a$
α	$b+\alpha$	b	$c+\alpha+\beta$	$b+\beta$	$b+\alpha+\beta$	α
$-a+\alpha$	$a+\alpha$		$a+\alpha$		$a+\alpha$	$-a+\alpha$
	$-d+\alpha$	b	$a+\alpha+\beta$	$b+\beta$	$-d+\alpha+\beta$	
		$-b$	β	$-b+\beta$		

Figure 11.34

The 37-hole board can be converted into the null-class annular board shown in Figure 11.35 by the removal of its central hole. All the single-vacancy complement problems on this board are soluble. L.-F.-J. Gardès suggested a similar class of problems in 1912: on the 37-hole board itself, vacate the centre hole and one other, and play to leave a single survivor in the other hole. This differs from the use of the annular board of Figure 11.35 only in permitting the use of the central hole during play.

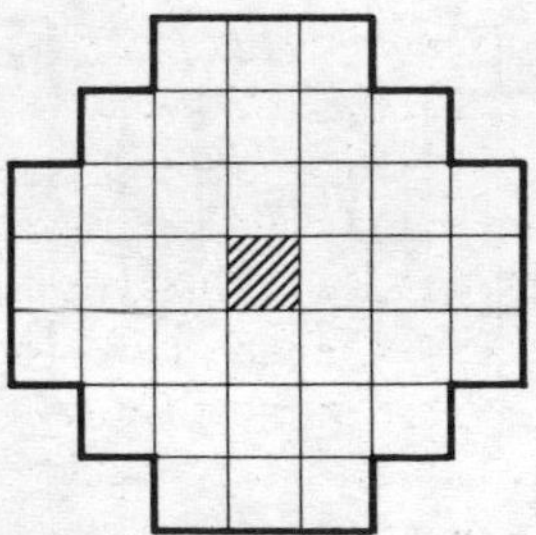

Figure 11.35

A related board considered by H.-A.-H. Hermary and others is the 41-hole draughtsboard shown in Figure 11.36. We follow the example of Lucas in retaining '*d*4' as the notation for the centre, denoting the new rows by 0 and 8, and the new columns by *z* and *h*. The 41-hole board is not a null-class board, and the only single-vacancy single-survivor problems soluble on it are those shown in Figure 11.37. All can be solved by adding suitable first and last moves to the quadruple-vacancy quadruple-survivor problem shown in Figure 11.38, an elegant condensation first discovered by Paul Redon in 1888 and reported by Lucas in the second edition of his *Récréations mathématiques* (1891).

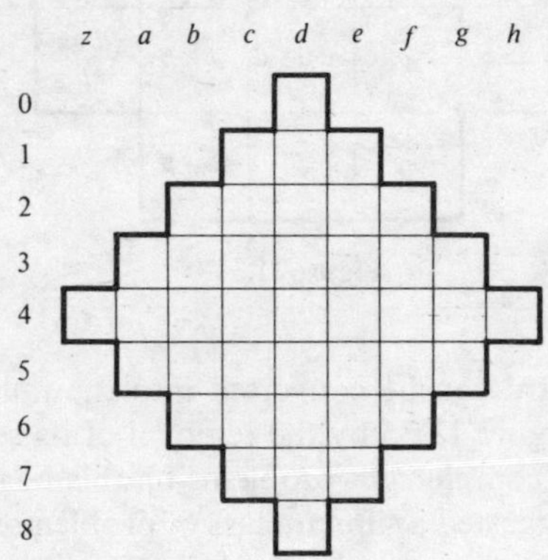

Figure 11.36

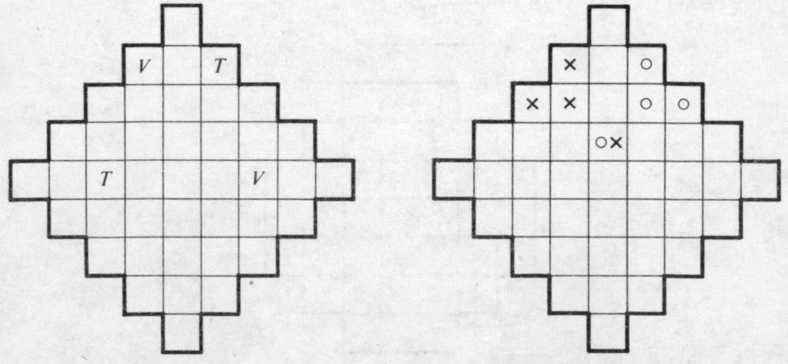

Figure 11.37 **Figure 11.38**

The 41-hole board can be converted into a null-class annular board by the removal of its central hole (Figure 11.39), but the only single-vacancy complement problem soluble on this board is the *c*3-complement. Hermary also suggests a conversion to a null-class board by removing two extreme holes, giving the 39-hole board of Figure 11.40. This board has only rectangular symmetry. All the single-vacancy complement problems on it are soluble except for the *a*4-complement (indicated by *N* in the figure), and all the other single-vacancy single-survivor problems with the target position in the correct fundamental class are soluble except for 'vacate *d*1, finish at *d*7'.

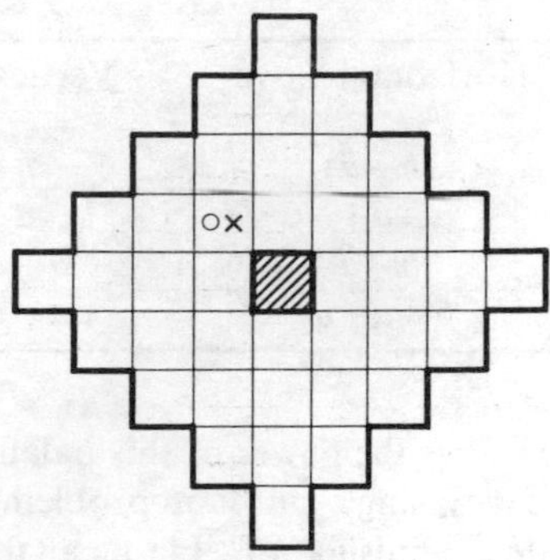

Figure 11.39

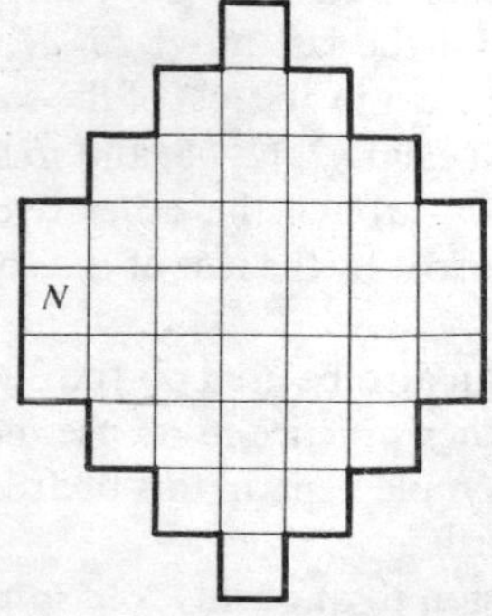

Figure 11.40

A powerful balance sheet for the 41-hole board can be obtained from that of Figure 11.19 by placing suitable negative values around the edge, but for many problems the simpler sheet shown in Figure 11.41 is adequate. This balance sheet is derived from that of Figure 11.20. The value of the full position according to it is $(2a+2b-4d+\omega)$, and the primitives are (a), $(a+\omega)$, (b), $(b+\omega)$, $(a-d)$, $(a-d+\omega)$, $(b-d)$, $(b-d+\omega)$, $(a+d)$, $(a+d+\omega)$, $(b+d)$, and $(b+d+\omega)$. This is an apparently forbidding list, but those involving $+d$ are rarely of importance. A solitary ω is irreducible, as is any value with a negative d component unbalanced by a positive a or b component, and the pattern of the moves losing $-d$ should be noticed:

Man	Horizontal move	Vertical move
*b*2	$b-d$	$a-d$
*f*2	$b-d+\omega$	$a-d$
*b*6	$b-d$	$a-d+\omega$
*f*6	$b-d+\omega$	$a-d+\omega$

A simple example shows the power of this balance sheet. Our list of soluble single-vacancy single-survivor problems on the 41-hole board omitted 'vacate *c*1, finish at *e*7'. Let us analyse this problem. The full position has value $(2a+2b-4d+\omega)$, the initial vacancy $(-b)$, and the target position $(-b+\omega)$, leaving $(2a+4b-4d)$ to be lost by the solution. To play *c*3–*c*1 as the first move or *e*5–*e*7 as the last would lose $(2b)$, which we cannot afford, so the first move must be *e*1–*c*1, losing (a), and the last move *c*7–*e*7, losing $(a+\omega)$. This leaves $(4b-4d+\omega)$ to be lost by the rest of the solution. In particular, this means that we must clear *b*2, *f*2, *b*6, and *f*6 by horizontal moves, but two of these lose $(b-d)$ and the other two $(b-d+\omega)$, leaving an inexpressible ω to be lost by the rest of the solution. The problem is therefore insoluble.

This balance sheet can also be used on the 39-hole board, and the reader wishing for further practice in its use may care to prove the insolubility of the *a*4-complement on this board, and also that of the problem 'vacate *d*1, finish at *d*7'.

In giving me permission to quote his solutions, Gordon expressed the hope that I would give the 37-hole board more than passing

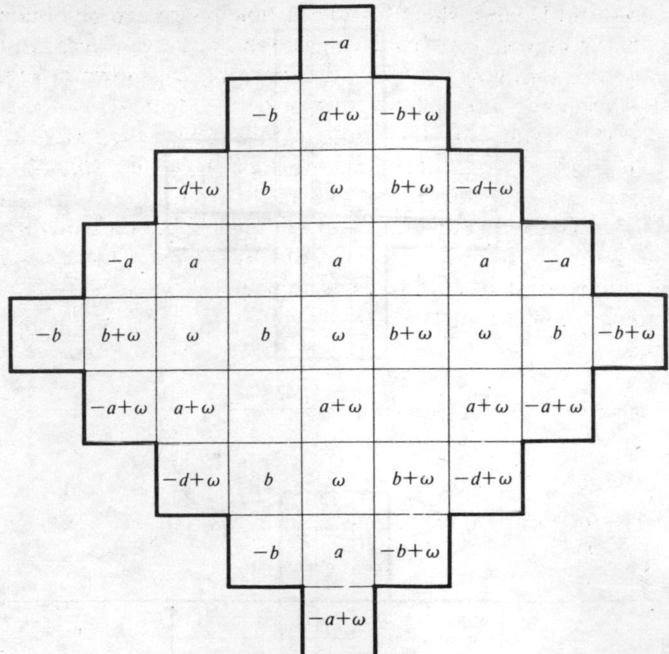

Figure 11.41

mention. He suggested that the reason I know of no other attempt to find minimal solutions is that no writer has stimulated such attempts. Perhaps this section will cause readers to look into it more deeply.

Wiegleb's 45-hole board

Wiegleb's 45-hole board (Figure 11.42) was one of the first boards to appear in print, but it seems to have received no subsequent attention. It has several features of interest.

One of the main differences from the 33-hole board is shown in Figure 11.43, in which it can be seen that the 'c', 's' and 't' men have changed roles: the 's' and 't' men now occupy the outside corners, and it is the 'c' men that we must use in order to clear them. The resulting shortage of 'c' men may be accentuated by the requirements of the arm-balance theorem (Chapter 6), which can be shown to apply to this board just as to the 33-hole board and states that an

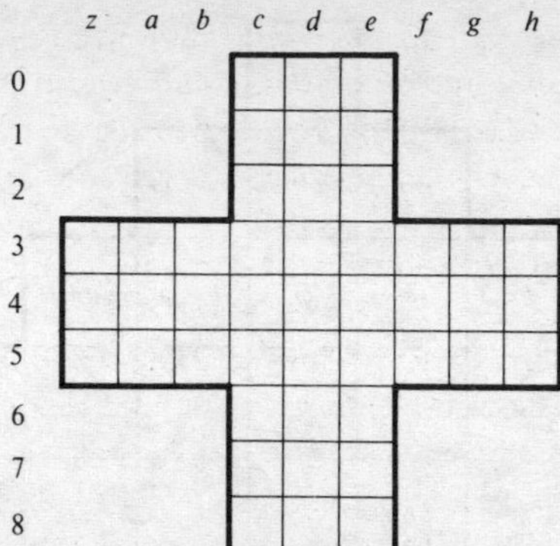

Figure 11.42

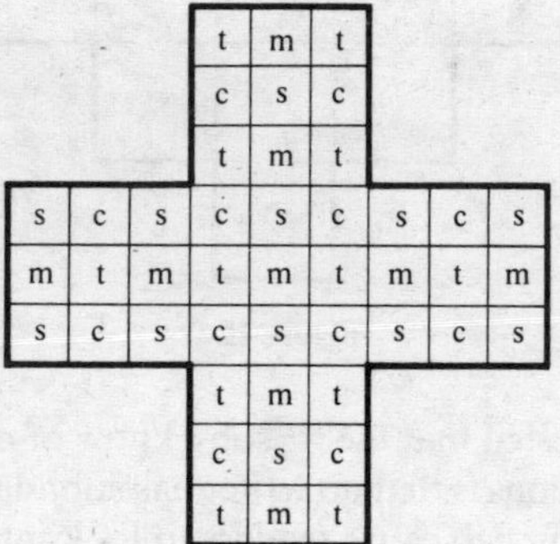

Figure 11.43

unbalanced move into or out of the centre must be accompanied in many problems by parallel moves across the adjacent inside corners. The requirements of the exit and delivery theorems of Chapter 7 may also cost 'c' men, and the overall effect is that play on this board can be quite difficult.

Wiegleb gives only a single solution (vacate *c*0, finish at *c*3), with a note that it can be played in reverse. In fact all the single-vacancy complement problems are soluble except for the *d*0-complement. We give solutions to the *c*0- and *d*1-complements at the end of the chapter, for he who can do these will have little difficulty with the rest. The insolubility of the *d*0-complement can be proved most simply (albeit rather tediously) by enumerating the possible move maps and showing that in each case there is a region for which an exit theorem is unsatisfied.

Whether Wiegleb knew of this impossibility himself is not clear. He uses a sequential notation for the holes (1, 2, 3, . . . from left to right and top to bottom), and gives three examples of play. Example 1, a solution to the *c*1-complement on the 33-hole board, is followed by the comment '*Wenn man Anfangs, das mittelste Loch (nehmlich 17) offen lässt, kann die letzte Spitze in allen Löchern, ausser in 9. 11. 23. 25 stehen bleiben*' ('If the game starts with the middle hole (namely 17) left vacant, the last peg may be left in any hole except 9, 11, 23, 25'). This is nonsense. Example 2, a solution to 'vacate *c*1, finish at *e*7' on the 37-hole board, is followed by the comment '*Wenn man Anfangs eines von denen Löchern 2. 14. 20. 32. offen lässet; so ist nicht möglich, dass die letzte Spitze, in einem derselben stehen bleibe*' ('If the game starts with one of the holes 2, 14, 20, 32 vacant, it is impossible for the last peg to occupy any of these holes'). This is true, for *every* complement problem on this board is insoluble, but it is not clear why holes 2 (*d*1), 14 (*f*3), 20 (*e*4), and 32 (*d*6) should have been singled out for particular attention. Example 3, a solution to 'vacate *c*0, finish at *c*3' on the 45-hole board, is followed by the comments '*Wenn ausser denen letzerwehnten vier Löchern 2. 14. 20. 32 eines Anfangs offen gelassen worden: so ist möglich, solcher Gestalt zu spielen; das die letzte Spitze in dem Loche stehen bliebe, welches man Anfangs offen gelassen*' ('If apart from the four last-mentioned holes 2, 14, 20, 32 one is left vacant at the start, it is possible to play in such a way that the last peg comes to occupy that hole which was left vacant at the start') and '*Man kann ferner leicht erachten, dass sich in allen drey Arten die Exempel umkehren lassen*' ('Further, it may easily be observed that in all three games illustrated the examples may be reversed'). The first of these comments is wrong as regards 2 (*d*0), the second correct. It seems clear to me that Wiegleb had the 33-hole board (or at least its notation) in mind throughout, for the selection of the combination 2, 14, 20, 32 makes sense on no other basis (they are *d*1, *a*4, *g*4, and *d*7 on the 33-hole board); but this does not explain the wildly inaccurate comment to example 1. The later editions throw no light; give or take an *umlaut*, the texts are identical.

The 6 × 6 square board

This board, shown in Figure 11.44, is the smallest board with the following property: Whatever the initial vacancy, we can mark *any* of the remaining men and play to leave it as the last survivor. Indeed we can do even better than this, for we can leave the marked man as a man on the watch and play to finish with at least an eight-sweep and in some cases a ten-sweep. The precise rules are given in Table 11.2. Note that *no dependence on the initial vacancy appears in this table*; final sweeps of the lengths stated can be achieved from *any* initial vacancy that produces a position in the correct fundamental class. The table is very much simpler than that which we gave for the 33-hole board (Table 9.2), reflecting the simpler geometry of the 6 × 6 board. Typical ten-sweep finishes are shown in Figures 11.45 and 11.46, and the reader may care to find solutions to the *c*1-complement problem ending with these sweeps.

This board offers less variety than the other boards we consider in this chapter, because each of the four classes of men forms the same geometrical pattern, but it permits some remarkably short

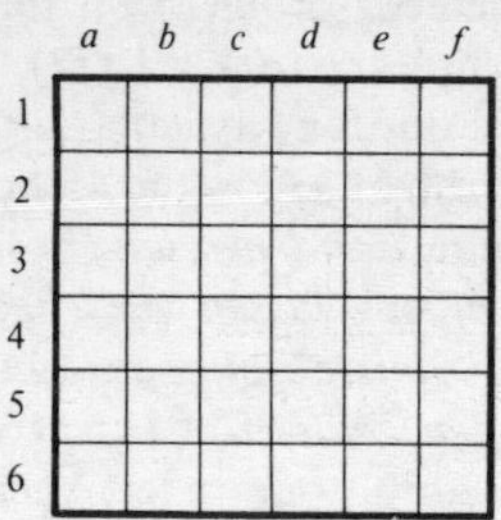

Figure 11.44

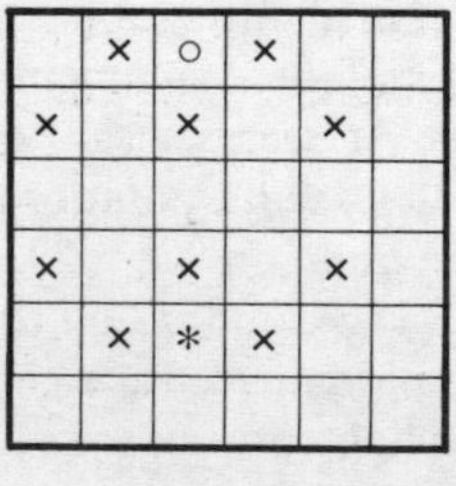

Figure 11.45

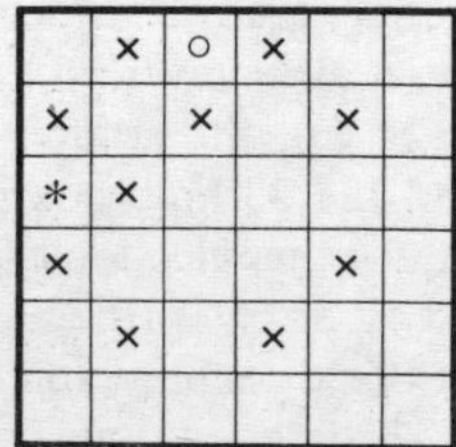

Figure 11.46

Table 11.2: Longest-sweep man-on-the-watch solutions in 6 × 6 Solitaire

Marked man	Final hole	Longest sweep
*a*1, *c*3, *e*5	*c*1, *e*3	9
	*a*1, *e*1, *c*3, *e*5	8
*c*1	*a*3, *e*3, *c*5	10
	*a*1, *e*1, *c*3, *a*5, *e*5	9
	*c*1	8
*e*1	*c*1, *a*3, *e*3, *c*5	9
	*a*1, *e*1, *c*3, *a*5, *e*5	8
*e*3	*c*1, *a*3, *c*5	10
	*a*1, *e*1, *c*3, *a*5, *e*5	9
	*e*3	8

solutions. John W. Harris found a 16-move solution to the *a*1-complement problem in 1962, and Harry O. Davis added 16-move solutions to all the other single-vacancy single-survivor problems between 1962 and 1964. Davis even found two such problems with *15-move* solutions: 'vacate *c*1, finish at *f*4' and 'vacate *c*3, finish at *f*6'. Wade E. Philpott also studied this board and found solutions ending with all the possible ten-sweep patterns, but a recent letter from him is interesting: 'While I frequently demonstrated solvability by analysis or an actual solution, it was always Davis who squeezed the excess moves out of the games.' Davis and Philpott became interested in Solitaire after retirement, an interest fostered by Martin Gardner's *Scientific American* column, and I have had pleasant correspondence with both.

An elegant proof that Harris's solution to the *a*1-complement is minimal was given by Robin Merson in 1962 as follows: one move must originate in each of the fifteen areas *A*...*O* of Figure 11.47, and another is needed to clear *a*1 after the first move. Davis's 15-move solutions can be proved minimal by a similar argument. The existence of this simple proof causes me to regard these solutions as comparable to the finest of Bergholt's and Davis's on the 33-hole board, for most similar arguments on the 33-hole board fail to get within two or three of the known or suspected minima.

We leave finite square lattice boards here; the underlying theory is no different from that of the 33-hole board, and the reader who wishes to explore further has the necessary tools at his disposal.

	A	*A*	*B*	*B*	*C*
D	*E*	*E*	*F*	*F*	*G*
D	*E*	*E*	*F*	*F*	*G*
H	*I*	*I*	*J*	*J*	*K*
H	*I*	*I*	*J*	*J*	*K*
L	*M*	*M*	*N*	*N*	*O*

Figure 11.47

Solutions to Chapter 11

The soluble single-vacancy complement problems on the various rectangular boards and draughtsboards should give no trouble to a reader who has come this far, so we content ourselves with two specimen solutions (Figures 11.48 and 11.49). In Figure 11.48, step 2*a*/2*b* is a double-six removal analogous to the double-three; the first two moves of the first six-removal (say *c*4–*c*2, *c*1–*c*3) create a catalyst for the second, so we break off the first, perform the second, and then resume and complete the first in the normal way. A similar technique can be used to solve single-vacancy complement problems on $n \times 3$ boards of arbitrary length. Step 5*a*/5*b*/5*c* in Figure 11.49 is a pointed ten (Figure 11.22).

The soluble single-vacancy complement problems on the 18-hole board of Figure 11.6 are shown in Figure 11.50. It is surprising that such a problem should be soluble if the initial vacancy is in a sharp corner but not if it is in a blunt corner.

Solutions to 'Le tricolet' and 'Le lecteur au milieu de ses amis' are shown in Figures 11.51 and 11.52 respectively. Both are transcriptions of the solutions in the *Dictionnaire des jeux mathématiques*; there is nothing new about block play.

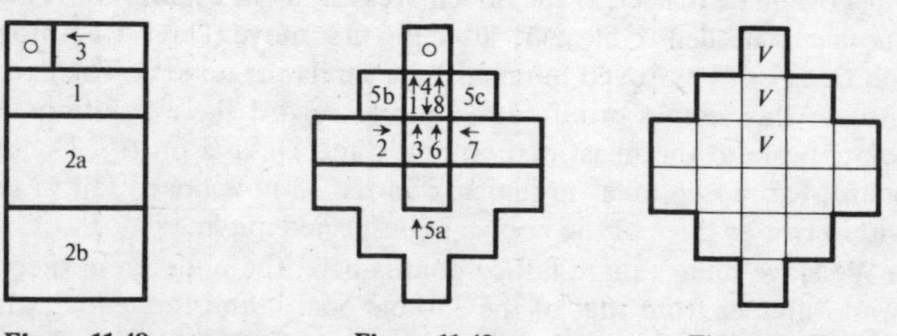

Figure 11.48 **Figure 11.49** **Figure 11.50**

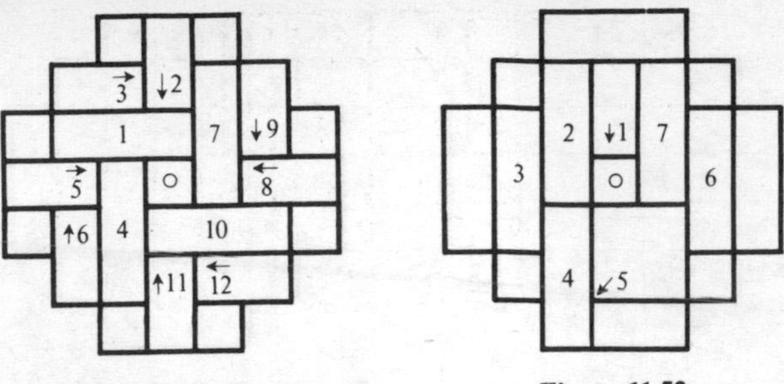

Figure 11.51

Figure 11.52

The three nine-man squares which can be reached from a central-vacancy start on the 37-hole board are shown in Figures 11.53 to 11.55, Figure 11.53 being given by Busschop. None of them is difficult. A simple way of solving the problem of Figure 11.55 is to start by playing to the position of Figure 11.56, which can be done by the play which reached Figure 10.1 from a central-vacancy start on the 33-hole board, and then to play the four quartets typified by *e*1–*e*3, *f*2–*f*4, *g*4–*e*4–*e*2.

Of the six other nine-man squares which can be placed on the board, four clearly cannot be reached in play because we do not have enough 's' and 't' men to form the square after making the initial move and clearing the perimeter. The other two are shown in Figures 11.57 and 11.58, and are more difficult to prove unreachable. Figure 11.57 in fact yields to the balance sheet of Figure 11.34, while each of the move maps that liquidate the debts and surpluses of Figure 11.58 contains a region for which the first exit theorem is not satisfied.

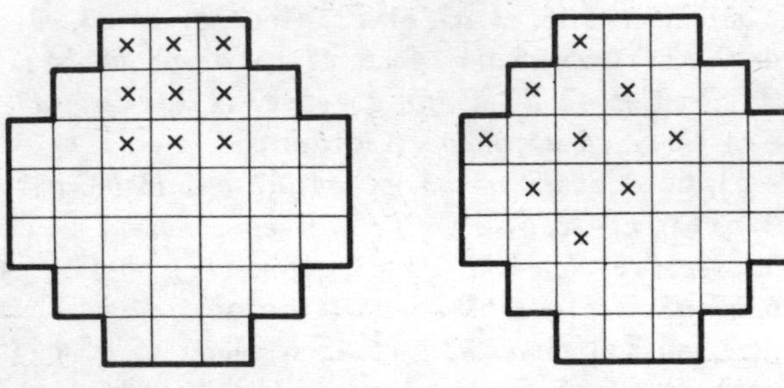

Figure 11.53

Figure 11.54

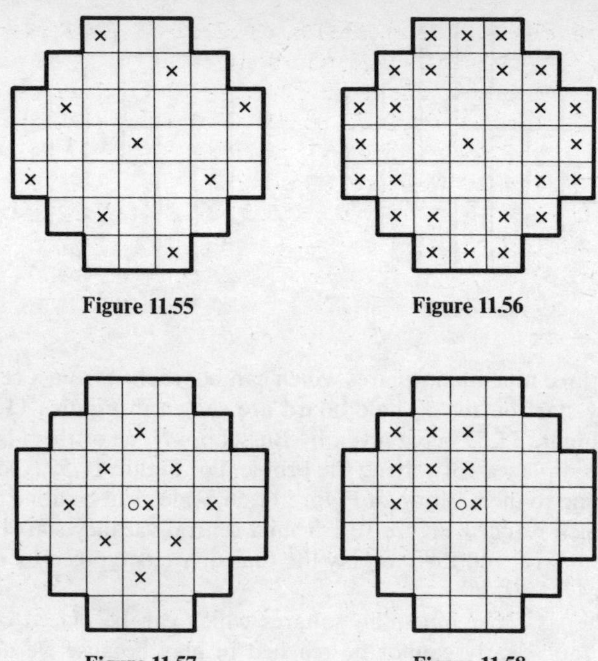

Figure 11.55

Figure 11.56

Figure 11.57

Figure 11.58

Solutions to the single-vacancy single-survivor problems are as follows:

Vacate *a*3, finish at *d*2: *a*5–*a*3, *c*4–*a*4, *b*6–*b*4, *d*5–*b*5, *f*5–*d*5, *a*3–*a*5–*c*5–*e*5 (6), *c*7–*c*5, *b*3–*b*5–*d*5–*f*5, *d*3–*b*3, *b*2–*b*4, *c*1–*c*3 (11), *d*7–*d*5, *g*5–*e*5–*c*5, *e*7–*e*5, *f*3–*d*3–*b*3–*b*5–*d*5–*f*5–*f*3 (15), *e*1–*e*3–*e*5, *d*1–*d*3–*d*5–*f*5, *f*6–*f*4, *g*3–*e*3, *g*4–*e*4–*e*2, *f*2–*d*2. (Gordon)

Vacate *a*3, finish at *a*5: *c*3–*a*3, *c*1–*c*3, *c*4–*c*2, *e*1–*c*1–*c*3, *e*2–*c*2, *b*2–*d*2, *c*6–*c*4–*c*2–*e*2 (7), *a*5–*c*5, *a*4–*c*4–*c*6, *c*7–*c*5, *d*5–*b*5, *b*6–*b*4 (12), *f*2–*d*2, *e*3–*c*3, *g*3–*e*3, *f*5–*f*3–*d*3–*d*5–*f*5, *g*5–*e*5–*e*3 (17), *e*7–*e*5, *d*7–*d*5–*f*5, *f*6–*f*4, *g*4–*e*4–*e*2–*c*2–*c*4–*a*4, *a*3–*a*5. (Gordon)

Vacate *a*3, finish at *d*5: *a*5–*a*3, *c*4–*a*4, *b*2–*b*4, *d*3–*b*3, *a*3–*c*3, *d*1–*d*3–*b*3, *c*1–*c*3 (7), *f*2–*d*2, *e*4–*e*2, *e*1–*e*3, *g*4–*e*4–*c*4–*c*2–*e*2–*e*4 (11), *c*5–*a*5–*a*3–*c*3, *c*7–*c*5, *e*6–*c*6, *e*4–*e*6, *g*3–*e*3, *g*5–*e*5 (17), *d*5–*f*5, *f*6–*f*4, *e*7–*e*5, *b*6–*d*6, *d*7–*d*5–*f*5–*f*3–*d*3–*b*3–*b*5–*d*5. (Gordon)

Vacate *a*3, finish at *g*5: *a*5–*a*3, *c*4–*a*4, *c*6–*c*4, *e*5–*c*5, *g*5–*e*5 (5), *d*3–*d*5–*f*5, *b*6–*b*4–*d*4, *b*2–*b*4, *f*3–*d*3–*b*3, *a*3–*c*3 (10), *e*1–*e*3, *e*4–*e*2, *e*7–*e*5, *g*4–*e*4–*e*6, *c*7–*e*7–*e*5, *c*1–*e*1–*e*3 (16), *c*2–*e*2, *f*2–*d*2, *f*6–*f*4, *a*4–*c*4–*c*6–*e*6–*e*4–*e*2–*c*2–*c*4–*e*4–*g*4, *g*3–*g*5. (Gordon)

Vacate *d*3, finish at *d*2: *d*1–*d*3, *b*2–*d*2, *c*4–*c*2, *c*1–*c*3, *e*2–*c*2–*c*4 (5), *e*4–*e*2, *e*1–*e*3, *e*6–*e*4–*e*2, *f*2–*d*2, *a*3–*c*3, *g*3–*e*3, *g*5–*e*5 (12), *c*4–*c*2–*e*2–*e*4–*e*6, *e*7–*e*5, *g*4–*e*4–*e*6, *c*7–*e*7–*e*5, *c*6–*e*6–*e*4–*c*4–*c*6 (17), *b*6–*d*6, *a*5–*c*5, *a*4–*c*4–*c*6–*e*6, *f*6–*d*6–*d*4–*d*2. (Gordon)

Vacate *d*3, finish at *a*5: *d*5–*d*3, *d*7–*d*5, *f*6–*d*6–*d*4 (3), *e*4–*e*6, *b*6–*d*6, *c*4–*c*6, *c*7–*c*5, *e*7–*e*5, *g*4–*e*4–*c*4–*c*6–*e*6–*e*4 (9), *f*2–*f*4, *d*3–*f*3, *g*3–*e*3, *g*5–*e*5, *a*5–*c*5, *b*3–*d*3–*f*3–*f*5–*d*5–*b*5–*b*3 (15), *e*1–*e*3, *a*3–*c*3, *d*1–*d*3–*b*3, *b*2–*d*2, *e*4–*e*2–*c*2, *c*1–*c*3–*a*3–*a*5. (Davis)

Vacate *d*3, finish at *d*5: *d*5–*d*3, *d*2–*d*4, *b*2–*d*2, *c*4–*c*2, *c*1–*c*3, *c*6–*c*4–*c*2, *e*1–*c*1–*c*3 (7), *a*5–*c*5, *e*2–*c*2–*c*4–*c*6, *a*3–*c*3, *e*4–*e*2, *f*2–*d*2 (12), *g*3–*e*3, *c*7–*c*5, *e*6–*e*4–*c*4–*c*6–*e*6, *f*6–*d*6 (16), *g*5–*e*5, *g*4–*e*4–*e*6, *e*7–*e*5, *a*4–*c*4–*c*2–*e*2–*e*4–*e*6–*c*6, *b*6–*d*6, *d*7–*d*5. (Gordon)

Vacate *d*6, finish at *d*2: *b*6–*d*6, *c*4–*c*6, *c*7–*c*5, *c*2–*c*4–*c*6, *a*3–*c*3, *e*7–*c*7–*c*5 (6), *e*6–*c*6–*c*4–*c*2, *c*1–*c*3, *a*5–*c*5, *e*4–*e*6, *f*6–*d*6 (11), *g*5–*e*5, *g*4–*e*4–*c*4–*c*2, *f*2–*f*4, *d*5–*f*5–*f*3 (15), *e*2–*e*4, *g*3–*e*3–*e*5, *e*1–*c*1–*c*3–*e*3, *a*4–*c*4–*c*6–*e*6–*e*4–*e*2–*c*2, *b*2–*d*2. (Gordon)

Vacate *d*6, finish at *a*5: *b*6–*d*6, *c*4–*c*6, *c*7–*c*5, *e*4–*c*4–*c*6, *e*7–*c*7–*c*5 (5), *e*6–*c*6–*c*4, *g*4–*e*4–*e*6, *f*6–*d*6–*d*4, *f*2–*f*4, *d*3–*f*3 (10), *g*3–*e*3, *g*5–*e*5, *a*5–*c*5, *d*1–*d*3–*f*3–*f*5–*d*5–*b*5 (14), *e*1–*e*3, *b*2–*d*2, *c*4–*c*2, *c*1–*c*3, *a*4–*c*4–*e*4–*e*2–*c*2–*c*4, *a*3–*c*3–*c*5–*a*5. (Gordon)

Vacate *d*6, finish at *d*5: *b*6–*d*6, *c*4–*c*6, *c*7–*c*5, *c*2–*c*4–*c*6, *e*7–*c*7–*c*5 (5), *a*3–*c*3, *d*3–*b*3, *a*5–*a*3–*c*3, *e*6–*c*6–*c*4–*c*2, *c*1–*c*3 (10), *e*2–*c*2, *b*2–*d*2, *e*4–*c*4–*c*2–*e*2, *f*2–*d*2, *g*4–*e*4–*e*2–*c*2, *e*1–*c*1–*c*3 (16), *g*3–*e*3, *f*6–*f*4, *d*5–*f*5, *g*5–*e*5, *b*5–*b*3–*d*3–*f*3–*f*5–*d*5. (Gordon)

Gordon's solution to 'vacate *a*3, finish at *g*5', rotated through 90 degrees, solves 'La corsaire', but it is perhaps more pleasant if the man making the nine-sweep does not move previously. The *Dictionnaire des jeux mathématiques* gives the following solution: *e*3–*e*1, *g*3–*e*3, *f*5–*f*3, *f*2–*f*4, *g*5–*g*3, *d*3–*f*3, *g*3–*e*3 (7), *e*4–*e*2, *e*1–*e*3, *b*3–*d*3, *b*5–*b*3, *d*5–*b*5, *d*7–*d*5 (13), *c*1–*c*3–*c*5, *a*3–*c*3, *d*3–*b*3, *b*2–*b*4, *a*4–*c*4, *c*5–*c*3 (19), *a*5–*c*5, *d*5–*b*5, *b*6–*b*4, *c*7–*c*5, *f*6–*d*6 (24). We can reach the eight-sweep of Figure 11.33 by a variation of this: play *f*6–*f*4, *e*4–*e*6, *e*7–*e*5, *e*2–*e*4, and moves 2 to 23 inclusive of the above solution.

The various single-vacancy single-survivor problems on the cousins of the 37-hole board should give no trouble, and we confine our attention to Redon's problem on the 41-hole board (Figure 11.38). An elegant block-play solution to this is shown in Figure 11.59, steps 1 and 3 being nine-removals (Figure 11.21) and step

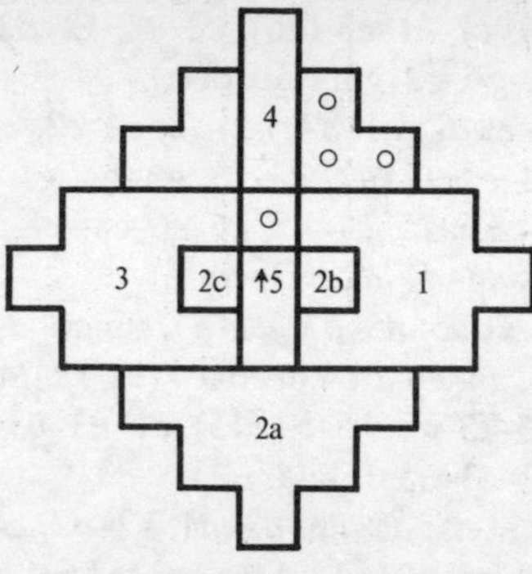

Figure 11.59

2a/*2b*/*2c* an eleven-removal (Figure 11.23). The complementary nature of the nine-removal and the eleven-removal is clearly shown in this solution.

Solutions to the *c*0- and *d*1-complements on Wiegleb's board are shown in Figures 11.60 and 11.61. The reader who masters these should have no difficulty with the other single-vacancy single-survivor problems on this board (except of course for the insoluble *d*0-complement).

Solutions to the ten-sweep problem of Figures 11.45 and 11.46 are shown in Figures 11.62 and 11.63 respectively. Step 4 of Figure 11.62 swallows the man that was delivered to *c*1 by the first move. Figure 11.63 shows several block moves useful in long-sweep prob-

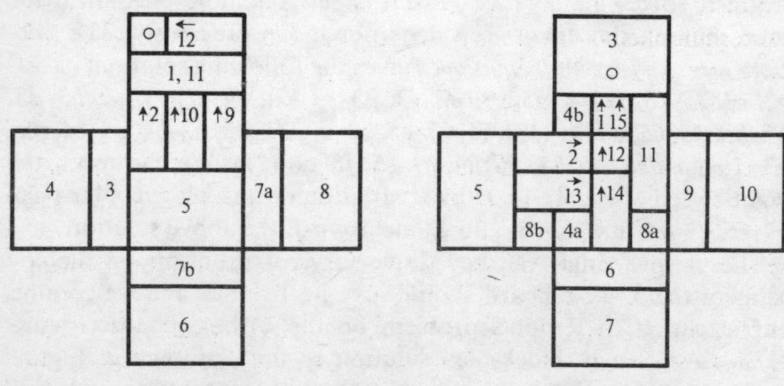

Figure 11.60 **Figure 11.61**

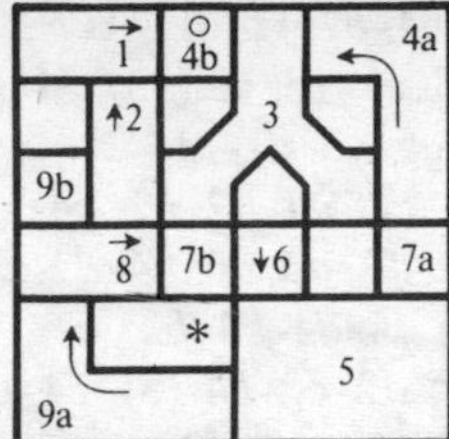

Figure 11.62

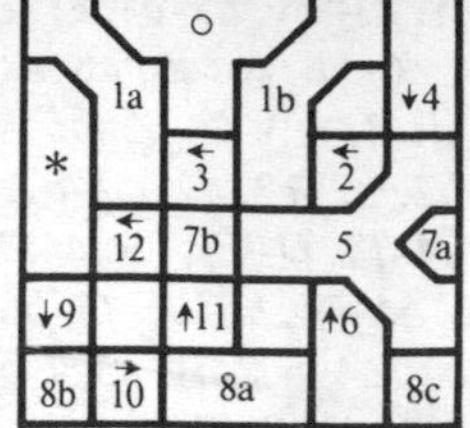

Figure 11.63

lems on the 6 × 6 board: the double-Y (step 1*a*/1*b*), the five-two (step 8*a*/8*b*/8c), and the ordinary four-chain (steps 9 to 12).

The other long-sweep solutions on the 6 × 6 board are generally similar to these, and many can be obtained each from another by modification of a few moves. For a particularly simple example, consider the *a*3-complement problem with a man on the watch at *c*5. If we start by playing *a*1–*a*3 and *c*2–*a*2, then we have the same position as that after steps 1 and 2 of Figure 11.62, except that there is a man at *b*3 instead of *c*2. We can now play steps 3 to 9 of Figure 11.62, performing step 3 by the moves *c*4–*c*2, *e*3–*c*3, *c*2–*c*4, *d*1–*d*3 instead of *d*3–*b*3, *d*1–*d*3, *e*3–*c*3, *b*3–*d*3, and we have set up a ten-sweep to deliver a man to *a*3 instead of *c*1. The reflection of this solution in the diagonal *a*1–*f*6 produces a solution to the *c*1-complement problem with a man on the watch at *e*3, completing the set of ten-sweep solutions to this problem. The reader may care to obtain ten-sweep solutions to the *c*2-complement problem similarly, by modifying the play of Figure 11.62 to start with the vacancy at *e*3 and that of Figure 11.63 to start with it at *e*3 or *c*5, and then re-orienting the board. None of these is quite as easy as the example above, but none is difficult.

Harris's sixteen-move solution to the *a*1-complement problem on the 6 × 6 board is as follows: *a*3–*a*1, *c*2–*a*2, *c*4–*c*2, *c*6–*c*4, *a*5–*a*3–*c*3–*c*5, *a*6–*c*6–*c*4–*a*4 (6), *e*5–*c*5, *d*3–*d*5, *f*4–*d*4, *e*6–*c*6–*c*4–*e*4 (10), *f*3–*d*3, *f*1–*f*3, *f*6–*f*4–*f*2, *c*1–*c*3–*c*5, *d*1–*f*1–*f*3–*d*3–*d*1, *a*1–*c*1–*e*1–*e*3–*e*5–*c*5–*a*5–*a*3–*a*1. It finishes with a circular eight-sweep.

Sixteen-move solutions to the other single-vacancy complement problems on this board are as follows:

*b*1: *d*1–*b*1, *f*1–*d*1, *a*1–*c*1–*e*1, *c*3–*c*1, *f*3–*f*1–*d*1–*b*1, *a*3–*a*1–*c*1 (6), *a*5–*a*3, *c*5–*c*3, *e*2–*c*2–*a*2–*a*4–*c*4–*c*2, *b*6–*b*4–*b*2–*d*2 (10), *d*6–*b*6, *f*6–*d*6, *e*4–*c*4, *a*6–*c*6–*e*6–*e*4, *e*3–*e*5–*c*5–*c*3–*e*3, *f*5–*f*3–*d*3–*d*1–*b*1.

*c*1: *a*1–*c*1, *d*1–*b*1, *a*3–*a*1–*c*1, *c*2–*a*2, *b*4–*b*2, *f*1–*d*1–*b*1–*b*3, *b*6–*b*4–*b*2 (7), *d*4–*b*4, *d*6–*b*6, *f*6–*d*6, *a*6–*c*6–*e*6, *e*3–*e*1, *c*3–*e*3 (13), *f*4–*f*6–*d*6–*d*4–*f*4, *f*3–*d*3–*d*1–*f*1–*f*3–*f*5–*d*5–*b*5–*b*3–*b*1, *a*5–*a*3–*a*1–*c*1.

*b*2: *d*2–*b*2, *a*2–*c*2, *f*2–*d*2–*b*2, *a*4–*a*2–*c*2, *d*4–*d*2–*b*2, *c*4–*c*2–*a*2, *a*1–*a*3–*c*3 (7), *f*4–*f*2, *f*1–*f*3, *f*6–*f*4–*f*2, *d*1–*f*1–*f*3–*d*3, *d*6–*d*4–*d*2, *b*1–*d*1–*d*3–*b*3 (13), *a*6–*a*4–*c*4, *b*5–*d*5–*f*5, *b*6–*d*6–*f*6–*f*4–*d*4–*b*4–*b*2.

*c*2: *a*2–*c*2, *a*4–*a*2, *a*1–*a*3, *c*4–*a*4–*a*2, *d*2–*b*2–*b*4 (5), *e*4–*c*4–*c*2, *c*1–*c*3, *c*6–*c*4–*c*2, *f*2–*d*2–*b*2, *e*1–*c*1–*a*1–*a*3 (10), *f*4–*f*2, *f*1–*f*3, *e*6–*e*4–*e*2, *f*6–*f*4–*f*2–*d*2–*d*4, *a*5–*c*5–*e*5, *a*6–*c*6–*e*6–*e*4–*c*4–*a*4–*a*2–*c*2.

*c*3: *c*1–*c*3, *a*2–*c*2, *a*4–*a*2, *a*1–*a*3, *c*4–*a*4–*a*2 (5), *e*4–*c*4, *e*6–*e*4, *c*6–*e*6, *f*6–*d*6, *a*6–*c*6, *d*2–*b*2–*b*4–*b*6, *f*2–*d*2–*d*4–*b*4 (12), *c*6–*c*4–*a*4–*a*6–*c*6–*e*6, *f*4–*d*4–*d*6–*f*6–*f*4–*f*2, *f*1–*f*3–*d*3–*b*3, *e*1–*c*1–*a*1–*a*3–*c*3.

Davis's 15-move solutions are as follows:

Vacate *c*1, finish at *f*4: *a*1–*c*1, *d*1–*b*1, *a*3–*a*1–*c*1, *f*1–*d*1–*b*1 (4), *c*2–*a*2, *c*4–*c*2, *c*6–*c*4, *a*5–*a*3–*a*1–*c*1–*c*3–*c*5, *a*6–*c*6–*c*4–*a*4 (9), *e*3–*e*1, *e*5–*c*5–*a*5–*a*3–*c*3–*e*3, *f*3–*d*3–*d*5, *d*6–*d*4, *f*5–*f*3–*f*1–*d*1–*d*3–*d*5, *f*6–*d*6–*d*4–*f*4.

Vacate *c*3, finish at *f*6: *c*1–*c*3, *a*1–*c*1, *d*1–*b*1, *f*1–*d*1, *a*3–*a*1–*c*1–*e*1 (5), *a*5–*a*3, *c*4–*a*4–*a*2–*c*2–*c*4, *e*2–*c*2, *d*4–*d*2, *f*3–*f*1–*d*1–*d*3 (10), *d*6–*d*4–*d*2–*b*2–*b*4–*d*4, *f*5–*f*3–*d*3–*d*5–*f*5, *c*6–*c*4, *a*6–*a*4, *f*6–*f*4–*d*4–*b*4–*b*6–*d*6–*f*6.

12

THE SOLITAIRE ARMY

There is no reason why Solitaire play should be restricted to a finite board. In this chapter we consider an infinite board and discover some surprising results.

How much support does a man require?

Let us take an infinite board, draw a line across it parallel to a lattice line, and start with all our men behind this line. How many men do we need to send one man forward a given number of holes?

Clearly two men are needed to send a man forward one hole (Figure 12.1), and four men to send him forward two holes (Figure 12.2).

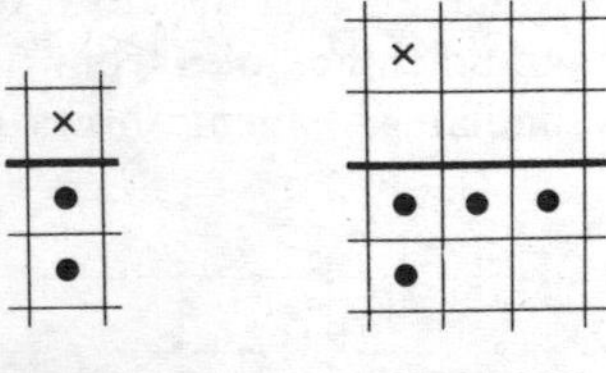

Figure 12.1 **Figure 12.2**

Eight men are needed to send a man forward three holes. The two possible configurations are shown in Figure 12.3, *PP* and *QQ* being alternatives. That eight men are indeed necessary can be seen from the resource count shown in Figure 12.4, for the target position has value 21 and the highest value that can be achieved with only seven men below the line is $1 \times 5 + 3 \times 3 + 3 \times 2 = 20$. (Although resource counts such as that of Figure 12.4 have values in every hole, we show only the important values above the line. To satisfy the demands of pedantry, the remaining values above the line may be filled in by forming each as the sum of the two values immediately below it. We shall follow this convention throughout the chapter.)

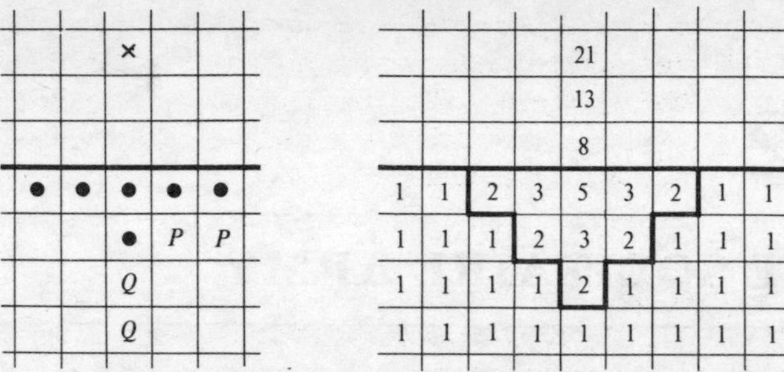

Figure 12.3 **Figure 12.4**

Two, four, eight, sixteen? No. To send a man forward four holes requires *twenty* men. The two possible configurations are shown in Figure 12.5, *PP* and *QQ* being alternatives. The proof that twenty men are necessary is not difficult. The resource count of Figure 12.6 shows that an eighteen-man configuration is impossible and that a nineteen-man configuration, if one exists, must occupy the sixteen holes marked *A* in Figure 12.7 and three of the holes marked *B*,*C*, . . ., *J*, for $89 = 1 \times 13 + 3 \times 8 + 5 \times 5 + 7 \times 3 + 3 \times 2$. The resource count of Figure 12.8 now shows that *B* must be occupied, for we need a position with value at least 55, the sixteen holes marked *A* contribute only 48, and no three holes from *C* . . . *J* can contribute the remaining 7. A similar argument shows that *C* must also be

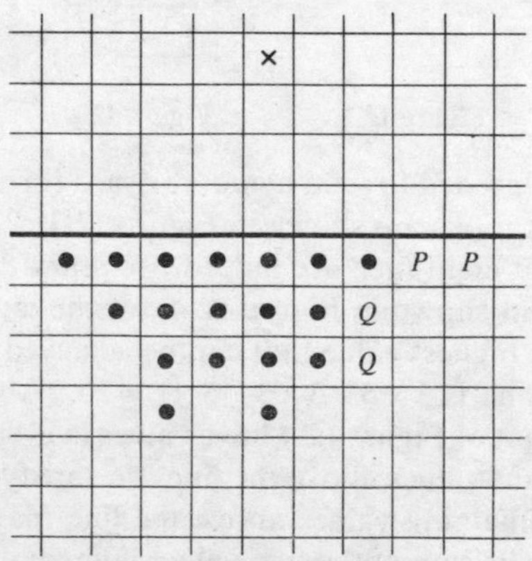

Figure 12.5

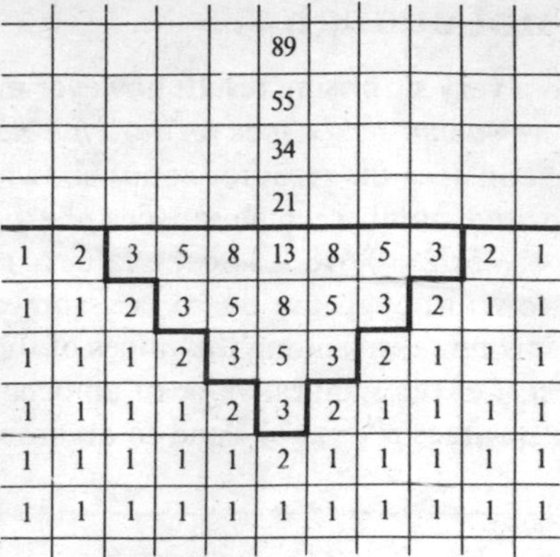

Figure 12.6

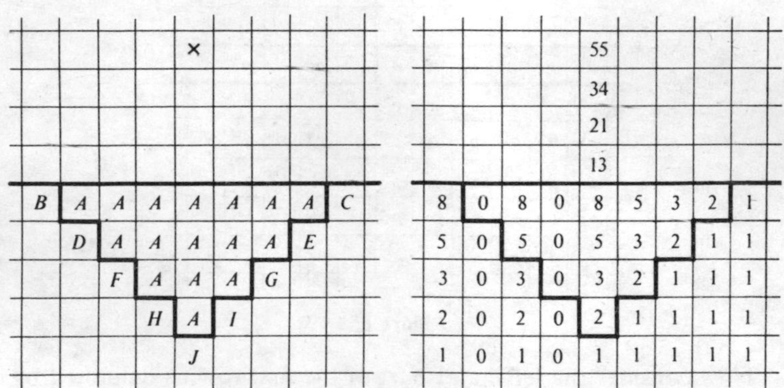

Figure 12.7 **Figure 12.8**

occupied, and there is no way of placing a nineteenth man so as to give a position in the correct fundamental class.

There is no proof which uses a single resource count, however, so we may suspect that a nineteen-man configuration is possible in Fractional Solitaire. This is indeed true; we can put whole men in *A* . . . *A*, *B*, and *C*, and half-men in *D* and *E*, giving a configuration totalling nineteen 'men' from which a man can indeed be sent forwards four holes.

Infinity is not enough . . .

We now come to a very surprising result: however many men we put behind the line, *we cannot send a man forward five holes.*

To prove this, consider the resource count shown in Figure 12.9, where p is the positive number which satisfies $p^2 + p = 1$. (The actual value of p is $(-1+\sqrt{5})/2 = 0.618\ldots$, so the value of p^N decreases with increasing N.) Now although the board is assumed to be infinite, any position on it is finite, so among the values of the occupied holes there is a smallest. Let the smallest value of an occupied hole be p^N; then all holes with values p^{N+1}, p^{N+2} and so on are vacant.

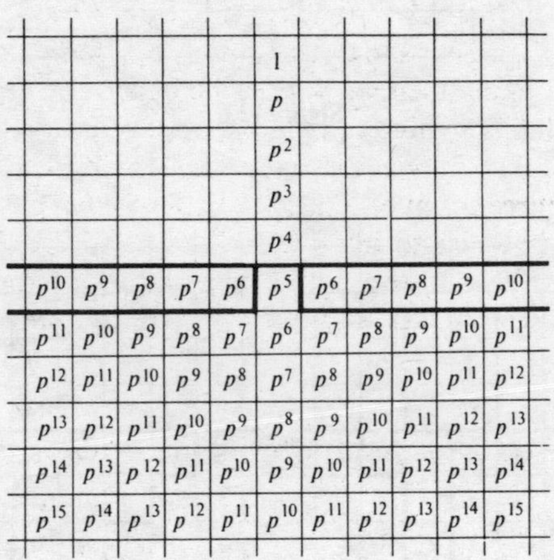

Figure 12.9

Now consider the left-hand part of the first row as delimited by the thick line in Figure 12.9. The holes with values smaller than p^N are unoccupied by virtue of what we have just said, so the sum of the values of the occupied holes is at most

$$p^6 + p^7 + \ldots + p^N.$$

By the normal formula for summing a geometrical progression, this expression is equal to

$$(p^6 - p^{N+1})/(1-p)$$

and therefore is certainly less than

$$p^6/(1-p) = p^6/p^2 = p^4.$$

By the same argument, the sum of the occupied holes in the right-hand part of the row is also less than p^4, and the central hole in the row has value p^5, so the sum of all the occupied holes in the row is less than

$$p^4+p^5+p^4=p^3+p^4=p^2.$$

Similarly, the sum of the occupied holes in the row whose central hole has value $p^n (n \leqslant N)$ is less than p^{n-3}, and rows whose central hole has value $p^n (n > N)$ are empty by the definition of N. Hence the entire position has value less than

$$p^2+p^3+\ldots+p^{N-3},$$

and the same argument shows that this is less than 1.

So however many men we put on the board, we cannot obtain a position which has a value equalling that of our target hole.

This beautiful result was discovered in 1961 by J. H. Conway. He called the resource count of Figure 12.9 'the golden pagoda': 'golden' because $1{:}p$ is known to mathematicians as the golden ratio, and 'pagoda' because it towers like a pagoda above the surrounding plain. A picture appears in *Winning ways for your mathematical plays*.

. . . Yet infinity plus one will do

If we allow one hole to contain two men, however, then we *can* send a man out five rows. This is true *however far back the doubly occupied hole may be*. The reader may care to prove this.

In a very real sense, therefore, we may say that we can 'almost' send a man out five holes beyond a given line.

Solutions to Chapter 12

Since we start this problem with a doubly occupied hole, we content ourselves with a solution in Unconstrained Solitaire. It is possible to play the moves of this solution without placing a second man in any hole other than that doubly occupied at the start, but this avoidance of multiple occupation complicates the solution and obscures its systematic pattern.

Let us suppose that the line comes between rows 4 and 5, so that our target row is row 0, that the hole doubly occupied is in column

x and row N, and that we have single men in as many other holes below the line as we choose. We shall denote the hole in column x and row n by X_n, so the hole doubly occupied is hole X_N. Our object is to place a man in hole X_0.

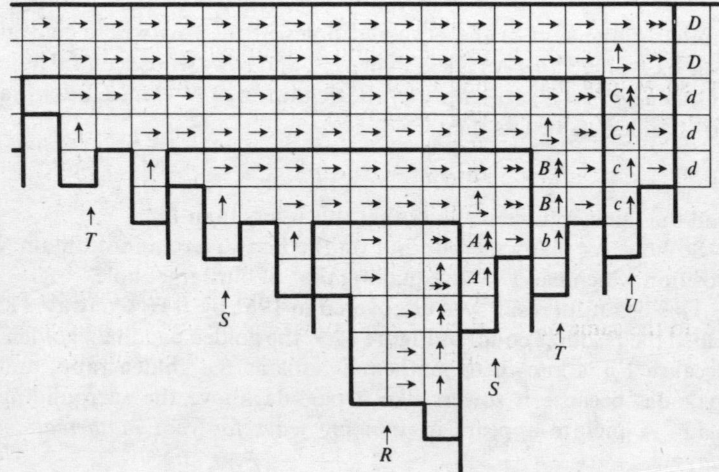

Figure 12.10

Our technique is iterative. Consider Figure 12.10. The following play is possible:

(a) if the 18-hole region R is initially full, then the moves shown clear it and deliver two men to each of the holes AA;

(b) if the 26-hole region S is initially full and step (a) has delivered two extra men to each of the holes AA, then the moves shown clear it and deliver two men to each of the holes BB and one man to hole b;

(c) if the 40-hole region T is initially full and step (b) has delivered two extra men to each of the holes BB and one extra man to hole b, then the moves shown clear it and deliver two men to each of the holes CC and one man to each of the holes cc;

(d) if the 54-hole region U (whose left-hand 'tail', not shown in the figure, is assumed to be the same as those of regions S and T) is initially full and step (c) has delivered two extra men to each of the holes CC and one extra man to each of the holes cc, then the moves shown clear it and deliver two men to each of the holes *DD* and one man to each of the holes *ddd*.

And so it goes on. The progression *S*, *T*, *U*, . . . is completely systematic, each step clearing a region of fourteen more holes than its predecessor and delivering one more man.

We can now outline a solution. Hole X_N contains two men initially and we can assume the rest of column x occupied as far as is necessary, so we can play a man from X_{N+1} to X_{N-1}, a man from X_N to X_{N-2}, and so on, finishing by playing a man from X_5 to X_3. This clears holes X_5 to X_{N+1} inclusive and places a man in X_3. We now use the play described above to clear a region of the left-hand side of the board, delivering two men to holes X_5 and X_6 and one man to each of holes X_7 to X_{N+3} inclusive. This is possible provided that we start at the correct place; to be precise, the holes *AA* must be in rows $2N-1$ and $2N$, and must be $2N-6$ columns to the left of column x. We do the same on the right. The men initially in holes X_{N+2} downwards have not been disturbed, so column x now contains the following:

X_0	0
X_1	0
X_2	0
X_3	1
X_4	0
X_5	4
X_6	4
X_7 to X_{N+1} inclusive (if $N>5$)	2
X_{N+2}	3
X_{N+3}	3
X_{N+4}	1

Holes X_{N+5} downwards do not matter. The final play is similar to the initial play; we play one man from X_{N+4} to X_{N+2}, two from X_{N+3} to X_{N+1} and so on until we reach X_6, two from X_7 to X_5, four from X_6 to X_4, two from X_5 to X_3, two from X_4 to X_2, one from X_3 to X_1, and finally one from X_2 to X_0.

Solutions involving fewer men are possible; in particular, we can make more use of column x and its near neighbours, and we can use narrower though more complicated 'tails' at the left-hand ends of regions *S*, *T*, *U*, and their successors. The systematic solution above is however sufficient to establish the required proof.

13

INTO THREE DIMENSIONS

Solitaire, like many other games, can be played in more than two dimensions. We obtain some simple results in this chapter.

Board, rules, notation, and history

The 'board' consists of a set of cells arranged in a cubic lattice as in Figure 13.1, and the 'move' of a jump in any of the three orthogonal directions. We use a similar notation to that for two dimensions, denoting planes by *A*, *B*, *C*, . . . from the front, and rows and columns by 1, 2, 3, . . . and *a*, *b*, *c*, . . . as usual.

The derivation of three-dimensional Solitaire from ordinary Solitaire is so obvious that it is difficult to write with confidence about its history. It was first suggested to me by John Conway in 1961, but only to the extent of pointing out that the 'plane removal' which we shall derive in the next section seemed to make it rather trivial. Harry O. Davis considered it more extensively in 1965 and coined

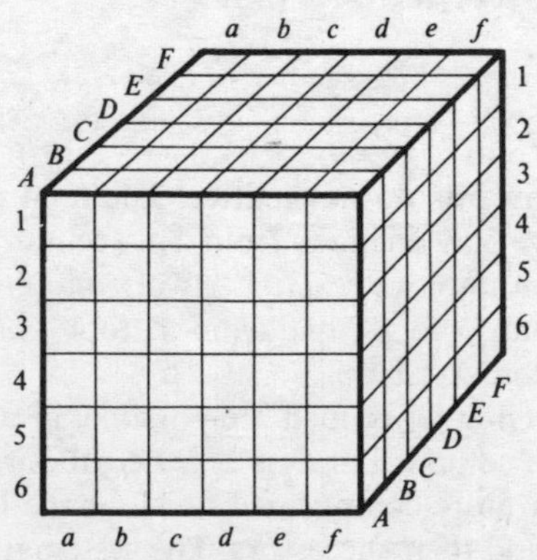

Figure 13.1

the name 'Solidaire' for it. The first mention in print appears to have been by Donald C. Cross in 1968, but this was only a passing reference in an article focused elsewhere. I find it difficult to believe that it did not receive at least occasional attention in earlier years, but no information appears to have survived.

Basic principles

Much of the theory of two-dimensional Solitaire carries over into three dimensions with only slight changes of detail. There are eight classes of men instead of four. There are 256 fundamental classes instead of sixteen. The same basic principles nevertheless apply, and resource, parity, and combined counts can be derived in the same way that they were in earlier chapters.

The block removals which we developed in two dimensions can also be used in three, and a very useful addition can be made to their number: the *full plane removal*, first shown to me by Conway. Suppose that we have a full plane in which at least one single-vacancy complement problem (say the *P*-complement) is soluble, and suppose furthermore that the adjacent planes provide a pair of unlike cells (one full, one empty) on either side of *P*. Then we can make a jump across *P*, solve the *P*-complement problem in the plane, and make a jump back, removing the whole plane and restoring the catalyst as usual.

In Figure 13.2, for example, we consider the *Ac*1-complement problem in the 6 × 6 × 6 cube. We start by noting that *Ac*1 is empty

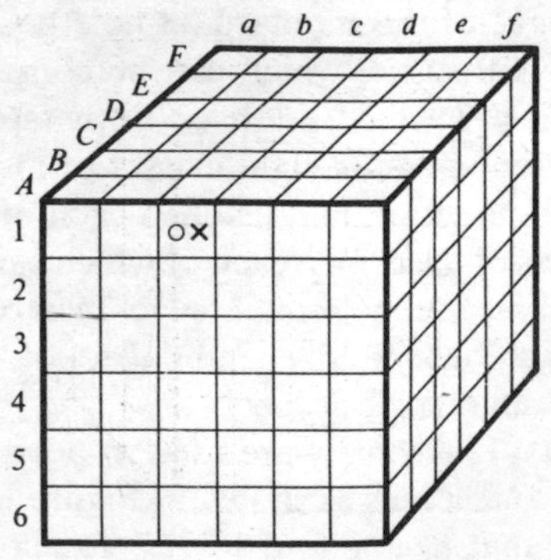

Figure 13.2

	a	*b*	*c*	*d*	*e*	*f*
1	•	•	(•)		•	•
2	•	•	•		•	•
3	•	•	•		•	•
4	•	•	•		•	•
5	•	•	•		•	•
6	•	•	•		•	•

Figure 13.3

and *Ae*1 full, and that the *A*1-complement problem is soluble in plane *d* (which is an ordinary 6 × 6 plane). So we can remove plane *d* by playing *Ae*1–*Ac*1, solving the *A*1-complement problem in plane *d*, and playing *Ac*1–*Ae*1. Figure 13.3 now shows a typical plane parallel to plane *A*, cell *c*1 being empty in plane *A* and full in planes *B* to *F*. We can now jump every man in plane *f* to plane *d*, clearing planes *f* and *e* and refilling plane *d*, and then perform another plane removal to clear plane *d* again. This deals with the right-hand half of the board. To deal with the left, we can perform an *A*1-complement solution in plane *c*, jump every man except *Aa*1 from plane *a* to plane *c*, remove plane *c*, and finally play *Aa*1–*Ac*1.

The other single-vacancy complement problems in the 6 × 6 × 6 cube can be solved in a similar manner.

The 135-cell board

The natural analogue of the standard 33-hole board is the 135-cell board shown in Figure 13.4, which can be considered either as a 3 × 3 × 3 cube with a 3 × 3 × 2 knob on each face or as three intersecting 3 × 3 × 7 cuboids. Its eight classes of men can be characterised as follows: one set of 'middle' men each of which can reach the centre, three sets of 'face' men each of which can reach the centre of an outside 3 × 3 face, three sets of 'edge' men each of which can reach the centre of an outside edge, and one set of 'corner' men each of which can reach an outside corner.

For practical play, I personally use a flat wooden board with holes clustered in threes and sevens as shown in Figure 13.5. I assume the board oriented so that *a* . . . *g* and 1 . . . 7 go across and down as usual, and represent planes *A* . . . *G* by the different holes in each

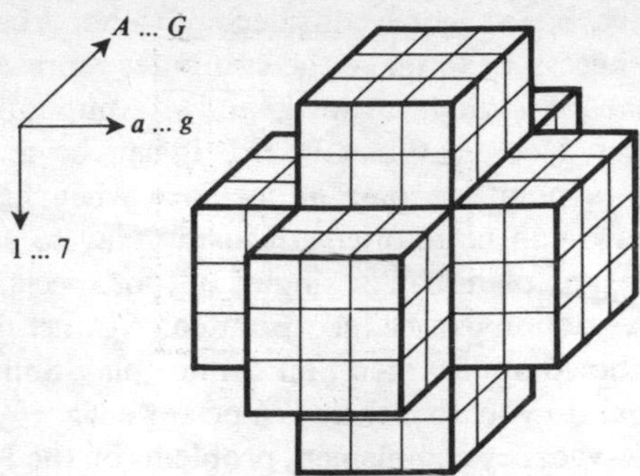

Figure 13.4

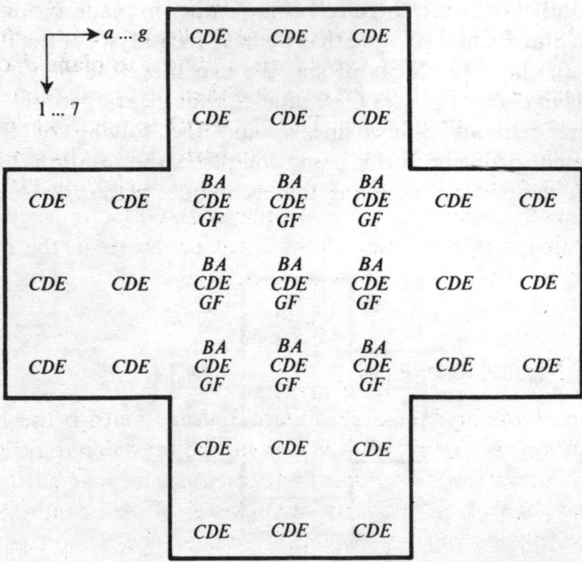

Figure 13.5

cluster. The S-shape assumed for the seven-hole clusters may be noted; these clusters might have been straight lines, as the three-hole clusters are, but the little rosettes are more attractive and one soon remembers which way the line goes. An afternoon's work suffices to make such a board.

An alternative 'board' worth considering is a home computer. The programming necessary to make the computer represent the board and obey moves is straightforward, and a computer has certain advantages over a conventional board: it can be made to reject invalid moves (a point of some importance when first trying the game), the board can be re-oriented during play to allow viewing from any angle, any plane can be singled out for special display, and a facility for retraction can be incorporated. Against this, if Father wants to use the computer then Son cannot play Solitaire (or vice versa), and what do you do if there is a power cut?

All the single-vacancy complement problems on the 135-cell board can be solved by a technique similar to that described for the 6 × 6 × 6 board. To solve the *Dd*4-complement problem, for example, we can start by removing planes *c* and *e*. Figure 13.6 now shows a typical plane parallel to plane *D* (cell *d*4 being empty in plane *D* and full in planes *C* and *E*), and we note that we have a catalyst for the removal of each of the side blocks of six. We can therefore play two six-removals in each of planes *C*, *D*, and *E*, thus clearing knobs *ab* and *fg*. There remains only plane *d*, and the solving of the *D*4-complement problem in this plane completes the solution. I cannot resist the temptation of calling this technique 'planar removal with knobs on'.

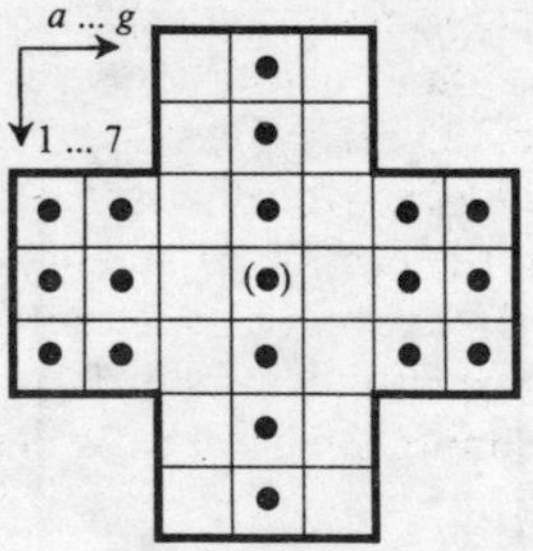

Figure 13.6

Many other problems can be solved by similar techniques. I believe all the double-vacancy and triple-vacancy complement problems on this board to be soluble, though I have not verified every case, and the only insoluble quadruple-vacancy complement problems that I know are those in which the initial vacancies are in four of the seven 'middle' cells. Even the apparently tough *Dd*1/

2/3/4/5/6-complement problem is soluble, and the reader may care to try it. Plane *D* of this problem is shown in Figure 13.7, and the rest of the board starts full and must finish empty. (The full *Dd*1/2/3/4/5/6/7-complement problem can be proved insoluble by a simple resource count, however: give value 1 to each of the seven 'middle' cells and also to *Dd*1 and *Dd*7, resulting in an initial value of 4 and a target value of 5.)

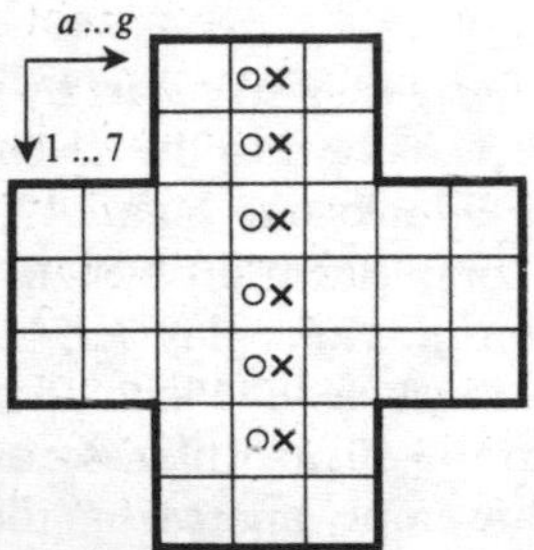

Figure 13.7

Short solutions

In comparison with two-dimensional Solitaire, little work has been done on the finding of short solutions in three dimensions. When he first considered the 135-cell game, Davis combined his minimal solutions in 33-hole Solitaire with efficient knob-clearances to obtain a 70-move solution to the central game and a 63-move solution to the *Cc*3-complement. I have since used this technique in a slightly different way to obtain a 63-move solution to the central game, but I am sure that further improvement is possible.

Long sweeps

Although it is more complex than ordinary Solitaire, three-dimensional Solitaire offers nothing new in principle, and in many respects it may be thought that the increased complexity does not bring increased pleasure with it. One area in which three dimensions undoubtedly do offer greater scope than two is that of long-sweep solutions to problems. The longest final sweeps in solutions to single-vacancy complement problems on the standard 33-hole board involve eight men. The longest final sweeps in solutions to such problems on the 135-cell board are as follows:

(a) with a face man, 14 (the *Dd*3-complement with a man on the watch at *Dd*7);
(b) with an edge man, 29 (the *Cc*2-complement with a man on the watch at *Ce*2);
(c) with a corner man, 37 (the *Cc*3-complement with a man on the watch at *Cc*1).

The first of these is fairly easy. We start by playing all but the last move of an eight-sweep solution to the *d*3-complement problem in plane *D*, so that plane *D* looks like Figure 13.8. Then we play *Bd*3–*Dd*3 and solve the *d*3-complement problem in plane *C*, so that plane *C* is cleared apart from *d*3, and play *Fd*5–*Dd*5 and solve the *d*5-complement problem in plane *E*. Plane *D* now looks like Figure 13.9, plane *d* like Figure 13.10, and planes *c* and *e* like Figure 13.11, and knobs *ab* and *fg* are empty apart from the men in *Db*4 and *Df*4 which contribute to plane *D*. We now remove the side sixes in planes

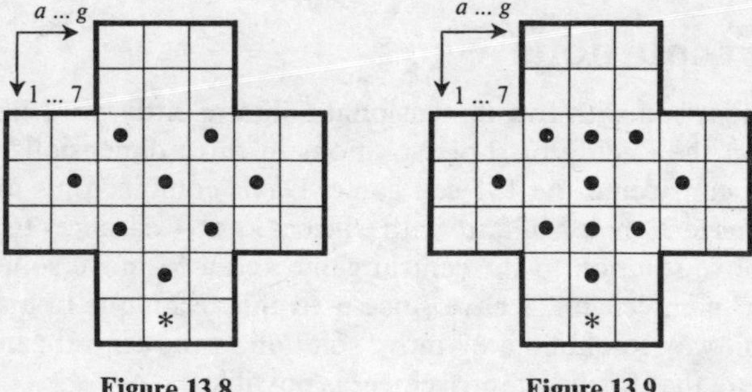

Figure 13.8 **Figure 13.9**

c and *e*, and play the obvious L-moves in plane *d* (*G*3–*E*3, *D*3–*F*3, *G*5–*G*3–*E*3, *A*5–*C*5, *D*5–*B*5 and *A*3–*A*5–*C*5). This leaves planes *D* and *d* both looking like Figure 13.8 and the rest of the board empty, and round we go.

The other problems do not yield so easily and we leave them for the pleasure of the reader. Suitable patterns for the final sweeps are shown in Figures 13.12 and 13.13.

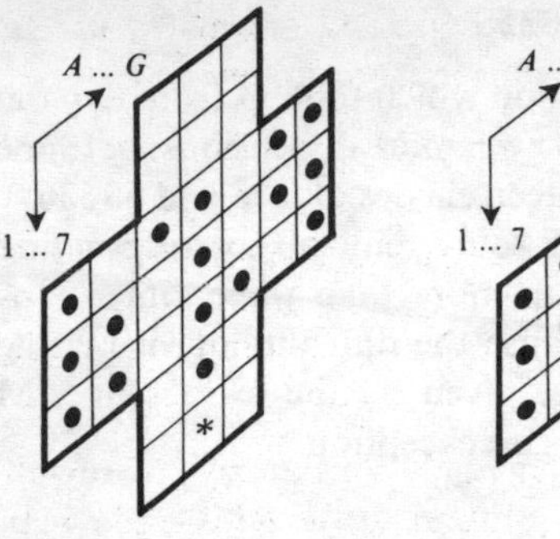

Figure 13.10

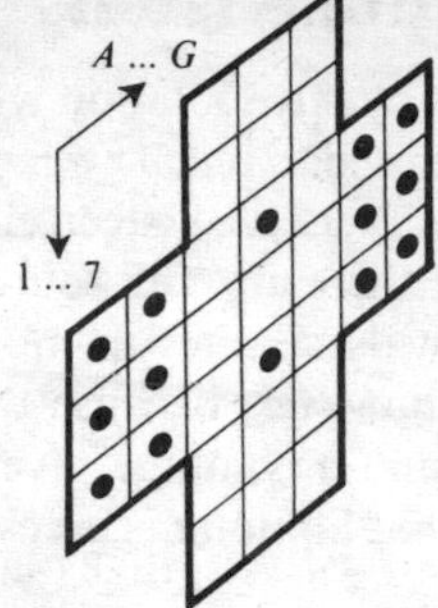

Figure 13.11

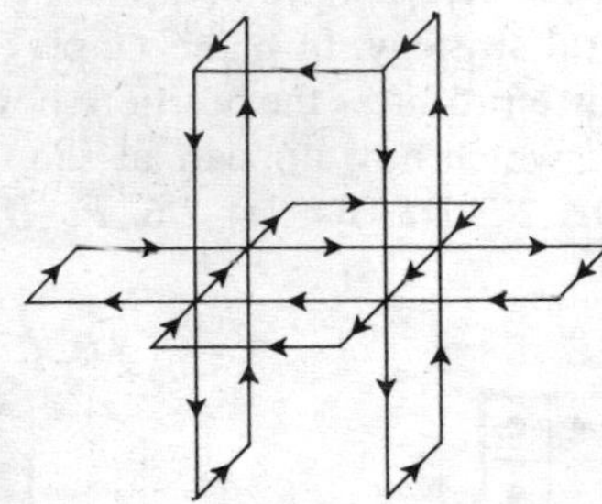

Figure 13.12

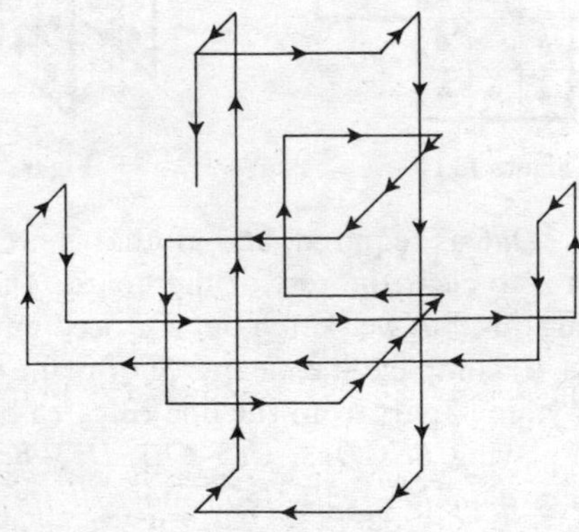

Figure 13.13

Higher dimensions

The process of extrapolation which took us from two dimensions to three can be used to reach even more dimensions. In four dimensions, for example, there are sixteen classes of men and 65 536 fundamental classes, and there are 'full solid' removals corresponding to our full plane removals. Games in more than three dimensions are rarely successful, however, because the difficulty of visualising the board outweighs any advantage given by the extra scope. My personal opinion is that Solitaire is no exception.

Solutions to Chapter 13

Complement problems with fewer than five initial vacancies should give no trouble. The *Dd*1/2/3/4/5/6-complement can be solved by following this general strategy: in plane *D*, play *b*3–*d*3, *b*4–*d*4–*d*2, *f*3–*d*3–*d*1, *f*4–*d*4, which produces the position shown in Figure 13.14, and then in plane *d*, which now appears as shown in Figure 13.15, play *B*3–*D*3, *D*4–*D*2, *B*5–*D*5, *B*4–*D*4–*D*6, *F*3–*D*3, *F*4–*D*4, *F*5–*D*5.

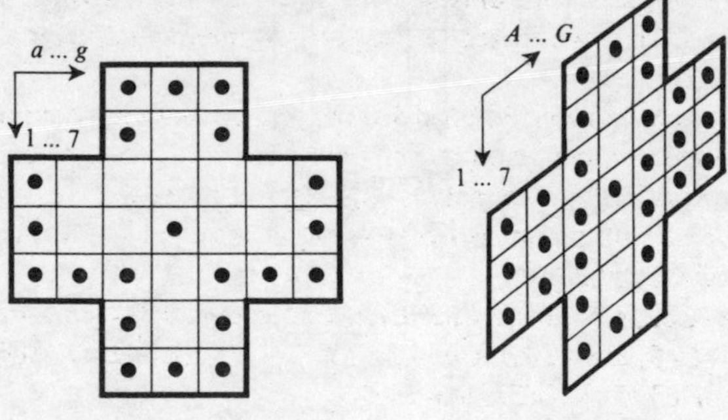

Figure 13.14 **Figure 13.15**

This fills *Dd*1 . . . *Dd*6 as required, and all that is necessary to complete a solution is to clear the rest of the board. There is no great difficulty in doing this, but we sketch out a procedure in the interests of completeness: (i) complete the clearance of plane *C*, for example by clearing everything apart from the line *c*3/*c*4/*c*5 by moves in the plane and then playing *Bc*3–*Dc*3, *Cc*5–*Cc*3, *Dc*3–*Bc*3; (ii) in plane *D*, clear the lines *a*3/*a*4/*a*5, *g*3/*g*4/*g*5, and *c*7/*d*7/*e*7 by play such as *Ea*3–*Ca*3, *Da*5–*Da*3, *Ca*3–*Ea*3; (iii) complete the clearance of plane *E* in a similar manner to step (i); (iv) in plane *c*, remove the sixes *A*3/*A*4/*A*5/*B*3/*B*4/*B*5 and *F*3/*F*4/*F*5/*G*3/*G*4/*G*5; (v) in plane *d*, remove the lines *A*3/*A*4/*A*5 and *G*3/*G*4/*G*5; (vi) in plane *e*, remove the sixes *A*3/*A*4/*A*5/*B*3/*B*4/*B*5 and *F*3/*F*4/*F*5/*G*3/*G*4/*G*5; (vii) in plane *D*, play *c*6–*c*4, *e*6–*e*4, *c*1–*c*3–*c*5–*e*5, *f*5–*d*5, *e*1–*e*3–*e*5–*c*5, *b*5–*d*5, completing the solution.

The central game can be solved in 63 moves as follows: (i) play *Bd*4–*Dd*4; (ii) in plane *C*, play the first 17 moves of a Bergholt 18-move *d*4-complement solution, leaving men in *b*4 and *c*4; (iii) play *Ac*3–*Cc*3, *Ae*3–*Ce*3, *Ac*5–*Cc*5, *Ae*5–*Ae*3–*Ac*3–*Ac*5–*Ae*5–*Ce*5, *Ed*3–*Cd*3–*Ad*3–*Ad*5–*Cd*5, clearing plane *A* and leaving only *c*4 and *e*4 occupied in plane *B*; (iv) in plane *E*, play a 16-move *d*3-complement solution; (v) play *Gc*3–*Ec*3, *Ge*3–*Ee*3, *Gc*5–*Ec*5, *Ge*5–*Ge*3–*Gc*3–*Gc*5–*Ge*5–*Ee*5, *Ed*3–*Gd*3–*Gd*5–*Ed*5, clearing plane *G* and leaving only *c*4, *d*4, and *e*4 occupied in plane *F*; (vi) in plane *D*, only *d*3 currently being vacant, play a 17-move solution to leave a single survivor at *d*6, picking up the chains *Cc*3/*Bc*4/*Cc*5/*Ec*5/*Fc*4/*Ec*3 and *Ce*3/*Be*4/*Ce*5/*Ee*5/*Fe*4/*Ee*3 on the way; (vii) play *Cb*4–*Cd*4–*Cd*6–*Ed*6–*Ed*4 and *Fd*4–*Dd*4. This solution should be regarded as a joint product of Davis, Bergholt, and myself. The Law of Murphy states that either Davis or I will discover an improvement just after this book has gone to press.

The long-sweep solutions with edge and corner men cannot readily be visualised without board and men, so we do not attempt a description and content ourselves with lists of moves.

The *Cc*2-complement problem with a man on the watch at *Ce*2 can be solved as follows:

*Cc*4–*Cc*2, *Cc*6–*Cc*4, *Ce*5–*Cc*5, *Cc*4–*Cc*6, *Ac*3–*Cc*3, *Cc*2–*Cc*4;
*Ec*5–*Cc*5, *De*5–*Dc*5, *Cc*5–*Ec*5, *Ec*3–*Cc*3, *De*3–*Dc*3, *Cc*3–*Ec*3;
*Fc*3–*Dc*3, *Ee*3–*Ec*3, *Dc*3–*Fc*3;
*Cc*7–*Cc*5, *Cc*4–*Cc*6, *Ec*7–*Cc*7–*Cc*5, *Ce*7–*Cc*7, *Ed*7–*Cd*7, *Cc*7–*Ce*7;
*Ce*7–*Ce*5, *Ce*4–*Ce*6, *Ee*7–*Ce*7–*Ce*5, *Ec*5–*Ec*7, *Ee*6–*Ec*6, *Ec*7–*Ec*5;
*Ec*1–*Ec*3, *Ec*4–*Ec*2, *Cc*1–*Ec*1–*Ec*3, *Ce*1–*Cc*1, *Ed*1–*Cd*1, *Cc*1–*Ce*1;
*Ee*1–*Ee*3, *Ee*4–*Ee*2, *Ce*1–*Ee*1–*Ee*3;
*Ed*5–*Ed*3, *Ed*4–*Ed*4, *Ed*3–*Ed*5, *Cd*6–*Ed*6–*Ed*4, *Cd*2–*Cd*4, *Ed*2–*Cd*2;
*Cb*5–*Cd*5, *Ac*5–*Cc*5, *Cd*5–*Cb*5;

*Fc*3–*Dc*3, *Ea*3–*Ec*3, *Dc*3–*Fc*3, *Fc*5–*Dc*5, *Ea*5–*Ec*5, *Dc*5–*Fc*5;
*Ef*3–*Ed*3, *Ge*3–*Ee*3, *Ed*3–*Ef*3, *Ef*5–*Ed*5, *Ge*5–*Ee*5, *Ed*5–*Ef*5;
*Be*3–*De*3, *Cg*3–*Ce*3, *De*3–*Be*3, *Be*5–*De*5, *Cg*5–*Ce*5, *De*5–*Be*5;
*Be*3–*Bc*3, *Bd*5–*Bd*3, *Bc*3–*Be*3, *Cb*3–*Eb*3, *Db*5–*Db*3, *Eb*3–*Cb*3;
*Fc*3–*Fe*3, *Fd*5–*Fd*3, *Fe*3–*Fc*3, *Ef*3–*Cf*3, *Df*5–*Df*3, *Cf*3–*Ef*3;
*Ae*3–*Ce*3, *Ae*5–*Ac*5–*Ac*3–*Ae*3–*Ae*5–*Ce*5;
*Ca*3–*Cc*3, *Ca*5–*Ea*5–*Ea*3–*Ca*3–*Ca*5–*Cc*5;
*Gc*3–*Ec*3, *Gc*5–*Ge*5–*Ge*3–*Gc*3–*Gc*5–*Ec*5;
*Eg*3–*Ee*3, *Eg*5–*Cg*5–*Cg*3–*Eg*3–*Eg*5–*Ee*5;
*Ce*2–*Ce*4–*Ae*4–*Ac*4–*Cc*4–*Ec*4–*Gc*4–*Ge*4–*Ee*4–*Ce*4–*Cc*4–*Ca*4–*Ea*4–*Ec*4–*Ee*4–*Eg*4–*Cg*4–*Ce*4–*Ce*6–*Ee*6–*Ee*4–*Ee*2–*Ce*2–*Cc*2–*Cc*4–*Cc*6–*Ec*6–*Ec*4–*Ec*2–*Cc*2.

The *Cc*3-complement problem with a man on the watch at *Cc*1 can be solved as follows:

*Ca*3–*Cc*3, *Cd*3–*Cb*3, *Cf*3–*Cd*3, *Ce*1–*Ce*3, *Ac*3–*Cc*3, *Cd*3–*Cf*3, *Cb*3–*Cd*3;
*Bc*5–*Bc*3, *Dc*5–*Bc*5, *Fc*5–*Dc*5, *Cc*7–*Cc*5, *Ea*5–*Ec*5, *Dc*5–*Fc*5, *Bc*5–*Dc*5;
*Ca*5–*Cc*5, *Dc*5–*Bc*5, *Ac*5–*Cc*5, *De*5–*Dc*5–*Bc*5;
*Be*5–*De*5, *Cg*5–*Ce*5, *De*5–*Be*5, *Fe*5–*De*5, *Ee*7–*Ee*5, *De*5–*Fe*5;
*Eg*5–*Ee*5, *Ee*4–*Ee*6, *Ee*2–*Ee*4, *Ge*3–*Ee*3, *Ge*5–*Ee*5, *Ee*4–*Ee*2, *Ee*6–*Ee*4;
*Dc*3–*Dc*5, *Fc*3–*Dc*3, *Ec*1–*Ec*3, *Dc*3–*Fc*3;
*Ea*3–*Ec*3, *Ed*3–*Eb*3–*Eb*5, *Gc*3–*Ec*3, *Ed*5–*Ed*3–*Eb*3–*Cb*3–*Cb*5;
*Gc*5–*Ec*5, *Dc*5–*Fc*5–*Fe*5, *Ec*7–*Ec*5, *Da*5–*Dc*5–*Fc*5–*Fc*3–*Fe*3;
*Ce*7–*Ce*5, *Ce*4–*Ce*6–*Ee*6, *Ae*5–*Ce*5, *Cc*4–*Ce*4–*Ce*6–*Cc*6–*Ec*6;
*Eg*3–*Ee*3, *Cd*3–*Ed*3–*Ef*3–*Ef*5, *Cg*3–*Ce*3, *Ee*1–*Ee*3, *Ed*1–*Ed*3–*Ef*3–*Cf*3–*Cf*5;
*Cc*2–*Ec*2, *Ee*4–*Ce*4–*Ce*2–*Ee*2, *Ae*3–*Ce*3, *Ae*4–*Ce*4–*Ce*2–*Cc*2;
*Bc*3–*Be*3, *Bc*5–*Be*5;
*Dd*1–*Dd*3, *De*3–*Dc*3, *Dd*7–*Dd*5–*Dd*3, *Dc*3–*De*3;
*Ad*4–*Cd*4, *Da*4–*Dc*4, *Dg*4–*De*4, *Gd*4–*Ed*4, *Ec*4–*Cc*4–*Ce*4–*Ee*4–*Ec*4;
*Ge*4–*Ee*4, *Dg*5–*De*5, *Ed*7–*Ed*5;
*Cc*1–*Ce*1–*Ee*1–*Ee*3–*Ee*5–*Eg*5–*Eg*3–*Cg*3–*Cg*5–*Ce*5–*Cc*5–*Ca*5–*Ca*3–*Ea*3–*Ea*5–*Ec*5–*Ee*5–*Ge*5–*Gc*5–*Gc*3–*Ge*3–*Ee*3–*Ce*3–*Ae*3–*Ac*3–*Ac*5–*Ae*5–*Ce*5–*Ee*5–*Ee*7–*Ce*7–*Cc*7–*Ec*7–*Ec*5–*Ec*3–*Ec*1–*Cc*1–*Cc*3.

14

SOLITAIRE UNLIMITED

We said in Chapter 1 that the essence of Solitaire is that it is a puzzle game played with board and men, the move being a jump by a man over one or more other men. In this chapter we look at some alternative rules of play, while preserving this fundamental essence.

Triangular Solitaire

The game of Triangular Solitaire differs from ordinary Solitaire only in being played along the lines of a triangular lattice, each hole having six neighbours. A suitable board is shown in Figure 14.1. The natural diagrammatic representation of the holes is as hexagons, which leads to the alternative name 'Hexagonal Solitaire'.

All the principles of ordinary Solitaire carry over into Triangular Solitaire, though there are naturally differences of detail. In particular, there are only four fundamental classes of positions, as can be shown by applying the arguments of Chapter 4 to the lines *A*, *B*, *C* in Figure 14.2.

It is natural to select three kinds of board for particular attention: the equilateral triangular boards typified by Figure 14.1, the equilateral hexagonal boards typified by Figure 14.3, and the equilateral

Figure 14.1

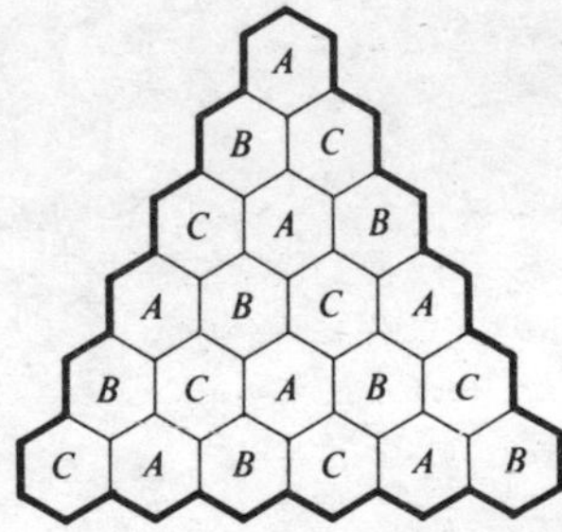

Figure 14.2

stellar boards typified by Figure 14.4. We characterise these boards by the length of their edges; an equilateral triangular board with edge n has $n(n+1)/2$ holes, an equilateral hexagonal board with edge n has $3n^2-3n+1$ holes, and an equilateral stellar board with edge n has $6n^2-6n+1$ holes (an edge being counted from an outside corner to an adjacent inside corner, both corners inclusive).

An *equilateral triangular* board is a null-class board if and only if the length of its edge is of the form $3n$ or $3n+2$. The smallest on

Figure 14.3

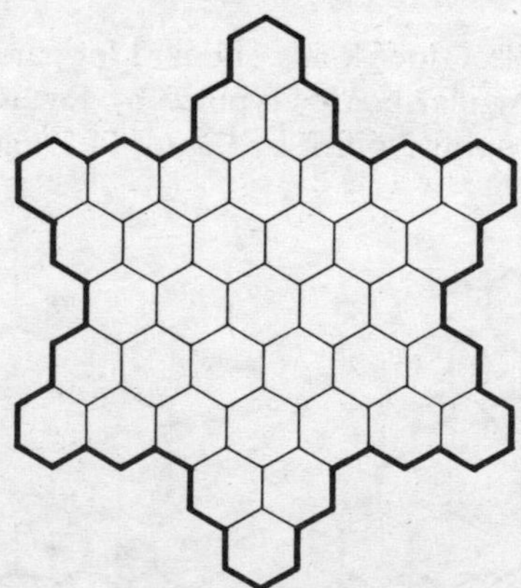

Figure 14.4

which a complement problem is actually soluble is the 15-hole board of Figure 14.5, a single-vacancy complement problem on this board being soluble if the initial vacancy is one of the holes marked *V*. The reader may care to try the problem in which the initial vacancy is at the top, which is the hardest of the set. The smallest equilateral triangular board on which every single-vacancy complement problem is soluble is the 21-hole board of Figure 14.1. The problem in which the initial vacancy is at the top is again the hardest of the set, though that in which it is in the middle of a three-hole line is also quite tough.

The condition for an equilateral triangular board to have a unique central hole is that the length of its edge be of the form $3n+1$. It follows that *no central-vacancy complement problem is soluble on an equilateral triangular board.*

An *equilateral hexagonal* board is a null-class board if and only if the length of its edge is of the form $3n+2$. The smallest on which a complement problem is actually soluble is the 61-hole board shown in Figure 14.3. In particular, every single-vacancy complement problem on this board is soluble, none being difficult.

An *equilateral stellar* board is a null-class board if and only if its edge is of the form $3n+2$. The smallest such board is the 13-hole board shown in Figure 14.6. A single-vacancy complement problem on this board is soluble if the initial vacancy is either of the holes marked *V*. The smallest equilateral stellar board on which every single-vacancy complement problem is soluble is the 121-hole board with edge 5.

Triangular Solitaire is certainly old; Jerry Slocum, a puzzle collector of Beverly Hills, sent me an American patent of 1891, and I presume that the basic idea is much older. Nevertheless little appears to have been published on it. Martin Gardner mentioned it in his

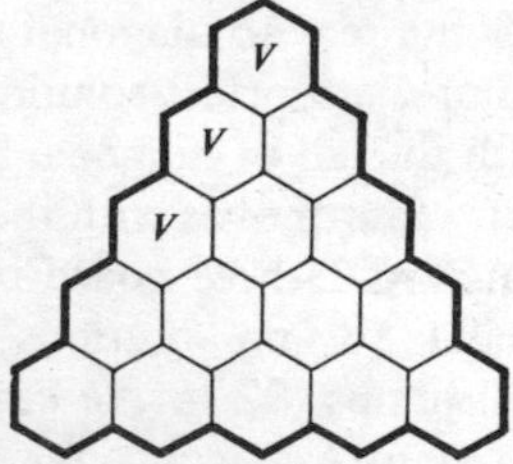

Figure 14.5

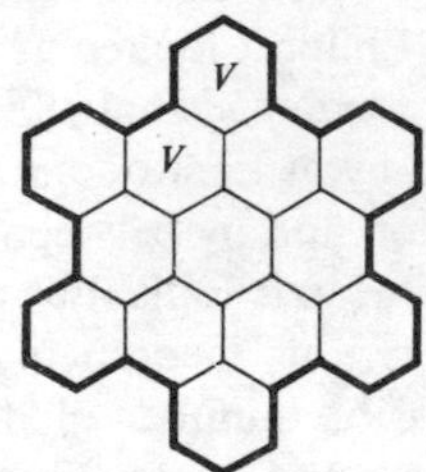

Figure 14.6

Scientific American column in 1966 (since reprinted in *Mathematical carnival*) and I. R. Hentzel wrote a paper in 1973, but the field remains almost unexplored. Perhaps readers will be tempted.

Beginner's licence

An extension frequently made by beginners to the rules of Solitaire is to allow diagonal moves as well as ordinary orthogonal moves. The immediate reaction of the expert is that this makes the game too easy. Well, perhaps, but there is a little more to it than meets the eye. The problem shown in Figure 14.7 is hopelessly insoluble using ordinary moves alone, since there is no way of dealing with all the outside men. The reader may care to try it with the help of diagonal moves. We leave our discussion of the fundamental theory of Solitaire with diagonal moves until the solutions at the end of the chapter, since to give it now would compromise this problem.

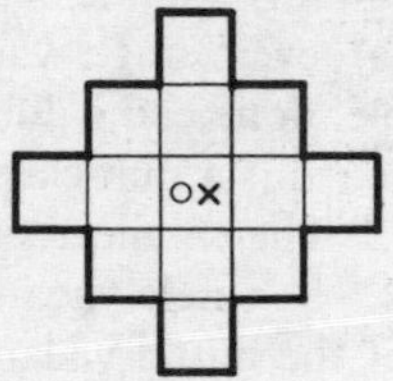

Figure 14.7

Little work has been done with diagonal moves. Several old problems exist with small numbers of pegs, but these were not normally called 'Solitaire'. The American booklet 'Problems in Puzzle-peg' (sixth edition, 1929) includes several 33-hole Solitaire problems requiring diagonal moves, but a note discourages readers from submitting any more 'as the fans prefer straight moves'. Harry Davis and Wade Philpott looked at 6×6 Solitaire with diagonal moves in 1966, and concluded that the length of the shortest solutions could be reduced by at least one move with the aid of diagonal moves in one direction and by between two and four moves with their aid in both. John Harris looked at the standard 33-hole board in 1970–1 and used various theoretical arguments to find solutions with the largest possible number of diagonal jumps (22 in the case of the central game and up to 27 in other single-vacancy single-survivor problems). The shortest solution that I have seen to the 33-hole central game with diagonal moves takes only 16 moves, but I suspect that this can be improved.

We may note that Triangular Solitaire is equivalent to ordinary Solitaire with the addition of diagonal moves in one direction but not the other. Philpott has accordingly suggested the terms *6-move Solitaire* for Triangular Solitaire and *8-move Solitaire* for Solitaire with diagonal moves in both directions. It seems likely that diagonal moves will receive greater attention in future and this terminology might reasonably be adopted as standard, ordinary Solitaire becoming *4-move Solitaire*.

Linear Solitaire

In Chapter 13, we went from two dimensions to three. It might seem that the inverse change, from two dimensions to one, should be similar; we should drop from sixteen fundamental classes to four, a board should be a null-class board if and only if its length is a multiple of three, and so on. The resulting game appears to be so limited in scope as to be almost trivial.

The ordinary game is indeed fairly trivial. There are indeed only four fundamental classes and a board whose length is a multiple of three is indeed a null-class board, but the only single-vacancy complement problems actually soluble are the 1-complement on a board of length 3 and the 2-complement on a board of length 6. No other single-vacancy single-survivor problem on a board of odd length is soluble, and a single-vacancy single-survivor problem on a board of even length $2n$ ($\geqslant 4$) is soluble if and only if the initial vacancy is hole 2 or 5 and the target hole is hole $2n-1$ or $2n-4$ (or vice versa).

If we play Up-and-down Solitaire, however, we find it not quite so trivial. In two dimensions, there are sixteen immovable positions and any two other positions in the same fundamental class can be transformed into each other by a succession of ordinary and inverse moves. In one dimension there are only four immovable positions, as we would expect, but to play from the position with only hole 2 occupied (Figure 14.8, top) to that with holes 1 and 3 occupied (Figure 14.8, bottom) proves to be impossible however long the board, despite the fact that the positions are in the same fundamental class. So the fundamental classes do not provide the complete criterion for solubility in one dimension that they do in two.

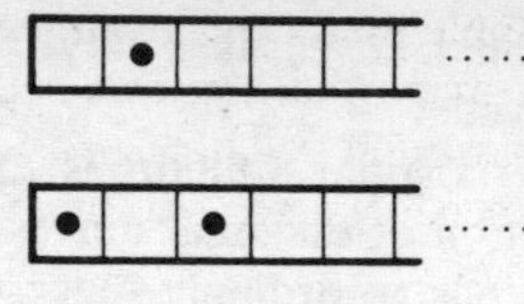

Figure 14.8

To discover the whole truth, let us consider the transformations of Suremain de Missery. The most important of these are repeated in Figure 14.9, the others being expressible in terms of these. It will be noticed that they are of two kinds: types (a1) and (a2), which are ordinary or inverse Solitaire moves and which we call *unbalanced* since they feature unlike outside holes, and types (b) and (c), which are not Solitaire moves and which we call *balanced* since they feature like outside holes.

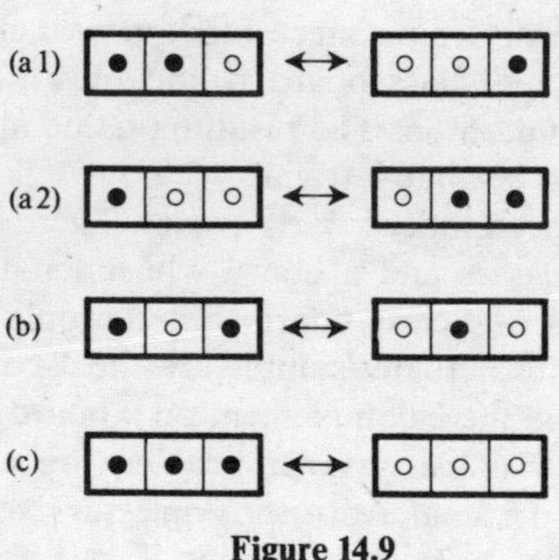

Figure 14.9

The division of these transformations into balanced and unbalanced leads to a division of each fundamental class into four subclasses. This is illustrated in Table 14.1, which shows all the possible positions on a board of length 6, '1' representing an occupied hole and '0' a vacant hole. From each position, a single unbalanced transformation produces a position in the subclass horizontally adjacent and a single balanced transformation a position in the subclass vertically adjacent. (There are two unimportant exceptions: no unbalanced transformations are possible between the upper subclasses of Class 0, since these contain the four immovable positions, and no vertical transformations are possible between the right-hand subclasses of Class 2, since these contain the four positions which are immovable under balanced transformation.) It follows that any chain of transformations between a position in the top half of a fundamental class and one in the bottom half must contain an odd number of balanced transformations, and so cannot consist entirely of Solitaire moves.

A similar result can be shown to hold for any longer board, with the unimportant difference that no subclass on a board of length greater than 6 consists entirely of immovable positions.

Table 14.1: The fundamental classes on a board of length 6

Class 0			Class 1		
000000		010101	000001	$\leftrightarrow U$	000110
111111		101010	001000		100010
			011010		101011
$\updownarrow B$		$\updownarrow B$	101100		110000
			$\updownarrow B$		$\updownarrow B$
000111	$\leftrightarrow U$	001001	001111	$\leftrightarrow U$	010011
001110		010010	010100		100101
011100		011011	011101		110111
100011		100100	111001		111110
110001		101101			
111000		110110			

Class 2			Class 3		
000010	$\leftrightarrow U$	001100	000011	$\leftrightarrow U$	000100
001011		110011	010001		001101
010000			011000		010110
101111			110101		100000
110100					
111101			$\updownarrow B$		$\updownarrow B$
$\updownarrow B$					
000101	$\leftrightarrow U$	011001	011111	$\leftrightarrow U$	001010
010111		100110	101001		100111
011110			110010		101110
100001			111011		111100
101000					
111010					

Multiple-removal Solitaire

The essence of Solitaire does not appear to be seriously changed if we require the jump to remove two or more adjacent men instead of just one. Such a game was indeed considered briefly by Hermary.

Nevertheless, though the change in the rules may be small, the difference in effect is substantial, and the game proves to be clumsy and inflexible. As an example, we consider Twin-removal Solitaire, in which the jump must remove *two* adjacent men (*d*1 to *d*4 removing *d*2 and *d*3, for example).

We note first that the number of men on the board can change only by an even number, so that a position with an odd number of men cannot be derived from one with an even number nor vice versa. Positions can therefore be divided into two 'fundamental superclasses' according as the number of men in them is odd or even.

Within each superclass are 64 'ordinary' fundamental classes. This is easily proved by considering the labelling of diagonals in Figures 14.10 and 14.11 and applying the same arguments as in Chapter 4. Because each move now removes two men, we say that a diagonal is 'in phase' if and only if it holds an even number of men when the total on the board is of the form $4n$ or $4n+1$, and 'out of phase' otherwise. This is a natural analogy of our definition in Chapter 4. The phases of any three of the diagonals *A* to *D* are independent, as are those of any three of the diagonals *E* to *H*. This gives 64 classes in each of the two superclasses, making 128 fundamental classes in all.

D	*A*	*B*	*C*	*D*	*A*
A	*B*	*C*	*D*	*A*	*B*
B	*C*	*D*	*A*	*B*	*C*
C	*D*	*A*	*B*	*C*	*D*
D	*A*	*B*	*C*	*D*	*A*
A	*B*	*C*	*D*	*A*	*B*

Figure 14.10

E	*F*	*G*	*H*	*E*	*F*
H	*E*	*F*	*G*	*H*	*E*
G	*H*	*E*	*F*	*G*	*H*
F	*G*	*H*	*E*	*F*	*G*
E	*F*	*G*	*H*	*E*	*F*
H	*E*	*F*	*G*	*H*	*E*

Figure 14.11

Most of our play in this book has used boards with square symmetry. A disappointing result applies here: *No single-vacancy complement problem on a board with square symmetry is soluble in Twin-removal Solitaire.*

This result is obviously true for an odd–odd board, because the number of holes in such a board is odd and hence no position is in the same fundamental superclass as its complement. To prove it for an even–even board, let us suppose, without loss of generality, that diagonal *A* in Figure 14.10 is one of the axes of symmetry. The other diagonal axis of symmetry then consists only of *B* and *D* holes and contains no *A* or *C* holes. It follows that the total number of *A* holes is even, since every hole not on the other diagonal axis of symmetry is accompanied by its reflection in that axis. This implies that the parity of the number of occupied *A* holes is unchanged by complementation, so complementation must involve an even number of moves. But the total number of holes on the board must be a multiple of four, $4n$ say, so the number of men to be removed in a single-vacancy complementation must be $4n-2$, implying precisely $2n-1$ moves. A single-vacancy complement problem is therefore insoluble on such a board.

The clumsiness of Multiple-removal Solitaire increases with the number of men to be removed by a move, and we shall not consider it further. An alternative, in which we allow a move to jump over any number of adjacent men (as in some forms of Draughts), might be called Arbitrary-removal Solitaire, but this proves to be disappointing for the opposite reason: it is too easy. For example, there is no satisfactory concept of 'fundamental class', and every single-vacancy single-survivor problem is soluble on many boards.

Geometrical frolics

We have assumed so far that two-dimensional play is on a flat board. There is no reason (apart from the practicalities of marketing) why it should be, and those with a taste for such things can have fun on the surfaces of cylinders, tori, Möbius strips, wild-horned spheres, and other exotica. No new principle is involved, though it should be noted that the different classes of men may no longer number four nor the fundamental classes sixteen. For example, the flat 4×4 square board is not a null-class board, but if it is bent into a cylinder, columns 1 and 4 being made adjacent, then it becomes such a board, and indeed all the single-vacancy complement problems on it become soluble.

It is also possible to play enjoyably on abnormal arrangements of lines in two dimensions. The reader may care to try the attractive little board shown in Figure 14.12, which was suggested to me by Martin Gardner, and its pentagonal analogue shown in Figure 14.13. The board of Figure 14.12 was developed for the game Solomon, and Gardner therefore suggests that this variant should be called 'Solomon Solitaire'.

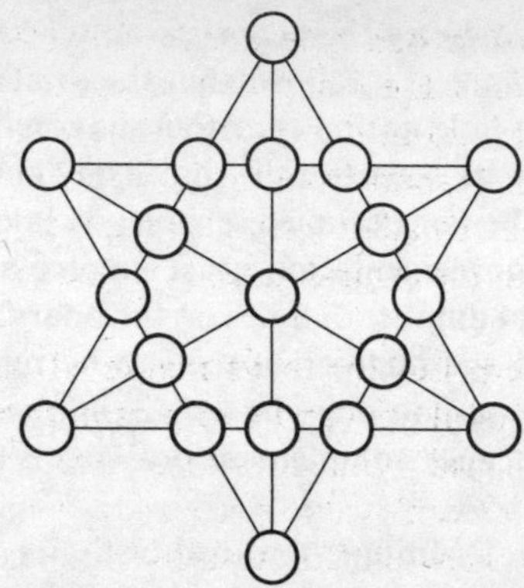

Figure 14.12

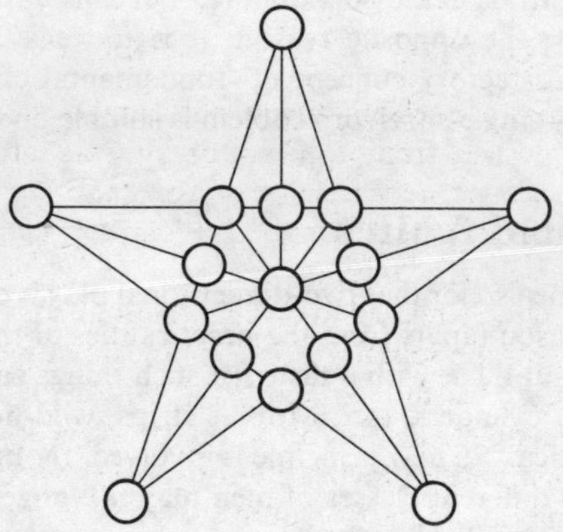

Figure 14.13

Extended Solitaires

Various extended forms of Solitaire have been invented over the years, and several games have been marketed which amount to extensions or modifications of Solitaire. The following brief selection does no more than reflect my personal fancy.

(a) T. R. Dawson suggested playing Additive Solitaire with consecutively numbered counters, the objectives being both to fill all the board apart from one hole and to leave specific counters in pre-assigned positions. His first proposal was to leave the five square numbers 1, 4, 9, 16, 25 in the central cross *d*3/*cde*4/*d*5, the rest of the board being filled apart from the inevitable single vacancy. This can actually be done by a fairly simple adaptation of our first block-removal solution to the central game, the final vacancy being left at *d*1.

(b) Kadon Enterprises Inc. have marketed 'Leap™', which is a compendium of several one- and two-person games with numbered counters on a 6 × 6 grid. It includes some excellent solitaires devised by Wade Philpott. ('Leap' is a proprietary trademark of R. E. Jones.)

(c) John Maltby devised Colourtaire (marketed by J. Spear and Co. Ltd), in which the player is presented with multi-coloured lay-outs for the central game and has to remove one colour at a time.

Solitaire for two

Although Solitaire is essentially a one-person game, two-person games can be derived from it. The most obvious of these is for the players to move alternately, the first person unable to move being the loser. Although not without interest, this game has almost nothing in common with ordinary Solitaire.

Much more closely related to ordinary Solitaire is a game in which the players choose a Solitaire problem and then move alternately, each player after his move having the option of challenging his opponent to complete a solution to the problem from the position left to him. This game is practicable only between proficient Solitaire players, but may be found of interest where two or more such are gathered together. As a simple exercise, the reader may care to find out who should win if the problem to be solved is the *d*1-complement on the standard 33-hole board. (As a research project, he might care to find out who should win if the problem is the central game; I started an analysis many years ago but did not complete it.)

A final challenge

We leave the reader with a final challenge: What is the smallest board on which every single-vacancy complement problem is soluble?

Solutions to Chapter 14

Many problems in Triangular Solitaire can be solved by block removals similar to those which have proved so effective in ordinary Solitaire. The call and answer, three-removal, six-removal, and L-removal prove particularly useful.

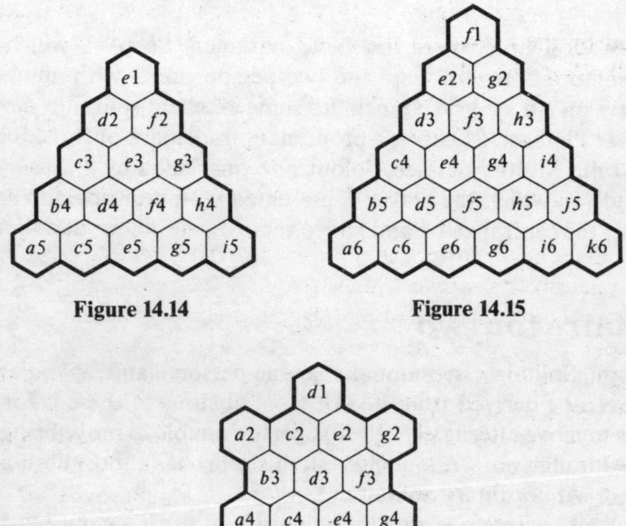

Figure 14.14

Figure 14.15

Figure 14.16

For problems which cannot be solved easily by block removals, we use the notations shown in Figures 14.14 to 14.16, denoting rows and *vertical* columns by numbers and letters respectively. The top row is always denoted by 1 and the left-most column by *a*. The topmost hole of the 15-hole triangular board is therefore *e*1 (Figure 14.14). The toughest soluble single-vacancy problem on this board is the *e*1-complement, which can be solved by the moves *c*3–*e*1, *g*3–*c*3, *b*4–*d*2, *c*5–*e*3, *g*5–*c*5, *i*5–*g*3, *f*2–*h*4, *a*5–*e*5–*g*3, *h*4–*f*2, *e*1–*g*3–*c*3–*e*1. Davis found a different 10-move solution in 1966 and proved that no shorter solution is possible.

The toughest single-vacancy complement problem on the 21-hole triangular board (Figure 14.15) is the *f*1-complement, which can be solved by the moves *d3–f1*, *h3–d3*, *c4–e2*, *e6–c4*, *a6–e6*, *g6–c6*, *k6–g6*, *c4–a6–e6–i6*, *h5–f3–d5*, *i4–k6–g6–e4*, *d5–f3*, *f1–d3–h3–f1*. The *f3*-complement, which is the other tough one, can be solved by the moves *d5–f3*, *i4–e4*, *h5–d5*, *d3–f5*, *d5–h5*, *g2–e4*, *c4–g4*, *k6–i4*, *h3–j5*, *g6–k6–i4–e4*, *a6–c4*, *f1–d3–b5*, *e6–a6–c4–g4*, *h5–f3*.

The toughest soluble single-vacancy complement problem on the 13-hole stellar board (Figure 14.16) is the *d1*-complement, which can be solved by the moves *d3–b1*, *g2–c2*, *a2–e2*, *d5–b3*, *a4–c2*, *e2–c4*, *g4–e2*, *d1–f3–d5–b3–d1*.

The important point about 8-move Solitaire is that *a move along a diagonal changes the phases of the two other diagonals in the same direction*. It follows that if the initial and target positions are in the same fundamental class in 4-move Solitaire, then any diagonal move in 8-move Solitaire must be balanced either by another move along the same diagonal or by moves along each of the other two diagonals in the same direction. Once this is realised, the problem of Figure 14.7 becomes quite easy, a solution being given by the moves *c1–c3*, *c4–c2*, *a3–c3*, *d3–b3*, *c5–a3–c1–c3*, *d2–b4*, *e3–c5–a3–c3*. It will be noticed that we have two moves along the diagonal *c5–a3* and one along each of the NE–SW diagonals.

The central game in 8-move Solitaire on the 33-hole board can be solved in 16 moves as follows: *d2–d4*, *b4–d2*, *a3–c3*, *f3–d3–b3*, *e1–c3*, *g5–e3*, *d6–b4–d2–f4–d6* (7), *c1–e1–e3*, *g3–g5–e5–c5–c3*, *e7–e5*, *e4–e6*, *c7–e7–e5* (12), *b5–d7–d5*, *c2–c4*, *a5–a3–c3*, *d4–d6–f4–d2–b2–d4*.

The construction of invariant parity counts on general boards is not difficult; the rule to remember is that if a line of play contains any marked hole at all then it must contain the sequence mark, mark, blank, mark, mark, blank, and so on. A corollary is that holes a distance of three apart along a line of play must be alike (both marked or both blank). It is thus easy to show that the Solomon Solitaire board (Figure 14.12) has three non-null invariant parity counts, one being shown in Figure 14.17 and the other two being rotations of this. Only two of these counts are independent, and they divide positions on this board into four fundamental classes. Each class contains at least one single-man member, the single-man positions and their classes being shown in Figure 14.18. The board is a null-class board, and a single-vacancy single-survivor problem is soluble if and only if the starting and finishing holes are in the same class. In particular, if the starting vacancy is at the centre then the

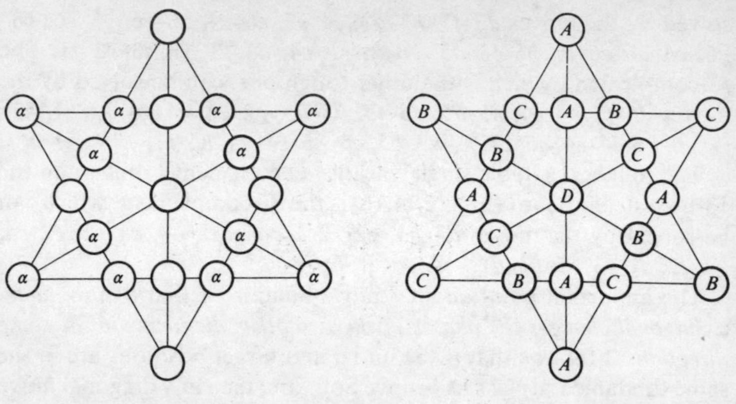

Figure 14.17 Figure 14.18

last survivor must finish in the centre. Finding the actual solutions should give no trouble.

The pentagonal board of Figure 14.13 has a subtly different structure. There is only one non-null invariant parity count, shown in Figure 14.19, and it divides positions into two fundamental classes. Each class contains some single-man members, these being shown in Figure 14.20. The board is not a null-class board, however, and a single-vacancy single-survivor problem is soluble if and only if the finishing hole is *not* in the same class as the starting hole.

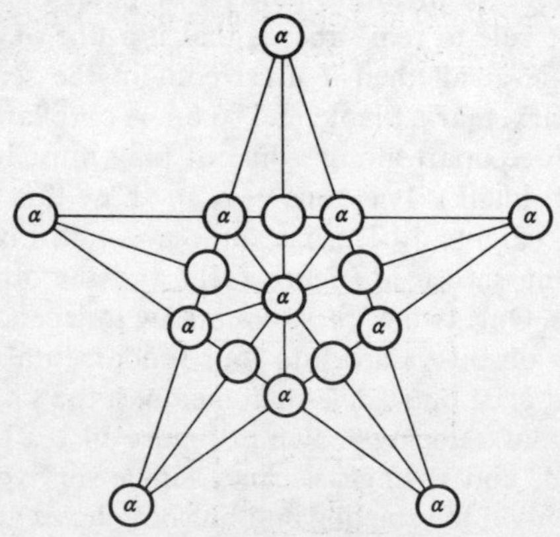

Figure 14.19

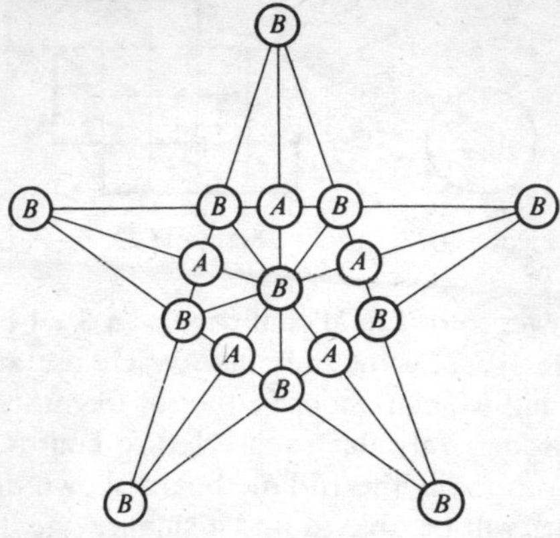

Figure 14.20

The reader may enjoy designing other boards and analysing them similarly.

Playing Solitaire for Two using the 33-hole *d*1-complement problem, player 1 must start *d*3–*d*1 and player 2 should reply *d*5–*d*3 (Figure 14.21). To reply *b*3–*d*3 instead would allow player 1 to play *e*3–*c*3 and challenge. Player 1 now has a dolorous choice. If he moves *b*4–*d*4–*d*2 then player 2 should move *d*1–*d*3 (or *f*4–*d*4) and challenge; if he moves *b*4–*d*4 then player 2 should move *d*3–*d*5 (or *e*4–*c*4) and challenge; if he moves *b*5–*d*5 then player 2 should move *e*5–*c*5 (or *d*6–*d*4, or even *d*6–*d*4–*d*2) and challenge; and if he moves *d*7–*d*5 then player 2 should move *b*4–*d*4–*d*6 and challenge. So player 2 should win.

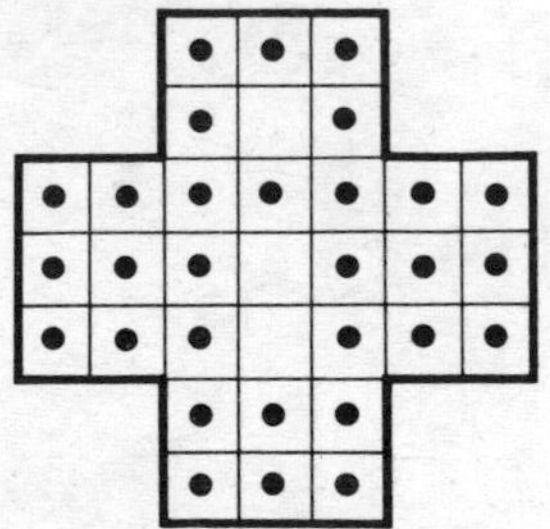

Figure 14.21

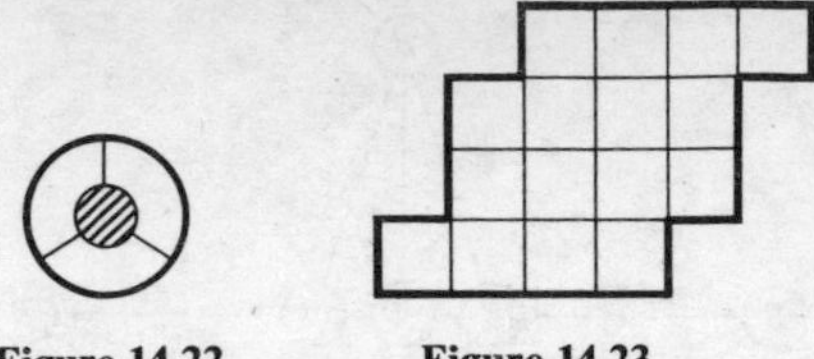

Figure 14.22 **Figure 14.23**

The trick answer to our final challenge is ‘A 3 × 1 board bent into a circle’ (Figure 14.22). Not only can we choose any hole as the initial vacancy but we can choose either of the other men to finish in it. If we consider only flat square lattice boards, however, the smallest known to me is the 16-hole board shown in Figure 14.23. Perhaps a reader will be able to find a smaller one, though there is little scope for reduction since the board must be at least four lines wide in each direction. (If it is only three lines wide and the initial vacancy is on the middle line, then there is no way of removing a man from an outside line.) This task was suggested to Martin Gardner by Derham Giuliani in 1962 and may well have been studied before, but I know of no previous appearance in print.

15

A LOOK TO THE FUTURE

In this last chapter, we summarise the present state of Solitaire knowledge and suggest possible future developments.

Theoretical summary

We have shown that the *holes* in a standard 33-hole board can be divided into four classes such that no man is able to move to a hole in a different class from that in which it starts.

We have shown that the *positions* possible on a standard 33-hole board can be divided into sixteen classes such that no play is possible between positions in different classes. We have called these classes 'fundamental classes'.

We have examined the game of Up-and-down Solitaire, in which both ordinary and inverse moves may be made, and noted that a problem in it is soluble if and only if its initial and target positions are in the same fundamental class (unless either is one of sixteen exceptional positions to or from which no play is possible).

We have developed measures of the resources contained in a position. These measures, which we have called 'resource counts', are such that no play can increase the value of a position as measured by them. In particular, the initial position of a problem always has at least as high a value as any position derived from it.

We have examined the game of Unconstrained Fractional Solitaire, in which fractional moves may be made and a hole may contain any number of men whether positive, negative or zero. We have shown that a problem in this game is insoluble if and only if there exists a resource count according to which the target position has a higher value than the initial position.

We have identified various measures whose parity can be changed only by certain moves, if at all, and have shown how they may be combined with resource counts to resolve difficult problems.

We have shown how to derive one or more 'move maps' for a problem from an analysis of its debts and surpluses, and have demonstrated conditions which a move map must satisfy if it represents a realisable solution.

We have developed some techniques for assigning lower limits to the number of moves that a solution must take.

Finally, we have shown how these techniques may be used on other boards and with other rules of play.

Suggestions for further research

Some readers will regard this book not merely as a record of things known but as a springboard from which to make new discoveries. There are several possibilities.

The puzzle enthusiast will wish to find some of the attractive problems that surely still await discovery both on the standard board and on other boards. He may also wish to look more deeply into the history of the game, for the picture revealed here is plainly incomplete. Much of the missing material is no doubt irretrievably lost, but there is no reason to suppose that it all is.

The mathematician will wish to close some of the remaining gaps in the underlying theory of the game. Three stand out: the absence of a simple discriminant for Unconstrained Solitaire, for Conway's balance sheet, although powerful, is not quite a complete discriminant; the absence of a simple discriminant for ordinary Solitaire; and the absence of simple general methods for determining the minimum length of solutions. Considerable progress has been made in all these directions, but we have not yet reached a position where we can *guarantee* to decide the solubility of a problem without an enumeration of variations.

The mathematician and the puzzle enthusiast may both wish to investigate complete classes of problems. Several past theoretical developments were sparked off by such investigations; for example, the theory of Suremain de Missery was quite probably stimulated by an attempt to list all the soluble single-vacancy single-survivor problems on a particular board, and the theory of Conway and Hutchings, which ultimately led to Conway's balance sheet, was developed during an investigation of the double-vacancy complement problems on the 33-hole board. The multiple-vacancy complement problems on this board are indeed not yet fully resolved, and such resolution appears impracticable without more powerful discriminants than are available at present.

Can the computer help?

The results described in this book were obtained without the aid of a computer. In the absence of discriminants suitable for use by hand, is it reasonable to press one into service?

At first sight it seems unfair that the achievements of solvers such as Bergholt and Davis should be subjected to possible eclipse by computer, but there is a little more to the matter than this. Men are better than computers at finding patterns. Computers are better at exhaustive calculation. So if no perceptible pattern can be found and the proving of a theoretical result appears to require exhaustive calculation, a situation which does arise from time to time, then there is a case for performing the calculation by computer rather than attempting it by hand or leaving the result unproven. The area in which the computer is likely to be most useful is in the establishment of minimum lengths of solutions, for this is the area in which current theoretical techniques are least effective. It may seem crude to tell a computer to try and beat an existing record, but at least if it verifies the record then the truth is known and no more effort need be wasted on fruitless search for better solutions by hand.

A brief look at possible computing techniques therefore seems appropriate, if only to see what a computer might be expected to achieve and what its limitations might be. Readers familiar with computers are asked to bear with a fairly elementary level of exposition for the benefit of those who are not.

The play possible from a given position can be represented by a tree as shown in Figure 15.1, and the most obvious way to search such a tree is by branches, looking in order at positions 1, 1.1, 1.1.1, 1.1.2, 1.1.2.1, 1.1.2.2, 1.2, 1.2.1, 1.2.2 and so on. In due course we should either find the solution required or 'prove' that it does not exist. 'Proof' by failure to achieve is not entirely satisfactory since the possibility of machine or program error cannot be ruled out, but several such 'proofs' now appear in the literature of mathematics.

Unfortunately 'in due course' may mean 'after a very long time'. It will be noticed that positions 1.2.3 and 1.3.1 in Figure 15.1 are the same, so the positions 1.2.3... and 1.3.1... derived from them are also the same. Figure 15.1 shows a very simple tree, and far more

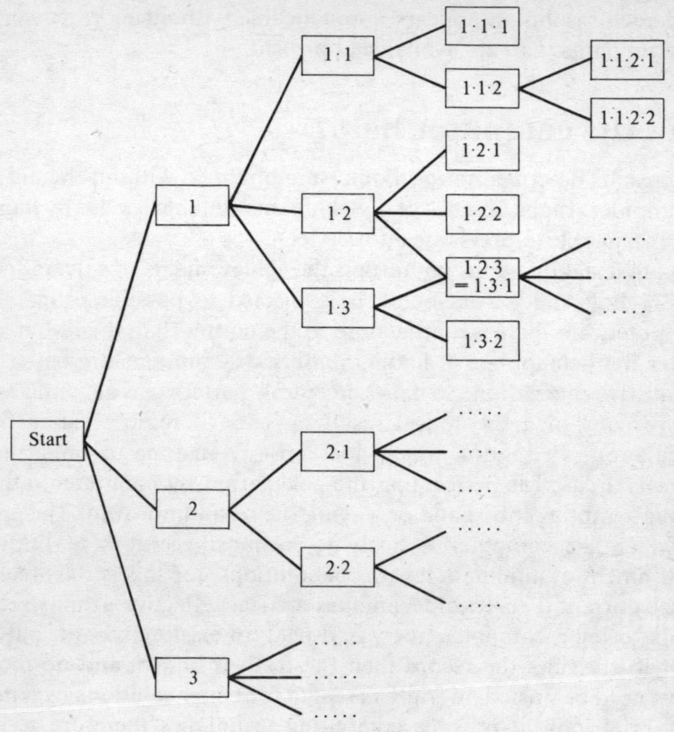

Figure 15.1

repetition occurs in real Solitaire trees; it may be possible to reach a position in a million or more different ways. A computer may be very fast, but to expect it to do a million times as much work as necessary is not the way to make progress.

It is therefore necessary for the computer to maintain a list of the positions already analysed, which brings us to the question of how a computer stores information. The basic unit of storage within a computer is the 'bit' (binary digit), which can be regarded as a box which can hold one of the two numbers '0' and '1'. A hole in a Solitaire board can therefore be represented by one bit in a computer, the bit containing '0' if the hole is vacant and '1' if it is occupied. A complete position in 33-hole Solitaire therefore seems to require 33 bits of computer storage, but in the case of a position *reached in play from a given starting position* we can manage with 29, for the position must be in the same fundamental class as the starting position and so we can infer the state of the holes in a given 2×2 square from the rest of the position.

Computer memory is normally organised in 'bytes' (a byte being eight bits), and measured in 'kilobytes' or 'Kb' (a kilobyte being 1024 bytes, not 1000, since computers like to count in powers of 2 and $2^{10} = 1024$) and 'megabytes' or 'Mb' (a megabyte being $2^{20} = 1\,048\,576$ bytes similarly). To put these units into perspective, let us consider the storage of written text by computer. Each separate typographical character (letter, punctuation mark or space) is normally stored in a separate byte, so a typical full sheet of typed paper (fifty lines each containing sixty characters) would occupy about three kilobytes, while the complete text of this book, excluding the figures, would occupy about a third of a megabyte.

We have seen that a 33-hole Solitaire position in a given fundamental class can be stored in 29 bits, and so can be fitted comfortably into four bytes of computer storage (32 bits). The three unused bits could in principle be used for part of another position, but the benefits of such condensation are rarely worth the effort entailed. So we need four bytes for each 33-hole position, and it looks as if we can get 256 positions into a kilobyte and 262 144 into a megabyte.

Unfortunately matters are not quite as simple as this. When we perform an analysis by branches, studying the positions in the order 1, 1.1, 1.1.1, 1.1.2, 1.1.2.1, 1.1.2.2, and so on, we must organise our list of positions so that we can quickly both identify a position already analysed and add a new position to our list. Techniques for doing this exist (readers expert in computing will not need reminding about the use of 'balanced' or 'AVL' trees and 'B-trees'), but all involve the storing of additional information with the positions. The amount of storage needed for this additional information varies according to the precise technique and computer used, but typically it increases the total storage required by a factor of two or three. Some computer storage is also needed for the program, and the computer requires some for its own internal use. So a computer with 64 kilobytes of storage cannot hold 16384 Solitaire positions together with the additional information required for an efficient search by branches; 5000 is a more realistic expectation.

The first of these difficulties can be overcome by analysing the problem by *levels* rather than by branches, studying the successive positions in the order 1, 2, 3, then 1.1, 1.2, 1.3, 2.1, 2.2, 3.1, 3.2, 3.3, then 1.1.1, 1.1.2, and so on. The general procedure is as follows: (i) given all the positions at one level, form a complete list of those at the next level without worrying about duplication; (ii) sort the newly formed positions into order, removing duplicates; (iii) go to the next level and repeat. No additional information need be stored with the positions, so we do get a position for every four bytes of storage (though we must still allow storage for the program and for the computer's own internal use); furthermore, the process can make effective use of 'backing store' (second-level storage, larger but slower than the main store, used on many computers to extend the amount of storage available). A search by branches is less well suited to backing store, though it can also be performed using it.

Searching by levels offers other advantages. We can stop the process after any level and restart it later. We can work backwards from the target position as well as forwards from the initial position, proceeding a certain number of levels in each direction and seeing if we reach a common intermediate position. And perhaps most importantly of all, we can print out parts of our lists of positions and perform spot checks by hand, verifying that all the positions which can be obtained from a given position do indeed appear in the analysis. Such checks may go a long way towards eliminating 'program or machine error' as a possible cause of failure to achieve a solution. There is only one small disadvantage, in that a successful search by levels merely shows that a solution exists and does not list its moves, but the moves can be found by a detailed examination of the lists of positions, starting from the common intermediate position (in the case of a search from both ends) and proceeding outwards towards the starting and finishing positions.

The most probable future use of computers is in the finding of solutions with minimum moves. Table 8.3 showed such an analysis performed by hand, but this was done in 1964 when a central university computer had little more power than the personal microcomputer which I am using as a word processor to prepare this text, and there is little doubt that a computer is better suited to such a task than the human brain. However, Table 8.3 was kept to a reasonable size by subjecting each position to complicated and sophisticated 'acceptance tests', and such a strategy is not ideally suited to automatic computation. (Computers are good at doing simple things quickly and reliably. They are not good at doing complicated things unless these can be broken down into simple things, and such breaking down is not always as straightforward as might at first be thought.) If I were analysing the central game in 33-hole Solitaire by computer, I would use simpler acceptance tests and accept more positions in the analysis as a result. I would also search by levels, whereas Table 8.3 shows a search by branches.

Computers can also be used for problems in which the number of moves is not an issue, though the potential gains here seem less since most such problems can be resolved by hand. The technique of Chapter 5 is particularly well suited to use by computer, since the finding of a resource count to prove a problem insoluble in Unconstrained Fractional Solitaire can be performed by a standard computing technique known as 'linear programming'. Bob Hutchings has indeed used a computer manufacturer's standard linear programming package for this purpose. The techniques of Chapters 6 and 7 are also suitable, in so far as a computer can easily be programmed to evaluate *predetermined* parity counts and to examine *predetermined* areas to see if they are full or empty, but a computer is not so good at looking at a position and *then* determining a suitable parity count to be evaluated or area to be examined. A reasonable strategy is therefore to perform a search by levels, checking a few predetermined parity counts and perhaps areas at each stage, and using linear programming to find resource counts by which positions having lower values than the target position may be rejected.

We conclude that a computer can indeed help, provided that it has enough storage to hold all the positions likely to be generated in the course of the analysis. Mike Beeler programmed small Solitaire boards many years ago, and Leonard Gordon tells me that his computer has found 268 nine-move solutions to single-vacancy single-survivor problems on the 15-hole board of Figure 14.5. Larger boards will undoubtedly be attacked in the future. It can only be a matter of time, for example, before Table 8.2 is replaced by a table of proven minima established by computer, though I shall be surprised if much improvement is made on the actual solutions discovered by Bergholt and Davis.

RECENT DEVELOPMENTS

Several minor but interesting developments have occurred since this book was originally written. Some computer calculations which I reported in a last-minute note to the original edition showed Table 8.2 indeed to be optimal; they have still to be confirmed by an independent worker, but I like to think they will stand up. Subsequently, John Harris has found all possible 15-move solutions on the 6 × 6 board, one by hand and the rest by computer; Rob Hutchings has done elegant theoretical work on the multiple-vacancy complement problem, on up-and-down linear solitaire, and on multiple-removal solitaire; and Len Gordon has invented some interesting games with non-linear jumps. I give no details, since these gentlemen may still wish to publish on their own account.

Regarding the early history of the game, it has become clear that the view I took when writing Chapter 1 was altogether too cautious. A volume written by Henri d'Allemagne for the Paris Exhibition of 1900, *Musée rétrospectif de la classe 100/Jeux/Tome II*, contains not only the Berey engraving of 1697 and a similar engraving of 1698 by Trouvain but also a separate engraving, *Nouveau jeu du Solitaire*, by Berey, which contains all the material that subsequently appeared in the *Dictionnaire des jeux mathématiques* of 1799. There is also a reference to a work of 1713 by Remond de Monmort (Leibniz's correspondent) which I have not seen. All this indicates that Solitaire was not merely played at the court of Louis XIV but was highly fashionable, and my interpretation of the Walpole letter of 1746 (see bibliography) may also have been too cautious. We may note, incidentally, that the rules do appear always to have demanded orthogonal play, contrary to my conjecture on page 4; that Berey gives my Figure 11.30 as 'Le triolet'; and that the 'lecteur' in Figure 11.31 should finish in the middle of his 'religieux' and not his 'amis'. Do I detect revolutionary anti-clericalism in the *Dictionnaire* of 1799?

Nevertheless, I remain sceptical about the alleged North American Indian origin of the game (it may be cited by Berey, but it still has the air of picturesque invention rather than fact); and I shall remain even more sceptical about the prisoner in the Bastille until somebody can show me a more convincing source than an English book written in 1801. Perhaps a reader with the leisure to explore the *Bibliothèque Nationale* and other French sources will be able to throw light on this.

SELECTED BIBLIOGRAPHY

The literature of Solitaire is fragmented and repetitive. Many encyclopaedias and books on games and puzzles contain a description of the game, and many isolated problems have appeared in newspapers and other periodicals; but much of this work has made no claim to novelty, and some which has made such a claim has unwittingly repeated older work. Furthermore, the name 'Solitaire' was formerly used in England as a generic name for card games for one player, a usage still current in America, and references in eighteenth- and early nineteenth-century literature should normally be construed thus. To cite everything that has been written would therefore produce a bibliography whose length would not be matched by its usefulness. I have accordingly included everything known to me that was written before 1850 and clearly relates to our game, but have been increasingly selective thereafter, concentrating on (i) historical landmarks, (ii) material likely to be of interest to teachers of mathematics, and (iii) convenient collections of puzzles that may interest readers who have been stimulated by this book to investigate further. 'Cited by . . .' means that I have not seen the item myself.

Ahrens, W. (1910/18). Das Nonnen- oder Einsiedler-(Solitär-)spiel. *Mathematische Unterhaltungen und Spiele* **1**, 182–210; **2**, 337–8. Teubner, Leipzig and Berlin. An excellent source for historical matters. Volume 1 (1910) contains the main article; Volume 2 (1918) cites further references and includes a pointer to the work of Suremain de Missery. This is the second edition; the Solitaire article in the first (1901, pp 94–113) is much less comprehensive.

——(1927). Solitär- oder Einsiedlerspiel. *Mathematische Spiele* 25–34. Teubner, Leipzig and Berlin. This is the fifth edition; its Solitaire article is much shorter than that in *Mathematische Unterhaltungen und Spiele*, but it contains an illustration of a presentation set which was given to Kronprinz Friedrich in 1883 and shows the legendary hermit playing in his cell. Solitaire appears to have been a hobby of the German royal family; the 1910 edition of *Mathematische Unterhaltungen und Spiele* (see above) quotes a statement of 1844 that King Friedrich Wilhelm IV was in the habit of playing it at tea-time instead of conversing politely with his guests as a well brought-up monarch is supposed to do.

Anon. (1807). *Neueste Anweisung zum Kreuz- Einsiedler- oder Kapuziner-Spiel.* Regensburg. A pamphlet cited by Ahrens, who attributes some of the traditional classics to it. Its size is not known to me, but Ahrens cites page numbers up to 41.

Anon. (1929). *Problems in puzzle-peg*. 24pp. Lubbers and Bell, Clinton, Iowa. The sixth edition of a booklet distributed with 'Puzzle-peg' sets, which were popular American Solitaire sets of the period. The booklet contains 113 problems, mostly contributed by readers and only of moderate quality. Its main present interest is in the light it throws on the use of diagonal moves, as described in Chapter 14.

Baslini, F. (1970). *Il 'Solitaire': 200 problemi risolti*. 176 pp. Il Campo, Firenze. A quadrilingual book (Italian, English, French, German) containing some good problems, though none with marked men. Its historical introduction is suspect. Baslini claims that the game was known in ancient Rome, and cites a passage from Ovid as proof: 'Si dispongono alcune palline (pilae) su di una apposita tavoletta recente numerosi incavi, e, all'inizio del gioco, bisogna toglierne una' ('Some marbles (pilae) are disposed on a proper board which has many hollows and at the beginning of the game the player has to take one off'). Unfortunately none of the uses of 'pila' cited in the standard concordance of Ovid (DeFerrari, Barry, and McGuire, Catholic University of America, 1939) matches this, nor can I find a matching passage elsewhere in Ovid. The nearest, perhaps, is *Ars amatoria* **3**, 361–2: 'Reticuloque pilae leves fundantur aperto, Nec, nisi quam tolles, ulla movenda pila est'. This passage is somewhat obscure, but most authorities regard it as describing a game related to spillikins, and the Loeb Classical Library (Mozley, revised Goold) translates it thus: 'And let the smooth balls be flung into the open net, nor must any ball be moved save that which you will take out'. In any case, the context is that of advice to young ladies to play games as a weapon of seduction, so the game, whatever it may be, is for more than one player. R. G. Austin's articles on Roman board games in *Greece and Rome* **4**, 24–34, 76–82 (1934–5) make no reference to Solitaire.

This mystery inevitably throws doubt on another of Baslini's statements, which is that the modern form of Solitaire was developed by a French mathematician named Pellisson at the order of Louis XIV, who wanted something simple and relaxing to pass his time during long carriage journeys. This has the air of a tale invented by a manufacturer of traditional French hand-held sets, and 'Pellisson' is presumably Paul Pellisson or Pellisson-Fontanier (1624-93), who was Louis XIV's historiographer and not a mathematician. But Pellisson-Fontanier was a prisoner in the Bastille from 1661 to 1666 and was acquainted with Leibniz, so it may just be that a search of his works would throw light on the legend of the noble French prisoner after all.

Beasley, J. D. (1962). Some notes on solitaire. *Eureka* **25**, 13–18. The original report of the work done at Cambridge in 1961–2. Now only of historical interest, having been completely superseded by Conway *et al.* (1982) and by this book.

Berey, C.-A. (1697). *Madame la Princesse de Soubize joüant au jeu de Solitaire*. Berey, Paris. The earliest Solitaire document known to me: an engraving of a lady with a classical French 37-hole board. See van Delft *et al.*

Bergholt, E. (1912). English solitaire. *The Queen* **131**, 666–7, 807. The source for the first 18-move solution to the central game, the problem having been posed in the issue of April 20 and solved in that of May 11.

——(1920). *Complete handbook to the game of solitaire on the English board of thirty-three holes*. 96pp. Routledge, London (American edition by Dutton, New York, 1921). Not really a 'complete handbook' since it contains little theory, but a fine compendium of problems. Much use is made of marked men and dead men, and there is a strong emphasis on the minimisation of moves. The more elementary material appears to owe a lot to Bizalion's 'Gentleman's Journal' articles (see below), but the long-sweep and minimal-move solutions are almost wholly Bergholt's own.

'Berkeley' (a pseudonym for W. H. Peel) (1890). Solitaire. *Dominoes and solitaire* 48–56. Bell, London (American edition by Stokes, New York). A booklet containing the earliest reasonably short solutions known to me, including a 19-move solution to the central game.

Bestelmeier, G. H. (1803). *Magazin von verschiedenen Kunst- und andern nützlichen Sachen* 6. Bestelmeier, Nürnberg. An extract from a manufacturer's catalogue. It describes 'Ein Solitair- oder Nonnenspiel' ('A Solitaire or nun's game') as consisting of a wooden cross with 33 holes and an equal number of small pegs (*Kegeln*); cost, in a small box, 24 kr. There is a 1979 reprint of this catalogue by Olms (Zürich). The British Museum used to have a copy of the 1799 edition, but it was destroyed during the war.

Bizalion, C. (1870-2). Solitaire. *Gentleman's Journal Recreation Supplement* **1**, 103–4, 124–5, 150–1, 176–7, 201; **2**, 10, 28, 64–5, 77–8, 105, 131; **3**, 24–5, 56, 88–9, 120–1, 152–3, 185; **4**, 358; **5**, 20, 53, 80, 116, 190, 215; **6**, 19–20. This particular 'Gentleman's Journal', which ran from 1869 to 1872, was actually a weekly paper for boys and included a monthly supplement on pastimes and puzzles. The Solitaire articles appeared in the latter from March 1870 to July 1871 and from Christmas 1871 to September 1872 (omitting June). Bizalion was described by his editor as having made a ten-year study of Solitaire. 121 problems appear in the articles, including some by J. Alcorn, J. Black, D. Fawcett, J. Lord, and N. M. Panday (or Pauday).

de Brujin, N. G. (1972). A solitaire game and its relation to a finite field. *Journal of Recreational Mathematics* **5**, 133–7 (subsequently reprinted in *Mathematical solitaires and games* 12–16, Baywood, 1980). An alternative derivation of the fundamental classes, making use of the finite field with four elements.

Busschop, P. (1879). *Recherches sur le jeu de solitaire.* 345 pp. Daveluy, Bruges. A collection of over 300 problems on the 37-hole board, published after Busschop's death by his brother. None of the problems makes any use of special features such as marked men and there is no apparent attempt to minimise moves, but it is nevertheless a fine collection.

Charosh, M. (1962). Peg solitaire. *The Mathematics Student Journal* **9**, 1-3. One of the many rediscoveries of some of the work of Suremain de Missery. This article, and its subsequent popularisaton by Gardner, had a significant effect in arousing modern American interest, though its content has since been found to reproduce material available elsewhere.

Conway, J. H., with Berlekamp, E. R., and Guy, R. K. (1982). *Winning ways for your mathematical plays* **2**, 695-734. Academic Press, London and New York. Conway's only published writing on the game to which he has made such a large contribution.

Crelle, A. L. (1852). Zwei Zahlen-Aufgaben. *Journal für die reine und angewahlte Mathematik* **44**, 317-34 (only pp. 332-4 being relevant). The earliest solution to the central game that I have seen.

Cross, D. C. (1968). Square solitaire and variations. *Journal of Recreational Mathematics* **1**, 121-3. A short article containing possibly the first published reference to three-dimensional Solitaire (though unpublished work by Davis predates it).

Davis, H. O. (1967). 33-solitaire: new limits, small and large. *Mathematical Gazette* **51**, 91-100. Davis's only published paper, containing amongst other things the first 15-move solution to a single-vacancy single-survivor problem on the standard board. (Davis actually discovered two significantly different 15-move solutions, both of which are quoted in our Chapter 8, and his correspondence with Gardner dates the discoveries to 1963.)

Dawson, T. R. (ed.) (1943-50). *The Fairy Chess Review* **5**, 42-3, 53-4, 58-9, 69-70, 138; **6**, 3, 6, 16, 18, 26, 56, 66; **7**, 34, 45, 65, 68, 102, 106, 128, 130, 140. Dawson's magnificent 'FCR' appeared every alternate month from 1930 until his final illness in 1951, and then continued until 1958 in other hands. Although based on the study of unorthodox extensions to Chess, it offered space to many forms of recreational mathematics and was one of the few periodicals frequently to feature Solitaire problems. The above references cite problems by Dawson himself, H. D., Mrs D., and Miss J. Benjamin (a family hobby), and W. H. Reilly. See also Willcocks.

van Delft, P., and Botermans, J. (1978). Peg solitaire. *Creative puzzles of the world* 170-5. Cassell, London. My source for the Berey engraving.

Deveau-Carlier, A. (1884). *Le solitaire amusant; règle de ce jeu et quatre-vingt-onze combinaisons*. 139 pp. Renaut, Cambrai. Cited by Redon.

Dudeney, H. E. (1908). Puzzles from games. *The Strand Magazine* **35**, 339–44, 455–8. Only pages 344 and 458 of these articles are relevant to Solitaire; they pose the central game and answer it by the well-known 'Dudeney' solution, which is actually very similar to one given by W. H. Peel.

——(1917). *Amusements in mathematics* 63–4, 107–8, 195, 234. Nelson, London. A few problems including perhaps the first uses of numbered counters (though little advantage is taken of their scope).

Encyclopédie méthodique (1797). Solitaire. *Dictionnaire des jeux familiers* 155. An article which mentions only the 37-hole board and gives no specimen play, but states that sets can be bought at the stationer's in the *rue des Arcis* at the sign of the Green Monkey. I haven't been to see if they still can.

——(1799). Solitaire. *Dictionnaire des jeux mathématiques* 200–3. Another article which mentions only the 37-hole board, though it gives several examples of play (including some classic problems) and cites the legend that a Frenchman learned the game from the North American Indians. This appears to be the earliest surviving statement concerning the origin of the game, but it is too remote from the event to have any primary evidential value. Bizalion thought it an improbable tale, and I am inclined to agree.

Gardès, L.-F.-J. (1913). Contribution à l'étude du solitaire. *Compte-rendu de l'association français pour l'avancement des sciences* **41**, 80–7. Paris. An analysis of the general 37-hole problem 'vacate the centre and one other hole, and play to leave the last survivor in the other hole'.

Gardner, M. (1969). Peg solitaire. *The unexpected hanging and other mathematical diversions* 122–35. Simon and Schuster, New York (British edition entitled *Further mathematical diversions* by Allen and Unwin, 1970, and subsequently by Penguin Books). Gardner's regular column 'Mathematical Games' in *Scientific American* aroused immense enthusiasm for recreational mathematics. This book and the next contain Solitaire material which appeared in it between 1962 and 1966.

——(1975). Penny puzzles. *Mathematical carnival* 12–26. Knopf, New York (British edition by Allen and Unwin, 1976, and subsequently by Penguin Books). One of the few published works to include problems in Triangular Solitaire.

Gerhardt, C. I. (ed.) (1887). *Die philosophischen Schriften von Gottfried Wilhelm Leibniz* **3**, 667–9. One of several sources for the 1716 letter from Leibniz to Remond de Montmort.

Hentzel, I. R. (1973). Triangular puzzle peg. *Journal of Recreational Mathematics* **6**, 280–3 (subsequently reprinted in *Mathematical solitaires and games* 16–19, Baywood, 1980). A short paper outlining the basic 'Suremain de Missery' theory.

Hermary, H.-A.-H. (1879). Sur le jeu du solitaire. *Compte-rendu de l'association français pour l'avancement des sciences* **8**, 284–94. A paper containing the first reference to Multiple-removal Solitaire. (Hermary's other pioneering work, on the 41-hole board, is not mentioned here but is quoted by Lucas.)

Honsberger, R. (1976). A problem in checker-jumping. *Mathematical gems II* 23–8. Mathematical Association of America (number 2 of the Dolciani Mathematical Expositions). An article which describes the solitaire army. This example might be followed by other mathematical books, for it is just as elegant as the more frequently quoted theory of Suremain de Missery.

de Jaucourt, L. (1765). Solitaire. *Encyclopédie, ou dictionnaire raisonné des sciences, des arts et des métiers* **15**, 324–5. Faulche, Neufchastel. An article which describes the 37-hole board. The article in the 1775 edition (p. 322) is identical. De Jaucourt was sadly unimpressed by the game: 'Ce jeu n'a pas grand attrait quand on en ignore la marche, et n'en a point quand on la sait' ('This game has no great attraction when you don't know how to do it, and none at all when you do').

Kowalewski, G. (1930). Das Solitärspiel. *Alte und Neue Mathematische Spiele* 126-45. Teubner, Leipzig. An article including a description of a 'grid' which may be used to identify potential starting and finishing holes.

Langman, H. (1962). *Play mathematics* 203–6. Hafner, New York. An analysis of an ancient Draughts problem topologically equivalent to Solitaire: 'Can you place 24 Kings two deep around the outside of a standard draughtsboard and then play to leave only a single King?' (You can't.)

Leibniz, G. W. (1710). Annotatio de quibusdam Ludis; inprimis de Ludo quodam Sinico, differentiaque Scachici & Latrunculorum, & novo genere Ludi Navalis. *Miscellenea Berolinensia ad incrementum scientiarum* **1**, 22–6. The earliest description of the game known to me, the relevant passage being quoted (with its misprints) at the front of this book.

——(1716). Letter to Remond de Montmort. A frequently quoted reference: 'Le jeu nommé le Solitaire me plut assez' ('The game called Solitaire pleases me greatly'). See Gerhardt.

Lewis, E. R. (1978). Solitaire. *Solitaire and fox and geese* 1–21. Shalbury Games, Auckland. A collection of 118 problems with a strong emphasis on long sweeps attainable from a single-vacancy start.

Lucas, É. (1882/91). Le jeu du solitaire. *Récréations Mathématiques* **1**, 87–141, 232–5. Gauthier-Villars, Paris. A fairly complete survey of the knowledge of the time, including the first mention of the 41-hole draughtsboard. Pages 232–5, which report additional work by Mantel, Chicandard and Redon, appear only in the second edition (1891). There have been several reprints: by Blanchard (Paris), Dover (USA), and Constable (London) in 1960, and by Blanchard again in 1977.

McKerrell, A. (1972). Solitaire: an application of the four-group. *Mathematics teaching* **60**, 38–9. One of several papers based on the premise that games can be an effective sugar for the pill of serious mathematics.

Maltby, J. (1974). The solitaire revival. *Games and puzzles* **30**, 8–9. London. An article written for the novice, which gains its place here on account of its description of Colourtaire.

Peel, W. H. (1890). See Berkeley.

Ramsay, D. (1974–5). Solitaire. *Games and puzzles* **31**, 6–13; **35**, 8–11. Two articles written for the novice but covering a lot of ground and containing some interesting problems. The second includes a brief description of some two-person games using Solitaire equipment. Ramsay attributes to me some results which were actually discovered by Conway, Hutchings, and M. Guy.

Redon, P. (1893). *Le jeu de solitaire*. 120 pp. Tablettes du chercheur, Paris. An attractive collection of problems for the 37-hole board, though less extensive than that of Busschop.

Reiss, M. (1857). Beiträge zur Theorie des Solitär-Spiels. *Journal für die reine und angewahlte Mathematik* **54**, 344–79. Long thought to be the earliest exposition of the theory underlying the game. It derives the fundamental classes and gives solutions to all the single-vacancy single-survivor problems on the 33-hole board. See also Ruchonnet.

Routledge, E. (ed.) (1875–6). The solitaire board. *Every boy's annual* (1875–6) 88–95. A typical short collection of puzzles.

Ruchonnet, C. (1877). Théorie du solitaire, par feu le docteur Reiss, librement traduite de l'allemand. *Nouvelles correspondance mathématique et physique, Bruxelles* **3**, 234–41, 263–8, 289–94. A translation of Reiss's paper which may have been one of the triggers that sparked off the French and Belgian writing of the next sixteen years.

Schmolck, A. W. (ed.) (1815). Das Solitärspiel und die Promenade des Springers. *Thee- und Caffee-Zeitvertreib für Herren und Damen* (2 Jan) 2–6. Cited by Ahrens.

Stewart, B. M. (1941). Solitaire on a checkerboard. *American Mathematical Monthly* **48**, 228–33. A paper which gives solutions to all the single-vacancy single-survivor problems on the 32-hole draughtsboard (length 8, width 7).

——(1952). *Theory of numbers* 20–6. Macmillan, New York. Probably the first textbook in which a section on Solitaire is used to illustrate a mathematical point rather than as an end in itself. It uses the idea of 'exceptional diagonals' which is essentially the same as that of our phase relations, and considers among others the 7 × 5 rectangular board.

Strutt, J. (1801). The solitary game. *Sports and pastimes of the people of England* **4** 238. A short and uninformative article, which refers to a circular board perforated with fifty to sixty holes; 'a certain number of pegs are then fitted to these holes, but not enough to fill them all'. This article contains the earliest reference I know to the legend of the prisoner in the Bastille.

Suremain de Missery, A. (1842). See Vallot.

Tissandier, G. (1882–3). *Les récréations scientifiques* 164–70; translated as *Popular scientific recreations* 735–9. Masson, Paris; Ward Lock and Bowden, London. A short article which includes pictures of a ball-board and a hand-held peg-board. The French page numbers refer to the third edition (1883); the Solitaire material is not in the first French edition (1881) and I haven't seen the second.

Vallot, J.-N. (1824). Sur le jeu du solitaire. *Bulletin des sciences mathématiques, astronomiques, physiques et chimiques* **1**, 137–8. Paris. An extract from a letter which cites work by Leibniz and 'Wiegles', the latter apparently in error (see Wiegleb below).

——(1842). Rapport sur un travail de Suremain de Missery: Théorie générale du jeu de solitaire, considéré comme problème d'analyse et de situation. *Compte-rendu des travaux de l'académie des sciences, arts et belles-lettres de Dijon 1841–2*, 58–70. The earliest surviving report of an investigation into the theory underlying the game. No copy of Suremain de Missery's own paper is known to me and it may never have been published, but this report highlights its main features and shows that he discovered at least the essentials and probably the whole of the theory now normally attributed to Reiss.

Walpole, H. (1746). Letter to George Montagu, Nov 3: 'Has Miss Harriet found out any more ways at *solitaire*?' I suspect that this reference is to a card game, but cite it in case any reader takes a different view. The context gives no clue.

Wiegleb, J. C. (1779). Anhang von dreyen Solitärspielen. *Unterricht in der natürlichen Magie* (*J. N. Martius*) 413–6. Nicolai, Berlin and Stettin. A short section at the end of a book of scientific recreations, containing the earliest examples of play known to me: a single solution on each of the 33-hole, 37-hole and 45-hole boards, in each case starting with a vacancy in the top left-hand corner and finishing with a single survivor. There are also some curiously inaccurate remarks concerning the existence of further solutions. The Solitaire material is repeated in the 1782 and 1789 editions (pages 458–61 in each case, the 1789 edition calling itself 'Volume 1'). I am grateful to John Maltby, to the Joseph Regenstein Library of Chicago, and to the Library of Congress for bringing this work to my attention, for there is no direct reference to it in the rest of the Solitaire literature. Vallot (1824) quotes some remarks by 'Wiegles' as appearing in '*Naturliche Mag. von Christ. Bened. Funck., Berlin, 1783*'. Lucas misconstrues this as an abbreviation of '*Natürliche Magazine*', but in fact it can only refer to the book *Natürliche magie* by Christlieb Benedict Funk, published by Nicolai in 1783 with a second edition in 1806. The Joseph Regenstein Library and the Library of Congress searched Funk 1783 for me and found no reference to Solitaire, but they did find a reference in it to Wiegleb 1779/82 and searched their copies of Wiegleb 1779, and the Regenstein Library sent me a copy of the relevant pages. Maltby's investigations preceded mine and followed a different trail; he told me that Funk 1806 contains no material on Solitaire, and gave me a copy of the relevant pages from Wiegleb 1789. (All three editions of Wiegleb are in the British Library, as it happens, but Funk isn't, which is why we enquired abroad.) Vallot's citation of Funk must therefore be in error, but his quotation fits a passage from Wiegleb and we conclude that he has confused two works with similar titles.

Willcocks, T. H. (1950-2). *The Fairy Chess Review* **7**, 115, 138; **8**, 25, 36–7, 52. These pages contain the first published solutions to all but one of Bergholt's 'special problems'; **7**, 138 (February 1951), in particular, gives the first published nine-sweep finish.

A few *patents* have come to my notice: Edson (American 47 491, 1865) for a hole in the groove surrounding a standard ball-board, together with a pivoting drawer to catch the balls; von Kosiński and Wolfsberg (German 42 919, 1887) for a wooden peg-board for the 33-hole game; Smith (American 462 170, 1891) for a 16-hole null-class board for Triangular Solitaire (*ceg*1/*df*2/*acegi*3/*bdfh*4/*cg*5 in our notation); Law (American 463 425, 1891) for a marked-man version of the 33-hole game; Maltby (British 1 251 254, 1970) for Colourtaire. There are doubtless others.

In the course of writing this book, I have accumulated a small file of notes (for example, on sources, red herrings, and blind alleys) which are not suitable for inclusion in the book itself but will save a future researcher a few days of work. It is my intention, when the book has been put to bed, to deposit this file in the Bodleian Library, which has agreed to receive it. If any reader is tempted to continue where I have left off, he is warmly invited to make use of it.

GLOSSARY

This Glossary includes a few terms which are used by other authors though not by ourselves, but omits terms whose meanings are obvious from the everyday usage of the words forming them. Terms in *italics* are defined elsewhere in the Glossary.

4-move Solitaire. Ordinary Solitaire, played on a square lattice.

6-move Solitaire. Solitaire played on a triangular lattice.

8-move Solitaire. Solitaire played on a square lattice using both orthogonal and diagonal moves.

33-hole board. The standard *English* and *German board* shown in Figure 1.1.

36-hole board. The 6 × 6 square board.

37-hole board. The classical *French board* shown in Figure 4.6.

41-hole board. The draughtsboard shown in Figure 11.36.

additive Solitaire. Solitaire in which the move is to jump a man over an empty hole, a man being inserted. Ordinary Solitaire is *subtractive.*

anvil. The *block move* shown in Figure G.1. It requires an *arbitrary catalyst AA*. See Chapter 11.

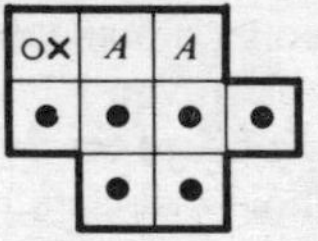

Figure G.1

arbitrary calatyst. A *catalyst* whose initial state of occupancy is unimportant.

arm-balance theorem, arm-crossing theorem. Theorems relating to play on the *standard board.* See Chapter 6.

balance sheet. A combined *resource count* and *parity count*. See Chapter 6.

ball. Synonym for 'man'.

beginner's licence. Solitaire in which diagonal moves are permitted.

block move, block removal. A set of moves which performs a simple and clearly defined operation. See Chapter 2.

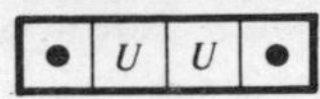

Figure G.2

call and answer, two-removal. The *block removal* shown in Figure G.2. It requires an *unlike pair UU*. See Chapter 2.

catalyst. A set of holes which are used by a *block move or removal* but are left in their original state of occupancy at its end. Catalysts are of two types: *arbitrary catalysts*, whose initial occupancy is unimportant, and *unlike sets* (pairs, triples, and so on), which must include at least one occupied hole and at least one vacancy.

chain-removal. A *block removal* typified by Figure G.3. This figure shows a 'six-chain', which requires an *unlike sextet UUUUUU*. Other chain-removals are similar. See Chapter 2.

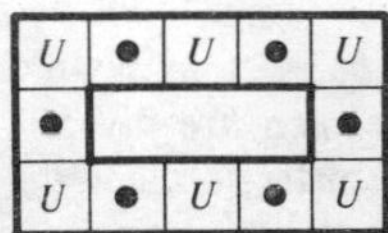

Figure G.3

complement, complement problem. The *complement* of a position is the position which has vacancies where the given position has occupied holes and occupied holes where the given position has vacancies. A *complement problem* is a problem in which the target position is the complement of the initial position.

complementary class theorem. A theorem relating the *fundamental classes* of a position and its *complement*. See Chapter 4.

constrained Solitaire. Solitaire in which the number of men in a hole is either 0 or 1. Ordinary Solitaire is constrained.

Conway's balance sheet. The *balance sheet* shown in Figure 6.15.

Conway's modified balance sheets. The *balance sheets* typified by Figures 6.32 and 6.33.

corner man. On the *standard board*, a man which can reach an outside corner hole.

cross-count. The *resource count* shown in Figure 5.8.

dead man. A man which does not move in the course of a solution.

debts and surpluses. The holes to which men must be delivered (debts) and from which they must be removed (surpluses) in the course of play. See also *task map*, *move map*.

double-three. The *block removal* shown in Figure G.4. It requires an *unlike triple UUU*. See Chapter 2.

double-two. The *block removal* shown in Figure G.5. It requires an *unlike triple UUU*. See Chapter 2.

double-Y. The *block removal* shown in Figure G.6. It requires an *unlike triple UUU*. See Chapter 11.

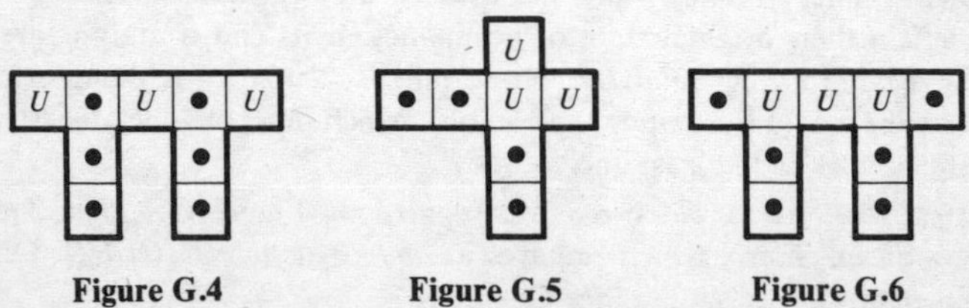

Figure G.4 Figure G.5 Figure G.6

edge man. On the *standard board*, a man which can reach a hole adjacent to an outside corner. Edge men are divided into two classes: 's' men, which must be removed in order to clear the side corners, and 't' men, which must be removed in order to clear the top and bottom corners. See Chapter 2.

elbow. See *L-removal*.

eleven-removal. The *block removal* shown in Figure G.7. It requires an *unlike triple UUU*. See Chapter 11.

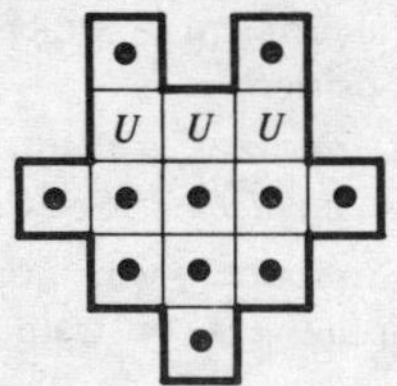

Figure G.7

empty position. The position with every hole vacant.

English board. See *standard board*.

equivalent positions. A term used by some authors to denote positions in the same *fundamental class*.

exit theorems. Theorems which a *move map* must satisfy if it represents a valid solution. See Chapter 7.

flat ten. The *block move* shown in Figure G.8. It requires an *arbitrary catalyst AA*. See Chapter 11.

four-move. The *block move* shown in Figure G.9. It requires an *arbitrary catalyst AA*. See Chapter 2.

four-three. The *block move* shown in Figure G.10. It requires an *arbitrary catalyst AAA*. See Chapter 2.

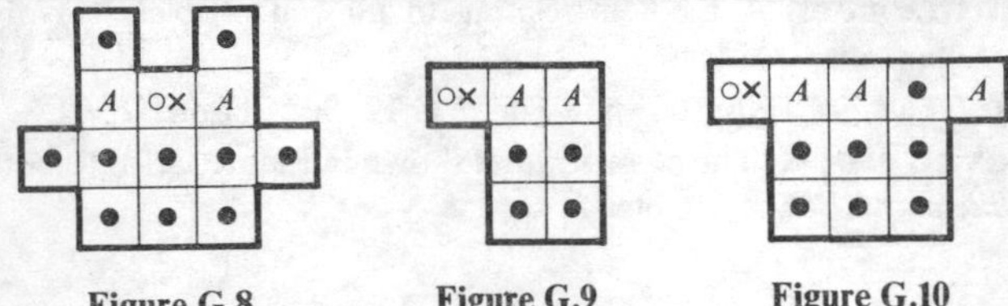

Figure G.8 Figure G.9 Figure G.10

fractional Solitaire. Solitaire in which fractional moves are permitted. See Chapter 5.

French board. The 37-hole board shown in Figure 4.6.

full position. The position in which every hole is occupied.

fundamental class. On the *standard board*, one of sixteen classes into which positions can be divided, play between positions in different fundamental classes being impossible. Analogous classes exist on other boards. See Chapters 4, 11, 14.

German board. The *standard board* of 33 holes. This term should really be preferred to 'English board' since the board was current in Germany long before its first recorded use in England.

golden pagoda. The *resource count* (pagoda function) shown in Figure 12.9. See Chapter 12.

gongoozler. An idle and inquisitive person who stands staring for prolonged periods at anything out of the common. My authority for this splendid word is H. R. de Salis (*Bradshaw's canals and navigable rivers of England and Wales*, 1904), who attributes its origin to the Lake District.

hexagonal Solitaire. *Triangular Solitaire*.

i-move. The *block move* shown in Figure G.11. See Chapter 11.

initial delivery theorems. Theorems which a *move map* must satisfy if it represents a valid solution. See Chapter 7.

Figure G.11

integral Solitaire. Solitaire in which only whole pegs may be used. Ordinary solitaire is integral.

invariant parity count. A *parity count* which cannot be changed by a Solitaire move. See Chapter 4.

inverse move. A jump over an empty hole, putting a man in. See *additive Solitaire*.

isometric Solitaire. *Triangular Solitaire*.

jug-top theorem. A theorem relating to play in problems involving marked men. See Chapter 7.

L-move. The *block move* shown in Figure G.12. See Chapter 2.

L-removal, elbow. The *block removal* shown in Figure G.13. It requires an *unlike pair UU*. See Chapter 2.

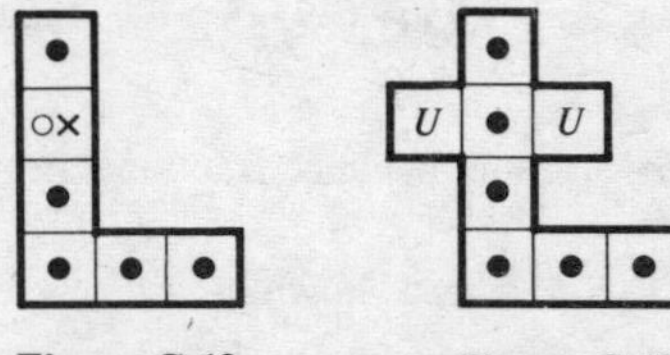

Figure G.12 Figure G.13

man on the watch. A *marked man* which remains stationary until the very end of a solution, when it clears off all the other remaining men to become the last survivor.

marked man. A man distinguished in some way, normally to ensure that it is not accidentally removed during a solution.

middle man. On the *standard board*, a man which can reach the centre.

modified cross-count. One of the *resource counts* typified by Figures 5.45 to 5.47.

move map. A representation of the moves needed to liquidate all the *debts and surpluses* of a problem. See Chapter 5.

nine-removal. The *block removal* shown in Figure G.14. It requires an *unlike triple UUU*. See Chapter 11.

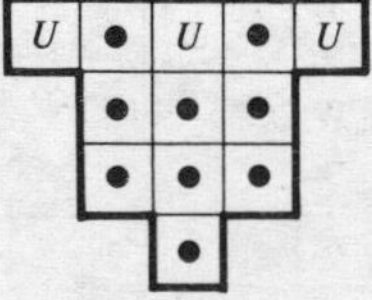

Figure G.14

null-class board. A board in which the *full position* is in the same *fundamental class* as the *empty position*. See Chapter 4.

pagoda function. Conway's original name for a *resource count*.

parity count. An assembly of values, one for each hole, such that the sum of the values of the occupied holes is relevant only in so far as it is odd or even. See Chapter 6.

peg. Synonym for 'man'.

pointed ten. The *block move* shown in Figure G.15. It requires an *arbitrary catalyst AA*. See Chapter 11.

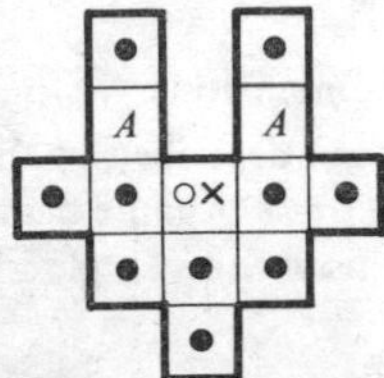

Figure G.15

raffle. Synonym for *sweep*.

Reiss class. A term used by some authors for *fundamental class*. In view of the prior work of Suremain de Missery, it should be abandoned.

resource count. An assembly of values, one for each hole, such that if the values of the occupied holes are added before and after a move then the sum after cannot exceed the sum before. See Chapter 5.

's' man. See *edge man*.

seven-plus-one. The *block move* shown in Figure G.16. See Chapter 11.

shifted six. The *block removal* shown in Figure G.17. It requires an *unlike pair UU* or *VV*. See Chapter 3.

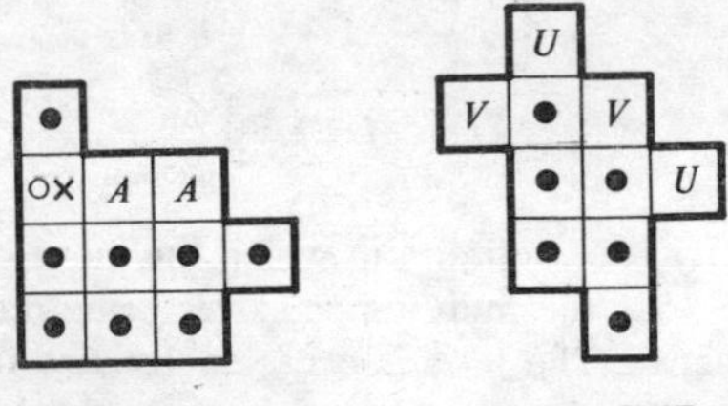

Figure G.16

Figure G.17

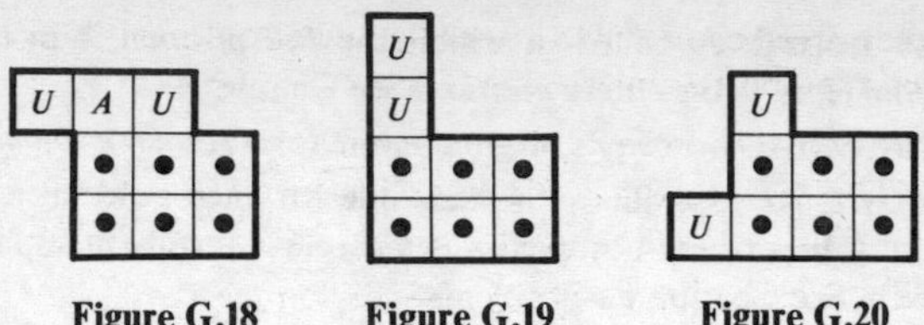

Figure G.18 **Figure G.19** **Figure G.20**

six-removal. The *block removal* shown in Figures G.18 to G.20. It requires an *unlike pair UU*, *A* in Figure G.18 being *arbitrary*. See Chapter 2.

slice. See *three-removal.*

Solidaire. Solitaire in three dimensions.

Solitaire. In Britain, the game described in this book. In America, any single-player card game, the present game being called 'Peg Solitaire'. In former years, the word was used for a single-player card game in Britain also.

Solomon Solitiare. Solitaire on the 19-hole board shown in Figure 14.12.

spine-count. The *resource count* shown in Figure 5.1.

square lattice board. A board in which the holes lie at the points of a square lattice. The term refers to the local arrangement of the holes, not to the overall shape of the board, so the *standard board* is a square lattice board.

standard board. The normal 33-hole board. See Chapter 1.

stellar board. A star-shaped board used in *triangular Solitaire*. See Chapter 14.

straight six. The *block removal* shown in Figure G.21. It requires an unlike pair *UU*. See Chapter 11.

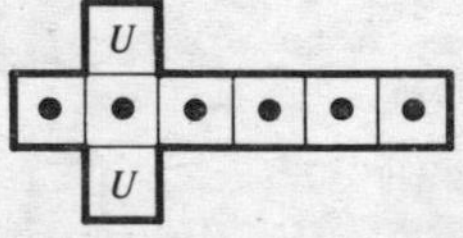

Figure G.21

subtractive Solitaire. Solitaire in which the move is to jump a man over an occupied hole, the man jumped over being removed. Ordinary Solitaire is subtractive. The term is occasionally used in contrast to *additive Solitaire*.

sweep. A move which captures a specific number of men; for example, a nine-sweep captures nine men.

't' man. See *edge man*.

tally. The *block move* shown in Figure G.22. See Chapter 11.

task map. A representation of the *debts and surpluses* which must be liquidated in order to solve a problem. See Chapter 5.

three-removal, slice. The *block removal* shown in Figure G.23. It requires an *unlike pair UU*. See Chapter 2.

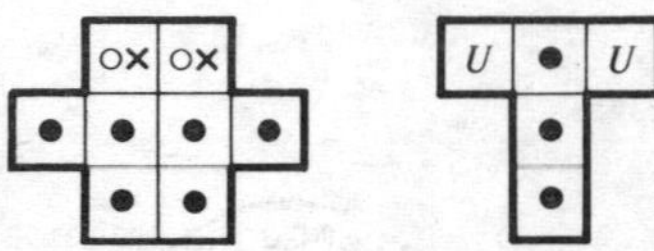

Figure G.22 Figure G.23

transformations of Suremain de Missery. Transformations which can be applies to a position to obtain another in the same *fundamental class*. See Chapter 4.

trellis, trellis map, trellis theorem. A *trellis* is a set of non-adjacent rows and columns. A *trellis map* is a *task map* whose non-zero elements lie on a trellis. The *trellis theorem* states that a debt in a trellis map can be liquidated only by a move along a line of the trellis. See Chapter 5.

triangular Solitaire. Solitaire played on a locally triangular lattice. See Chapter 14.

two-five. The *block removal* shown in Figure G.24. See Chapter 11.

Figure G.24

two-removal. See *call and answer*.

unconstrained Solitaire, unconstrained fractional Solitaire. In *unconstrained Solitaire*, the number of men in a hole can be any integer, positive, negative or zero. In *unconstrained fractional Solitaire*, fractional numbers are also permitted. See Chapters 5 and 6.

unlike pair, triple etc. See *catalyst*.

up-and-down Solitaire. Solitaire in which both ordinary (subtractive) and inverse (additive) moves are permitted. See Chapter 4.

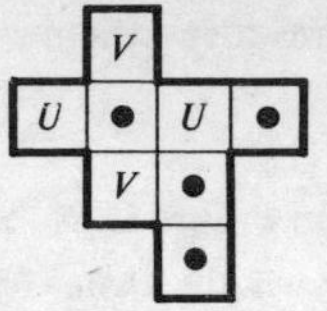

Figure G.25

Wiegleb's board. The 45-hole board shown in Figure 11.42.

Y-removal. The *block removal* shown in Figure G.25. It requires an *unlike pair UU* or *VV*. See Chapter 3.

YY-removal. See *double-Y*.

INDEX